W9-BYL-728

DATE DUE

Demco, Inc. 38-293

RESISTING ETHICS

SCOTT SCHAFFER

5279920 1

HM
665
S35
2004

c. 1

3-7-06

RESISTING ETHICS
© Scott Schaffer 2004

All rights reserved. No part of this book may be used or reproduced in any manner whatsoever without written permission except in the case of brief quotations embodied in critical articles or reviews.

First published 2004 by
PALGRAVE MACMILLAN™
175 Fifth Avenue, New York, N.Y. 10010 and
Houndmills, Basingstoke, Hampshire, England RG21 6XS
Companies and representatives throughout the world

PALGRAVE MACMILLAN is the global academic imprint of the Palgrave Macmillan division of St. Martin's Press, LLC and of Palgrave Macmillan Ltd. Macmillan® is a registered trademark in the United States, United Kingdom and other countries. Palgrave is a registered trademark in the European Union and other countries.

ISBN 1–4039–6443–2 hardback

Library of Congress Cataloging-in-Publication Data
Schaffer, Scott.
    Resisting ethics / Scott Schaffer.
        p. cm.
    Includes bibliographical references and index.
    ISBN 1–4039–6443–2
      1. Social ethics. I. Title.

HM665.S35 2004
303.3′72—dc22   2003060146

A catalogue record for this book is available from the British Library.

Design by Newgen Imaging Systems (P) Ltd., Chennai, India.

First edition: March 2004
10 9 8 7 6 5 4 3 2 1

Printed in the United States of America.

TABLE OF CONTENTS

For those who struggle where I cannot,
And for the future.

Preface and Acknowledgments

This project, even though I didn't know it, began on a dare over a decade ago, when someone told me that no one wrote political or social theory on Jean-Paul Sartre anymore. So I didn't—until 1997, when the real work began on this book.

Perhaps a few words are in order as to what this book is *not*; I leave it to the rest of the work to say what it is. This book resides firmly in the realm of sociology, not philosophy, despite its concerns with ethics and existentialism (something that most sociological theorists gave up on in the 1970s). Part of this is due to my training in the interdisciplinary Graduate Programme in Social and Political Thought, York University, Toronto; part of it is due to my commitment to crossing disciplinary boundaries in the search of integrating forms of knowledge for the betterment of our social lives. The approach I have taken here, though, is designed to represent a conversation between philosophy, sociology, and activism in the hopes of contributing something more than a simple theoretical treatise to the future.

A more youthful and insolent me saw other authors as primarily writing "theory on theory on theory." I didn't want this work to be a compilation and synthesis of secondary sources, a literature review, or a list. I wanted to take the original materials behind the names and use them to create something new. Indeed, I wanted this book to be a careful contribution to an ongoing debate. Hopefully, that has been achieved. The result of that approach is that this book, unlike many others in the American tradition, does not rely as heavily on secondary sources and does not attempt to contextualize itself vis-à-vis the countless other authors who have done, are doing, or are thinking about doing similar kinds of work. Instead, this book simply *is*. It is my attempt to contribute something to an ongoing and absolutely necessary discussion about a period of time where the many conflicts in the world, between poverty and wealth, under- and overdevelopment, North/West and South/East, *jihad* and McWorld (to borrow Benjamin Barber's phrase), and between preserving an unjust status quo and disturbing it for the sake of creating a new world for us all, are coming to a head. Where appropriate, I provide the details of works that are dealing with similar kinds of issues in similar kinds of ways. But rather than spending both our time going through the lists of works being produced on issues pertaining to resistance, social justice, and ethics, I felt it best to simply step up and say "this is what I see going on and what should be going on." I hope this doesn't offend the reader's sensibilities—too much.

Much of this book relies upon the American context for its criticisms of the current social order. In part, it is geographically convenient to do so, a vision supported by the relative dearth of real news about the rest of the world on the usual American media. However, there are countless parallels between what's gone on in the United States during the first years of the twenty-first century and what is happening in other countries in the "overdeveloped West," ranging from the increasing lack of attention paid by British Prime Minister Tony Blair to the wishes of his people, to the increasing moves toward privatization of social welfare systems by the French and German governments, to the growing predominance of right-wing and fundamentalist politics in Australia, Austria, and the Netherlands. Thus, even though there are not regular references to or analyses of other societies' problems, I believe that given these parallels, as well as the increasing willingness of the United States to impose its will onto other countries and their policies, the arguments made here are broad enough that they can be translated into other contexts. And in large part, it is precisely that translation process that I hope this work fosters; the use of the "extreme case studies," cases that, even though they are outside the conceivable realm of normalcy for some readers, have some bearing on the reader's own situation, is designed to make this mode of analysis more prominent. To put it another way, I see great value in taking an analysis of some other social setting that appears to have no parallel to one's own and trying to find something to learn and "bring home" from it.

Since the start of this project, this manuscript has gone through countless revisions, revisitations, and rethinking. Probably more than I care to admit, the completion of this book has had dramatic impacts on friends who wondered either where I disappeared to or how I could work every night, as well as on family, who always wanted to know when it would be done. In all cases, though, from near and afar, they have supported me through the six years of work on this book. Thanks are due, in ways I cannot fully express, to all of them, who get to see themselves in liner note form:

Family: Marsha Schaffer, Kim Davis, Gary Johnson, and Jim Schaffer, all of whom never cease to express how cool it is that this is finally in print; Thelma Carr and Louise Schaffer, who didn't get to see this work, though their support made me the author I am today; and Bela, whose presence curled up around my feet or next to me on the couch was sorely missed during the last two years of this project (though Sabia has done yeoman's work in her stead).

Friends: Kristin Anderson, Jessica Veitch, Natasha Pravaz, Kirsten Stolte, Lisa Wunder, Amy Huwel, Sandra Willis, Mary-Angela Willis, Thamora Fishel, Frederika Schmitt, Jenna Stoltzfus, and Cesar Dominguez, for pressing me forward on the project; Joel Schalit, Naomi Mandel, Brian Martin, Doug Anthony, Myron Orleans, Allen Shelton, and Susan McManus, all of whom were either sounding boards, critical devil's advocates, or readers of various versions of this work; the folks at the cafés mentioned here, who were always interested in what I was writing—until I told them; and all the people over the last seven years who have told me that it's time to take a break.

Cafés: The Coffee Table in Silver Lake, California, and Square One Coffee in Lancaster, Pennsylvania, both provided me safe and consistently available places to work and lots of caffeine. Without them (and their owners, Mike Zamarripa and Lane Levengood, respectively), only two pages of this book would have ever appeared. Other establishments in Los Angeles and Lancaster provided me with the space to reflect, consider, and complain. Much gratitude (in most cases) is owed them as well.

Colleagues: My colleagues in the Department of Sociology/Anthropology at Millersville University of Pennsylvania and the Department of Sociology at California State University, Fullerton both deserve *muchos kudos* for their support, comfort, and various and random kicks in the bum to keep me going on the project.

Students at Millersville University, Cal State Fullerton, and Indiana University of Pennsylvania all provided crucial insight and helped me make ideas that seem lofty at times understandable and palpable for people who do not specialize in this kind of work. Special thanks go to my student assistants, Sarah Jacobson and Holly Nagy, whose efforts during the last year of work on this book—always last-minute, and always impeccable and life-saving—were of great help in this project's completion.

Advisors and Mentors: Alec Stone Sweet, for providing me with the dare in the first place; David Easton, for reminding me to write for the sake of my readers; David McNally, whose continued support and guidance and political engagement are an inspiration to me on a regular basis; Gottfried Paasche, whose fatherly advice and critical eye helped me more times than I care to count; Ato Sekyi-Otu and Lesley Jacobs, who provided key insights and direction during the dissertation phase of this project; and Helmar Drost and Edward Andrew, whose commentary on this work was extremely helpful and enlightening.

Elements of this book were presented at a variety of conferences over the years, including conferences held by *Rethinking Marxism*, the International Social Theory Consortium, the American Sociological Association, and the Radical Philosophy Association. Many thanks go to those who provided critical commentary and important insights on earlier versions of this work. Gratitude is also due to the number of anonymous reviewers who read preliminary versions of this work for a variety of presses and journals; your insights helped me refine this work substantially, and it would not be what it is without you. Particular appreciation is extended to Ron Aronson, whose keen insights into the intricacies of these problems deepened the analysis in chapter 5, and who unwittingly gave me a way of talking about what this book was trying to do—to be both Camus and Sartre without making the mistakes of either.

An earlier version of chapter 4 was published in *Research and Society*, the Graduate Journal of Marxist Studies at SUNY Buffalo. Their feedback and the comments I've received from readers of that article were of tremendous assistance.

Present in the text are selections from referenced works that appear in the original language. All translations are provided either in the text itself or in the notes at the end of the book, and all translations are mine, with assistance from native speakers of both French and Spanish and other resources. Of course, translation is never an exact science, so any issues in translation reside solely with my interpretation of the work.

Research support was provided by the Faculty Grants Committee and Dean of Humanities and Social Sciences at Millersville University through a variety of research and publication completion grants. Without their assistance, this manuscript would not be as complete as it is. Similar tons of thanks go to the Beinecke Manuscript Library at Yale University and to the Bibliothèque Nationale de France for granting me access to and citation permissions for two unpublished manuscripts by Jean-Paul Sartre. To the best of my knowledge, this is the first book written in English by a sociologist to utilize the 1964 *Conférence à l'Institut Gramsci* (otherwise known as the *Rome Lectures*) or the 1965 *Cornell Lectures* (never given due to Sartre's protest against American involvement in Vietnam) in its development. Countless thanks go to Thomas C. Anderson, who advised me of their existence and my need for them, and Betsy Bowman, who helped prepare me for the adventure the BNF posed.

Finally, great thanks go to Anthony Wahl, Heather Van Dusen, and Ian Steinberg of Palgrave Macmillan for taking a risk on this project and guiding me through the process. Their assistance—and apparently infinite reserves of patience—regularly and continually calmed and inspired a rookie author.

With all this support, one might expect perfection. However, any and all mistakes are my own. Even an embedded network such as the one I have benefited from can't watch everything.

CHAPTER 1
COMPLICITY, ETHICS, AND RESISTANCE

Think about the first years of the twenty-first century for long enough, and one will get the sense that the world has gone seriously wrong, even more wrong than it has been in the past. Start with the "election" of U.S. President George Bush in 2000, move to the U.S. response to the attacks of September 11, 2001, and on through the second war on Iraq, and one finds an increasingly unilateral and imperial American government working to impose its conception of "the good" on the rest of the world, either through heavy-handed arm-twisting in international institutions, thumbing the proverbial nose at other countries and their rights to self-determination, or through outright military force. Work from the treatment of members of minority groups around the world—Turkish *Gastarbeiter* (guest workers) in Germany, North African immigrants and the *sans-papiers* living in France, West Indians living in poorer parts of London—and one will end up looking at America's imprisonment and suspicion of immigrants from Islamic countries in 2002 and 2003. Begin at the U.S. removal of itself from the Kyoto Protocols in 2001, or its increasing attempts to turn the world into a "free trade" zone, or its contempt for the French and German governments' exercise of their democratic right to hold their own opinion in the UN Security Council in 2002, and one sees an increase in the number of situations that would violate many definitions of "social justice."

There are countless numbers, though, who resist this trend toward the dismissal of the concerns of the many for the sake of the few. Millions of people worldwide have gone into the streets to protest globalization and the activities of the World Trade Organization, the International Monetary Fund, and the World Bank, as well as efforts to institute a "Free Trade Area of the Americas." Likewise, tens of millions around the world rose up to protest the U.S. war on Iraq, just as many are criticizing the American and British governments for what has turned out to be trumped-up evidence of the crimes of the Iraqi regime. Thousands struggle against fundamentalist and oppressive regimes in the Middle East; Chechen "freedom fighters" battle against the Russian forces that prevent them from establishing their own independent republic; and rebels in Liberia are locked in a civil war against a democratically elected warlord. Still others in the United States and elsewhere have been utilizing the Internet to express their views and demands to their elected representatives and then calling on those representatives to account for their actions when they fail to represent their constituents' wishes.

Yet, there are countless people around the world who look out their window at breakfast and wonder how much worse things can get. They *know* the world is not the place it could be, that their political institutions do not do what they were designed to do, that the economy runs for the benefit of the few and that they are not part of that "few," and that they are rendered apparently powerless by the structures in which they find themselves. They either take this powerlessness to heart, feeling depressed about the state of things, wondering whether they should bring new lives into the world, or they simply ignore all the atrocious things people do to other people in the world. Those in the former group grow increasingly embittered as time goes on, feeling that as much as they would like to protest against wars, support liberation movements, and struggle for social justice, "it won't mean anything anyway." This group feels their inertia, their adherence to a rule-bound morality that requires that they not rebel against the status quo, negatively, progressively growing more alienated. The latter group simply stops caring and starts looking out for "number one," lifting a finger in the political sense only when someone wants to build a homeless shelter or landfill in their neighborhood; they live up to the rules that say, explicitly or implicitly, "take care of yourself, because no one else will and no one else should." The first group eventually gives up; the second group becomes increasingly selfish and self-interested; and both groups of people end up ensuring that things will simply stay the course, and the world will become a more unjust and unfree place to live. They are, in essence, complicit with the powers that be, part of that set of inertial structures that ensures that very few among us can make decisions that affect everyone, and that those decisions will benefit the very few who made them.

There are still others, though, people who want to support or at least validate the claims of those groups and individuals around the world who say, "I am not treated fairly, ethically, or justly." This group wants to see everybody have "equal opportunities," receive just pay for their work, and be able to improve themselves in the ways they see fit. These people may not, however, have any idea about how to do this, or whether it matters that they do or not. They want the Zapatistas to gain their autonomy, the Israelis and Palestinians to work things out, the Iraqis to build their own democratic social order, and for all people to be treated in the way they wish to be treated. For this group of people, acting ethically is a real concern: they check the tags of their clothing to ensure they weren't made in sweatshops; they only buy "fair trade," shade-grown coffee; they recycle; and they write letters when Amnesty International asks it of them. They wish they could do more on behalf of those made subaltern in society and around the world, but feel like doing more would either disrupt their lives too much or would get them into trouble somehow. They want to be *really* ethical, but that comes into conflict with the other ethics present in the overdeveloped West: work hard, consume, vote when asked to, and take care of your own affairs. Doing anything else, acting in any other way, gets in the way of profit, productivity, or "the good life."

Every day sees new varieties of issues regarding social ethics arising, even though most revolve around questions that Enlightenment-era philosophers had supposedly solved. Should the First Nations be entitled to possession of lands their ancestors lived on well before Europeans arrived in North America? Or should they be limited to owning casinos and taking their revenge on the white man through 5-to-2–odds at video poker? Is self-determination a natural right, inherent to the human species by fact of birth (as stated by the Universal Declaration of Human Rights), or is it a socially constructed notion of how people should treat one another, one that can do more harm than good? Such questions are not the only ones that appear to us at the dawn of the millennium. Other questions, more local in scope (and yet paralleling more global issues), show up when we least expect it. As a recent NAACP-sanctioned survey reports, 50 percent of American youth would support the segregation of the "races" so long as every group had "equal opportunities." Two questions arise from this: Is "separate but equal" an ethical standard so long as the "equality" between separated groups is ensured? And what would be equality along this line of thinking? Is women's labor equal in social worth to the labor of men? Or should their 3 : 4 income ratio be translated into all areas of social life, including buying groceries at a 25 percent discount? Can there ever be a widely accepted version of "equality"? Or does Orwell's prophetic saying, "All animals are equal; some are just more equal than others," really hold? Who should be engaged in bringing about more equal, more equitable, or more humane forms of social relations and institutions—those who are directly wronged by those institutions, or those of us who have for so long enjoyed the privileges ascribed to our status through the blood, sweat, and tears of others?

It is these kinds of issues that I tackle here. Overall, this book is about one key question: What would we need to do in order to create a more just social order for others and ourselves? In order to answer this question, I work between two realms of social action—resistance and ethics. Both types of social action have become more prominent in the hidden transcript of social discourse (to use Scott's [1990] term); more and more people are thinking about what would be needed to improve the state of affairs and about what a "better state of affairs" might look like. In dealing with these two areas of social life, this book essentially works to integrate the two, to see the connections between resistance and ethics, and to understand the social practice of each as necessarily involving the other.

The *double entendre* in the title *Resisting Ethics* reflects this two-fold intention: to show how "ethics"—that form of behavior that we commonly equate with "good behavior" or "good treatment of others"—can be used to justify resistance by all of us against the multiple forms of oppression present in the world today; and to convey the notion that Ethics, in the rule-bound and universalizing sense in which the subject is usually discussed in philosophy seminars, is something that needs to be resisted in favor of the development of more humane and situationally appropriate and ethically radical ways of being toward others and being with others. As well, and more importantly for this work, resistance requires a form of ethics that motivates the resisters and determines not just the way in which they want a new social order to operate, and ethics as such requires a type of resistance not generally recognized. Part of this analysis, then, is to show how resistance in its actual lived form (as opposed to the ossified version generally studied in academia) requires and in fact presupposes a nascent ethics that many resistance movements strive to bring into being, and to show how ethics, in the way Aristotle describes it (*ethos*, a way of being in the world), necessitates a type of resistance in its own way, one which brings the ethical actor to transcend the habitual basis of most of our actions.

Our trek, then, begins with two simple premises: first, resistance exists. All over the world, groups are actively engaged in struggles for their liberation from a variety of forms of oppression, ranging from race, class, gender, and sexual oppression, to the exercise of political tyranny, to the rule of multinational corporations and Western ideas of capitalist development. From North America, though, there seem to be two perspectives on these struggles. The first could be characterized as a universalizing one, one that parallels the way in which we handle economic development: why is it that these people are resisting the path of social progress that we have tried and proven to be good? From this perspective, resistance movements are seen as the knee-jerk reactions of "backward" people who do not understand the goodness of the path the overdeveloped West has laid out for the rest of the world. The second perspective would be the "terrorist" interpretation: those who are engaged in resistance are "terrorists," intent on "getting their way," regardless of the potentially destructive impact it has on others (generally us). The discourse surrounding the September 11 attacks on the United States, the Palestinian *intifada*, and anticapitalist and anti-globalization protestors all highlight this tendency to turn resisters into "terrorists," especially when those who resist do so against the United States. As such, it becomes difficult for us to understand why people resist, but we need to in a deeper way.

The second premise is nearly as clear and obvious: Ethics, which I define as a collectively determined and reproduced rule-bound morality turned into a guide for practical everyday conduct, is a social matter, not one merely for individuals.[1] Even in societies characterized by more or less extreme versions of individualism such as those of the West, ethical codes, including those that emphasize the fulfillment of individual desires or the ignoring of the needs of others even when the satisfaction of those needs would better us all, are produced and reproduced by the social order. From the moment children are born into Western societies, they are taught in the ways of the West, both good and bad: merit, competition, satisfaction of individual goals and desires, the elevation by both individuals and societies of the needs of the one over the needs of the many, and individuals as privileged over collectives.

Reinforcing this is the rise of the notion of our "postmodern" times. Originally arising in the humanities, this strain of thought has made its way into both philosophy and the social sciences and into the larger collective consciousness. Premised as it is on the "death of metanarratives," the slippery slope of identity politics, the increasing speed and virtuality of our "everyday existence," and the apparent groundlessness of modern life, the collective notion of postmodern experience, I would argue, has undermined our quotidian concept of sociality. Works such as Bauman's *Intimations of Postmodernity* and *Postmodern Ethics* claim to show, even as our lives become increasingly globalized, that the "local" is the only way in which we can even conceive of the remains of "society." For Bauman, it is only within our "habitat," the local space of our existence, that we are able to be social. And yet, technologies such as the

Internet make it possible for us to have lengthy social relations with people across the world we've never met in person; we watched in awe as the clock struck 12 on the "new millennium" in every time zone around the world (twice, no less); we are increasingly affected by economic and political events in countries many have never heard of; and our work life is fully implicated in the expansion of the global capitalist system. Yes, we can be anywhere in the world without really "being there"; but more and more of our lives is imbued with a globalism that leads in many ways to our dependence upon people thousands of miles away we will never meet.

The reaction of various notions of postmodernity to this challenge of globalism shuts down any appreciation of its importance. In postmodernity, after all, we are all nothing more than appearances, blips on the radar of people we run into on the path of life; and anything resembling "social structures" that are potentially or actually oppressive disappears from view, leaving any kind of dissatisfaction about as efficacious as screaming at the curtain shielding the Wizard of Oz. This makes conceiving of anything we might know as "society" extremely difficult: because all we are is appearance (or presentation, though this may imply too much agency on the part of the individual), we can create ourselves almost out of nothingness; because we are anything to anyone, we have little if anything in common with them, save for a fleeting bond with the "Other" in the moment, so we owe no social obligation to them because we are not bound up in a "society" with them. Since we have lost the concept of society in recent years, we also lose the concept of Ethics. As Caputo claims in *Against Ethics*, Ethics as a universal set of maxims governing our relations with one another ceases to exist once societal bonds are eliminated; thus, what we are left with is obligation to particular individuals rather than the kind of categorical imperatives presented to us by traditional forms of ethics. In some sense, this development is liberatory, in the sense that ethical codes or philosophies that come to us from past social orders and historical timeframes present us with a version of "the good" that is out of sync with our own time. The intention of this may be laudable: one, after all, now has the ability to "bend" ethical "rules" for the benefit of another, a more situationally appropriate ethical maxim, whereas the quasi-bureaucratic ethical principles such as the categorical imperative might prevent this. Caputo's claim is that the reliance on Ethics is even more dangerous than this:

> Ethics lays the foundations for principles that *force* people to be good; it clarifies concepts, secures judgments, provides firm guardrails along the

slippery slopes of factical life. It provides principles and criteria and adjudicates hard cases. Ethics is altogether wholesome, constructive work, which is why it enjoys a good name.

The deconstruction of ethics, on the other hand, cuts this net. Or rather, since deconstruction is not some stealthy, cunning agent of disruption, is not an agent at all, is in a sense nothing at all, it is much more accurate to say that a deconstructive analysis shows that the net is already torn, is "always already" split, all along and from the start. The deconstruction of ethics is ethics' own doing, ethics' own undoing, right before our eyes. It is something that happens to ethics and in ethics, something going on in ethics, with or without Jacques Derrida. In any possible deconstruction of ethics, one would be simply passing the word along that one is rather more on one's own than one likes to think, than ethics would have us think. (Caputo 1993: 4)

In claiming that Ethics has essentially duped us, that all along we were on our own, merely mollifying our consciences with Ethics, Caputo leaves us with no clear way of being at all. Rather, *Against Ethics* leaves us with the unsettling feeling—one I would argue rarely felt by even the most selfish individual on the planet—that we are obligated to nothing higher than another person. And even Bauman's *Postmodern Ethics*, which engages rather than deconstructs *in toto* thousands of years of ethical thought, still leaves us with a strange tension between socially given rules regarding action and our conscience—strange, because any sociological standpoint begins with the premise that we are brought into the world *through* and not in spite of or against society. So, in our regular experience, we feel alone, trapped, with or without postmodern theory or theorists. Our ties with others are cut, and with those ties go our notions of Ethics. And with or without Ethics, we still reproduce those old rules of conduct—as much to our detriment, I would say, as it is in Caputo's deconstructive argument.[2]

Given the disappearance of society as an evident factor in our ordinary lives and the increasing importance of the individual above all else, we have a difficult time understanding resistance as more than either large-scale revolution, as processes that appear to happen without people, or small-scale protestation and/or performances, as people acting without processes.[3] Against both notions, I mean "resistance" as collective sociopolitical actions that are geared first and foremost to the liberation of an oppressed group.[4] In the classic sense of the term, resistance involves a group of people who are in some way subordinated within their society, and who, instead of waiting to have their social and political needs met through the extension of rights and freedoms to them by the dominant group, have chosen to formulate a collective project geared toward their individual and collective liberation. Resistance is necessarily a social act; it requires a large number of people, a group choice to act, and participation by the collective in the act. Resistance is also geared toward freedom for both the individual and the collective. This is not to say that individuals participate in resistance movements for themselves first, or solely for *le peuple*; rather, this is to say—and this will be dealt with in detail through the course of this work—that liberation is both the transformation of a social and political order so that an oppressed group is no longer oppressed *and* a transformation of the individuals within that group, so that what is created is both a new society and new socially oriented individuals. Finally, resistance is also inherently normative; the choice to overturn a social order is one that does not happen without a plan, but also entails a collectively determined concept of how people should relate to one another and the institutions that should mediate these social relations.

These criteria, though, are not all that is indicated by "resistance." As the description of resistance just given indicates, there are a wide variety of acts that are included, ranging from outright revolution to protest movements to social dissent. What is important, though, is that resistance does not simply indicate dissatisfaction with a sociopolitical order's particular policies or actions. One can express their disgust with a particular policy, for example, by engaging in a letter-writing campaign that floods political representatives with expressions of dissent. This, though, is not resistant by the definition used here. Resistance here also refers to the concept, lost to many social and political theorists in recent times,[5] of consent, the ability to actively participate in the continued construction, enforcement, and evaluation of social rules, groupings, and institutions. The resisters' idea that we should actively be participating in the creation and mediation of our social relations is an important one, and indicates both the normative nature of resistance and, as I will argue through the development of this work, the ethicality of resistance. Consent, then, would include not simply the structural possibility of actively agreeing to the form of the dominant social order, but also the freedom and the agency to do this in a consistent and processual manner. The question of the ethicality of resistance revolves around this point, then: if resistance is a social act that reclaims a group's agency and allows them to create conditions of increased individual and collective freedom where people have a regularized capacity to consent to the rules governing their social lives, then is it not *necessarily* ethical? And further, does the maintenance of this capacity for consent over the life of a social grouping not require that we resist any tendency to ossify the social order? This book, to give the short answer up front, argues yes.

Figuring Out How to Survive

I take seriously the notion that, put bluntly and colloquially, we need to get our individual and collective acts together. There are significant problems with how the social orders of the overdeveloped West operate, and this book works to offer up one possible solution for creating a more ethical social order.

In chapter 2, I present key aspects of the works of Sartre and Merleau-Ponty. Taken together, their works provide an excellent understanding of the relationships between the individual as an agent and a subject in relation with the social, the material, and the existential conditions in which we exist. I first discuss the ways in which this "philosophical" body of work is actually strongly sociological (in spite of the critique leveled herein against *Being and Nothingness*) and in itself represents a form of ethics. I then detail their theories of action, sociality, and history in order to show that an existential theory of action also serves as a theory of freedom, critical to a theory of resistance, *and* a theory of ethics. In chapter 3, I outline a theory of an existential ethics, one that is dramatically different from our current conceptions of ethics. Specifically, this chapter details the perspective that Ethics as we know it now, being embedded in the practico-inert social order within which we exist, serves as a form of inertia, carried down from the past into our own lives, leaving us unable to do much but to "act ethically" by echoing the past into our future. This treatment of ethics as inertia highlights the problems briefly mentioned here regarding the state of ethics and its relationship with theories and practices of resistance, and provides us with a crucial insight into this relationship—namely that resistance requires ethics, and that in fact, ethical action, at least in the sense of bringing about a more humane social order, *requires resistance*. This discussion will draw in particular on the issues of existential freedom, the paradoxes of ethical action, and the concept of "ethical radicalism," the act that presents to the world a glimmer of what future, truly ethical life would look like.

Chapter 4 presents a discussion of Pierre Bourdieu's work, taken in the context of an examination of the ways in which the possibility for human agency is suppressed or minimized in a hegemonic social structure. I begin there by highlighting the linkages between Bourdieu's conception of the habitus, which I take as the sociological "site" of the individual's encounter with the world, and the version of existentialism developed in chapters 2 and 3. I then bring in Antonio Gramsci's conception of hegemony to show that the habitus is capable both of reinforcing the dominant social order through the reenactment of practico-inert structures and alienated concepts of "freedom" and of providing the basis upon which an ethical form of resistance can be built through the "decolonization" of the habitus and the reclamation of human agency, crucial components of the development of a resistant project and, I would argue, necessary for the conceptualization of an ethical orientation toward those in our social field.

Chapter 5 presents a detailed case study of French colonial rule in Algeria and the process of the Algerian Revolution. After presenting a brief history of French rule in Algeria, focusing primarily on the ways in which French conceptions of humanism work together with actual physical and military force to subjugate the Algerian people, I go on to utilize Frantz Fanon's works as a phenomenology of Algerian oppression. I then employ the theoretical framework developed in chapters 2 and 3 to show the ways in which the armed resistance that began in 1954 provided the possibility for the decolonization of the Algerian habitus, a necessary aspect of the development of a social ethics in the specific context of colonial rule. Taken as such, the violence of the Algerian Revolution can be seen as a necessary element in this historical instance of an ethics of freedom, providing the mechanism by which the Algerians could collectively develop a project of human liberation, one that serves as the basis for the development of a new society. The *Front de la Libération Nationale* (FLN), however, betrayed the possibilities inherent in a revolutionary ethics of freedom through the *praxis* it used to ensure its dominance in Algeria. In violating all that Fanon said on the necessities for the *social* liberation of a people, the FLN set up a situation in which the revolution could not truly come to pass. Put briefly, the FLN's structuring of the Revolution ensured that no *real* revolution could occur. In spite of this historical shortcoming, though, the Algerian case study provides us with a set of tools we can utilize in the development of a social ethics in our time.

The *Ejército Zapatista de Liberación Nacional* (EZLN, or "the Zapatistas" as they are more colloquially known) provide the case study for chapter 6, an examination of one way in which the kind of ethics of freedom I see at work in the Algerian Revolution has been put into practice. Focusing primarily on the form of social organization the EZLN utilizes, this chapter deals with the issue of what a society motivated by an ethics of freedom might look like. The EZLN's key organizational principles of *mandar obedeciendo* (to command by obeying) and *preguntando caminamos* (asking while we walk), I argue, incorporate the key concerns of an ethics of freedom into their theorizing and practice by ensuring that the organizational structures of both the military and political aspects of the Zapatista National Liberation Army continually rely upon and foster the active participation of its membership. In doing so, the EZLN ensures that its primary concern, the expansion of dignity and freedom for all subaltern peoples, is met in a processual manner; put another way, the EZLN's structural norms foster an active, concrete version of freedom that yields a radicalized form of democracy. This chapter works to translate these structural norms from the revolutionary context of the rebellion in Chiapas into our own nonrevolutionary context, in part by showing how the linkage between means and ends makes this an easier task than in the case of the Algerian Revolution.

Chapter 7 provides my insights into how this social ethics would operate and how it can be brought about. This section unifies three key insights from this book, and argues that our complicity with the status quo makes it incumbent on us in the here and now to create a solution to the "problem of others" plaguing Western neoliberalist societies today. First, it deals with the idea that our action/inaction/non-choice to act stems from the situation in which we find ourselves and experience within that situation. Second, our action/inaction/non-choice to act always positions us in relation to practico-inert social structures, in a way that clearly places us in a political alignment with regard to all others in the world. And third, whatever course of action or inaction we choose, our hands are dirtied by our involvement in the situation (however benign), so our choice as to whether or not to act with those who would bring about a situation of concrete freedom in essence pits us either for the development of freedom or for the maintenance of the status quo structures of oppression. The combination of these insights, as well as lessons learned from the extreme case studies of the Algerian Revolution and EZLN, are integrated into the framework of a social ethics predicated on the practice of resistance, the ultimate goal of this book and the way to overcome our complicity with forms of oppression.

This issue of complicity, then, is an important one for the development of an existential social ethics; as we will see in the concluding chapter, the fundamental question that faces us—or rather, the question that almost six billion people face us with—is whether we want our hands dirtied by action or through inaction. Our choice in that matter could determine our very survival.

CHAPTER 2

AS FRAGILE AS GLASS: BALANCING
THE INDIVIDUAL AND
THE SOCIAL

In order to embark on this examination, we must first do more to show how an individualistic (or, at the very least, individualized) concept of ethics fails to illuminate how resistance can be seen as not only normative but also ethical. Rather than dealing with authors external to this work, though, I feel it to be more productive to deal with an author whose later works are crucial for the development of this project— Jean-Paul Sartre. His early work, especially *Being and Nothingness*, displays what I would argue are the root problems with much of Ethical theory: a reliance upon the Cartesian dualism revolving around the *cogito*; the Kantian movement toward a universal, ahistorical concept of morality; and the reliance upon the presocial individual that makes problematic not only recent ethical theory, but also a good deal of social and political theory, especially that of the "social contract" or contractarian schools of thought. This early version of Sartre, the one that is usually criticized for being nihilistic or unproductive as far as social relations go, presents us with a way into the causes of the problems discussed in chapter 1.

Sartre *contre-soi*: The "First Ethics"

The direction in which this work is heading—the examination of existentialism for the development of an ethics that can be both socially and historically oriented and can deal with the difficulties posed by and necessity of resistance—might invite the response, "well, Sartre makes the same abstract individualist moves in his ethical thought." Indeed, I would argue that one of the necessary difficulties with postmodernist versions of ethics stems from a correct reading of a work that to my mind represents one of the least successful examples of ethical theory in existentialist thought, *Being and Nothingness*. The asociality, resignation, and surrender that characterize postmodern ethics as well as the abstractness of traditional ethics both appear in force in Sartre's early and most widely read work. The existence of the individual *sui generis*, regardless of the presence of others, is a fundamental premise of *Being and Nothingness*, one that is ultimately translated (either directly or indirectly) into the work of postmodern theorists of ethics.[1] This, though, is the "straw man" version of existentialism, and one of my first tasks, then, is to defend existentialism from itself so that I can move into what I believe are the most important insights of Merleau-Ponty and Sartre— namely, that we exist with others, have a necessary ethical orientation to them (sometimes in spite of ourselves), and that our actions in the world bear out this ethical orientation to these others.

We can begin this examination of Sartre's early existentialism with the "catch-phrase" most frequently used to describe his philosophy: Existence precedes essence. Opposed to the Cartesian "I think therefore I am," by which Descartes deduced the nature of human existence through thought, the existentialists began with the brute facts of human existence. First and foremost, we exist and define ourselves in an *ex post facto* manner; in other words, we do something and then work to construct an "essence," a meaning that we attribute to our action. This is because, as Sartre points out, we are nothing in the beginning: "If man, as the existentialist conceives him, is indefinable, it is because at first he is nothing. Only afterward will he be something, and he himself will have made what he will be. Thus, there is no human nature, since there is no God to conceive it. Not only is man what he conceives himself to be, but he is also only what he wills himself to be after this thrust toward existence" (Sartre 1993a: 35–36). Even if God were to exist, according to Sartre, our attribution to Him or Her of the creation of our "nature" would be a human construct and, as we will see later, an act of "bad faith" by which we deny our responsibility for our action (here, this action of attribution). As such, our existence is meaningless until we create a meaning for it. We are, as it were, the sole agents responsible for our lives, the only ones who can involve ourselves in the world and construct meaning for our lives (ibid.: 36, 48).

In this way, Sartre argues that there are two particular aspects of our existence: Being and Nothingness. Being is the brute facticity of our existence, that which undergirds all existence. Contrary to earlier depictions of being, such as those of philosophers going all the way back to Plato, Sartre argues that being is what appears to us as the world: "For the being of an existent is exactly what it *appears*" (Sartre 1973 [1956]: 4). The relation between being and "the phenomenon" that is the object of phenomenological discovery is not one of presence and absence, but rather is one in which the being of the phenomenon is not reducible to the phenomenon of being; or, rather, the "phenomenon *is* as it *appears*" (ibid.: 9). Nothingness, on the other hand, is not the total negation of the world; the spelling Sartre occasionally uses, "No-thingness," shows that Nothingness is that which willingly negates itself in order to transcend its "thingness." As such, nothingness is the awareness of a lack, of desire, of the permanence of this lack and desire—something that cannot be posited by or as a thing. As Sartre puts it, "Nothingness is not, Nothingness 'is made-to-be,' Nothingness does not nihilate itself; Nothingness 'is nihilated' " (ibid.: 57). In other words, Nothingness is a complement to Being: "*The being by which Nothingness comes to the world must be its own Nothingness*" (ibid.: 57–58; emphasis in original). Sartre argues that this nothingness by which being comes to the world is the human individual, capable of willing certain acts, ideas, and so on, to a distance from it in order to become something else. Nothingness provides the human individual with the ability to act, because if everything were given in the world (existent), there would be no desire or lack and therefore no motivation to act.

We find, then, two aspects of human existence, which Sartre calls the *en-soi* and the *pour-soi* of being. Being *en-soi* (or "in-itself") is the being of the phenomenon as it is—as a fact in the world. As the glossary to *Being and Nothingness* puts it, "strictly speaking we can say of it only that it is" (Sartre 1973 [1956]: 800). Being for-itself (*pour-soi*) is the reflective aspect of being; the human consciousness, which has the quality of constructing a particular meaning for something in the world, distances itself from the thing, makes of the thing a no-thingness, and places it in a certain relationship to itself. The consciousness, as Sartre puts it, is a "for-itself . . . perpetually determining itself *not to be* the in-itself" (ibid.: 134). The human individual necessarily posits itself as the object of its consciousness, making the for-itself the adjudicator of what the in-itself is and is not, and leaving one's awareness of reality as the awareness of something lacking (ibid.: 135). Both the *pour-soi* and the *en-soi* are orientations to our being: the former takes our being as "missing something," as a lack of something for something else (ibid.: 147), while the latter takes our being as a fact; the *pour-soi* reflects on the *en-soi* in order to determine what is missing from the *en-soi* and thereby determines its future actions. In this way, negation, the process of making the *pour-soi* no-thing, is the fundamental act of being. We observe the world and notice that something is not there (for our consciousness); and it is this judgment that something is lacking that inspires us to act in the world.

Thus, we have two different axes of existence that lead to two different orientations toward that existence: Being and Nothingness refer explicitly to the facts of our condition, with nothingness seen as the malleable aspect of our existence, that aspect which can change, and being taken as the aspect of existence that *is*; while the *en-soi* and the *pour-soi* relate to the pre-reflective and reflective orientations we take vis-à-vis our condition.

In spite of himself, Sartre reenacts Descartes's *cogito* even while purportedly opposing it. Sartre takes as fundamental the *cogito*, that thinking "being" without which any awareness of the world would be impossible, assuming that consciousness appears prior to (or at least, simultaneous with) being, even in spite of his claim that "existence precedes essence." As he puts it in "The Humanism of Existentialism,"

> There can be no other truth to start from than this: *I think, therefore, I exist.* There we have the absolute truth of consciousness becoming aware of itself. Every theory which takes man out of the moment in which he becomes aware of himself is, at its very beginning, a theory which confounds truth, for outside the Cartesian *cogito*, all views are only probable, and a doctrine of probability which is not bound to a truth dissolves into thin air. In order to describe the probable, you must have a firm hold on the true. Therefore, before there can be any truth whatsoever, there must be an absolute truth; and this one is simple and easily arrived at; it's on everyone's doorstep; it's a matter of grasping it directly. (Sartre 1993a: 50–51)

To put it another way, Sartre presumes that our ability to think is proof of our existence: because we think, we must necessarily exist. But what is it that we think of ourselves? Our essence. Therefore, for Sartre, we exist in the world (through doing) and reflect upon this action at some later point, "back-writing" as it were, what our "essence" is (at least until we decide to change it). Problematically, though, the separation of the human existence Sartre makes parallels the split Descartes makes between the being in the world and the thinking being, the latter of course being privileged over the former. There is first and foremost for Sartre the thinking being who constitutes their "existence" through their awareness of their existence; but this thinking being is wholly dependent upon the existing being-in-the-world. In other words, because Sartre begins with the Cartesian mind/body dualism, he is left attempting to explain the being/no-thingness dualism along the lines of the chicken or egg question, answered with *pollo ex nihilo*—the chicken out of nothingness.

Beyond this, though, is the difficulty surrounding the conception of freedom that predicates his entire analysis of our existence. In Sartre's early works, freedom is the fundamental condition of human beings; it is, as he puts it, "not *a* being; it is *the being* of man—i.e., his nothing-ness of being" (Sartre 1973 [1956]: 569). Freedom is the nothingness that makes possible the distinction between the *en-soi* and the *pour-soi*; it makes possible our ability to reflect upon the world and upon our facticity. Keeping in mind that the human condition is one marked by the desire for something, Sartre argues that freedom is that characteris-tic of the human condition that makes us desire for something, that forces us to make ourselves to be everything that we are:

> Human-reality is free because it *is not enough*. It is free because it is perpet-ually wrenched away from itself and because it has been separated by a nothingness from what it is and from what it will be. It is free, finally, because its present being is itself a nothingness in the form of the "reflection-reflecting." Man is free because he is not himself but presence to himself. The being which is what it is cannot be free. Freedom is precisely the nothingness which *is made-to-be* at the heart of man and which forces human-reality *to make itself* instead of *to be*. (Sartre 1973 [1956]: 568)

It is the *pour-soi* aspect of our existence that constitutes our freedom: if we were pure facticity, then we could not be free because our being was limited; but as the "reflection-reflecting," the being that can reflect upon itself, we are free because there is always something absent to us in our existence. In our reflection upon ourselves, we note that we are not the absolute foundation for our existence (the God complex Sartre refers to throughout *Being and Nothingness*), so we strive to be more than we are, to "nihilate" our facticity in order to try to become that absolute foun-dation. Freedom, then, "is nothing but the *existence* of our will or of our passions in so far as this existence is the annihilation of facticity; that is, the existence of a being which is its being in the mode of having to be it" (ibid.: 573). In other words, we freely transcend our facticity in order to become more than we are; and the result of our transcendence, obvi-ously, becomes a return to facticity, inspiring the continuation of the cycle of freedom.

For Sartre, though, this is an absolute kind of freedom: We appear to be able to completely become something else than we are because of the nature of our consciousness. Because Sartre relies upon the Cartesian *cogito* (the "I think, therefore, I exist") as the foundation of conscious-ness for his early existentialism, there is an absolute nature to our ability to reflect upon our existence. The ability to think for Sartre ultimately grounds our awareness of existence; because we can think about our existence, we exist. This thinking, though, is ungrounded except in the human individual's ability to think, thereby making thought the ultimate foundation for existence. Since we are the absolute foundation for our own existence because of our absolute ability to think our existence, we are therefore also absolutely free. In the same manner that Descartes describes the expurgation of his passions in *Discourse on Method*, Sartre's work argues that because we think our existence, we can completely rethink our existence as well; and since this change of thought would change the nature of our existence, we are absolutely free (Sartre 1973 [1956]: 612). It is by this logic that Sartre is able to claim, "This means that no limits to my freedom can be found except freedom itself or, if you prefer, that we are not free to cease being free" (Sartre 1973 [1956]: 567); we can decide to pursue another project, another form of transcendence, that directly contradicts or annihilates the original project in terms of its existence to us in the present.

This should not be taken, though, as a depiction of freedom as bourgeois freedom, which is seen as "freedom to possess." For Sartre, freedom is the ability to "determine oneself to wish (in the broad sense of choosing)" (ibid.: 621). So, to take the example of a prisoner, they are not necessarily free to go out of prison or simply to long for release, but *are* free to try to escape or be liberated: "whatever his condition may be, he can project his escape and learn the value of his project by undertaking some action" (ibid.: 622). There is, then, a certain determination of the limits of our freedom by our situation, but only in the sense—and this becomes important for us when we turn to Merleau-Ponty—that the details of our action are determined by the obstacles that appear to us by virtue of our situation. In other words, the facticity of our situation provides us the awareness of what is lacking to us and gives us the impetus to formulate a plan of action:

> Thus the empirical and practical concept of freedom is wholly negative; it issues from the consideration of a situation and establishes that this situation *leaves me free* to pursue this or that end. One might say even that this situation conditions my freedom in this sense, that the situation *is there in order not to constrain me*. Remove the prohibition to circulate in the streets after the curfew, and what meaning can there be for me to have the freedom (which, for example, has been conferred on me by a pass) to take a walk at night? (Sartre 1973 [1956]: 624–625)

It appears, then, that freedom is resistant, that freedom gives me a negative incentive to act in certain ways, to be in certain ways. Freedom would, by this account, be that quality which allows us to see certain aspects of the world and to act in accordance with (in either a positive or a negative light) that world as it is illuminated through reflection. Once we posit an end we want to achieve (as we will discuss in the next section), we see the world in a particular way, as having certain lacks for us that we want to fill in; as such, the situation constrains us, but only insofar as we want to create something that does not yet exist. There is, then, freedom "only in a *situation*, and there is a situation only through freedom" for Sartre (1973 [1956]: 629), at least in the first version of freedom he provides us.

What Sartre gives us in this aspect of what Anderson (1993) has called his "first ethics" is a notion of freedom that is fundamentally ungrounded and totally disclosed to the free human individual. Because the ability to think and reflect—that is, self-consciousness—is the basis for Sartre's idea of existence, it would be absurd, both philosophically and pragmatically, to claim that some people do not have the ability to think and reflect. At the end of *Being and Nothingness*, though, Sartre begins to see that certain social and political situations hide our awareness of our intrinsic freedom by compelling us to deny or ignore that freedom in "bad faith." But, to put it as Anderson does (1993: 26), changing structures of oppression is not necessary in Sartre's first version of freedom; rather, one needs to conquer themselves, to change their perspective upon the world, in order to change their relation with their situation. If one is poor and fails in one's choice to live the "high life," one merely needs to freely choose to live an ascetic lifestyle and everything will be fine. As well, Sartre argues that freedom is the primary moral value: because freedom, as the fundamental aspect of the human condition, is the only source of meaning and value (and hence of action), "strict consistency" calls for taking it as the primary value, meaning that we should act in order to bring freedom into being (Sartre 1993a: 57–59). But, this makes "freedom" abstract; it gives the idea no content. How, then, do we know when freedom has been brought into being? Or, as Anderson puts it, "what is liberated freedom for; what is its positive goal? To say that it is for freedom is not particularly enlightening" (Anderson 1993: 148).

Sartre's first conception of freedom seems to have no content, no goal, and no relation with how we live our lives. Since Sartre claims that even our freedom can elude us through our denial of it, either intentionally as in "bad faith" or unintentionally in an oppressive situation, we seem to have no basis for envisioning what this freedom might be. As well, this concept of freedom is ahistorical in the worst sense. In spite of the early Sartre's claim that freedom can exist only in and through a situation, it becomes clear that the sociohistorical particularities of that situation have no real bearing on that freedom. Put another way, for Sartre, we can be "free in the mind" at best, but only if we conquer our desire to be free in the world. Furthermore, since Sartre's first ethics posits that we exist outside history (or, rather, that history does not exist for us) and that history has no bearing upon our freedom, we can also see that this notion of freedom and ethics assumes a presocial human being. In just the same way that Descartes's development of rationalism led to the conceptualization of a "state of nature" from whence we come to form a society on the basis of a contract (as Hobbes, Locke, and Rousseau put it), Sartre's argument that our freedom is absolute leads us to see neither history nor society as having an impact upon our situation. In other words, the fact that we can praise being free in the mind and accept the quietism that results from this position implies that we can come to the world having created ourselves out of nothingness with no regard for the "problem" of others who are in the world with us. Obviously, though, as Durkheim points out in "Individualism and the Intellectuals" (1973: 47–48), we do not come to the world out of nothingness; rather, we are made in the image of the world around us—and in our time, we happen, as a result of being "social facts," to believe that we do come into society as individuals first, only to join with others when it suits us. As such, Sartre's first ethics enacts three difficulties for my examination here (as well as for his own work): he divides the individual human being into fact and the annihilation of that fact, into Being and Nothingness; he presumes, à la the "social contract theorists," that we exist as presocial individuals first and then move into society as the result of some form of self-interest; and he builds his entire understanding of the human condition upon this subdivided creature that he takes from its habitat only to say later, "well, they'll go back if they feel like it."

Thus, we see different conceptions of freedom existing in relation to the two aspects of being: existential freedom in relation to the *en-soi*, and Sartre's "actual" freedom in relation to the *pour-soi*. I would argue that each conception of freedom reflects the human individual's orientation to their situation, and all three are interrelated. The *en-soi* intends itself as facticity, and can absolutely, according to Sartre, freely remake itself. The *pour-soi* orients to its situation reflectively, and attempts to construct the world in relation to its project, its idea of how it wants to see itself *en-soi* at a future time. But, as they stand at the end of *Being and Nothingness*, the Kantian and Cartesian tendencies of Sartre's work are overwhelming. It is not until his "second ethics" that Sartre begins to recognize the necessity of the social individual—thanks greatly to the challenge posed by Merleau-Ponty.

Sartre's "second ethics," beginning with *Existentialism and Humanism* and continuing into his last works (cf. Anderson 1993), provides us with a more empirical conception of what freedom is and its relation to our everyday lives. Starting in the 1960s, Sartre begins to see that freedom is an essential value for our existence, but not the only one. Instead, freedom begins to be taken by Sartre in conjunction with our other needs: food, clothing, and shelter; the love of others; for knowledge, culture, and a meaningful life. Freedom in this latter sense, as Sartre points out in his preface to Fanon's *The Wretched of the Earth*, functions as a part of a process of self-determination:

> The native cures himself of colonial neurosis by thrusting out the settler through force of arms. When his rage boils over, he rediscovers his lost innocence and he comes to know himself in that he himself creates his self. Far removed from his war, we consider it as a triumph of barbarism; but of its own volition it achieves, slowly but surely, the emancipation of the rebel, for bit by bit it destroys in him and around him the colonial gloom. (Sartre 1963: 21)

The freedom that Sartre denies to the prisoner in *Being and Nothingness*—the freedom to radically convert their situation rather than adjusting to incarceration—is heartily given over to the Algerian rebels, as they are in the process of liberating their individual freedom for the sake of collective self-determination. Freedom in Sartre's later works, as Anderson argues in reference to the unpublished *Rome Lectures*, in a surprisingly instrumental way, and is appealed to as a means to an overarching existential condition (Anderson 1993: 157). This is not to say that the basic ontic-ontological structure Sartre attributes to freedom in *Being and Nothingness* has changed. It is only to say that as Sartre's work matured, freedom became more important as a tool for achieving a more fundamental value, the idea of "integral humanity," in which our needs prove to be mutually satisfying and our ability to achieve the ends we set ourselves simultaneously have the effect of helping others to have the freedom to achieve their ends. We can see, then, that there are for Sartre two types of freedom: the ontological, existential freedom to posit anew a particular set of circumstances; and the freedom to actualize the values we posit (cf. Stewart 1998b: 202).

The problems with Sartre's "first ethics"—its reliance on the Cartesian dualism of body/soul in the form of Being/Nothingness; its Kantian ahistoricism; and its dependence on the idea of an individual who preexists society at all stages—all manifest themselves in various ways in most versions of ethics: either we exist outside of the world and come into it with an already-determined set of moral principles we have developed in a historical and political vacuum, or we rely upon an ethics that predicates our existence before the others toward and with whom we are supposed to be "ethical." However, not all existentialist thought is plagued by these difficulties. Sartre's later work (in particular, *Critique of Dialectical Reason*) provides a clear insight into the way social structures and groupings are created and maintained in the world. As well, Merleau-Ponty's work *begins* from the presumption that we are by virtue of our very existence social creatures and moves from there to attempt to understand *how* we are social, in what ways our relations with others are tainted, and how it is that we can reclaim a more humane set of social relations for ourselves. Reading these theoretical moves together, I argue, provides us with an excellent existential social theory, one that becomes a theory of ethics by virtue of the individual's participation in the world. Thus, this brief examination of Sartre's problematic early work has given us one important insight that makes all the difference for the study herein: we must never forget that we are always in the world, even if we think we are individuals first and members of society only afterward.

Le vrai Sartre: Existence as Both Social and Individual

As this discussion of *Being and Nothingness* has shown, it is easy to dismiss existentialism as the source of a socially oriented ethics if one relies solely on Sartre's *Being and Nothingness*. As that text suggests, our existence is lonely and filled with angst at the failure of our "God project" at best, and characterized by a clash between consciousnesses who see the Other as a threat to their very existence as a subject at worst. However, those who would characterize existentialism solely in terms of this early, individuated work miss an important point, at the very least in the tone of existentialism, namely that while our current condition is one in which dread and despair are fundamental conditions of existence, we are not doomed by any essential property of existence to live in such a way. They see the "regressive" side of existential analysis but miss the more important "progressive" aspect, the one that provides us with the material to devise a new form of ethics grounded in the practice of resistance and an existential analysis of our interrelations in and through this important form of social practice.

The choice of existentialism for the basis of this work is not an arbitrary one; there are many aspects of existentialist philosophy that have, to a large extent, been ignored in the formulation of social theory. First, while someone shopping for books by Sartre, Merleau-Ponty, de Beauvoir, and others would most likely find them in the philosophy section, their work, as we will see below, is strongly sociological. Second, the methodological framework used by the existentialists—phenomenology of the Husserlian sort—allows for linkages to be drawn between apparently disparate social forces (such as "resistance" and "ethics") by breaking down the political aspects of any situation into describable phenomena in themselves. Third, the French existentialists saw a necessary engagement in everyday affairs as a result of and a cause for their philosophical, methodological, and political outlooks. The "immoralisms" Merleau-Ponty (Merleau-Ponty 1973a: 144) cites as a necessary aspect of divining social ethics were often the characterization of their actions as "public intellectuals." These, then, form the primary reasons for embarking on an examination of existentialist thought as the basis for developing a socially oriented ethics, and each will be expanded on in the course of this chapter. The goal of this phase of the work, then, is two-fold. The first is to develop an existentialist concept of society, action, agency, and human freedom. Second, I work to show that the analysis of our embeddedness in a social field provided by Merleau-Ponty, Sartre's examination of the ways in which practico-inert social forms and practices structure our existence so that through our very conception of "agency" they are surreptitiously reenacted over and against us, and the insights into an existential ethics provided by both Merleau-Ponty and Sartre, all work together to lead to an important conclusion for this work: namely, that to be ethical from an existential point of view requires action and, very often, outright resistance to the dominant social order.

The path of the remainder of this chapter, then, will be as follows. First, I will further develop the brief justification for the use of existentialism as a basis for the development of a social ethics by outlining the importance of its phenomenological makeup, the "regressive-progressive" method often used by existentialists, and the political and historical conditions in which French existentialism came about. Then, I will work to integrate the views of Sartre and Merleau-Ponty on the individual, its relations with others, its capacity for action, and both possible and problematic conceptions of "the social." The views of Sartre and Merleau-Ponty often diverge; I see this divergence as both a fruitful foundation for the development of a social ethics within an individualistic society and as a way of covering "all the bases." After this existential sociology, I will then develop the conceptions of ethics, resistance, and history that occupy such an important place in this school of thought, as well as the interrelations between the individual, the social, and the historical, in chapters 3 and 4. These analyses will become crucial in the discussion in the final chapter, where I discuss how we can bring about a more socially oriented ethics.

Why Existentialist Theory?

As I have already hinted, there are a number of reasons to base my development of a socially oriented ethics on the works of the French existentialists. These include the sociological framework inherent in the works of Sartre and Merleau-Ponty; the phenomenological basis of existential thought; and the political and historical aspects of the development of existentialism, which move dialectically from the conditions of the development of this school of thought into the operation of Sartre and Merleau-Ponty as "public intellectuals" and back into the further development of existentialism. This discussion shows the linkage between theory and *praxis* in existentialism, both in the school of thought that we call "existentialist" and in the mode of existentialist engagement. It is ultimately here that I find inspiration in their work for the development of this ethics.

Existentialism as Sociology

There are a number of ways in which the classic texts of French existentialism are good sociological theory. First, while philosophically interrogating the character of human existence, these works are primarily studies of the individual's existence *in* and *with* the world. Sartre's social thought was not the typical "technical" analysis that focuses on description, the treatment of social phenomena as "facts," or a positivistic analysis of the It that is "the human individual." Rather, Sartre proposed to invert the usual sociological hierarchy of "world over humanity," characterized as it is by what he called a "spirit of seriousness," by proposing a theory of existence as social action, one in which "the individual actor, his social group, and the field of his practical action are interconnected" (Hayim 1980: xii). Sartre's philosophy constructs a solid sociological analysis of how human beings interact in the world, examines how social institutions work to hinder the true humane potential of our interactions, and speaks directly to the potential for the creation of a human world and begins (though it is prevented from completing) a "progressive" analysis of how a more humane world can be constructed.

Merleau-Ponty's thought is similarly sociological, exploring the entire gamut of our existence in and with the world. By beginning with an analysis of the mediator between our consciousness and the world around us—the body—Merleau-Ponty is able to construct a philosophical analysis of our potential for acting in and on the world, a theory of how the world aids in constructing who we are as individuals, and provides the basis for the phenomenological development of our key characteristic—freedom. It is, in sum, an analysis of our experience in the world (Spurling 1977: 4–5). As with Sartre's thought, Merleau-Ponty is oriented toward uncovering the ways in which human interaction is both possible and changeable. Given existentialism's credo of "existence precedes essence," the works of both Sartre and Merleau-Ponty set out the characteristics of human existence and the paths by which an "essence" is given to that existence. Since human existence is first and foremost an existence with other human beings, their work necessarily takes on as a primary task the study of sociality—the ways in which we interact with others, the bases of human social groupings, and the possibilities for social change.

Another way the French existentialists' works are sociological is in their implicit exploration of the agency/structure problem (see Giddens 1979; Sewell 1992). This problem, which plagues much of sociological thought to date, is one that separates the human individuals that make up society from the social structures that appear to dictate the forms of human social existence. Decades before Giddens's discussion of what he calls "structuration"—the way in which the practices of human individuals display and replicate what sociologists analyze and describe as "structures"—the works of Sartre and Merleau-Ponty sidestep the agency/structure problem by examining the *social situatedness* of human beings. This issue of situatedness in existentialism allows us the chance to see that resisters intuit the existence of linkages between resistance and ethics through the lived practice of resistance. For both Sartre and Merleau-Ponty, it is the social, whether conceived of institutionally as by Sartre or as a field of meaning in Merleau-Ponty's Weberian–Marxist conception of it (Wolin 1992: 107), that provides us with our actual, existential agency as well as our understanding of the degree to which we have agency. At the same time, it is our agency that either constructs new social forms and structures or reproduces the practico-inert structures in which we already exist.

This notion of situatedness represents the way in which theory and *praxis* are integrated throughout their studies. Both Sartre and Merleau-Ponty take ways of being—a mode of action or *praxis* according to both of them—as the locus of their philosophy and work to theorize these forms of being (or be-ing, to make the actional aspect of this term more clear). The choice to "be," for both of them, is one of the most fundamental choices we make as human beings, as the option to stop being (i.e., to commit suicide) is an ever-present part of our existence. These ways of being happen at a number of different levels and in varying degrees of sociality, and provide the basis for their theorizing. As we will see, the intimate bond between theory and *praxis* provides us with the basis for exploring not only the theoretical elements of ethics and resistance, but also the ways in which that theory can be put into practice.

Existentialism and "the Public Intellectual"
Because of its emphasis on the situatedness of human existence and experience, then, we should not conceive of existentialism, especially that of Sartre and Merleau-Ponty, as coming to fruition in the proverbial vacuum. Rather, French existentialism developed its particular form of *engagement* as a direct result of the experience of its proponents during World War II, when the "abstract consciousnesses" that seem to populate Sartre's early work *L'Être et néant* became objectified in the colonized situation of France under Nazi occupation. Sartre and Merleau-Ponty's experiences as members of the *Résistance* and as the colonized French proved greatly constitutive of the path that French existentialism took in the postwar period.

Here, I borrow from Schalk's illuminating discussion of *engagement*, the involvement of intellectuals during the Algerian Revolution and during the U.S.–Vietnam conflict, especially as he attributes the translation of the concept into English to Sartre's essay, *What is Literature?* (Schalk 1991: 41). According to Schalk, *engagement* is the process by which intellectuals "descend" from the ivory tower and participate in political affairs, most often through participation in or support of protests or "social movements." This participation, he is careful to point out, is not coerced; rather, it "is derived from reflection on the external political and social situation, and a conscious and reasonably free decision to become involved" (loc. cit.). The process of *engagement* follows three steps: the pedagogic stage, characterized by calm, scholarly writings intended to educate the public and political leaders with regard to the error of their ways; the moral stage, in which "ethically based protest and a growing sense of outrage and shame" is incorporated into the educational process; and the "counter legal" stage, in which intellectuals participated in actions their respective nation-states deemed illegal (Schalk 1991: 48–52). Sadly, as Schalk contends, most intellectuals who became *engagé* ended up *embrigadé* (blindly committed to a particular cause) by the end of the conflicts concerned, and ultimately became *dégagé*, leaving behind their critical spirit in order to return to a disengaged life (ibid.: 52–53). It is the process of *engagement*, though, that characterizes the notability of the works of Sartre and Merleau-Ponty; both had a long-lasting commitment to the improvement of the human condition through their philosophical and political involvement in the world. They are, to be sure, not the only scholars to become involved in public and political affairs (Durkheim's engagement with the Dreyfus Affair in "The moral responsibility of the intellectuals" and Chomsky's activism against the Vietnam War and on behalf of the sovereignty movement in East Timor provide two clear examples of *engagement*); however, Sartre's and Merleau-Ponty's participation in public affairs is crucial for the clear understanding of the fundamental claim of their existentialisms—namely that one is always positioned in the world, and an ethics is only comprehensible in relation to what one does in the world and for or with others.

Prior to the outbreak of World War II, the work of Sartre in particular had a slightly political dimension, as is evinced by some concluding remarks in "The Transcendence of Ego" and other works around the events of the Spanish Civil War (in particular, "Le Mur," a short story published just after *Nausea*) (McBride 1991: 24–25). However, most of Sartre's works prior to 1945 contributed little to what we would call a Sartrean political theory (ibid.: 28). It is after the experience of being a German prisoner-of-war, of participating in the *Résistance*, and of being colonized by the Germans that Sartre's work takes on an explicitly political dimension that we could identify by the term *engagement*, a kind of directedness characteristic of his later works. This engagement with the political begins to appear with the founding of *Les Temps modernes*, the politico-literary journal Sartre founded along with Merleau-Ponty in 1945. While the collective, consisting of Simone de Beauvoir, Jacques-Laurent Bost, Merleau-Ponty, and Jean Pouillon, was formed as early as 1941 (just after Sartre's release from a POW camp), the journal only appeared in its public form in 1945. Sartre's directorship of *Les Temps modernes*, quite clearly, shows the first instance of his increasing engagement with current affairs. The journal, oriented as it was (and continues to be) to providing current commentary on social and political affairs and to promoting a socialist revolution, gives us a prime example of Sartre's developing "synthetic anthropology," what Davies calls the journal's *raison d'être* (Davies 1987: xi–1).

The second aspect of Sartre's writings, the "literature of commitment" (McBride 1991: 51), in which politics and literature, author and public come together and realize the bonds that should link them, places him squarely in the camp of individuals committed to social change. His essay *What is Literature?* (Sartre 1948b) identifies the problematic relationship between the engaged author and their public in the postwar period: there is no natural audience for the committed author who wants to bring about a socialist revolution as did Sartre, since the bourgeoisie, the usual readers of an author, are the targets for the author's political attacks (McBride 1991: 57–58). Over the years, Sartre's engagement with the variety of political conflicts in the Cold War situation—Algeria, Vietnam, and the continuing attempts of both the United States and the USSR to culturally and economically colonize France—continued to blossom, and Sartre took great pains to engage his fellow existentialists, especially Merleau-Ponty and Camus, in political affairs, even giving rise to heated public debates between them and the end of Sartre's friendship with Camus (Sartre 1965; Aronson 2004). Thus, we can see from this brief review of Sartre's life that the goal of *Les Temps modernes*—the development of the public intellectual, committed to social change and a continuous *autocritique*—was actualized throughout Sartre's life; from the manifesto presented in the first number of *Les Temps modernes*, we find that "*Notre revue voudrait contribuer, pour sa modeste part, à la constitution d'une anthropologie synthétique. Mais il ne s'agit pas seulement . . . de préparer un progrès dans le domaine de la connaissance pure: le but lointain que nous nous fixons est une libération*" (Sartre 1948a: 26; in Davies 1987: 3; italics in original).[2]

Merleau-Ponty, as well, was continuously engaged in postwar social and political affairs, working to make politics "thinkable" (Whiteside 1988: 3).

> Before the war, politics seemed unthinkable to us because it treats men as statistics, and we saw no sense in treating these unique beings, each of whom is a world unto himself, according to a set of general rules and as a collection of interchangeable objects. Politics is impossible from the perspective of consciousness. But the moment came when our innermost being felt the impact of these external absurdities. (Merleau-Ponty 1964c: 145)

The Occupation seemed to have more of an impact upon the writings of Merleau-Ponty than it did on others, as Merleau-Ponty became one of the few to engage in a discussion of the complicity of the French in the Occupation. Sartre, de Beauvoir, and Camus saw their decision to remain in Paris during the Occupation as an act of resistance, even while attempting to live their lives as normally as possible, with Sartre, for example, continuing to teach philosophy during the Occupation (McBride 1991: 26). Merleau-Ponty, however, felt the extreme guilt of not having done "enough" to resist German oppression, partly because the situation of the Occupation did not offer anyone an efficacious choice: "It is true that we are not innocent and that the situation in which we found ourselves admitted of no irreproachable conduct. By staying here we all became accomplices to some extent, and we must say of the Resistance what the combatants said about the war: no one comes back except the man who at some moment or another reduced the risks he was running, who, in that sense, elected to save his life" (Merleau-Ponty 1964c: 147). As he struggled with the political dimension of existence, Merleau-Ponty noted with some regret that some forms of philosophy do not allow for political thinking. Descartes and Kant, in particular, are condemned by Merleau-Ponty for this failing of modern philosophy. Being at the center of modern political thought as they are, Cartesian and Kantian modes of thinking—namely the taking of the *cogito* as the foundation of the world and the universalization of norms that, when combined, result in a "statistical treatment of man" and the treatment of human beings as "substitutable objects" (Whiteside 1988: 5)—obliterate the possibility of thinking politically or of making politics thinkable and able to be experienced. This, in part, explains the existentialist reliance on phenomenology. By using a method that is peculiarly able to study the ambiguities, contingencies, and vicissitudes of everyday life, one can develop a philosophical perspective that makes possible what Whiteside claims are Merleau-Ponty's three goals of philosophy: understanding the difficulties of everyday situated life, evaluating the various choices presented to us by our situation, and acting to bring about humanistic values. It is after the realization by Merleau-Ponty that the main philosophical trends of his time cannot serve as a foundation for a politics that his work begins the same process of engagement we have identified in Sartre.

Individuals, the Conditions of Existence, and Action

Those who decry existentialism for its dread, despair, nausea, and other seemingly unappealing aspects of existence focus on the conditions of existence of the modern individual. The human condition is, for both Sartre and Merleau-Ponty, characterized by massive burdens: the ethical responsibility to act according to the one aspect of our existence that could be called "essential," that is, freedom; the massive responsibility for our actions that both writers attribute to the human condition; and the essential meaninglessness of our existence that provides us with the root of the despair and nausea that even Sartre attributes to our condition. Rather than constructing what some critics have called "quietism," a charge Sartre spent a great deal of time arguing against (e.g., Sartre 1993a: 47), these conditions lead to the fundamental claim of existentialist theory: that human beings are first and foremost characterized by their capacity for agency (ibid.: 48–49) and that they should act upon this capacity, bearing in mind their full responsibility for their actions.

Even in this limited claim, the connections with the other aspects of existentialism start to become clear. Once we realize our capacity for action and engage in the world, we realize that others are present in our situation, others who are affected by the results of our action; hence, we have a responsibility for them that I would call ethical. Put another way, the presence of others in our situation (at whatever sociological level of analysis we posit "the situation") creates for us an opportunity in which we can act toward them in a number of ways, ranging from cooperation in the fight against oppression to the attempt to dominate them. The term "responsibility for others" does not necessarily imply at this point that we are beholden to treating others as ends, à la the Kantian categorical imperative; rather, our orientation to others, even if it is a neutral or disengaged orientation, is an ethical relation of some sort, and it is our orientation to others in the formulation and actualization of our project that determines the ethicality of our actions. Once we know that others are present with us, other forces, such as the social group in which we exist, also become present to us, as do aspects of our situation for which we bear responsibility. Once we experience the social group, we also experience the material conditions of that social group (what Sartre calls "scarcity"; Sartre 1985 [1960]: 123), as well as the historical conditions that produced that group *and* the human *praxis* of others and myself that reproduces that group. We also realize our responsibility for all of these aspects of our existence, and respond to this responsibility either by turning toward it in our "authenticity" or by turning away from it in "bad faith," both of which lead to another set of actions on our part, and so on. It is because of this interconnectedness that the analytic separation I am forced to make between the individual, the social, and the historical is an awkward and arbitrary one.

To proceed, then, I will begin with Merleau-Ponty's depiction of the human condition—the fact of our embeddedness in the world with others and our necessary being-with-others that results from our mere existence. I will then discuss the characteristic aspects of the human condition: our innate freedom, our embeddedness in a particular concrete situation, our responsibility for the construction of meaning in the world, and the ambiguity that inheres to the effects of our action. Third, I will outline what I see as the existentialist understanding of how we envision the possibilities for our action in the world. Next, I will discuss the particular aspects of our *praxis* and show how *praxis* in some respects is a form of resistance (though I will not make the claim that all human action is resistance). Finally, I will discuss our orientations to the effects of our actions, namely ambiguity, responsibility, and "authenticity," and how these lead to the development of an existential social ethics.

Orientations to the Human Condition

Over and against the Cartesian dualism between *en-soi* and *pour-soi* in Sartre's philosophy that we saw in chapter 1, Merleau-Ponty explores a "third term *between* the for-itself and the in-itself" (Merleau-Ponty 1962: 122n1), the realm of perceptual experience. This third term is the structure of the relationships between the perceiving subject and the perceived object, a structure that is the result of the for-itself's multiple and partial perspectives on the object, the taking of these partial perspectives as the grounds for the development of a *sens* (sense or meaning) of the object, and the unification of these partial perspectives into the "in-itself" meaning of the object. This *intermonde* ("inter-world") is the pre-reflective perspective the individual takes on objects within their world:

> I do not need to take an objective view of my own movement, or take it into account, in order to reconstitute the true form of the object behind its appearing: the account is already taken, and already the new appearance has compounded itself with the lived-through movement and presented itself as an appearance of a cube. The thing, and the world, are given to me along with the parts of my body, not by any "natural geometry," but in a living connection comparable, or rather identical, with that existing between the parts of my body itself. (Merleau-Ponty 1962: 204–205)

Merleau-Ponty's depiction of the "unthought" aspects of his perception of a cube shows explicitly the way in which the *intermonde* appears to us; that is, it does not explicitly appear to us in the way that Being does to Sartre, but rather *grounds* our ability to unify the six sides of the cube into what we perceive as "a cube" in an almost unconscious manner (ibid.: 440). Hence, for Merleau-Ponty, the possibility of having a consciousness of the world is predicated not upon my absolute consciousness (nor, as we will see next, upon my absolute freedom), but rather upon my ability to integrate my sense perceptions of the world in ways that are particular to me as a result of my experience in the world. The mechanism by which these sense perceptions are able to be integrated is not merely the consciousness or *cogito*; Merleau-Ponty also claims that there is a core set of meanings that inhere to the human species as a whole, a common set of intentions that, by virtue of the similarities of the human body, "define the general contours of the environment for human beings as a species" (Merleau-Ponty 1962: 440; Whiteside 1988: 55). The cube in this example serves the same function as anything in the world—a fact to which we *must* orient by virtue of our existence. As such, this species-based mode of relating to the world fundamentally grounds us in our situation, both in our environment and our relationship with others by virtue of this visceral commonality. As well, this embeddedness in the world and understanding of the commonalities of *l'intermonde* provides us with the basis for understanding the nature of freedom.

Freedom and the Situation

For Merleau-Ponty, freedom is neither a characteristic of human existence that exists as opposed to the situation in which we find ourselves, nor merely a tool in the positing and achievement of some other end. While Sartre's early work posits freedom as the fundamental choice of values (or, as we see in the later Sartre, as the question of succeeding in creating fundamental values in the world in the face of ossified social formations), Merleau-Ponty sees freedom as an intentional quality of actions we take. While for Sartre we might freely flee a mugger who approaches us, for Merleau-Ponty this flight is not a free choice; put another way, for Merleau-Ponty freedom cannot be the same in all actions, else there would be no freedom whatsoever (Merleau-Ponty 1962: 436–437). For Merleau-Ponty, concrete freedom "rests upon our voluntarily mobilizing *in*voluntary, body intentions into generalized attitudes toward the world which themselves function involuntarily as background for, while being modified by, specific choices" (Compton 1998: 181). This development of an intentional orientation to the world that results in an act, one which leads to a further modification of this structure of intentionality, is the manifestation of freedom. Over and against Sartre's claim that freedom can "fundamentally choose" values, Merleau-Ponty argues that it is our orientation to our situation that characterizes freedom. Our freedom is not absolute in the way that Sartre describes it in *Being and Nothingness*; we cannot absolutely change our situation or create a new one *ex nihilo*:

> If freedom is doing, it is necessary that what it does should not be immediately undone by a new freedom. Each instant, therefore, must not be a closed world; one instant must be able to commit its successors and, a

decision once taken and action once begun, I must have something acquired at my disposal, I must benefit from my impetus, I must be inclined to carry on, and there must be a bent or propensity of the mind. (Merleau-Ponty 1962: 437)

The temporality Merleau-Ponty attributes to freedom—the quality of freedom as a historical and historicizing process that motivates and makes possible action in the world—makes this conception of freedom quite different from that of Sartre, who sees freedom as a kind of radical negation. For Merleau-Ponty, freedom is appropriation rather than negation: freedom adjusts itself to the situation rather than attempting to destroy its particularities; and freedom, rather than creating meaning in the world through a particular nihilistic choice of meaning, sees a meaning-laden field in its situation and options off a particular kind of meaning in its adjustment to the situation (Merleau-Ponty 1962: 441; Hall 1998: 188–194). As such, freedom presupposes a pre-reflective understanding of the potential variety of meanings in the world and, as a result of our gradual inculcation into social and historical processes, adjusts itself to the meanings present to the individual in the world, who then appropriates one type of meaning as its own.

There is, then, an interdependence in Merleau-Ponty's conception of freedom that corresponds directly to his conception of existence in *l'intermonde*. Freedom actually presupposes the existence of meanings in the world that we pre-reflectively understand as a result of our similarities with other human beings. At least in the beginning, Merleau-Ponty means our physiological and psychological makeup; human beings can see and hear at certain frequencies, have certain pain tolerances, and the like, and will therefore respond similarly to similar stimuli. But, we can also see that these similarities extend into more social realms as well: we are situated not only in our body in-the-world, but also in a certain set of relations with the world and the others who are in it with us. As such, we exist in a sociohistorical situation with its own temporality, and therefore perceive meanings in the world similarly to those who are in that situation with us. ("Culture shock" is a good negative example of this pre-reflective understanding.) So the meanings in the world are, to some extent, already constructed, and we act as agents in the appropriations of these meanings based upon our situation: "we are entangled in *real* relations, i.e., relations of *reciprocal determination of meaning*, with the order of nature, with other persons, and with institutions, through our bodies" (Compton 1998: 179). And it is our embodiment, our embeddedness, in a particular situation that gives our freedom the quality it has by orienting us to certain meanings that exist in the world and constituting the site by which we can act on them.

I would argue that each version of freedom presented above presupposes our ability to take from our past and project a future state of existence, one that can be actualized through *praxis* in the present. What I have called the "potential" version of freedom, that appropriate to the *en-soi*, operates in such a way that it orients to the past, intending itself as the negation of "that which was." The "situated" freedom of Merleau-Ponty is oriented to the present, in the sense of "what meanings exist in the world as it is now?" and draws from that situation the "tools," for lack of a better word, it needs to create the meanings it would like to see in the world. And the "actual" version of freedom posited in Sartre's "second ethics" is one that intends to bring about some entirely new state of affairs, but cannot because of the historicity of the subject and the residuum of history in the current situation; as such, it orients to both the present and the future.

Each aspect of existential freedom fits into a particular temporal frame in the human individual's existence: the *en-soi* to the past; *l'intermonde*, the present; and the *pour-soi* to the future. This is not, though, a strict temporal limitation, as each temporal aspect of the modes of existence also refers to the others, so that the *en-soi* orients to the present insofar as it is facticity and to the future as the individual wants to be "more than it is"; *l'intermonde* is situated in the present, but is the "sedimentation" of the past of a social and historical context and the site for future intersubjective action; and the *pour-soi* reflects upon the past *en-soi* or facticity in order to figure out how it is able to act in the present in order to achieve its intended result. Put another way, "The idea of an initial, instantaneous, reflective choice of a self-constituting consciousness is a confusion, since choice presupposes a prior commitment and future consequences, i.e., continuity" (Hall 1998: 192; cf. Merleau-Ponty 1962: 437). So because of the temporal conditioning of the three modes of existence, we also have a temporal conditioning of the three aspects of freedom; that is, the continuity of our subjectivity provides us with limitations on our perceived possibilities for action. Taking from Merleau-Ponty, we can see that our past, which is ever-present with us, helps determine the mode by which we encounter or intend the present situation; if we have a certain set of experiences, such as being abused, then our actions in the present are in part determined by the way in which we intend in the present the set of meanings surrounding this abuse. As well, the future state of affairs we wish to create—continuing the example above, transcending our existence as "a victim of abuse," for example—is one that cannot be actualized without a set of actions in the present that will bring us to a point where we can act to transcend this "victim" status. Our motivations for action, then, depend simultaneously on the meanings we intend our past experiences to have for us, the horizon of possibilities we envision in the present for acting to bring about another set of meanings (and, as we will see later, the impact of others on this horizon and the set of meanings we wish to intend), and the set of meanings we intend to experience in the future. It is in this way that we begin to formulate what could be called "motivations" for action.

But, according to Merleau-Ponty, these motive forces are constructed after the fact in a justificatory manner. That is, we reconstruct the *sens* or meaning we intend our actions to have in the world after we have engaged in them as a way of making others understand what we are doing (and, thereby, to make ourselves understand our actions). The action, it seems, occurs pre-reflectively; we experience a particular situation and respond to that situation in a particular way that can be narrativized (in becoming part of the *en-soi* or our facticity) and explained to others as part of our project. The "figure-background" relationship Merleau-Ponty lays out in *The Phenomenology of Perception* helps to explain this. Merleau-Ponty's example of the development of class consciousness shows that once the worker realizes that their particular "lot in life" is not fate, but is rather the result of their activity in conjunction with the "background" of their situation (in other words, they are workers because they act in accordance with the way in which "workers" are situated), they can begin to realize the intersubjectivity of their structural position and can act in accordance with others in the same structural position. Prior to this realization—that is, prior to the bringing to the foreground of what was formerly in the background of the individual's perception—the individual could call "their lot in life" (their structural position as "worker") the motivation for their action, even if they intended to act in a way that would bring them out of the structural position of the proletariat; after this realization, they can intend their future actions as oriented toward bringing about a socialist society.

The transition here is important for Merleau-Ponty. Without the realization that their actions were creating "their lot in life," the worker is in a sense "back-writing" their fate; after the realization, though, they begin to orient more to a future state of affairs and intentionally intend their actions to bring about this state of affairs. As such, the phenomenology of this awareness becomes crucial, not merely for bringing about social change but also for acting in accordance with their freedom. Freedom, as we have seen, requires an orientation to the conditions of one's existence or one's situation; what Sartre would call "stupidity" (Sartre 1993b: 312), and what we might otherwise call "bad faith," would be the absence of this orientation to the phenomenology of one's situation, to the unfree manner in which they acted, and to the future, as there is no project with which one acts in the present. This absence of a project that serves as an expression of the creativity and spontaneity of the individual leaves them acting in accordance with what Sartre calls practico-inert structures, the sedimentation of the *praxis* of individuals in the form of unthought social and cultural practices; and this mode of action can and often does serve as a way of maintaining an oppressive status quo situation for an entire society through the actions of the individual. In this way, we can see a distinction that will become important for the next section—the consequential aspect of our *praxis*.

Praxis *and Resistance*

One of the important aspects of existentialist thought that Merleau-Ponty's discussion of the development of class consciousness raises is the relation of *praxis* to the human individual's situation. Sartre and Merleau-Ponty take two different approaches to this problem. For Sartre, the essential tension that exists is between *praxis*, the actual work that human beings do upon the world, and the practico-inert, the end product of every bit of *praxis* in which we engage. For Merleau-Ponty, the figure/background issues in perception as well as the temporal orientations that the individual must engage in govern the way in which we see our possibilities to engage in a particular kind of action. The effect of these insights, though, is the same: Whatever we do in the world will ultimately become sedimented in the common set of meanings that frame us in our situation, and what we do will end up working, in some sense, against us. It is here that we can begin to see the issue of resistance coming to light, though in this first individuated instance, resistance is a matter of our ability to act upon the world; it functions as a tension between our intentions toward the world and our ability to actualize the meaning we want our actions to have in the world and for others.

Sartre's *Critique of Dialectical Reason* is the work in which he begins to explicitly deal with the issue of *praxis*. For Sartre, *praxis* follows the traditional Marxist definition; it refers to the labor we do in and on the world, "an activity which organises a field in the light of certain objectives" (Sartre 1985 [1960]: 328). In accordance with his existentialism, though, Sartre argues that *praxis* is the means by which we create our being. As he puts it:

> But all these manipulations, which make freedom into a curse, presuppose that the relation of men to matter and to other men resides above all in *doing*, as synthetic creative work. And the *being* of man, as inorganic passivity, comes to him *in* his action from the fact that every individual undertaking is forced by its dialectical freedom to interiorise a double inert materiality. . . . But if he can reinteriorise this reciprocity of materiality as the *untranscendable being* of his activity, this is because other activities have already interiorised and re-exteriorised it *as other*. (Sartre 1985 [1960]: 328)

This passage reflects the double way in which our actions become our "being," our project, our expression of ourselves in the world. Our actions in and on the world construct a mode in which we can "back-write" our "essence" as our project, the way in which we express ourselves through our *praxis*. This being or essence comes about according to Sartre as a result of an interiorization of what we do and what we will for all others in the world. In "The Humanism of Existentialism," Sartre argues that when we engage in an act, we will that act for all humankind (Sartre 1993a: 37). This process becomes interiorized by the *pour-soi*: we take our action as the site of reflection and internalize the effects and the efficacy of our action, in effect appropriating our action to ourselves, making it a part of "who we are" and what we want others to be. In effect, what we do according to Sartre is add our action to ourselves as a quality of us, relying upon a new notion of the human individual as a fully material being (Anderson 1993: 89). This quality added by Sartre in the *Critique* is meant to reflect the embeddedness of the human being in a particular sociohistorical situation; in other words, by adding materiality as a quality of the human individual, what Sartre has done is to take into account what he calls the "practico-inert"—the sedimentation of past human *praxis*.

The practico-inert—and this is the second way in which our *praxis* comes back upon us—is the sum total of past *praxis* (in effect, History). The creation of the practico-inert is the result of two complementary processes. First, the interiorization of *praxis* by the human agent as "their project," the construction of the facticity of the *en-soi* through reflection by the *pour-soi* so that "what is" can be transcended, constructs the past *praxis* of the agent as a thing, something upon which further work can be done. Just as the situation the human agent encounters provides them with the "inert materiality" that is worked upon through *praxis*, the past *praxis* of the individual becomes matter upon which they can add, subtract, and so on. Since our *praxis* has an effect upon our situation and the world, it is accessible to and has a variety of effects on others, including the "universalization" process Sartre refers to in "The Humanism of Existentialism," making possible a commitment to a project and therefore to ethics. But, our *praxis* reaches the others in our situation as facticity, as a thing, just as their *praxis* in response reaches us as a "brute fact" of our existence: "But if he can reinteriorise this reciprocity of materiality as the *untranscendable being* of his activity, this is because other activities have already interiorised and re-exteriorised it *as other*" (Sartre 1985 [1960]: 328). Others in the world take what we do as exterior to them, do work upon the results of our *praxis*, and internalize that *praxis* to them, leaving our *praxis* inert to them and their *praxis* inert to us. This reciprocity of facticity leaves us in paradoxical circumstances: no matter what we do in the world or what *sens* we try to give our *praxis*, it returns to us as something other than us, regardless of our intention.

It is in this way that we construct the practico-inert field through our *praxis*. As Sartre points out, and I quote at length:

> The practico-inert field is the field of our servitude, which means *not* ideal servitude, but real subservience to "natural" forces, to "mechanical"forces, and to "anti-social" apparatuses. This means that everyone struggles against an order which really and materially crushes his body and which he sustains and strengthens by his individual struggle against it. Everything is born at this line which simultaneously separates and unites huge physical forces in the world of inertia and exteriority (in so far as the nature and orientation of the energy transformations which characterise them give a definite statute of improbability to life in general and to human life in particular) and practical organisms (in so far as their *praxis* tends to confirm them within their structure of inertia, that is to say, in their role as converters of energy). This is where the change from unification as a process to unity as an inert statute occurs, and where inertia, as a moment which has been transcended and preserved by life and practice, turns back on them so as to transcend them and preserve them in the name of their dialectical unity. . . . (Sartre 1985 [1960]: 332–333)

Our free *praxis*, by which we unite the "practical field" or situation we encounter in the world in order to do work upon it in light of the project we intend to bring about, has the result of being turned against us as a unified structure that operates in a way akin to the "obstacles to freedom" discussed by Merleau-Ponty in *The Phenomenology of Perception*. We do work upon the world by negating the current state of affairs in order to bring about a new state of affairs; and yet, this new state of affairs reappears to us as an inert materiality upon which we are forced to do more work (ibid.: 335). The world offers us a "passive resistance"; it works against us while at the same time we work to negate it through the *praxis* inspired by our project, placing us in a situation of servitude.

Being a practical, actional being entails facing down a world that passively struggles against us at every turn. The world offers us something that is not ours as the matter upon which we are supposed to do work; and the more we do work upon the world, the more it appears that even the work we do is alienated from our intended project. As our *praxis* is interiorized and re-exteriorized as it is returned to us in practico-inert structures, it becomes "not ours," and threatens to completely negate us as we intend ourselves to be through our project. In this way, the transition from *praxis* to practico-inert is, for Sartre, something to be resisted.

We can see that the experience of the conversion of our *praxis* into the practico-inert structures that recondition our situation is a universal experience, one that characterizes our everyday life (Sartre 1985 [1960]: 336). Sartre's presentation of this fundamental characteristic of our experience leads us to envision one particular question that is important for the task at hand: How is actual social and political resistance possible? How is it that we can act in such a way that the results of our *praxis* do not reinforce the practico-inert structures of existence and at the same time do not involve working against the *praxis* of others? To begin to respond to this question, we must turn to other aspects of this conversion. The figure/background issue brought to light by Merleau-Ponty will help us develop an idea of how resistance in the sense of group actions oriented to radically changing the social conditions of existence is conceivable.

(Fore)grounding Resistance

Recall that for Merleau-Ponty the figure/background issue refers to the way in which we constitute a group of sense perceptions as field or as a unified structure that has meaning for the individual who perceives the phenomena and who intends the various sense-perceptions to have a particular unity. In this view of how we perceive the world, we develop a certain set of relationships between the elements that make up the "system," foregrounding some of the elements while backgrounding others (Merleau-Ponty 1963: 47). It is in this way, Merleau-Ponty argues, that class consciousness can "spontaneously" develop where previously the individuals who gain this consciousness only saw their situation as "fate." If we perceive the requirement that I sell my labor power to another in order to earn a salary that supports me as "my lot in life," then I do not perceive this situation as one that I continue to support through going to work each day. The "class" aspects of my situation then exist for me in the background, as unnoticed, unmarked aspects of the conditions of my existence:

> My fellow workers in factory or field, or other farmers, do the same work as I do in comparable conditions; we co-exist in the same situation and feel alike, not in virtue of some comparison, as if each one of us lived primarily within himself, but on the basis of our tasks and gestures. These situations do not imply any express evaluation, and if there is a tacit evaluation, it represents the thrust of a freedom devoid of any project against unknown obstacles; one cannot in any case talk about a choice, for in all three cases it is enough that I should be born into the world and that I exist in order to experience my life as full of difficulties and constraints—I do not choose so to experience it. But this state of affairs can persist without my becoming class-conscious, understanding that I am of the proletariat and becoming a revolutionary. How then am I to make this change? . . . If [class consciousness] does [arise], it is not because the day-laborer has decided to become a revolutionary and consequently confers a value upon his actual condition; it is because he has perceived, in a concrete way, that his life is synchronized with the life of the town laborers and that all share a common lot. (Merleau-Ponty 1962: 443–444)

As Merleau-Ponty puts it, class consciousness begins to arise when the commonality of the larger-scale forces characterizing the situation are perceived as part of the foreground, as opposed to the earlier perception of the mere tasks people perform as being the foreground aspects. This change in focus provides us with the ability to perceive aspects of our situation that were disguised to us before, and enables us to conceive of resistance.

Our action, insofar as we see it operating at the level of the individual, tends to lead us to believe that we focus solely upon our own project when we engage in forms of *praxis*; that is, we act in accordance with the meaning we want to see in the world, so the larger-scale issues that characterize our situation tend to fall away into the background. This leads to the result of alienating ourselves through our *praxis*, that is, through the return of our *praxis* to us as something Other than us in the practico-inert. However, if we follow Merleau-Ponty's logic, by changing the focus of our perception (and, I would argue, our intentionality toward our situation), we can see the common situation or facticity we share with others in the same or similar situations—workers, members of visible minority groups, or oppressed social subgroups—thereby making it possible to begin to conceive of a way of acting in which our *praxis* does not have the effect of reinforcing the status quo practico-inert structures of the world.

There is still, though, the issue of the conversion of *praxis* into the practico-inert. Even with our awareness of the process by which our *praxis* is turned against us and is often used to support our "servitude," to use Sartre's word, how is it that we can turn our *praxis* against the status quo? Two issues relating to this question have yet to be discussed: the issue of our orientation toward the future, posed in terms of "responsibility," "ambiguity," "bad faith," and "authenticity"; and the issue of our orientation toward and cooperation with others, including the issues of group formations and relations and the possibility of common *praxis*. Obviously, *praxis* can be done in a revolutionary manner; it has happened and continues to happen in countless different circumstances. The issue, though, is how this change in perception benefits us in terms of engaging in practices of resistance. As Merleau-Ponty's discussion of the impossibility of merely willing ourselves as "bourgeois" or "proletarian" shows, it is not merely the desire to "be" one or the other that makes us that type of person, but rather the way in which we act upon this desire through our *praxis*; our project must orient itself to our particular situation (e.g., one in which we can barely keep food on our table). By bringing to the fore the characteristics of our situation and the way in which our *praxis* is turned against us or reinforces the status quo, we can intend a project that is oriented to bringing about the kind of world we envision for ourselves, one that we intend for others as well. Sartre refers to this as "hope": "Hope means that I can't undertake an action without expecting that I am going to complete it. And, as I told you, I don't think that this hope is a lyrical illusion; it is in the very nature of action. In other words, action, being at the same time hope, cannot be in principle doomed to absolute inevitable failure. This doesn't mean that it must necessarily achieve its end, but it must present itself in a realization of the goal posited as future" (Sartre and Lévy 1996: 56). Put another way, the realization of the paradoxical limitations placed on our *praxis* by the existence of others and a preexisting set of practico-inert structures should not doom us to the quietism so frequently attributed to existentialism, but rather should make us act toward and with others so that our projects can potentially be achieved, to act with the hope of achieving the goal as it is posited as a future. This leads us to the issues of our orientation to the present situation and the future state of affairs we want to bring about—to the questions of responsibility and ambiguity.

Problematic Orientations: Ambiguity, Responsibility, and Authenticity

The paradoxical conditions that constrain our individual *praxis*—the presence of others, the conversion of our *praxis* into practico-inert structures that turn against us, and our inability to rely upon the success of our projects in the world—force us to consider the orientations we have toward the present, the past, and the future. Incorporating the notions of temporality and historicity that are part and parcel of our embeddedness in the world, we will see that in our encounter with the world and in our willing of a project that will determine our actions in and on the world, we are forced to orient to all three time frames simultaneously. Going beyond the usual notions of ethicality we see in traditional philosophy, existentialism forces us to take on a view of ourselves as acting individuals in terms of who we are, who we were, and who we envision ourselves being in the future. In other words, the issues of ambiguity, responsibility, and authenticity seen as characteristics of our existence all result from and orient us to our temporality, our place within the development of History as the sum total of human *praxis*, and ultimately, as we will see in a later section, to others as an existential form of ethics.

We have seen that one of the difficulties of formulating *praxis* as the development of our project and hence of our being is that we can never be sure that what we intend in our action is what will come about; that is, the results of our actions may be not be the results we intended. This can be as small a matter as not winning the affections of someone we admire even though we "did everything right," or as historically grave a matter as being labeled "traitors to the revolution" even though we followed through on a revolutionary program, as was the case of those convicted in the Moscow Trials Merleau-Ponty writes about in *Humanism and Terror* (Merleau-Ponty 1969). This *ambiguity* is a fundamental problem in the development of a life-project and its actualization in the world. In the first instance, this ambiguity in the first instance is the result of the tension between the three aspects of human existence: the *en-soi*, the *pour-soi*, and our being-in-the-world (Bell 1989: 30). Because the choice of any meaning for our existence is a human choice, making us the basis of our meaning in the world, we exist in an ambiguous state: the meaning we create in the world is such that it is not always the same for us across time, and the meaning we give to ourselves may not be the same as the meaning others give us in the world. Therefore, we must constantly strive to create meaning for ourselves in the world: "What we maintain is that one must not expect that this goal be justified as a point of departure of a new future; insofar as we no longer have a hold on the time which will flow beyond its coming, we must not expect anything of that time for which we have worked; other men will have to live its joys and sorrows" (de Beauvoir 1994 [1948]: 128). So, in addition to the ambiguity that is the result of the brute fact of our existence, we see that there is also an ambiguity when it comes to the temporal effects of our action. We must constantly act in accordance with the project we intend for ourselves in order to continuously create the meaning we want to see in the world. However, the meaning we want to see in the world may not be the meaning that others want to see in the world and in fact may not be the meaning our actions have in their conversion into the practico-inert. Thus, there is the potential for conflict based on the values that separate individuals attempt to bring about in the world as the result of their action. Put another way, the notion of ambiguity as being rooted in the conditions of existence leads us to see that negation (as a result of our freedom) becomes the dominant mode of our action.

In addition to the possibility of a tension between different individuals' projects, there is also an ambiguity that occurs in a temporal fashion because of the results of our actions taking on the form of facticity. When the results of our actions become a factual part of the situation others and we encounter, they can have impacts upon them and upon us that we never expected:

> In the end everyone agrees that political acts are to be judged not only according to their meaning for the moral agent but also according to the sense they acquire in the historical context and dialectical phase in which such acts originate. . . . In a world of struggle—and for Marxists history is the history of class struggles—there is no margin of indifferent action which classical thought accords to individuals; *for every action unfolds and we are responsible for its consequences.* (Merleau-Ponty 1969: 23)

As such, there are two temporal and historical spaces in which ambiguity exists for us: the moment at which the act is done, and the future, after the impacts of the act have unfolded. Neither of these spaces have a guaranteed meaning: we create the meaning in the present we want our act to embody, but that act can, through its unfolding and its impact upon others as a result of the conversion into the practico-inert, end up with a very different meaning than we intended.

Merleau-Ponty's claim that we are responsible for the results of our actions introduces an element of *historical responsibility* into the development and implementation of our project. Since History is the result of our actions, actions that are translated into practico-inert structures that impact upon individuals in the future, it is predicated upon the same ambiguity that characterizes the conditions of our existence. As such, we cannot simply engage in an action and then dismiss the results as "not what we intended." Rather, because our actions are ours, we are responsible for the impact of those actions, regardless of how messy the consequences may be or how much they sully our soul. A historical responsibility, then, develops the idea of what I call the "ripple effect" of our *praxis*, one that embraces our responsibility for the effects, including any unintended consequences, of our actions.

This ripple effect has three main aspects. First, the conversion of our *praxis* into the practico-inert often results, as I said earlier, in the turning of our actions against our intentions. Second, our actions do not have effects in a vacuum; instead, they impact directly upon the people closest to us and indirectly upon potentially the entire population of the planet. As such, if the intentions of our action are meant to improve our situation but result in great harm being done to everyone else on the planet, then we would be responsible for this. The third aspect of this ripple effect is a truly historical one. The two aspects of the ripple effect just described occur in an almost contemporaneous fashion; the impacts of the actions undertaken show themselves almost immediately. But longer-term effects also travel with the path of history; we can think of the impact of Puritanism upon both the development of American culture and on the progress of "Western rationalized capitalism" as Weber argued in *The Protestant Ethic and the Spirit of Capitalism*. As such, we can see that the fundamental ambiguity that characterizes our condition of existence—the indeterminacy of our choice to create meaning in the world through our *praxis* or of the effects of our *praxis*—also brings a great responsibility upon us, not only in the present but also long after we have engaged in a particular form of *praxis*. As Merleau-Ponty points out, "Historical responsibility transcends the categories of liberal thought—intention and act, circumstances and will, objective and subjective. It overwhelms the individual in his acts, mingles the objective and the subjective, imputes circumstances to the will; thus it substitutes for the individual as he feels himself to be a role or phantom in which he cannot recognize himself, but in which *he must see himself, since that is what he was for his victims*. And today it is his victims who are right" (Merleau-Ponty 1969: 43; my emphasis).

The difficulty here is that History *is* ambiguity; that is, we can never fully know the impacts of our actions or whether or not the path *we see* in History is the path that History will actually take. As Merleau-Ponty notes,

> History offers us certain factual trends that have to be extrapolated into the future, but it does not give us the knowledge with any deductive certainty of which facts are privileged to outline the present to be ushered in. What is more, at certain moments at least nothing is absolutely fixed by the facts and it is precisely our absence or intervention which history needs in order to take shape. *This does not mean that we can do whatever we please*: there are degrees of probability and these are not nothing. But that means that whatever we do will involve risk. Not that one should hesitate and avoid decision but that a decision can lead political man to his death and the revolution into failure. (Merleau-Ponty 1969: 65; cf. 93)

This highlights the interconnections between ambiguity and responsibility as well as the difficulties they present for the formulation of our project and its actualization in *praxis*. Ambiguity as a condition of our existence forces us to take responsibility for our actions, no matter what the consequences, and hence goes against the Kantian notion of responsibility as embodied in intentionality. And our responsibility for even the unintended consequences of our actions tempts us to avoid ambiguity altogether by resorting to quietism, something Sartre and Merleau-Ponty argue we cannot do, since even the choice not to act is an act. Hence, we are forced to orient to time frames other than the present in formulating our project; namely, the future becomes something to which we are held accountable and to which we must orient in deciding our path of action.

There are, though, two forms of this orientation: "bad faith" and "authenticity." Bad faith, for Sartre, is a lie to oneself, an attempt to deny one's responsibility for their actions, and an attempt to avoid the ambiguity that each of our actions brings to the fore for us. As Bell succinctly puts it, "In bad faith, individuals try not to acknowledge the extent of their freedom and responsibility" (Bell 1989: 32). Bad faith is also an attempt to implicate others in one's denial of their responsibility; we attempt to defer responsibility for ourselves and our actions onto others and their actions insofar as they involve us. As Sartre points out, bad faith requires a denial of "what we are," namely, beings that are forced to constantly make themselves "who they are":

> If man is what he is, bad faith is forever impossible and candor ceases to be his ideal and becomes instead his being. But is man what he is? And more generally, how can he *be* what he is when he exists as consciousness of being? . . . In this sense it is necessary that we *make ourselves* what we

are. But what *are we* then if we have the constant obligation to make
ourselves what we are, if our mode of being is having the obligation to be
what we are? (Sartre 1973 [1956]: 101)

The individual in bad faith attempts to constitute themselves as something they are not—as courageous when they are cowardly, as hetero-
sexual when they are homosexual, as unfree when they are free. As such,
by diverting the responsibility for who they really are onto others or
onto an essentialized version of some aspect of their lives, they try to
escape the need for them to act and their responsibility for that action.

The authentic action is one that asserts our being (and becoming),
our project, our capacity and need for the construction of meaning
through action, and our orientation to others through the action. As
McBride shows us, "Authenticity, says Sartre, involves at once recognizing the ultimate gratuitousness of all human projects and yet devoting
oneself to one's freely-chosen project with full reflectiveness" (McBride
1991: 63). Authenticity, Sartre claims, comes from the negating aspect of
the *pour-soi*; we see in the state of affairs we encounter a lack, and we
negate part of what exists in order to bring about a change in that state
of affairs. As such, we can see that *authenticity involves resistance*; that is,
it involves a choice to negate a part of the *status quo* in favor of developing new meanings in and through one's situation. The situation of
oppression is one in which an individual's freedom is often limited to "no
choice other than resignation or revolution" (Sartre 1966), and for Sartre
it is "revolution," or action designed to bring about a "pure future," if
only in a limited capacity, that characterizes the authentic choice:
"*L'avenir pur* de l'impératif n'est *ni connaissable ni prévisible*. Son caractère
de pur avenir, c'est-à-dire avenir que rien n'a préparé, que rien n'aide à
réaliser, en fait *un avenir à faire*" (Sartre, in Contat and Rybalka 1970:
739).[3] Hence, we can see that because of the ambiguities in our situation
and the ensuing responsibility we hold for the effects of our actions, we
have two choices in the development and actualization of our project:
quietism or struggle, bad faith or authenticity, the maintenance of the
status quo or work intended to bring about a new state of affairs.

We have seen, then, that the position of the individual is one fraught
with contradictions. We are simultaneously self-determining actional
creatures and facticities in the world. We strive to construct our own
absolute meaning, only to find that we can never achieve this total foundation for our existence except through our constant action. We find
that everything we do has an ambiguous meaning in the world because
our *praxis* is turned against us; it becomes part of the situation that faces

not only ourselves but also others in our situation and in the future; and it takes on a meaning in the world that we could never have foreseen. Yet, it is *our praxis* that does this, and so we have complete responsibility for whatever happens to and because of our project. And we find that others are ever-present, and our responsibility for and with them cannot be avoided except in bad faith and in complicity with a system that most would characterize as oppressive. These tensions do not cease once we leave the site of the individual and move on to the level of the social; rather, they multiply in a number of ways. Not only do the antinomies that characterize the conditions of existence of the individual multiply once we examine the sum total of others in the world with us, but new forms of tensions and, ultimately, of violence appear once we move to the next level.

Relations with Others and Conceptions of the Social

In describing patterns of social relations, I use the term "social" rather than "society" for two reasons: first, the "the social" highlights the idea that forms of social life exist at all levels of "society," ranging from the family and close friendship networks to the population of the planet; and second, the term "society" brings to mind not only the group of people who comprise the entity that we call "society," but also the institutions and structures that govern the society (what some would call the "polity"). From an existentialist perspective, the problem of social life is not the explanation of the existence of the polity, which can be easily explained through a restatement of the process by which *praxis* becomes converted into practico-inert structures. The problem, rather, is the formulation of the process by which social groupings that could be called "authentic" and who could act authentically in common *praxis* come into being.

Initial Orientations to Others: Being-for-Others, Being-with-Others

Other people are a fact of our existence and hence make up part of the situation that we encounter in different ways. Two primary orientations to the existence of others, each built upon different aspects of existentialist thought, are being-for-others, apparent in Sartre's earliest works, in which he claims we work to annihilate the *pour-soi* of others in an attempt to reclaim our own freedom, and being-with-others, described by Merleau-Ponty as cooperation in the construction of the world through *l'intermonde*. Being-for-others is fully predicated upon the individualistic existentialism of *Being and Nothingness*, a version that places the sole responsibility for existence in the world on the individual and their attempt to construct themselves as a *sui generis* foundation for the world. Being-with-others, on the other hand, is founded upon the notion of the inter-mundane world, that aspect of intersubjectivity Merleau-Ponty attributes to our situatedness and the reliance of our freedom upon the freedom of others (cf. Merleau-Ponty 1964b: 68). These two orientations toward others result in two different aspects of social life—the first, violence; the second, the possibility of collectively engaging in a liberatory form of *praxis*.

"Being-for-others," as Sartre calls it in *Being and Nothingness*, is the result of an orientation to others that involves the absolute assertion of the individual's *pour-soi*. Because there is an aspect of the *pour-soi* that attempts to assert itself as the absolute foundation for its own existence, it begins to see all others in the world, who also want to establish themselves as their absolute foundation, as threats to the individual's existence. In a manner not unlike Hegel's version of the master/slave dialectic and the struggle for recognition (cf. Honneth 1995), Sartre argues that because we also exist in the world as factical *en-soi*, Others apprehend us from the outside as objects to be worked or worked upon. This is, in part, the result of the way in which we encounter ourselves: because we are "reflection-reflecting" beings (in other words, beings that simultaneously create and annihilate ourselves through the development of our project), we are for ourselves the authors of our own facticity. When we encounter others, though, we become "reflected-on" beings; in other words, our *pour-soi* is annihilated because the other can experience us only as an aspect of the situation they encounter (Sartre 1973 [1956]: 397). We become facts for-the-other rather than consciousness. The other cannot know us as we are, as we see ourselves to be, because they only encounter the veneer of who we are.

At the same time, though, the Other and I are the same; that is, we are equally imbued in the conditions of existence, namely that we are never "what we are," and we can never completely be the project we intend for ourselves. To accept the sameness of the Other, I would have to deny my own attempts to construct myself as the absolute foundation of existence. In other words, in a moment of reflection, I would have to deny my own ability to reflect on my existence, and I would have to deny my own agency in bringing about my being:

> By its effort to be self-consciousness the totality-for-itself would be constituted in the face *of* the self as a self-as-consciousness which has to

not-be the self of which it is consciousness. Conversely the self-as-object in order to *be* would have to experience itself as made-to-be by and for a consciousness which it has to not-be if it wishes to be. Thus would be born the schism of the for-others, and this dichotomic division would be repeated to infinity in order to constitute a plurality of consciousnesses as fragments of a radical explosion. (Sartre 1973 [1956]: 397–398)

Being-for-others, and this is how we generally experience social life, is the result of my *pour-soi* encountering another person as *en-soi*, and vice versa, with the concomitant effect of feeling as if the individual is constructed by Others and that Others have their facticity imposed on them by the individual instead of by themselves (Bell 1989: 75). This orientation is, in other words, the annihilation of consciousness in favor of facticity or alienation: "We have learned that the Other's existence was experienced with evidence in and through the fact of my objectivity. We have seen also that my reaction to my own alienation for the Other was expressed in my grasping the Other as an object. In short, the Other can exist for us in two forms: if I experience him with evidence, I fail to know him; if I know him, if I act upon him, I only reach his being-as-object and his probable existence in the midst of the world" (Sartre 1973 [1956]: 400). This alienation is a dual alienation; the individual is alienated from themselves and from Others, and "no synthesis of these two forms is possible" (loc. cit.). As such, Sartre's early version of this form of a social relationship results in no real relationship at all, but instead "the social remains the relationship of 'two individual consciousnesses' which look at each other" (Merleau-Ponty 1964c: 152). The possibility for violence in these encounters between *en-sois* seeing one another as an obstacle to their project should be clear.

So how can we conceive of a set of relations in which "being-for-others" is not the primary orientation of the individual to other people? The conclusion of Merleau-Ponty's *The Phenomenology of Perception* gives us the beginnings of the other kind of social relationship that I call "being-with-others." The corollary of Merleau-Ponty's claim that our freedom is predicated upon a field of meaning that preexists us is that we are already embedded in a larger social group and constructed in part as the embodiment of that social group (Merleau-Ponty 1962: 438). There is already in existence a set of meanings that my freedom gears itself to as it gears itself to our situation, and it is others who are in my situation who help bring about this set of meanings. As well, our interaction with others is not automatically determined by the Sartrean objectifying gaze; rather, instead of failing to understand an Other because we only see them as facticity, we can understand them because they are part of the field of meaning to which I adjust:

> . . . at the outset, I am not an individual beyond class, I am situated in a social environment, and my freedom, though it may have the power to commit me elsewhere, has not the power to transform me instantly into what I decide to be. Thus to be a bourgeois or a worker is not only to be aware of being one or the other, it is to identify oneself as worker or bourgeois through an implicit or existential project which merges into our way of patterning the world and co-existing with other people. (Merleau-Ponty 1962: 447)

It is thus my decision to intend vis-à-vis my existence or to appropriate a particular meaning that preexists me that already puts me in relation with others in the world. This "being-with-others" is therefore a result of our choice in the development of a project; by choosing one path of action as it has been influenced by our situation, we end up with some people over and against others, and vice versa. We are part of "the social" in the very act of choosing a project, through our intention of certain values in the world, and through our existence.

This is not to say that "being-with-others" results in a more idyllic social situation than "being-for-others." The simple act of realizing that we exist with others through the choice of similar projects influenced by our situation does not immediately make our social lives utopic, any more than "being-for-others" automatically actualizes the Sartrean maxim "Hell is other people." In the first instance, Merleau-Ponty is insisting on our intersubjectivity, on our existence as part of a larger social group. Rather than the absolute determinism of Durkheim's "individuals are social facts," though, Merleau-Ponty allows for the determination of the perception of possible projects by one's encounter with their situation while at the same time granting that we are embedded with others in a social world just as in a physical world. The intersubjectivity Merleau-Ponty identifies is one characterized by dialogue rather than "the gaze": using dialogue as an existentialist explanation of human relations explains how collective existence is possible, as it allows for both the individual's ability to give new meaning to worked matter through their project and the ability of others to understand the meaning given to such matter (Whiteside 1988: 82). At the same time, though, Merleau-Ponty's notion of dialogue as the foundation for social and cultural life does not "distort the nature of communication"; it allows for the development of both the commonality of social life and the explanation of violence. Put another way, while Sartre's notion of "being-for-others" tends to yield only one pessimistic version of human relationships, Merleau-Ponty's "being-with-others" results in an optimistic view of what social relations can be as well as a negative view of what they generally are—that is, characterized by violence.

Violence and the Forms of Social Relations

Neither "being-for-others" nor "being-with-others" guarantee a synchronicity between the values that different individuals want to actualize through their projects. Because there is no absolute foundation for values, either for individuals or for a social group, there is always the possibility of conflict and violence between individuals who are trying to actualize their projects. Individuals freely construct their projects in relation to their understandings of the situation they encounter; as such, there is neither a complete determinism of what we envision for the world nor a complete freedom. We do encounter a set of shared meanings in our situation in the world; however, as a result of our experiences in the past and the development of our particular project, we intend a different set of meanings in the world and formulate different projects that do not necessarily interact in a cooperative manner. Our project is our own, and we wish to assert it in the world, over and against all obstacles including other people, whose freedom to pursue their own projects is to be intended by us in the willing of our own projects. Violence, then, is in a perception of the world; we structure the world and others within it as facticity when we encounter them, thereby attempting to ossify their "essence," an essence that may be shattered at some future point (Merleau-Ponty 1962: 361). As well, after our encounter with the world, our *praxis* does violence to the world. Our perception of a "lack" in the world, the impetus for the development of our project, inspires us to change that world in order to be sure of it as the world we set out to create: "It is true neither that my existence is in full possession of itself, nor that it is entirely estranged from itself, because it is action or doing, and because action is, by definition, the violent transition from what I have to what I aim to have, from what I am to what I intend to be" (Merleau-Ponty 1962: 382). As such, our existence is characterized by a certain form of violence, one which can be counteracted only if we are aware of this phenomenology and only if we actualize other values that can override the violence we do upon the world and, ostensibly, to other people. Hence, because violence is rooted in a multiplicity of partial perspectives, the desire to impose a unitary meaning on the world results in the need to act to bring about domination by the individual (Whiteside 1988: 87). This phenomenon appears in both social orientations: the "gaze" in being-for-others attempts to objectify through perception, while the "dialogue" in being-with-others is subverted in favor of the suppression of dialogue and polyvocality.

In addition to this Ego-Alter formulation of violence, we must keep in mind that, at least for Merleau-Ponty, individual human beings are parts of and symbols of groups that may bear antagonistic values. When these groups come into conflict, they carry with them the institutions in which they are embedded (Merleau-Ponty 1962: 443). In this manner, the kind of social conflict we are more familiar with appears. "The War Has Taken Place," Merleau-Ponty's recounting of the disenchantment of France with its pre–World War II values, shows this quite clearly:

> We had to relearn all the childish behavior which our education had rid us of; we had to judge men by the clothes they wore, reply rudely to their well-mannered commands, live side by side with them for four years without living with them for one minute, feel ourselves become not men but "Frenchmen" beneath their glance. Had we looked more sharply, we could already have found masters and slaves in peacetime society, and we could have learned how each consciousness, no matter how free, sovereign, and irreplaceable it may feel, will become immobile and generalized, a "worker" or a "Frenchman," beneath the gaze of a stranger. But no enslavement is more apparent than that of an occupied country. (Merleau-Ponty 1964c: 142)

This "thingification" of identity is a form of violence; the construction of others as "things" means they can be worked, manipulated, or ignored, have no agency and therefore no longer "exist."

The violence that seems to inhere in social orders appears to counteract the Enlightenment values that we hold so dear to our existence as societies. We are enlightened, free, and able to decide for ourselves what our existence will be . . . or are we? For Merleau-Ponty, the answer is a resounding no:

> . . . it must be said that the Resistance experience, by making us believe that politics is a relationship between man and man or between consciousnesses, fostered our illusions of 1939 and masked the truth of the incredible power of history which the Occupation taught us in another connection. We have returned to the time of *institutions*. . . . those five years have not taught us to think ill of what we once judged to be good, and in the eyes of conscience it is still absurd to hide a truth because it harms one's country, to kill a man because he lives on the other side of the river, to treat another person as a means rather than

an end. We were not wrong, in 1939, to want liberty, truth, happiness, and transparent relations among men, and we are not now abandoning humanism. . . . It is a question not of giving up our values of 1939 but of realizing them. (Merleau-Ponty 1964c: 151–152)

The Occupation showed Merleau-Ponty (and ultimately Sartre, too) that there was a distance between the ideal version of relations between human beings and the violence that generally characterizes social relations. This implied a turn to history in order to examine the ways in which the violence of partial perspectives manifests itself in a variety of social forms.

For Sartre, there are essentially four types of social "ensembles," his preferred word for a social group (Sartre 1985 [1960]: 828). Seriality, the condition in which people are members of a group solely by virtue of their relation to an outside force, such as "waiting for a bus" (Sartre 1985 [1960]: 256), is a condition in which there is an absence of sociality. Relations to people within the series are by virtue of an outside third party; hence, people in a bus queue are related by virtue of waiting for a bus, radio listeners are related by virtue of the program they are listening to, and readers of this work are related by virtue of this text. For Sartre, the series cannot be considered a social grouping; the relations within the series are constructed by something outside the group and are not by virtue of any *praxis* done by any member of the series. This is not to say that people in a series are not social; rather, they are not social within this particular group of people, but are instead members of other groups that do not exist in and through this particular experience. It is, then, a "negative side of individual integration" that characterizes the series. This negative form of integration is such that one's membership in the series is only the result of a common interest (Sartre 1985 [1960]: 259). In this way, the "social" relationship in the series happens through alterity: one's membership in the bus queue is determined solely by one's relationship to others through their place in the queue (ibid.: 261). The unity of the series through its alterity is such that it does not symbolize anything, such as a common belief in a certain set of ideals; rather, this unity, this bus queue, *is* the social grouping (ibid.: 264). As such, then, we can see that the series embodies the orientation we have earlier called earlier "being-for-others," with a twist: in "being-for-others," the goal of the individual is to assert their freedom over and against all others, whereas in the series the orientation is one of "being-outside-themselves-in-the-other of the members of this practico-inert grouping" (ibid.: 268). Here, it is the presence of others—both other people and the *exis*, or the stasis, of the constitutive element—that determines one's membership in the series.

In this way, the series is not simply constituted in an innocuous fashion or situation; it also appears in situations in which individuals are essentialized in the same manner as in "being-for-others," situations often characterized by great violence:

> *The* Jew (as the internal, serial unity of Jewish multiplicities), or *the* colonialist, or *the* professional soldier, etc., are not ideas, any more than *the* militant or, as we shall see, *the* petty bourgeois, or *the* manual worker. The theoretical error (it is not a practical one, because *praxis* really does constitute them in alterity) was to conceive of these beings as concepts, whereas—as the fundamental basis of extremely complex relations—they are *primarily* serial unities. (Sartre 1985 [1960]: 267)

The orientation of "being-for-others," which allows the individual in bad faith (cf. Gordon 1994) to essentialize another in terms of some appearance the other presents to the individual, appears here in a manner that constructs a member of a particular group as a particular example of a group constituted by an outside factor. In the case of anti-Semitism, it is not for Sartre that the anti-Semite's desire for the annihilation of the particular Jew that motivates their hatred; rather, it is the anti-Semite's choice of a particular project, namely the social denigration through the essentialization of Jews, that makes all Jews "recognizable" by their physique, by their profession, and so on, and therefore members of the serial group the anti-Semite constructs as "the Jews" (Sartre 1976 [1948]: 26–35). In the series, then, the violence that is done occurs through the taking of a person as an example of a group. It is not what Jews do, says the anti-Semite; it is "who they are" that makes them deserving of hatred (ibid.: 22–23). But in addition to the violence characteristic of the "being-for-others" orientation, the series adds another violence—the violence of absence. Take the example of the radio listener. As Sartre points out, it is the absence of a reciprocal relation between the listener and the broadcaster *as well as* between listeners that characterizes the violence of this situation (Sartre 1985 [1960]: 271). This relation of absence means that as an individual I am completely impotent; I cannot silence the voice (even by turning the radio off, I recognize the power of the broadcaster to continue the broadcast), nor can I convince every single listener of the incorrectness of the information being broadcast because the broadcast continues, and because I can never know every member of the series constituted by the radio broadcast (Sartre 1985 [1960]: 273). As such, the absence of reciprocity in the serial relationship ensures that a particular form of violence, namely the taking of individuals as other through the existence of others and their enforced impotence through their ability to engage in *praxis*, continues to be done.

The second form of social ensemble, the gathering, marks for Sartre the beginning of the negation of seriality. While the gathering is an unorganized ensemble, it at least allows for the potential negation of the impotence produced by the serial collective. As we have just seen, the serial collective is constructed in such a way that its members can do no action against the external construction of the collective. The gathering, though, presents us with the first possibility of collective *praxis*. While for Sartre the gathering is not yet a collective agent, as it is usually represented by another grouping to which the gathering defers its agency, it is an actional ensemble by virtue of the individuals who make up the gathering, the reaction of others to the individual's attempt to act, and the mutual reciprocation of action within the ensemble. As Sartre puts it, "a *group* constitutes itself as the negation of this impotence, that is to say, of seriality: I feel my impotence in the Other because it is the Other as Other who will decide whether my action will remain an individual, mad initiative and throw me back into abstract isolation or whether it is to become the common action of the group. . . ." (Sartre 1985 [1960]: 277). The gathering provides every individual with the potential for action with others but only if those others engage themselves in the same act. *Praxis* in the gathering remains *praxis* through alterity; individuals still relate to one another through alterity, but in this case, the alterity is imposed from within the ensemble rather than externally as in the series (Sartre 1985 [1960]: 354–355). The motive force here, according to Sartre, is still "seriality": the individuals still respond to others as Other, and yet their actions in this context result in at least the possibility of the constitution of a group (ibid.: 355).

Once again, the "being-for-others" orientation appears in the gathering, but in a different manner. Rather than the serialization of others that would appear as a direct result of this orientation, a new intentionality appears, one that makes possible the development of group relations; looking at the French Revolution, Sartre claims,

> In so far as everyone wanted to defend himself against the dragoons. . . . the result, *in the field of praxis*, was that *the people of Paris armed themselves against the king*. In other words, the political *praxis* of the government alienated the passive reactions of seriality to its own practical freedom: indeed, from the point of view of this *praxis*, the passive activity of the gathering was taken from it in its passivity and inert seriality reappeared

on the other side of the process of alterity as *a united group which had performed a concerted action.* (Sartre 1985 [1960]: 355)

Sartre comes to this conclusion through the examination of the phenomenon of *praxis* and its collective result. Through the individual, serialized act of arming oneself to defend oneself against others, an armed gathering appears and decides to move against the king, resulting in a new social ensemble, one able to engage in a collective form of *praxis* and through this *praxis* creating a new type of social relationship. Reciprocity appears here as the result of each individual feeling themselves to be the "individual incarnation of the common person" (ibid.: 357); the unity that begins to characterize the gathering is one that begins to be present within the group rather than existing as an outside force. The orientation here, then, is the realization of the reciprocity of alterity, that is, that each individual is Other as himself. There is a synthesis of the individual and the other in the gathering, which makes possible the transition from the gathering to the fused group.

The third type of social ensemble, the fused group, which Sartre argues is "still a series" (Sartre 1985 [1960]: 358), is so only insofar as it is in transition. The fused group is a group in formation, with its dissolving seriality and its unity projected ahead of it, but is still dominated by its seriality. This seriality, though, is constituted by the situation rather than by an external "third party." The fused group's reason for coming into existence as the logical and temporal descendent of the gathering is a serial matter; as we saw in the example of the storming of the Bastille, people armed themselves only so they could be protected from others who were arming themselves. But, after this serialized action, the members of this ensemble realize that they are as a result of this action able to act freely; the intended object of their action is no longer their self-protection from one another, but the "enemy." Their "pure quantity" determines them to be a significant threat to their enemy, but they have not yet intended a project (Sartre 1985 [1960]: 359n10). The fused group, then, embodies not a common *praxis* in the form of a project but the realization of one's non-serialized freedom to act within the situation of a series; put another way, individuals realize their ability to be free only in and through their membership in a series. We have seen that the "being-for-others" orientation that characterizes the series results in the diminution of the individual's freedom through the other. In the fused group, the Other becomes the means by which one's freedom to act is affirmed while at the same time delimited; that is, the individual's choice to act (in Sartre's example, the choice to arm oneself and march on the Bastille) is confirmed by the Other's act, and yet the individual cannot storm the Bastille by themselves and must rely on the others present in the fused group to engage in this action, which does not yet have the character of the project.

In addition, we come to the fused group as a third party. Because we come to the group out of seriality, the action we undertake with the group is engaged in through two perspectives: our perspective as a member of the group, and our perspective as a third party to the relations set up between others and the group. As such, the group mediates relations between myself and another partly because the group's action and the object against which we act is what constitutes the group, not the relations between the members: ". . . the individual, *as a third party*, is connected, in the unity of a single *praxis* (and therefore of a single perceptual vista), with the unity of individuals as inseparable moments of a non-totalised totalisation, and with each of them as *a third party*, that is to say, through the mediation of the group" (Sartre 1985 [1960]: 374). In the fused group, we are integrated into the group by virtue of our participation in the group's action and separated from the members of the group through this same action, which is constitutive of our membership. Since it is the common *praxis* of the group that constitutes it as a group and not a set of relationships the members of the group establish among themselves in order to formulate a group project, we are left in a situation of "immanence-transcendence": we are interiorized by the group by virtue of our participation in its action, but we continue to transcend the group by virtue of the fact that its action can be carried on without us. Put another way, our membership in the group lasts only as long as our participation in its *praxis* lasts; once we choose not to participate any longer, we leave the group. As such, the fused group is transitional, existing only as long as its action since it does not have the structural aspects required to maintain its existence after its action has been carried out (ibid.: 378–379).

In this sense, then, the fused group begins to embody the "being-with-others" orientation. I am no longer completely "for others" in the sense that they construct my existence through the annihilation or serialization of my freedom. In the fused group, I am "with others" as I share a particular field or situation with them and realize it as long as I continue to participate in the group's actions: ". . . in this initial moment of the group, because the Other, by totalising the practical community through his regulatory action, *effects for me* the integration which I myself should have realised but was unable to. . . . I am *amongst* third parties and I have no privileged statute. But this operation does not transform me into an object, because totalisation by the third party only reveals a free *praxis* as a common unity which is already there and which already qualifies him" (Sartre 1985 [1960]: 379). The issue of "sovereignty," or the ability of an individual to freely manipulate series within a group, does not complicate matters here, since in the fused group the individual maintains their membership in the group through their freedom, that is, through their free *praxis* with the group. As such, individuals are integrated into the group through their *praxis* but are never completely totalized by the group; the lack of organization and structure in the fused group means that membership does not inhere to the individual as "essence," but rather as "existence," that is, through their free action. Over and against the series, the fused group has the unique characteristic of being "spontaneous." Whereas the serial relationship results in the impotence of individuals to affect their situation as part of the series, the fused group's status as a spontaneous agent results from the characteristic of freedom that each individual brings to the group. It is the spontaneity of free human action that makes possible the transition from the serialized gathering to the fused group.

But, in the same way that *praxis* is converted into the practico-inert, the spontaneity of the fused group is converted as the group organizes, assigns specific tasks to specific individuals, and begins the transition from a group based upon action to a group based upon the relationships between the individuals who make up the group. The pledged group *is* the converted *praxis* of the fused group (assuming that the spontaneous group decides to continue its existence beyond the spontaneous action). Once the members of the group decide to develop a project, a plan of action that expresses their common being as a group, they must organize and develop a specific organization in order to carry out the tasks that will make up their project. Since the first task is organization, a certain set of relationships, often hierarchical, must be established. This marks the first difference from other social ensembles: the fused group is now predicated on the relationship of the individual to others as they construct it rather than on a serialized task that becomes "common." As Sartre puts it, the members of the pledged group are "merged with everyone by a totalising third party" (Sartre 1985 [1960]: 381)—their pledge to the group as embodied by the individual's decision to follow a commonly chosen leader. The organization of the individuals who make up a group into a structure allows the group to engage in a certain project through the *praxis* of its members and places its members in the situation of having their *praxis* (as part of the group's project) mediated by their membership in the group. In other words, the task of organizing the group results in the group's definitions of its internal structures and its definition of itself as a practical activity. The development of the organization therefore results in a necessary ambiguity: the group only exists by virtue of its constructed relationships among the individual members *and* only exists in relation to the object of the group's *praxis* (ibid.: 446). Consequently, an examination of the development of the group leads us to study "the relation between *the action of the group on itself* and *the action of its members on the object*" (ibid.: 448); or, to clarify the sociological dynamics, to examine the way in which the members of the group maintain their cohesion as a group, how its members engage in the development of the group's project, and the relationship between the two.

The group exists, at the level of organization, through the allocation of functions to its particular members. To each member, the group assigns a particular task in the development of its project, one the individual experiences as a determination of their potential *praxis*. Rather than experiencing this determination of *praxis* as a limitation of their freedom, though, Sartre argues that the member experiences their function in a mostly positive manner:

> But in the normal exercise of organised activity, *function* is a positive definition of the common individual: either the group as a whole or some already differentiated "organ" *assigns* it to him. It is a determination of individual *praxis*: an individual belongs to the group in so far as he carries out a certain task and *only that task*. . . . Function is both negative and positive: in the practical movement, a *prohibition* (do not do *anything else*) is perceived as a positive determination, as a *creative imperative*: do *precisely that*. . . . Thus, he must actualise everything that *predetermines* his function (the common objective, practical problems, the conjuncture, the state of techniques and instruments) *in inertia* (as an inert possibility defined by discourse, for example, and which it realises in repetition), in the milieu of *sovereignty over things* (the dialectical freedom of organic *praxis*) and of *power over men* (social freedom as a synthetic relation based on the pledge), in short, in *freedom*. (Sartre 1985 [1960]: 449–450)

There is much going on in this passage. Sartre here argues that the individual, in carrying out the commands of the group to do a particular task, acts in freedom by working between the inert object on which the group wants to do work and the "social freedom" that derives from the pledge.

The pledge, the oath to participate in the bringing-about of the group's project, becomes the mechanism by which one's social freedom is actualized. We have seen already that there are for Sartre two forms of freedom: "potential" freedom, or the unlimited potential of an individual to intend their being through acting on a project; and actual freedom, wherein an individual is in a situational position in which they can actualize their project. In the pledge group, the latter becomes more important, though again with an ironic twist. The individual's active choice to pledge to the other members in the group allows them to freely act in conjunction with others in order to bring about a particular state of affairs. Yet, the decision to pledge oneself to others in the group defers the individual's sovereignty. Through the pledge, the individual gains freedom in the sense of being able to act with others in a common *praxis*, and yet those others gain authority and sovereignty over the individual's *praxis*, in that the group assigns the individual's tasks and enforces the performance of that task by the individual (Sartre 1985 [1960]: 577). What is left in ellipses in the long quotation above is the "fraternity terror" that accompanies the pledge (Sartre 1985 [1960]: 449–450). The terror that accompanies the pledge is such that one defers their sovereignty over themselves in favor of the group, and gains from the group sovereignty over others. As such, there is a more pronounced combination of the orientations of "being-for-others" and "being-with-others": in the pledged group, each has the power over others to determine their tasks only insofar as they derive from the group the responsibility to carry out their individual task or to face the consequences (of the failure of the task, of sanction, or of death). The pledge, in its conversion of the accidental common *praxis* of the fused group into the organized common *praxis* of the group actualizing its project, results in the conversion of *praxis* into the practico-inert; the act of pledging oneself to the group results in a set of structures that has dominion over the individual. For the group, the individual is constituted as a tool for the development of the group's project in the same way that the individual utilizes tools in the development of their project.

This, though, is not yet alienation, according to Sartre. The characteristics of freedom still pervade the pledged group: the individual still freely consents to the sovereignty of the group over their *praxis* and the group is still freely engaged in the development of its project. The pledged group is still engaged in characterizing itself over and against its former seriality (Sartre 1985 [1960]: 455). The difference here, at least for now, is in the intentionality of the group; that is, the pledged group at this stage still intends itself to be almost pure *praxis* by which it hopes to avoid the alienation that characterized its situation before the pledge. As a result, the members of the group carry out their authority over the individuals not by means of an institutionalized police force, but by utilizing the intention of actualizing the group's project as a way of leveraging the individual into continued compliance with the group's directives.

Once the group institutionalizes itself to such an extent that its *praxis* is almost completely limited to its reproduction as a group, we find the beginnings of alienation. As Sartre argues, both the pledge and the terror that ensues from the maintenance of the pledge reflect a fear of "a dissolution of unity" and a need to interiorise the group's status for others as "objectivity" (Sartre 1985 [1960]: 582). The group, once it reaches the stage at which its project is merely its own maintenance and reproduction, does not have the same meaning it once created through its *praxis*. As a result, a sense of malaise and a regularization of the integrative functions of the group comes about, a process that effects the Terror (Sartre 1985 [1960]: 583–584). So, as the group moves closer to organizing and integrating itself on the basis of the freely given pledge and the desire to enact a group project, it moves further away from these bases and goals and closer to the point of alienation. As individuals feel less a part of the group (what Durkheim referred to as *anomie*), the group works harder and harder to enforce the coherence of the group. The threat of exile poses for the individual the terror of having their *praxis* alienated from them, and the threat of secession poses for the group the need to enforce ever more rigorously its statute of fidelity.

This institutionalization of adhesion to the group (ibid.: 600, 602) results in the demise of the pledged group and the end of pure praxis. What was once created to actualize both group and individual projects ends up having to organize and institutionalize functions that each individual is to perform under threat of exile; the threat of exile is reacted to by the individual through their adherence to the group's sovereignty as the result of the individual's freely given pledge and by the group through the increasing enforcement of integration. As such, the group's energies are spent maintaining the inertia of integration through the enforcement of structural relations and not the project it wanted to bring about in the first place. By this point—and this is the danger Sartre seems to warn us of regarding the formation of new social groupings—the individual's freedom is once again gone. After having escaped from their seriality and unfreedom through the common *praxis* of the fused group and their fidelity to the pledged group, individuals find themselves alienated from their actual individual and social freedom through the group's inertia: ". . . the practice becomes an institution as soon as the group, as a unity which has been eroded by alterity, becomes powerless to change it without completely disrupting itself, that is to say, as soon as everyone comes to be conditioned by the shifting flight of others"

(Sartre 1985 [1960]: 602). As such, the institutionalization of a group is the transition from *praxis* to the practico-inert; the action of the group, the inertial maintenance of its existence, becomes the modality of its *praxis*, while at the same time the institution is the practico-inert residuum of its earlier project (ibid.: 603).

Once the group becomes institutionalized, the "being-for-others" orientation returns to the relationship between individuals in the group. Authority takes hold, and those in authority attempt to distinguish themselves from those they hold authority over. These individuals attempt to "liquidate the Other in himself so as to liquidate it in the Others" and "constitute himself as the absolute Other" (ibid.: 605). In doing so, though, the co-sovereignty that came about as a result of the spontaneous though serial action of the fused group disappears; the sovereignty of "institutional man" can now be expressed "only as a univocal relation of violence with a given multiplicity" (ibid.: 610). Individual freedom as it occurred through the common *praxis* of the group is liquidated, and the individual's *praxis* is limited to the instantiation of the common project presented as individual will (ibid.: 615). Hence, for the sake of the preservation of the group at least in its practical field (since it can never achieve its "ontological status" as "group"), the group destroys that upon which it was predicated—the development of the freedom of the individual. Sartre's summation of this situation is as follows:

> At this level, a double transformation takes place. (1) At the level of the *common individual*, my powers are conferred on me by all but only *through the mediation of the Other*; there is still reciprocal organisation, but it takes the form of a univocal rearrangement, without reciprocity; and common *praxis* manifests itself in the form of an untranscendable *praxis* of an individual in freedom. (2) At the level of my own individual activity, my freedom is stolen from me and I become the actualisation of the Other's freedom. . . . my freedom is freely lost and divests itself of its translucidity so as to actualise, here, in my muscles, in my body at work, the Other's freedom *in so far* as it is elsewhere, in the Other, and in so far as it is lived, here, by me, as an alienating signification, as a rigid absence and as the absolute priority, *everywhere*, of interiorised alterity—everywhere, that is, *except*, in the untranscendable Other, who is other than all precisely in being alone in being able to be himself. (Sartre 1985 [1960]: 616)

In this manner, the institution organizes our lives so that, while still feeling free to follow our own projects, we are only given that freedom insofar as it is consistent with the group project. The "institutional group alienates the practical freedoms of its members to the free *praxis* of the community," a *praxis* that no longer exists except as "the abstract, negative object of an empty intention" (Sartre 1985 [1960]: 620). The ambiguity of our freedom is resolved into the ambiguity of the freedom of the social, that is, into the self-defeating *praxis* of a set of practico-inert structures.

The pledge the individual freely gives in order to act freely with others becomes a tool of violence against them. Looking at the development of the group-in-fusion out of the series, we can see that the transition is defined by an Other, an enemy, against which people realize they need to act. The group-in-fusion is already created in part by the practico-inert structure of society, instantiated by the enemy of the nascent group-in-fusion. The group-in-fusion, therefore, is put in the paradoxical position of struggling against a system, all the while being prone to the same forces that helped create the system over and against human freedom in the first place: "The task is complex. Revolutionaries are in the contradictory position both of creating a system to combat a system and yet affirming the preeminence of humanity over all its systems. They must therefore struggle against both the system and the counter-system, even as they use the latter" (Bowman and Stone 1992: 188; cf. Sartre 1964a: 152–153). Emancipation, the goal of all counter-system actions, is thereby prone to being stolen from the very people who struggle for emancipation.

This is, of course, if we take these moments in the transition from series to group as discrete and separable moments, and it is here that Merleau-Ponty's phenomenology makes an additional contribution. We should recall that, for Merleau-Ponty, time is not a series of discrete instants, but rather a path through which we exist. As such, the transition from series to group that Sartre describes in the *Critique* ignores one important aspect of existential thought: responsibility. Responsibility is a brute historical fact for us; we are responsible for the impact and consequences of our acts, both for us and for others upon whom we act. In this way—and I believe Sartre forgets this in his discussion of fraternity terror—we are responsible for the pledge we make to the group. Sartre's presentation of the relations between individuals and the group has a clearly individualistic bent: the damning thing about joining a group is that one's freedom is delimited by membership in the group, and ultimately the group's inertia will have such an overdetermining impact upon the individual that there is little left to do but to go along with it. This brief summation of Sartre's position shows that it is not necessarily the formation and maintenance of the group that dominates his analysis, but rather its impact upon the individual and their freedom. Thus, the individual appears to take precedence in Sartre's analysis, leaving us to wonder how it is possible not simply to exist with others, that is, to bear the existence of others in our practical field given their limitations upon us and our freedom, but rather to *live* with others, contributing to a better life for one another through a socially oriented ethics. This is, to some extent, not a problem: a concern for the individual is an integral part of social analysis, and Sartre's unintended depiction of the dangers of postrevolutionary terror in the maintenance of the "group" adds a critical element to this analysis—that in any new form of social change, we must take great pains to guard against the repetition of the individual–group and individual–individual relationships Sartre describes in *Critique of Dialectical Reason*. Failure to do so, as Gorz has eloquently put it, leads directly to Stalinism: ". . . for Sartre the 'formal laws of the dialectic' always have inevitably led the fused group—a community which is active and sovereign through and through—to relapse into a diversified, opaque and alienated form of unity" (Gorz 1973: 264). An emphatic concern for the individual, though, cannot do us well without the balancing concern Merleau-Ponty has for the group, and so we return to *l'intermonde*.

The Social, Shared Praxis, and Collective Meaning

Recall the makeup of *l'intermonde*: it is the set of pre-reflective, preexisting meanings that we encounter with others within our situation. Once we recognize that there is a set of meanings we share with others in the world—that is, once we see the "figure" of commonality against the "background" of the seemingly infinite set of possibilities for our action— we can begin to intentionally exist "with-others." For Merleau-Ponty, this interdependence of meaning also brings about an interdependence of freedoms: because the field of meaning we encounter precedes our freedom and provides the ground by which we can formulate a project we intend to actualize, our freedom is as dependent upon our situation as that of others, making my freedom dependent on the freedom of others:

> I must apprehend myself from the onset as centred in a way outside myself, and my individual existence must diffuse round itself, so to speak, an existence in quality. The For-Themselves—me for myself and the other for himself—must stand out against a background of For Others—I for the other and the other for me. My life must have a significance which I do not constitute; there must strictly speaking be an intersubjectivity. . . . (Merleau-Ponty 1962: 448)

Following from this intersubjectivity of meaning and hence of freedom, we can see that for Merleau-Ponty a solution to Sartre's positing of the inherent conflict in human relations would be "mutual recognition" in the Hegelian vein (Whiteside 1988: 88; cf. Honneth 1995). As Merleau-Ponty points out, "I do not reduce [another] to a slave unless, in the very moment when I look at him as an object, he remains present to me as a consciousness and as a free being" (Merleau-Ponty 1964b: 68). The imposition of meaning that Merleau-Ponty claims is the source of human violence does not merely happen in the ontological realm; rather, if we follow the chain "meaning $\rightarrow$ freedom $\rightarrow$ action $\rightarrow$ history," we can see that the imposition of meaning has a potentially detrimental impact upon the other's freedom to formulate and enact a project and to participate in the creation of history. The struggle that results in the imposition of meaning and which comes from the partial "for-others" orientation that characterizes the human situation today is predicated upon a common ground for that struggle; that is, it is only by recognizing the sameness of the other in our desire for recognition that the struggle can even take place. It is in this way that a situation charac- terized by violence has the potential to yield mutual recognition. Mutual recognition would be, then, a relationship in which two individuals fore- ground the commonality of their situation instead of bringing about the egoistic tensions that the reliance upon their own projects would cause.

How would this occur in groups, though? We can envision two partic- ular individuals in either separate or similar situations finding a common ground of meaning based on which they can act together. But, according to the phenomenology of group formation presented by Sartre, we find that regardless of this intention of "mutual recognition" in the dyad, the group's formation seems to require that the inertial maintenance needs of the group counterweigh this set of intentions. There is, then, a need to maintain the mutual recognition in the group setting; that is, the group, even if it begins to slide into the practico-inert institutionalized forma- tions Sartre lambastes in the *Critique*, must maintain the sort of mutual critique and interrogation that Merleau-Ponty argues grounds *l'inter- monde*. Mutual recognition within a social grouping requires a commu- nication between the various members of the social group. The pursuit of collective meaning, the foregrounding of the sociality that is the basis of our encounter with our situation, would be another mode by which mutual recognition could come about in an ensemble.

Merleau-Ponty's discussion of the development of class consciousness, presented here in a brief form, gives us a clear example of the way in which mutual recognition can occur. As Merleau-Ponty points out, it is through the realizing of common actions, common situations, and common projects (to the extent that their class position allows them the free pursuit of a project) that class consciousness comes to fruition. Unlike Sartre, who seems to argue that class consciousness appears before the consciousness of class (i.e., the realization of the conditions of existence that delimits the "proletariat" as a class comes before the construction of the "essence" of the class), Merleau-Ponty argues that it is the existence of class as part of the field of meaning and a set of social structures in which we are embedded that allows us to recognize our membership in a class: "What makes me a proletarian is not the economic system or society considered as systems of impersonal forces, but these institutions as I carry them with me and experience them; nor is it an intellectual operation devoid of motive, but my way of being in the world within this institutional framework" (Merleau-Ponty 1962: 443). Once we recognize the similarities between our class positions, a common consciousness that we can call a "class consciousness" comes to fruition, not automatically, but through mutual discussion and dialogue. This collective meaning can lead therefore to the development of a common project, one that intends to bring about a certain type of social change, so long as we do not fall into the trap of institutionalization Sartre describes in the *Critique*:

> "A class *organizes itself,*" says Sartre, probably meaning to say, not that it organizes itself, not that others organize it, but that in a single movement which is without subject, being the exchange of the workers and the Party, the workers invent themselves as militants and pure action comes into being. Between the worker and the militant, the unbeliever and the converted, the militants and the Party which "tolerates" their discussion, the relationships are inflexible because they are inflexible to the highest degree between the proletariat and the bourgeoisie. It is the entire social fabric which becomes as fragile as glass. (Merleau-Ponty 1973b: 112–113)

The task, then, is to figure out how to bring about the goal of "mutual recognition" and the development of collective meaning, tasks that Merleau-Ponty sets us, while at the same time avoiding the dangers of the institutionalized, quasi-Stalinist group that Sartre highlights. In other words, we need to discern the ways in which a group dedicated in principle to freedom can maintain that ethical valuation of freedom in practice. We must, then, figure out what an existentialist ethics would be and how it would preserve both the freedom of the individual *and* the freedom of the group.

CHAPTER 3

METHODS, NOT RECIPES: RETHINKING ETHICS IN (AND THROUGH) RESISTANCE

Formulating *the* ethics of existentialism, as one might be wont to do with other philosophical systems, is a nearly impossible task. The philosophy of existentialism is not one that can provide us with hard-and-fast rules by which we can say we live "ethically"; we must construct, according to the existentialists, our own set of meanings in the world through the creation and actualization of our own project. To impose a set of rules upon a group of people would be tantamount to the elimination of the freedom of those who make up the group; as de Beauvoir reminds us, "Ethics does not furnish recipes any more than do science and art. One can merely propose methods" (de Beauvoir 1994 [1948]: 134). In fact, an existentialist ethics must necessarily *resist* rule-bound Ethics for these very reasons. And yet, we already exist in groups: we are members of a society and subject to its norms, mores, and sanctions even before we are born, and the situation today is such that we are left in the inertia of the institution described by Sartre: "It is too bad if I do not agree: I shall have to come to terms with it. And if I agree, so much the better: it is a fluke, an accident, crucial for me but indifferent for the practice itself, and might be expressed in these words: since it cannot be changed, it is just as well that I am willing to go along with it . . ." (Sartre 1985 [1960]: 602). Put another way, rule-based conceptions of ethics of whatever stripe represent a form of inertia, one that can serve as a form of violence to the freedom of individuals and groups. So how can we come to terms with society's ability to impose a set of rules upon us by which we live "ethically" through our tacit consent to the laws that maintain the status quo, *à la* Locke, *and* with the existentialist need to avoid the imposition of rules in favor of the development of collective meaning and *praxis* that leads to the creation of a more just society?

I argue that in order to begin to envision what a social ethics would look like, we need to examine a number of aspects of existential social theory to see their ethical import. We will be breaking down the ethical aspects of existentialism phenomenologically and, ultimately, reconstructing them as a phenomenology of social action. Continuing from the previous chapter's discussion of our social situation, this examination follows the chain of the regressive–progressive method: situation → intentionality → capacity for agency → action → history → advocacy for social change. One of the primary benefits of this method is critical for the argument of this book: it enables us to understand currently existing rule-based ethical codes as a form of practico-inert life; that is, Ethics, in the codes we live and in the philosophical descriptions we use for those codes, is a form of inertia. This method also allows us to see that an existential ethics goes beyond the traditional orientations of ethics; that is, rather than emphasizing one aspect of an action to which one orients as "the site of ethics," an existential ethics orients to *all* aspects of an action—to the situation, to the intention, to the action, and to the historical aspects of the action (both in the past and in the future). Ultimately, I argue that an existential ethics is an ethics of action, but a particular kind of action that transcends the inertial aspects of a social order. As such, an existential ethics is also an ethics of freedom, and the enhancement of human freedom and the improvement of human relations that this ethics of freedom should bring about is the goal of the existentialism of both Sartre and Merleau-Ponty.

Ethics and Intentionality

Given the existence of others in our situation, we can see that the first aspect of an existential ethics is going to involve our orientation to them. We have already described two particular orientations to others that, through our presentation of Sartre's discussion of the problematic nature of group formations, show two different ways in which we can treat others: "being-for-others," in which we attempt to assert our freedom and agency in the world by annihilating the freedom and agency of others; and "being-with-others," in which we recognize that our agency is dependent upon the agency of others to produce and reproduce meanings in the world that provide the basis for our agency. Neither of these, though, is necessarily a "good" ethical orientation. Being-for-others, as we have seen earlier, is implicated in "bad faith," through which we attempt to deny responsibility for our actions and their consequences; and being-with-others can appear even in the most alienated situations so long as we recognize that we share our situation with others. To boot, both of these orientations often occur within the same social ensemble and situation, and as such the claim for either as "the" ethical orientation is an ambiguous one at best. How is it possible, then, to identify an ethical orientation to others that the existentialists could defend?

There are, at first, two different problems that appear for us in considering the "intentional" aspect of an existential ethics. First, there is the phenomenological issue that arises here. Recall that for both Sartre and Merleau-Ponty, the mode of an existential analysis is a regressive–progressive analysis, that is, we are supposed to discern within a situation the way in which a certain set of phenomena are produced and potentially reproduced; only then can we suggest a direction in which to proceed. Hence, to say that *either* a "being-for-others" or a "being-with-others" is *the* ethical (or even unethical) orientation would be a "bad faith" prescription in that we would be ignoring the particular exigencies of the situation we are investigating. The situation, according to both Sartre and Merleau-Ponty, should determine the necessary orientation we should have toward others:

> [Freedom] is a dependence, but not a dependence like slavery. Because I believe this dependence itself is free. It is a characteristic of ethics that an action, while it seems to be subtly constrained, also presents itself as capable of not being undertaken. Therefore, in doing it one is making a choice and a free choice. What is surreal about this constraint is that it does not determine; it presents itself as a constraint, yet the choice is made freely. (Sartre and Lévy 1996: 71–72)

> But the point is that we are not spectators of a closed history; we are actors in an open history, our *praxis* introduces the element of construction rather than knowledge as an ingredient of the world, making the world not simply an object of contemplation but something to be transformed. (Merleau-Ponty 1969: 92)

Since the situation in part determines what we see as a possibility for action, and others help make up that situation, the particular others with whom we interact in the situation determine, by their orientation to the situation, the orientation we should have toward them and the trajectory that our action will take. As an example, if we benefit from a situation characterized by the oppression of a large group of people, and if we wish to continue that benefit, we are likely to see as "ethical" an orientation to them that would lead us to follow a project oriented toward the maintenance of that oppression. Conversely, if we are among the oppressed, we are more likely to orient toward those who oppress so as to eliminate our oppression through the prevention of their action:

> Pour mieux dire il ne l'oppose pas—comme si c'était une valeur à d'autres valeurs—c'est son besoin qui l'oppose à l'ordre des choses en étant à réclamer *aux hommes contre les choses* sa réalité d'homme. D'un côté, *l'homme mutilé* subordonne les hommes à la chose; de l'autre, l'homme opprimé subordonne les choses à l'homme comme un moyen de restituer l'humain. (Sartre 1964a: 102)[1]

In both these situations, our orientation is going to be one of "being-for-others": our project leads us to intend the "destruction" of the other, either through the elimination of their freedom in a practical and onto-logical sense or through their actual physical destruction. However, our orientation to those with whom we need to work to either reinforce the practico-inert structures of oppression or to overturn them is going to be one more along the lines of "being-with-others": we need to develop a collective *praxis* that is going to actualize the project we set ourselves.

The second issue that arises when considering the intentional aspect of an existential ethics is the issue of multiple orientations. There are obviously multiple types of social groups that exist within one "society," regardless of how large or small we envision it. Families often have multiple factions within them; there are a number of different social classes within a society; and in many places in the world, the intercon-nectedness of the global economy means that we can have multiple orientations toward one group at the same time. To illustrate this latter point, let us consider the example of sweatshop labor in a "Third World" country and the issue of a boycott against the company that employs this labor (and note that I am assuming that the members of the boycott are acting in good faith, i.e., with an authentic desire to help the workers and not simply to mollify their consciences). If a group of us dogmatically participate in the boycott, we can force the company to stop using sweatshop labor (obviously an ethical good), but perhaps at the cost of the livelihood and survival of the people who work in sweat-shops (not the intent we had in formulating the boycott).[2] So, to partic-ipate in the boycott could mean hurting the company (a good) while also hurting the people on whose behalf we are boycotting the company. The ambiguity that arises in this particular situation can lead us in one of three directions: sheer quietism, in which we do nothing because we cannot deal with the ambiguity this situation presents us (a bad faith response); to decide not to engage in the boycott because of the poten-tial harm it can do to the workers; or to decide to engage in it in order to harm the corporation that employs them in spite of the consequences. In any of these cases, harm is done to those we wanted to help. It is not, though, our intention that causes this harm, but the exigencies of the situation or the practico-inert structures of international capitalism. The ambiguity of this situation lies in both the consequences of our action and in the reception of our action by those for whom we act. The ambiguity that inheres to every such interaction with others is a force to be reckoned with: it is not simply our freedom that creates the world around us, nor are we merely reenacting the practico-inert structures of the social order; rather, it is our project mingling with other projects in the face of a world that is not known with any certainty but can be anticipated as existing in a particular way. The combination of a world that partially overdetermines us, that we partially construct, and that others construct around us (in spite of us and with us), all construct our field in ways we cannot completely know; and the ambiguity that arises is not merely in the consequences of our actions, but also in the reception of our actions by others in that field. As such, we must pay careful attention to the way in which we orient to others around us and take account of the pragmatics of the situation in formulating the action that this intention leads.

Merleau-Ponty's discussion of the ethics that undergirds Marxism and revolutionary violence provides us with substantiation for these views. As Merleau-Ponty argues, our situatedness puts us in conflict with some and in concert with others. As such, we must take into account the fact that, because of the intersubjectivity of *l'intermonde* and the interdependence of our freedoms stemming from their basis in *l'intermonde*, we are automatically implicated in our action through our intentions toward others: ". . . as soon as we begin to live, we lose the alibi of good intentions; we are what we do to others, we yield the right to be respected as noble souls. To respect one who does not respect others is ultimately to despise them; to abstain from violence toward the violent is to become their accomplice" (Merleau-Ponty 1969: 109). According to this logic, then, there is a mutual determination of our orientation toward the variety of others in our situation: the situation we encounter provides us with the material by which our orientation to others can be formulated, and at the same time our orientation to others implicates us in a plan of action that places us in a certain set of relations based upon that action. Merleau-Ponty's discussion of *Darkness at Noon* shows us this all too well. His presentation of the trials by which those who were committed to the historical *sens* of the Russian Revolution were judged to be counterrevolutionaries and therefore traitors shows us that the situation—the consolidation of power by a single leader, the Communist Party, and the mandatory nature of one's orientation to the Party as the sole voice of the people rather than to particular others—determines to a large extent the impact of the relationship between situation and orientation.

In sum, the question of the *directionality* of our orientation—that is, to whom we orient as the bearers of our ethical intention—becomes an important one for the formulation of a project. While we are free to intend any project as a result of our desire or our perception of a lack (for us) in the world, that project and the resulting *praxis* implicate us in a charged and potentially conflict-laden set of social relations. Through our project, we automatically intend a certain type of "singularized universal" who we hope to benefit from our project (and not simply ourselves). In the examples given, we intend for our boycott to result in the improvement of working conditions and wages for sweatshop laborers. Through these intentions, will for the sweatshop laborers a set of working conditions that parallels our own, even in their limited benefit. And yet, by willing this project and attempting to actualize it, we can end up doing harm to the very people we commit ourselves to aiding in their liberation.

As such, *our intention cannot merely be one antecedent to the act*: we cannot say "damn the consequences; we meant well," as if we had purchased the wrong gift for a family member. Our actions have a profound impact on others and as such go beyond deontological versions of ethics. There is a profound historical aspect to even our orientation to others in two ways. First, in taking account of the situation's impact upon our intentions and the potential for the practico-inert structures to turn our actions against us and those we want to help, we are taking the historical construction of the situation into account. Our relationship with sweatshop laborers is one that may be tainted with a history of colonialism, so that they would refuse our assistance through the boycott as being either neocolonialist or as an attempt to tell them how to change the nature of global capital on their end. The second historical aspect of our intentionality is the impact our action has upon the beneficiary of the act. If we intend to free sweatshop laborers from their wage slavery and end up running them out of work and into even more abject poverty, *we are responsible for this effect of our actions*, even when it runs in direct contradiction to our intention. A deontological or intentional ethical perspective would deny both these aspects of responsibility, arguing that by fulfilling our duty or by intending a certain outcome, we have done our job. The absence of any historical and historicized considerations in the ethical evaluation of our act leads us to the unethical avoidance of action that counters situations of oppression. Therefore we need to have as a key concern in the formulation of our action and in our evaluation of its ethicality the variety of parameters provided to us by the historical situation in which we act.

Ethics, Ambiguity, and Choice

As we have already seen, ambiguity absolutely characterizes the formation of a project we intend to be "ethical." The nature of our perspective on the world and its motivating force for our action enable us to see only part of the picture. Even, as Merleau-Ponty argues, the "scientific" foresight of a theory of action and history such as Marxism works beyond our knowledge; we can never know all the aspects of our situation, of the situation of those who we want our actions to benefit, or the results of our actions. As well, our encounter with the situation does not provide us with only one path of action, but a vast number of possibilities for action in the world and a vast number of "others" for and with whom we want to act. There are, therefore, a vast number of "variables" (for lack of a better word) that result in an ambiguity we can never eliminate: "History offers us certain factual trends that have to be extrapolated into the future, but it does not give us the knowledge with any deductive certainty of which facts are privileged to outline the present to be ushered in . . . . *This does not mean that we can do whatever we please . . .*" (Merleau-Ponty 1969: 65). As such, the unknowable nature of the future leaves us with a dilemma: either we act and bear total responsibility for what happens, or we do not act and bear total responsibility for what happens *because we did not act* (Merleau-Ponty 1969: 89). How do we orient to this total responsibility for the world, to the fact that the human being is "responsible [not only] for his own individuality, but that he is responsible for all men" (Sartre 1993a: 36)?

De Beauvoir's *The Ethics of Ambiguity* provides us with some insight into ways of orienting toward ambiguity as an aspect of an existential ethics. She reminds us that every action in which we engage sets up values (i.e., the value of the ends of our project), ones she argues must be commensurate with the means by which we want to actualize our project (de Beauvoir 1994 [1948]: 149). As such, we are already orienting to ambiguity; by acting, we have chosen the path we want to see come to fruition, the consequences we want our action to have for the world, and the state of affairs we want to leave to those who come after us. But, this is not a simple Machiavellian matter of the ends justifying the means, nor a mere cost/benefit analysis, as it might be for utilitarians; rather, there is a reciprocal, almost dialectical, relationship between means and ends for de Beauvoir:

> ... these qualitative considerations are insufficient. One can no more judge the means without the end which gives it its meaning than he can detach the end from the means which defines it .... Suppressing a hundred opponents is surely an outrage, but it may have meaning and reason; it is a matter of maintaining a regime which brings to an immense mass of men a bettering of their lot. Perhaps this measure could have been avoided; perhaps it merely represents that necessary element of failure which is involved in any positive construction. It can be judged only by being replaced in the ensemble of the cause it serves. (de Beauvoir 1994 [1948]: 146)

We are left, though, in the same situation: How do we take account of ambiguity in the formulation of our project? De Beauvoir's suggested method clarifies this somewhat: we are to take account of the others in our practical field as human beings, as freedoms who will freedom as their end through the formulation and actualization of their own projects, and act in accordance with this situation, that is, in order to ensure or bring about its existence. The intent here is clear. De Beauvoir wants us to evaluate for ourselves the meaning our choice will have for others as a methodology for evaluating the ethicality of our action.

But, this version of our orientation to ambiguity is not complete. While de Beauvoir's methodology is such that it allows us to preserve others as "ends-in-themselves," that is, people to be absolutely respected, the situation we encounter may be such that it might not be possible to do this. In other words, ambiguity forces us back into the sticky mess that the world presents to us, both in the present version of the situation we encounter and in the historical aspects of our situation. Just because our willing of others as freedoms to be preserved works in the short term does not necessarily mean it was what should have been. Merleau-Ponty deals with this "is/ought" trap in arguing that the success of any potential action does not legitimate it as the one true path; had any other person acted or not acted, any other potential action could have worked just as well (Merleau-Ponty 1969: 94). What is important, then, is that the actor take a historical perspective on the project they wish to bring about because, as I have hinted at earlier, there is no inherent meaning to history, only that which we create through our actions within a larger chain of events (ibid.: 94–96). As such, to return to de Beauvoir's discussion, the act of killing another human being has no inherent meaning; rather, it takes on that meaning through the act's insertion into a historical chain of human events in which the actors intend a certain meaning and project and hope for a certain outcome. Hence, the difference between the lynching of a black man in the American South and the killing of a soldier during a revolutionary struggle has everything to do with the situation at hand (the American version of *apartheid* versus a struggle for liberation), the intention of the act (killing a "lesser" human being versus killing a member of an oppressing class), *and* the ultimate result of the act.

Put another way, according to Merleau-Ponty, the project of bringing about a situation in which the taking of others as freedoms to be preserved may require the sacrifice of some. Merleau-Ponty's position is that the key question with regard to any revolutionary action is whether it can create more human relations (and often it does not; Merleau-Ponty 1969: xvii–xx). However, the potential in any revolutionary movement for the development of this project creates an ambiguous situation in which only a historical orientation can provide an adequate assessment:

> He who condemns all violence puts himself outside the domain to which justice and injustice belong. He puts a curse upon the world and humanity—a hypocritical curse, since he who utters it has already accepted the rules of the game from the moment that he has begun to live. Between men considered as pure consciousnesses there would indeed be no reason to choose. But between men considered as the incumbents of situations which together compose a single *common situation* it is inevitable that one has to choose—it is allowable to sacrifice those who according to the logic of their situation are a threat and to promote those who offer a promise of humanity. This is what Marxism does when it creates its politics on the basis of an analysis of the situation of the proletariat. (Merleau-Ponty 1969: 110)

As such, because of the ambiguity that occurs in multiple aspects of the development of the project—in the temporal realm, in the historical realm, and in the consequential realm—one must take into account further aspects of the "ripple effects" of one's project and the ensuing *praxis*.

Ethics and Action

This aspect of an existential ethics—that some might be harmed, done violence to, or even killed in the actualization of a project intended to increase human freedom—is one that causes some consternation. It is also one that even within existentialism is held with ambiguity. And while orientation and ambiguity are ontological in nature, pertaining to the kind of meaning that one wants to bring about in the social world, these aspects only come about through one's action. But, as opposed to most ethical theories, in an existential ethics the theorist does not construct the rules of conduct, but rather discerns them in the "regressive" part of their analysis and attempts to direct them through "progressive" prescriptions.[3] As such, the ethical aspects of orientation and ambiguity are only discernable through the action of a given person or social ensemble.

This is not to say, though, that an existential ethics is or should be constructed *ex post facto* or after a given action is completed. Rather, this kind of ethics is one that manifests itself through action; we can reveal or reconstruct the ethical framework through which a person developed a particular project and actualized it through the results of their action. It is in this way that the ethical aspects of action are also historical: there is an ethical framework that preexists the action; and we can investigate that framework through the results of that action or project as they play themselves out over time. This raises many of the issues Merleau-Ponty explains in his analysis of *Darkness at Noon*:

> How then does [Rubashov] see his life at this moment? Whether they realized it or not, he and his comrades had started from the affirmation of a value: the value of men. One does not become a revolutionary through science, but out of indignation. Science comes afterward to fill in and delimit that open protest. It taught Rubashov and his companions that the liberation of man presupposed a socialist economy and so they set to work. But he learned that in order to construct this economy in the particular circumstances of the land of the Revolution it was necessary to impose greater suffering than was known under the ancient regime; that in order to free men in the future it was necessary to oppress men in the present. . . . The consciousness of self and the other which had animated the enterprise at the start had become entangled in the web of mediations separating existing humanity from its future fulfillment. (Merleau-Ponty 1969: 11)

The actions Rubashov took later because of the increase of suffering (in other words, the "political violence" against the Party; Merleau-Ponty 1969: 8) that were intended to relieve that suffering (which is the goal of his revolutionary project) might end up being counterrevolutionary because they do not maintain the inertia of the Revolution. Ambiguity and orientation appear here, but it is through the actions Rubashov took that they appear to us. Rubashov clearly intends at the outset of his project to improve the lot of humanity, acts in accordance with this project, and ends up failing at the project because of the particular situation. When he acts to reinvigorate his project to relieve the people's suffering, he is judged to be a counterrevolutionary. But, had he not acted in either way, he would still be responsible and still be called to act.

To put this in another way, we can see that an existential ethics, one that maintains an orientation to others, to ambiguity, to action, and, as we will see shortly, to freedom, is one that can call us to resistance. It is often the case that the ethical project we construct for ourselves as a result of our encounter with others and the world necessarily leads to acting against the status quo social arrangement. Remember that the project we intend and work to actualize results from our observance of a lack of some particular kind of meaning in the world. Since the status quo has the wrong meaning (for us, i.e., violence and oppression), and since we share our situation with others who often see a similar lack of meaning in the world, it is clear that the status quo for some represents an absence of some particular kind of meaning that, for them, makes it either impossible to act in certain beneficial ways or necessary to act in a detrimental manner. This necessity for action may make resistance against the dominant order appear to be the only ethical option.

But what makes this option appear to be the only one and "ethical"? First, if the status quo prevents the formation of free projects by individuals or groups within a society, then the awareness of this path of action may not appear to the individual. It is within the social ensemble, though, that this awareness can come about. If we realize that we share with others a position within a set of practico-inert structures or practical fields (i.e., as members of a "proletariat"), then the construction of collective meaning through a process of mutual recognition may already be a form of resistance. The prevention of the development of free projects, if it is indeed an aspect of the existing social ensemble or order, is *intentional*. As Sartre claims in his discussion of colonialism, even though the racism that appears in the colonial order is a type of superstructural legitimation of the status quo, it is also reproduced through the actions of human individuals on both sides of the colonial dividing line, and on the part of the dominant party, is an intentional reproduction since it helps them pursue their project: "Circularity—as a structure of the social as a human product—produces its intelligibility through a double determination. . . . The racism which occurs to an Algerian colonialist was imposed and produced by the conquest of Algeria, and is constantly recreated and reactualised by everyday practice through serial alterity" (Sartre 1985 [1960]: 714). The situation of the Algerian *colonisés* is such that in their serial state, that is, as individuals, they do not explicitly realize the modes by which the actualization of their freedom is prevented. Once in contact with others, though, they can develop a collective set of meanings through the realization of their similar structural position. The assertion of collective meaning can be taken by the *colons* as a form of resistance, as a direct attack on the status quo producing and working to reproduce the *colonisés* as "sub-human."

Second, the development of collective meaning can and does lead to the development of collective *praxis* that often takes the form of resistance. Once the individual encounters the others in their situation and helps to collectively develop a project, their project can develop in conjunction with the collective and in opposition to the status quo. In the earlier discussion of the French Revolution, we saw that Sartre discounts the "collective meaning" aspect of this transition, one that Merleau-Ponty would hold up as exemplary: It is not merely the sudden realization by each individual that in a group they would be more effective against the soldiers that motivates the transition from seriality to the group; rather, it might very well be the realization that there are more people than just the individual who are in the same "situation" in both the term's senses. One more step, and we can see the development of collective *praxis* meant to storm the Bastille. It is, though, the transition from "collective meaning" to "collective *praxis*" that brings this act of resistance to fruition, and this transition can also lead to the perception of active resistance as "the only option." The mutual recognition of one another's situation and project and the transcendence of one's situation that can occur during this transition, as the Tennis Court meetings before the start of the French Revolution signified, can lead not simply to the perception of resistance as the only option, but also its actualization: "Faced with a still imprecise threat, but with an increasing hostility from the aristocracy and court, the deputies of the Third Estate swore *not to allow themselves to become divided*. They did not know what their tactics should be. And in fact it was the people of Paris who resolved the problem" (Sartre 1985 [1960]: 467). The construction of unity among the Third Estate's deputies (an already-constructed class, a definition of people who experienced their position of inferiority in pre-revolutionary French society) leads to a form of resistance. Because of the threat posed by the first two Estates, the Third Estate's decision to remain united against the first two becomes an oath to fight them after its translation into the larger group of "the people of Paris." As such, the Tennis Court oath becomes the way in which the collective meaning of their class position becomes the platform for a collective *praxis* on the part of the people of Paris and leads to resistance as the only option for this *praxis*.

At the same time, though, we cannot take the Tennis Court oath or the development of the foundations for resistance as an ethical justification for resistance or revolution. The ethical concerns we have raised already must be attended to. In other words, the group whose project it is to improve the condition of humanity must take into account the orientations among its members to one another and to the group being resisted, the ambiguity that their resistance brings about, and the fact that these ethical orientations have to take place through actions whose success is never guaranteed, whose results are never foretold, and which can be turned against the actors. These multiple aspects to which we must ethically orient further delimit at least the philosophical aspects of an existential ethics. And, as we have seen earlier, the situation in which we encounter others and from which we draw our abilities to develop and actualize a project helps to determine the practical aspects of a situated existential ethics. Taken together, we are beginning to develop a clearer picture of the complexities involved in developing an existentialist theory of ethics.

The Necessity of Resisting Ethics

There are, though, really two aspects of an existentialist theory of ethics. The first is what an ethics *ought* to be, which we have begun to elucidate here. The other, though, has to do with what ethics currently *are*—that is, with the nature of the forms of ethics we practice today. It is this aspect of an ethical theory that deserves to be addressed now.

Previously, we saw that the social world is, in part, determined by the practico-inert, that residuum of past *praxis* and past projects that create the meaning system from which we draw to develop our own projects today and obstacles to the enactment of our existential freedom. It would make sense, then, that the practico-inert would be made up not just of actions and their consequences, but also of the values and ethical codes that motivated past action and that result from that action. In other words, we can see that rule-based forms of ethics are inertial; in our current practice, we maintain ethical codes that motivated past actors, that are embedded in the residuum of their actions, and bring them to bear on our projects today. Sartre's *Rome Lectures*, as well as other unpublished works from the mid-1960s, provide a great deal of insight into the inertial aspects of ethics. In particular, three things are gleaned from that series of works: first, that the nature of the norm, the basis of any ethical code, is in fact inertia; second, that the imperative aspect of the norm in effect compels us to maintain the practico-inert social and normative structures that make up our social milieu, thereby maintaining the status quo; and third, that the ethical, the sense of what we *ought* to be doing, serves not only as an "extremely *pervasive* structure of everyday experience," but also as an effective historical tool in itself (Stone and Bowman 1991: 57).[4]

It is in social groupings in particular that we see the difficulties surrounding the practico-inert. Part of the difficulty surrounding group *praxis* relies upon the way in which it relies upon individuals to carry out their tasks: continuing to act in a revolutionary manner, for example, even after the group has moved to institutionalizing its own power, leads to being labeled as "counter-revolutionary," as in the case of Merleau-Ponty's discussion (1969) of *Darkness at Noon*. This is, in part, because the ethical code that motivated the revolutionary action—liberation, for example, or bread, or whatever—once achieved is no longer trusted. Those who act in accordance with principles, rather than with the group's requirements to maintain itself *qua* group, are mistrusted. Put another way, "social ensembles recognize themselves more in norms viewed as definite *tasks* for which people are the means than in the people who accomplish these tasks by realizing the unconditional—such people being unreliable in maintaining the status quo" (Stone and Bowman 1991: 72). The morality that inspires revolution, then, becomes institutionalized, set down in the form of particular requirements of individuals' action within groups in order to maintain the status quo, and removed from the realm of inspiring individuals to act freely. "The terror" of the institutionalized group works not only to compel individuals to act in accordance with its needs, but also turns those needs into norms that individuals are expected to uphold. Groups expect human beings to reproduce systems first and foremost, be it a capitalist system, a socialist system, or some other form of social structure. By turning the maintenance of a social structure into a normative value to be upheld, as Gramsci would argue in the case of hegemony, ensures that the threat of physical force or social exclusion does not necessarily have to be brought to bear upon individuals in the group; it is often enough to turn their pro-system, pro–status quo work into a normative virtue.

In this way, social structures can be seen as not only the residue of social action, but also the embodiment of norms. This normative content is as much a part of the practico-inert basis for a social order as the structures, institutions, and other apparatuses by which societies reproduce themselves. As Sartre points out, "La morale est un certain rapport de l'homme avec l'homme. Mais ce rapport n'est pas à l'origine une inerte relation d'intériorité. C'est un rapport actif de réciprocité qui se passivise et s'éternise (éternité de l'instant) par la médiation de la matière ouvrée" (Sartre 1964b: 476).[5] Because social orders contain this normative element, the products of that order also contain this element and maintain the normative value of upholding a particular mode of conduct in the world. The *values* embodied in the social order are transformed from an optional value to be upheld into an imperative: one *must* act in this way or be punished. As Sartre points out, this leads to an ethical paradox:

> Dans l'impératif de la coutume, le contenu de la norme me fixe un destin: je dois me produire à travers mon acte. L'intériorité est de temps à autre le sujet de mon acte possible et de la possibilité que je me fasse sujet, en un mot la possibilité *qu'une détermination quelconque de mon passé* soit sans rapport avec mon acte. On renvoie le passé au passé et l'impératif est une découverte de l'avenir en tant que disqualification du passé.
>
> Mais, simultanément, *cet avenir qui pose* la possibilité inconditionnée que je me produise en intériorité, la pose en tant qu'impératif qui a déjà été respecté par les individus des générations précédentes. Pour les hommes du passé, cela était un futur. En réalité, cet avenir est lui aussi un *futur antérieur*: pour l'agent moral que je suis aujourd'hui, il s'annonce comme *mon avenir* et comme un fait répétitif. (Sartre, in Contat and Rybalka 1970: 741)[6]

In acting in accordance with systemic norms and in following the imperatives of the system, the past comes back to life through our actions, which we see as "fulfilling our destiny," but in effect preventing us from realizing ourselves as autonomous beings by acting in a "future anterior" manner. We take on ethical codes that appear to us in our milieu, repeat the past and past *praxis*, and ultimately reproduce the status quo, all in the name of "acting ethically."

Sartre's analysis of the structure of the norm provides us with a better understanding of the tools used by social groupings to ensure our reproduction of systems. In particular, he focuses on the past production of the norm and its combination of a value to be upheld and an imperative to be followed. Social orders and groups, in creating themselves as social groups, rely upon a set of structural norms for the socialization of new individuals and the concomitant reproduction of the social order. In doing so, they work to embody in the individuals within the group a set of values—honesty, individuality, respect for private property, greed, and so on—that are seen as goods to be brought into being through individual action and in human relationships (Sartre 1964b: 380). For example, we may value honor in our relations with others, thereby enacting a socially defined value in our lives. However, this valuation and enactment of honor as a value is not autonomously decided; rather, we value honor because we think others value honor, and we act in accordance with the *imperative* of "be honorable": "L'impératif est donc la chose dictant ses lois à la *praxis* entant qu'elle est maintenu par *l'action des autres*. C'est si l'on veut, *la praxis cristallisée et refroidie au sens où le pareil humain s'emprisonne dans le produit manufacturé*" (Sartre 1964a: 42).[7] Because the system expresses "honor" as part of its morality, and because we expect that others will uphold this value by virtue of its imperative status, we act in accordance with it as well. In this way, an imperative serves as the expression of a system, and in fact operates as an *alienated morality*, alienated because it compels us to determine our *praxis*, our "interiority" or sense of self, on the basis of the "pseudo-interiority" of the *praxis* of Others (Sartre 1964a: 14, 22). Our reliance on the satisfaction of the expectations of others through our action—and their reciprocal reliance on our expectations of their actions—ends up reproducing the social milieu that constructs the normative elements in that practical field. Because others are seen to uphold a systemic imperative, and because others see us as upholding that imperative, the imperative, the kinds of actions demanded by that imperative, and the social structure that relies on that imperative are all reproduced, just to come back upon us in the future, which we live as a "past-future" (*futur antérieur*).

Social norms, comprising values and imperatives to uphold those values, determine the possibilities for our action. But, because these norms are the product of particular societies in particular historical phases of development, they are embedded in past practico-inert social structures that we echo or reflect into our own time frame. As Sartre puts it:

> Toute éthique particulière et datée est historique dans son contenu.
> Toute éthique particulière et datée se présente comme dépassement de l'historique.
> Toute éthique particulière et datée est arrêt de l'histoire et maintien d'une société par répétition.
> Toute éthique particulière et datée est dépassée par l'histoire.
> Toute éthique particulière et datée est aliénation (homme produit de son produit, homme fils de l'homme). . . .
> Toute éthique particulière et datée saisit radicalement fait éclater localement l'histoire d'un double point de vue: avenir (intégration de la mort); passé (répétition contre l'évolution). (Sartre 1964b: 427)[8]

We are, according to Sartre, not our own product when we act according to normative or ethical codes: we reproduce a set of norms that were unique to a particular time and place, halt the development of society, and act according to an alienated morality, one not of our own making. We simply live out the past and convince ourselves we are living out the future, and hinder ourselves from developing our own projects and futures.

The problem here is two-fold. First, the facticity of ethical codes and norms prescribes for us a particular kind of action, one that serves to delimit both our perceived possibilities for action. Second, they prevent us from formulating and realizing ourselves as fully human, since our actions are more prominently oriented to the production and reproduction of systems. Because the practico-inert structures of society both institutionalize and regularize patterns of action and prescribe those patterns of action as norms to be upheld, our perception of our field of action (*champ du pratique*) is delimited by a social form that needs us to follow its rules, its patterns of action, and its norms to be reproduced. Put another way, the social structure lives through individual human beings and needs them to reproduce itself; it thereby makes acting in such a way so as to reproduce the social order an ethical good, one to be upheld as both a value ("I am a law-abiding citizen") and followed as an imperative ("One must obey the law"). In order to do that—or rather, precisely because—the practico-inert residuum of the *praxis* of the past makes up the basis for the field of meaning from which we draw to develop our personal and collective projects, the normatively reproduced social order provides us with *only* the materials that go to serve its reproduction as a basis for the development of our own project. The result of this, then, is that without necessarily intending to reproduce a social order, we do so, if only because the materials we have to work with lead to that consequence. In doing so, we are valued as "ethical people" for acting in accordance with that order:

> Les morales comme *alibis*: "on doit, quand on aime, etc." En ce sens super-structures mais sont . . . déguisements des conduites réelles seulement ses conduites réelles sont elles-mêmes éthiques (ex: une morale de l'austérité ou de la générosité peut cacher une *pratique* intéressée.) Mais *l'intérêt* tant lui-même un impératif, on peut dire qu'une morale (comme simple verbalisme) en cache *une autre* (. . . le règne du simple fait). (Sartre 1964b: 456)[9]

We are drawn into a form of ethical conduct, one that reinforces and reproduces the existing state of social affairs whenever we act socially, and can use the ethical values embedded in this state of affairs as an alibi for our actions, as a way of legitimating ourselves in the eyes of Others who hold to these ethical values.

This, of course, presumes that we are simply acting in the world, following the inertia of our own projects as they are delimited by the status quo. What happens, though, when we look at conduct that is explicitly intended to be "ethical" in the definition of the status quo? We want to be "good people," so we act in accordance with an ethical code, philosophically formulated or not, that we expect others will recognize and respond to our actions as "ethical." But, are these ethical codes particularly appropriate to our conduct in the here and now? Yes and no: yes, because they are the ethical codes embedded in our particular social milieu and govern the conduct of others in whose eyes we wish to be judged as "good people"; and no, since those codes are the product of past times and social orders, *they are not of our making*, save in the sense of our echoing the past into the future through our conduct in accordance with them:

> On a compris que la praxis passée, inscrit dans l'inertie d'extériorité, se dissoudrent d'elle-même si elle n'était maintenue par ceux qui eu profitent. C'est donc *à travers* la lutte de classes (puisqu'ils la maintiennent contre ceux qu'elles frustrent) et *dans le mouvement même de l'histoire* que *l'emprisonnement de l'avenir éthique inconditionné et concevable.* (Sartre 1964a: 43; cf. Bowman and Stone 1991: 114)[10]

This "unconditioned future," a state of affairs characterized elsewhere in this work as "concrete freedom," is one in which individuals and collectivities are self-determining, not bound to blindly or semi-blindly reproducing the social order as is. This view of existing rule-based ethics as inertial and oppressive directly contravenes the possibility of developing *l'avenir pur*, the "pure future." We can see, then, that the ethics of already-existing social orders are those of the practico-inert, impelling us to act in accordance with something we call "freedom," but in actuality merely repeating the *praxis* of past social orders in inventive ways, freely alienating ourselves from the possibility of truly human *praxis*. We carry through the inertia of our forebears, taking that work on as our own through the desire to be ethical creatures. It is not the desire that is the problem here; it is the inertial, alienating, and ultimately oppressive tools with which we try to fulfill that desire.

By providing us with what are in essence someone else's tools for creating ourselves, tools created in another historical time and space and therefore not necessarily appropriate to our own, the existing social structures give us only so much room to act, a set of values created by others for us to uphold in our action, and the basis for ethical projects that prevents us from seeing possibilities other than those that serve to reproduce the social order (Stone and Bowman 1986: 203). It is no wonder, then, that even without a particular society in mind, Sartre calls the social order and its embedded ethical codes "alienating" and "inert." A "repetitive society" [*société répétitive*] would tend to alienate us from our own potential. Or, to put this another way, Ethics, whether the philosophical study of moral codes or the enactment of those moral codes in our daily lives, compels us to act to undermine our own freedom.

Ethics and Freedom

As yet, we have not talked about the value to which we should orient the development of our projects and their actualization—freedom. For both Sartre and Merleau-Ponty, freedom is the ultimate value. Sartre's early individuated and absolutist version of freedom, outlined in *Being and Nothingness*, is not the conception of freedom to which we need to orient our *praxis*. In this "potential" version of freedom, individuals in even the most oppressive situations are free in that they are self-conscious consciousnesses able to formulate projects that transcend their situation. The "abstract" morality from Sartre's early work corresponding with potential freedom ignores the situation in which the individuals find themselves. This version of morality parallels that of most ethical philosophers, such as Kant, in that it correctly posits that human beings are intrinsically free, but avoids the messy details of their particular situation and results in "inertia and resignation, since it does not challenge the status quo nor seek to change it, no matter how repressive or subhuman it may be" (Anderson 1993: 51). This situation of collective unfreedom, a state of both structured and individually enacted oppression in which human agency (the actualization of one's existential freedom) is severely restricted or stolen from some members of the social order by others, or, as a result of resignation on the part of oppressed individuals and groups, willingly (though not freely) given up, would by the argument I develop in this work require that we resist it in order to bring about a concrete state of individual and collective freedom and human agency. It is this type of freedom, which I have called concrete freedom, or *le futur pur*, that should be the ultimate value of our projects. A concrete morality, though, corresponds with actual freedom: this form of ethics focuses upon human beings situated in particular sociohistorical contexts and posits concrete goals that lead to the development of a realm of concrete human freedom.

The question arises, though, as to what a social order characterized by "concrete human freedom" would look like. To Sartre's mind, it would be one in which true socialism and a classless society—in other words, a "city of ends"—appears. We can and should expand this beyond the mere programmatic aspects to the characteristics of this "city of ends" by incorporating Merleau-Ponty's critique. In the writing of *Notebooks for an Ethics*, Sartre remained to a large extent within the philosophical framework outlined in *Being and Nothingness*, while at the same time combining this framework with Marxist goals such as the development of the classless society. Since the *Notebooks* are stuck within the ego-oriented conception of human relations put forth by *Being and Nothingness*, though, the desire still appears for the development of an existentialist version of Kant's categorical imperative: Do unto others as you would have them do unto you. As such, two issues arise. First, the obvious goal of this "first ethics" (as Anderson calls it) is to treat others as ends rather than means, that is, to avoid treating others as tools for the development of one's own project. This, though, as Merleau-Ponty points out, is one of the "ideals of 1939" that cannot be brought about until the social conditions of existence—namely the violence of class-, race-, and gender-based oppression—are changed: ". . . if men are one day to be human to another and the relations between consciousnesses are to become transparent, if universality is to become a fact, this will be in a society in which past traumas have been wiped out and the conditions of an effective liberty have from the first been realized" (Merleau-Ponty 1964c: 144). This of course would necessitate a change in Sartre's mind from an "abstract" morality to a "concrete" one. However, even the transition from a "city of means" to a "city of ends" will require more than just an attention to the particulars of an individual's or group's situation. It will require not simply the elimination of "scarcity" (Sartre 1985 [1960]: 113) so that the class struggle can be ended; it will also require a new orientation to others, a new reason for treating others as ends rather than as means. A new set of collective meanings, a new set of intentionalities, and a new orientation to others must come about, one that comes from the particular exigencies posed by a particular sociohistorical situation.

The second issue that arises in Sartre's transition from an abstract to a concrete morality is the continuing ego-orientation that exists in his existential categorical imperative. Treating others as ends instead of means can be taken in a way such that the value to be brought into being is one's freedom instead of the freedom of others. If we recall that our freedom is bound up with the freedom of others because each individual depends upon the situation they are in for the development of their freedom, then it becomes clear that one intention for working to develop the city of ends is to bring about or maintain one's freedom through working to bring about the conditions in which others' freedom can be actualized. This, though, does not move much past Kant's categorical imperative; the end result of both is the freedom of the individual, but in Sartre's plan, the freedom of the individual requires the freedom of others, so that working for the former requires working for the latter. The key, though, is that the individual's freedom becomes the primary value. As such, the ego-orientation still exists. This, though, can be taken care of by integrating Sartre's call for the development of a "city of ends" with Merleau-Ponty's position regarding our inherent sociality. For Merleau-Ponty, it is the social relationships that are primary. Because the social situation provides the basis upon which an individual develops their project and actualizes it, it is necessary for the social setting to be one of concrete freedom so that the individuals within it can be actually free (Whiteside 1988: 115). Put another way, while Sartre's task is to move from the individual's existence to the community's existence, Merleau-Ponty works in the opposite direction; while Sartre's problem is to bring about an ethical state of affairs to the group by working through the individual, Merleau-Ponty's is to see the community's conception of the good come into existence with the individuals in the group actualizing and living this state of affairs.

As a result, we have two different angles from which to approach the problem of the appearance of the "city of ends" and its concrete freedom. One important thing to remember, though, is the nature of freedom, a claim I draw from both Sartre and Merleau-Ponty's concept of action: *Freedom is a process.* Freedom is never an end in-itself, that is, a finality to be achieved, after which we can rest on our laurels; rather, freedom is to be processual, leading to new manifestations of freedom. As Sartre puts it:

> This is the ethics and tactics of freedom since it implies that one ought never to allow oneself to be caught up in one's undertaking, ought never to allow oneself to fall into it like into a well but always be able to contest it, to be able reflexively to get out of it in order to be able to make it appear before oneself for examination and to be able to modify it as one wills, or according to the circumstances. (Sartre 1993b: 392–393)

Freedom is therefore not an object, a facticity, or a slogan, but rather the ability to constantly strive to divert the conversion of free agency into inertia, to struggle against the transformation of *praxis* into the practico-inert. If I allow myself to fall into a project I know I can never accomplish and yet continue to do so, my freedom has become inertial; I have allowed myself to become an object whose sole reason for existence is to follow through on a project that is no longer mine. This is, though, an individualistic perspective, one Merleau-Ponty renders less important through his emphasis on the ambiguity of the social:

> . . . it is a question of knowing whether there is indeed a certain line of conduct which can justify each man in the eyes of his fellows or whether, on the contrary, our condition does not make all ways of behaving mutually unforgivable and whether, in such a situation, all moral principles are not merely a way to reassure rather than to save ourselves, a way to wave questions aside instead of answering them. (Merleau-Ponty 1964a: 4)

As Merleau-Ponty puts it, this kind of individualistic orientation to the construction of concrete freedom can be merely a placebo for a real ethics. One must conceive of the way in which a community or a social ensemble can bring about a concrete situation of freedom in order to think about an individual's real concrete freedom. It is possible to reclaim this intention to freedom as a social project by remembering that the individual's freedom is dependent upon the freedom of all others. Because our individual freedom for Merleau-Ponty is predicated upon the situation in which we find ourselves, it is at the level of the social that we must bring about concrete freedom; that is, we must find a way to make freedom processual at the social level and not just at the individual level. We will return to this issue in chapter 7.

For now, though, we can see the following with regard to the development of an ethics of freedom. First, our *praxis* must be such that it is oriented to the freedom-seeking activity of those who are embedded in a situation of oppression and/or are committed to overcoming it.[11] As such, our *praxis* (and hence our ethical orientation) is not simply intended to develop the freedom of everyone in a situation, including the oppressors. And this is not just the avoidance of doing violence to others in an attempt to treat others as ends in themselves; this is also the *praxis* of working for and with others in an attempt to develop actual practical freedom, the situational and situated ability to develop and pursue one's project, for all, and as such means that we cannot take all others as "ends rather than means." As Merleau-Ponty reminds us, our situation is one in which violence is part of the status quo, so the elimination of this violence as a systematic principle may very well require us to engage in a violent project (the ambiguity of revolutionary activity). To do this, though, we are not to take the freedom of others or the freedom of all as a programmatic statement; as Merleau-Ponty puts it, "We must remember that liberty becomes a false ensign—a 'solemn complement' of violence—as soon as it becomes only an idea and we begin to defend liberty instead of free men. . . . It is the essence of liberty to exist only in the practice of liberty, in the inevitably imperfect movement which joins us to others, to the things of the world, to our jobs, mixed with the hazards of our situation" (Merleau-Ponty 1969: xxiv–xv). Since freedom appears only in and through the practice of freedom, we must orient the practice of our freedom to others' practice of their freedom by working to bring about the conditions in which they can actualize their freedom. This aspect therefore eliminates the possibility of being ethical by oneself; one can only be ethical and act ethically with and toward others (Sartre 1993b: 471). Second, this ethics of freedom cannot be "abstract" or rule-bound, but rather must be oriented to the particular situation in which the actor and the recipients of the action exist. This "concreteness" is such that it would yield a framework of action that would emphasize the "finite" in the infinity of freedom (Sartre 1993b: 427). As well, an ethics of freedom would also highlight the relationship between history and ethics: as Sartre puts it, history implies ethics through the idea of "universal conversion," that is, that our project can be understood by others as a "singularized universal"; and ethics implies history, since "no morality is possible without systematic action in some situation" (ibid.: 471).

Third, an ethics of freedom takes account of the ambiguity of our existence and that of others; by calling us to engage in *praxis* that is intended to bring about the concrete freedom of all in our situation, an ethics of freedom calls us to recognize that our actions have unintended consequences, ones that can be detrimental for the situation of others, and as such forces us to take consideration of these consequences and their impact on the future of freedom and the free future. In sum, then, we can see that the ethics of freedom in the way I have developed it here meets what Sartre claims at the end of his life is his conception of ethics. To quote at length:

> All human beings will be in a state of fraternity with each other when they can say of themselves, through all our history, that they are all bound to each other in feeling and in action. Ethics is indispensable, for it signifies that men or submen have a future based on principles of common action, while a future based on materiality—i.e., on the basis of scarcity—is simultaneously being sketched around them, which is to say, what I have is yours, what you have is mine; if I am in need, you give to me, and if you are in need I give to you—that's the future of ethics. . . . (Sartre and Lévy 1996: 91)

> The question is to find the ultimate end, the moment when ethics will be simply and truly the way in which human beings live in relation to each other. The rules-and-prescriptions aspect of ethics that prevails today will

probably no longer exist—as has often been said, for that matter. Ethics will have to do with the way in which men form their thoughts, their feelings . . . . (Sartre and Lévy 1996: 106–107)

Given the current state of affairs, we can see that this kind of ethics would call us to resistance against the status quo and the practico-inert structures that prevent the concrete exercise of the freedom of many.

Ethics, Resistance, and Violence

At first blush, it might appear odd to have to discuss the issue of violence in a work devoted to the development of a socially oriented ethics. However, the problem of violence becomes paramount when examining both the development of an existential social ethics in terms of the philosophical makeup of the foundational material and in terms of the political affiliations of the two primary authors upon whose work I draw on here. The latter aspect is easy enough to detail. Both Sartre and Merleau-Ponty had affiliations with Marxism to varying organizational degrees, and as such saw that violence might possibly be necessary to bring about a classless society and a socialist order, not for the sake of violence as Alexander argues,[12] but because the existing social order is itself violent. And since the development of our individual or collective project is dependent on the situation in which we find ourselves, for both of them violence *can* be ethical. If the violence that is enacted is done in the context of a project that contributes to the liberation of humanity and the creation of concrete freedom in the world, and if the violence is limited to that which is necessary for this liberation, then it can be seen as ethical. Both paid careful attention to the revolutionary movements in Algeria, Vietnam, and other former French colonies, and noted that, in fact, the only way for colonized peoples to liberate them-selves from the violence of the colonial system is to engage in a violent revolutionary project:

> Of course, violence is not going to speed up the pace of history and draw humanity together. Violence merely breaks up a certain state of enslave-ment that was making it impossible for people to become human beings. When violence has destroyed the characteristics of the colonized person—that is, the characteristics of the slave—what you have are no longer just submen who are not suffering from certain constraints anymore—though they will find other constraints elsewhere, as in Algeria—but people who are trying to come closer to the active citizen, who himself is still as far removed from Humanity as he is from the colo-nized submen. (Sartre and Lévy 1996: 92)

For, by hiding violence, one grows accustomed to it and makes an institution of it. On the other hand, if one gives violence its name and if one uses it, as the revolutionaries always did, without pleasure, there remains a chance of driving it out of history. In any case violence will not be expulsed by locking ourselves within the judicial dream of liberalism. (Merleau-Ponty 1969: 34)[13]

With regard to the practical concrete situation of oppressed peoples, then, revolutionary violence can be seen as ethical since its goal is the liberation of humanity from oppression.

Developing the philosophical justification for the ethicality of violence, though, is a longer process. We must start from the practico-inert structures of society to find Sartre's and Merleau-Ponty's justifications for the use of violence in ethical action. For both Sartre and Merleau-Ponty, the practico-inert has an element of violence within it. The conversion of *praxis* into the practico-inert, once completed, also turns *praxis* into *exis*, or the realm of the mundane. Once the acts of individuals within a social ensemble are converted into *exis*, they take on the realm of the natural (Sartre 1991 [1985]: 359). Action is converted into naturalized essences that appear in the realm of the unthought and as such exert themselves on individuals within that social ensemble with the force of authority. If we remain in the realm of pure action and ignore the particularities of the types of action that become part of the practico-inert structures, this situation does not appear all that bad. The context of these actions, though—as we can see from any basic stratification, feminist, or antiracist text—shows that what is converted into the practico-inert is the stuff of oppression:

> . . . for the child of the colonialist, violence was present in the situation itself, and was a social force that produced him. The son of the colonialist and the son of the Muslim are both the children of the objective violence which defines the system itself as a practico-inert hell. But *if* this violence-object produces them, if they suffer it partly as their own inertia, this is because it used to be violence-*praxis* when the system was in the process of being installed. It is man who inscribed his violence in things as the eternal unity of this passive mediation between men. (Sartre 1985 [1960]: 718)

Even the normative elements of the practico-inert social order become violent if they make actions that reproduce that social order imperative. Once individuals encounter this situation and utilize it as the basis for the development of their "freedom" (and here, I keep "freedom" in quotation marks to show that it is merely potential or existential freedom and not the actual capability to act freely), both sets of children reenact the practico-inert structures of oppression in and through their *praxis* (ibid.: 714). The son of the colonialist will become a colonialist and will treat the colonized as the "dogs" he perceives them to be (because of his embeddedness in the position of "colonizer" in the colonial system), and the colonized will respond in the expected way to the practico-inert structures that oppress them—until they choose to develop a new liberatory project (ibid.: 720). In this way, the system is reenacted by its subsequent generations; the practico-inert is converted into an oppressive *praxis*; and yet this *praxis* in essence remains in the realm of *exis*, of habit. Our ability to envision a social order outside the one that exists, as well as our ability to bring about any sort of liberatory change, is removed here. All that we have left is the almost-ritualistic reenactment of the dominant social order, all the while envisioning ourselves as being "free," with dangerous consequences.

This *exis*-based action reinstates the violence of the *praxis* that brought the oppressive system into being. It must necessarily remain hidden from view, for it is the hiding of violence that allows it to become institutionalized. Through the process of institutionalization, the form that the violence of the system takes necessarily becomes less and less extreme. As Merleau-Ponty puts it, the unemployment, war, and imperialism that are the hallmarks of bourgeois society are violent (Merleau-Ponty 1969: 107), in spite of justifications that unemployment is the individual's fault, that wars can be fought in the present to prevent bloodshed in the future, and that imperialism is nothing more than the operation of the "free market" economy. We do not directly perceive the forms of oppression enacted by bourgeois society as "oppressive" or as forms of violence unless we are directly affected by them; we only see them as the downsides of a liberty held up as a commodity to be defended. Both these views are imbued with the normativity of the very liberalism that produces these forms of violence, and both demand the upholding of their ethical maxims.

These forms of inequality and oppression, though, are violent in one important way: they prevent individuals and groups from developing and actualizing free projects of their own. As we saw in the previous section on ethics and inertia, the dominant social order must necessarily compel us to reproduce it and the practico-inert structures that make it up, and one way in which it achieves this goal is through the maintenance of ethical codes and our expectation that we will meet these codes. Following these codes, though, impedes our ability to act freely or directly to create our own individual or collective projects; we "freely alienate" ourselves from our own freedom and human potential. This is but one instance in which the ontological possibilities given to us by our freedom and the possibility for acting upon these ontological possibilities diverge (and hence, the reason Sartre's claim that we are at the very least free in our minds leads us to nothing but the repetition of the status quo). If from the outset of the encounter with our situation we are essentialized (in other words, treated like an object prior to our action and delimited in such a way), we are prevented from ever acknowledging the unlimited nature of our potential freedom and thereby prevented from ever actualizing any real concrete freedom—in other words, we are alienated. Put another way, the status quo situation is one of "bad faith" on both sides of the oppressor/oppressed equation; the oppressor acts in bad faith by deferring responsibility for their construction of the oppressed as subhuman onto the oppressed; and the oppressed act in bad faith because the situation in which they are embedded, a situation pervaded by violence, prevents them from acting in an authentically human manner (cf. Gordon 1994). As such, the quest for authenticity—or, rather, the quest to make freedom processual rather than an object (Dufrenne 1998: 282)—would require that the oppressed, once they realize the true nature of their situation, resist in order to overcome their alienation from themselves.

This process is one that requires the construction of a common set of meanings within the resisting subgroup. It is here that we return to an ethics of freedom. Because the members of this subgroup act to construct a different practical field for themselves than the practico-inert one given to them, they are taking the first step in changing the situation in which they exist and act. As Sartre puts it, "There remains therefore just one path for the slave, if he does not want all his efforts (which are nothing more, by the way, than internal and idealistic adjustments) to turn into complicity with the enterprise of dehumanizing man. This is the concrete rejection *in acts* of the master's power" (Sartre 1993b: 398). Since the "master's" power is first and foremost the ability to dictate the field of meaning and *champ du pratique* that the "slave" encounters and is formed by, the rejection of this field is the first step toward the construction of a new order. But, the acceptance of the necessity of the destruction of the old order requires that, as Sartre points out, the oppressed choose "Evil":

> And since . . . the slave's violence is the discovering of subjectivity, the slave discovers his subjectivity and has to assume it within the element of Evil. Therefore he has to choose between consciousness of self as absolute

> Evil, that is, as freedom choosing Evil and choosing itself within
> the dimension of Evil, or as the grasping of oneself beginning from the
> Master's gaze. A thing or Lucifer. The myth of the revolt and fall of the
> Angels shows quite clearly the revolt of the slave as absolute Evil, yet it
> cannot be that this revolt should appear to itself as the choice of absolute
> Evil. (Sartre 1993b: 401)

This evil, though, is merely an "immoralism"; or, rather, the choice to
revolt against the oppressive order is the turning of that order's violence
against itself in order to destroy the binary dependence of "oppressor" and
"oppressed" (Sartre 1993b: 402, 404). As Merleau-Ponty puts it, "The
Revolution takes on and directs a violence which bourgeois society toler-
ates in unemployment and in war and disguises with the name of misfortune" (Merleau-Ponty 1969: 107). The immoralism inherent in the
revolutionary impulse is precisely this: that one is taking on the violence
of the status quo and turning it against itself in an attempt to construct a
new order. It is, in large part, the reclamation of freedom and human
agency. But, the revolutionary impulse is no longer innocent; its hands are
dirty, and the "dark feeling" that we identify with the taking-on of revolutionary violence (Sartre 1993b: 401) is this loss of innocence, gained at
the price of enacting precisely the acts and values that one wants to end:
". . . no one can feel justified in the eyes of those on whom he has inflicted
violence. . . . And yet it was precisely in order to liberate men that he had
used violence against some men. He does not think he was wrong. But he
is no longer innocent" (Merleau-Ponty 1969: 5; cf. Camus 1991: 10, 128;
Camus 1960: 93–94; Merleau-Ponty 1973b: 146–147).[14]
    Put another way, in order to attain the freedom to engage in self-
determining projects, it may very well be necessary for the oppressed in
a society to engage in violence. By Sartre's estimation, all of us are
oppressed by the practico-inert structures of society, though some of us
are considerably *more* oppressed by those who act to reinforce and reproduce their position in these structures. This form of "ethical radicalism,"
acting in an "unethical" way (from the point of view of the present) in
order to bring about a more ethical order in the future, may or may not
take the form of violence; however, there is violence within this form of
action from the perspective of the system.[15] Referring to the Liège,
Belgium, infanticides following birth defects resulting from the mothers
taking thalidomide, Sartre argues that these infanticides represent a
form of ethical radicalism that indicates the basis of a "dialectical ethics":

> Ou, si l'on préfère, l'avenir inconditionné ou *l'homme avenir de l'homme*
> et l'identification de la morale au sens de l'histoire ne peuvent être

produits, n'entant que tels, par la classe qui nie l'histoire. Cette norme rigoureuse est produite par les classes exploitées dans la mesure même où leur projet humain de produire des hommes est en contradiction avec les conditions inhumaines que leur sont faits. (Sartre 1964a: 59–60; cf. Bowman and Stone 1991: 114)[16]

It is in this desire for a "nonrepetitive" end—in other words, a situation in which our actions do not merely reproduce or repeat the past *praxis* of those who come before us, but rather enable us to conceive of and actualize our own freely chosen projects—that motivates Sartre and Merleau-Ponty's ethical legitimation of violence if the sociohistorical situation necessitates it. That is, if an unethical act in the present aids in bringing about a more ethical future, it should be endorsed. If that unethical act is liberatory violence, as in the case of the decolonization movement, or the horrific sacrifice of children with birth defects, and if the historical situation requires it, so be it.

Violence, though, is not intended for short-term gain in power or wealth. Its ultimate orientation is supposed to be the development of a future in which freedom concretely exists for all, or, as Camus puts it, "Freedom is nothing else but a chance to be better, whereas enslavement is a certainty of the worst" (Camus 1960: 103). The question, though, as to whether or not violence can be ethical (because clearly it is ambiguous as a phenomenon in itself) appears in both its orientation to the others with whom and on whose behalf one resists *and* in its historical *sens* or meaning. Three selections, taken from among many in Merleau-Ponty's work, should suffice to show the importance of intentionality and *sens* in the evaluation of the ethicality of violence and resistance.

> The Party's action is not to be judged on a detail any more than a man is to be judged on a tic or a mole; rather it is judged on a direction taken, on a way of doing things, and, in the last analysis, on the militant's relationships with it. (Merleau-Ponty 1973b: 128)

> Between these two fundamental choices, no reading of history can arbitrate, no truth can decide. The bourgeois choice is ultimately murder or, worse still, degradation of other freedoms. The revolutionary choice is ultimately freedom for all. The decisive reading of history depends, then, on a moral option: one wants to exist against others, or one wishes to exist with everyone; and the true perspective in history is not the one that accounts for all the facts, because they are equivocal, but that which takes into account all lives. (Merleau-Ponty 1973b: 146–147)

> But successful revolutions taken altogether have not spilled as much blood as the empires. All we know is different kinds of violence and we

ought to prefer revolutionary violence because it has a future of humanism. (Merleau-Ponty 1969: 107)

Again, though, the question of the ethicality of violence as in any other action is determined in a number of ways and at a variety of temporal junctures. The actor or group must evaluate whether or not their act or project as it is intended is ethical for both themselves (in terms of actualizing their free project, and acting authentically as opposed to in "bad faith") and others, as well as whether or not the act or project has the potential for unintended consequences that will counteract or overwhelm the intention of the act. The actor or group must also evaluate whether or not their act is in accordance with the historical situation in which they are acting. The ensemble that engages in a collective form of *praxis* must evaluate its ethicality at all of these points as well. And all actors must see themselves as responsible for their action, whatever the consequences might be. As such, an existential ethics, which leads one to consider whether revolutionary violence in the context of a liberatory project is ethical, requires a "nomadic" perspective that operates through a variety of experiences of the social order, takes account of a multiplicity of social conditions of existence, and has regard for others who will be affected by one's actions, be they present at the moment of action or existing in the future.

To Resist Ethics and a Resisting Ethics

Nous avons vu la contradiction de l'éthique. Nous avons vu le motif propre de l'éthique: la volonté de souveraineté dans la réciprocité.
—Sartre, "Conférence à l'Institut Gramsci," 1964a (445)[17]

What we have found, then, is that ethics as we commonly understand it—as an already-existing moral code, whether philosophically codified or merely practiced, best denoted as Ethics—represents and valorizes the reproduction of the dominant social order, thereby preventing us from freely acting in the world. Because past actions are turned into values, things to be upheld, and made imperative, thereby conditioning our action, we end up merely repeating the past *praxis* of old social orders, merely echoing the past into the present. This is not the kind of ethics Sartre or Merleau-Ponty envisioned; rather, they felt that freedom, the most basic human quality, was what should be valorized, whatever the cost. What is needed, then, is an ethical radicalism, a radical form of action designed to break down or overturn the practico-inert structures of our current social order, one in which we freely alienate ourselves, for the sake of creating a social situation in which freedom can be processual, that is, our freedom goes in large part to ensuring the continued freedom of the whole. This ethical radicalism represents a form of resistance; it requires us to contradict the normative nature of our current social order in favor of an undefined and unknowable future order in which "humanity" can take hold. Put another way, ethical radicalism appears in actions designed to bring about "th : will of sovereignty in reciprocity"—the capacity for all to reciprocaly be sovereign in their own projects, not over others (as in our society), but with others (Sartre 1964b: 450–451).

Problematically, though—as shown in Merleau-Ponty's "yogi and commissar" discussion as well as "the terror" inherent in Sartre's analysis of social groups—once liberatory *praxis* is undertaken (and assuming it is successful), the victorious group attempts to institutionalize its victory, thereby starting the cycle of "ethical radicalism"—liberation—terror over again. How is it that this can be prevented? One way is to remember Dufrenne's statement that freedom is processual; but how is it that this can ensure that the imperative of the "permanent revolution" does not prevent that revolution from actually achieving its goals? Part of the lessons of Sartre's *Critique of Dialectical Reason* come in here: "L'homme fils de l'homme peut exiger *négativement* dans la rétrospection (suicide), [ou] positivement par la praxis révolutionnaire, d'être réellement dans sa naissance même le produit de l'homme. . . . C'est-à-dire une société où le pratico-inerte est sans cesse dissous à mesure qu'il sa forme par l'union des hommes contre la médiation de l'inerte; société sans structure, économique produisant l'homme sans institutions (État) ni morale aliénée" (Sartre 1964a: 141).[18] Put another way, humanity entails the satisfaction of needs, self-production, group action, and *praxis* guiding the practico-inert (Bowman and Stone 1992: 175). The latter two elements of this humanity—group action (instead of serialized individual action) and the dominance of *praxis* give us the basis for envisioning how it is we can prevent "the terror" from returning upon us. By ensuring that we preserve the elements of ethical radicalism in quotidian individual and collective action, we can ensure that it is the *goals* of ethical radicalism that are preserved, *not* the institutions that bring it about:

> Le normatif inconditionnel et *aussi* le fondement de l'impératif. La transformation des structures fondamentales du système . . . en rend la Terreur inutile ne supprime pas son moyen, mais la fin inconditionnée de découvre de nouveau et la praxis se donne pour but, à partir de la poursuite vrai du but révolutionnaire réel de liquider les limites du Terrorisme. (Sartre 1964a: 161; cf. Bowman and Stone 1992: 186)[19]

The prevention of the Terror, the quashing of Liberation by the liberators, and the act of ensuring that freedom is allowed to become processual comes through *continued resistance*—not simply resistance against an oppressive practico-inert structure, but resistance against the tendencies in all of us to protect, ossify, and institutionalize any social grouping. In a word, then, the social ethics that is the thoughtful outcome of an existentialist analysis of the nature of society and ethics is a *resisting ethics*, in the double sense implied: we need to take on an ethics of resistance (against the practico-inert structures of society and our internalization of them and their tendencies), and we need to resist Ethics (the practico-inert rule-based ethical codes that delimit our possibilities for acting in ways that generally reproduce the status quo). We are in the world with others, make and remake the world with others, and determine our own sense of belonging with and orientation to others. We must make it one in which we all have the capacity for sovereignty with others.

"Existence Requires Resistance": Moving to a Place of Freedom

In sum, the theory of existence presented by Sartre and Merleau-Ponty is *at one and the same time* a theory of action *and* a theory of ethics. Put another way, existence *is* action, which *positions us ethically* with regard to the world and those in it. It is in this way that we can see the interconnectedness of ethics and resistance: resistance, which is a group's acting to concretize its freedom, is *praxis* intended to bring about the group's existence as freedom. Groups that resist or revolt are those whose existence (i.e., self-determined existence as a group of human beings relating to one another as human beings) has been denied by the practico-inert structures of a social order; in this way, their quest for existence as a self-determining process of *praxis* is a way of working to bring about a new, more ethical order; and those who would align themselves socially, politically, and historically with oppressed groups find that this intentionality is one that requires them to move against the dominant social order in the hopes of creating a more ethical order characterized by the creation and maintenance of a situation of concrete freedom.

This more ethical order, though, is not one in which resistance is merely a catalytic force that separates "the unethical past" from "the ethical future"; rather, in order to maintain the ethical orientations to others and to the development of concrete freedom, *one must always be in a state of resistance.* As we have seen in Sartre's discussion of group formation, there is a tendency for social ensembles as they move from seriality to pledged groups to institutionalize, to ossify the structure of the group and the assignment of functions to individuals in order to preserve the group's status as group and as the victorious group. This Terror, though, as we have seen, results in the elimination of precisely that which the group worked to bring about—the increase of human (i.e., individual) freedom. This ossification process, then, is what needs to be resisted in order to continue to act ethically: if a group's project is to bring about a concrete state of human freedom in which freedom is not a piece of propaganda but the ability to continuously act freely with others in "human" relationships (and as Sartre reminds us, "Essentially, ethics is a matter of one person's relationship to another"; Sartre and Lévy 1996: 68), then it cannot quit its struggle to bring about human freedom once it has achieved "victory" and begins to institutionalize the violence it used to gain this victory.

> Our problem today is simple. If the idea of revolution becomes identified with the idea of terrorism, it's done for. To restore meaning to the idea of revolution, if it's possible, one must do away with the concept of fraternity-terror. Of course, one can choose to abandon any idea of revolution by taking it for a very costly, poetic illusion. To this there are two objections. The first is factual: there are revolts. The second touches on the legitimacy of the revolts. It derives from what we used to call the desire for society. Against the illusion—and this one is in no way poetic—that human unity has been achieved in current social conditions, a revolt raises the real and profound issue of unification; the unity of the human enterprise is still to be created. . . . the revolt is an appeal to an ethical order: the forgotten are making themselves heard. . . . To say that the phenomenon of fraternity is sustained essentially by recourse to violence would be, in a way, like saying that for a child to be born doesn't call for the union of a man and a woman and the maturation of the embryo, but that what basically counts is the use of forceps. (Lévy, in Sartre and Lévy 1996: 96)

As such, ethics requires resistance (to the institutionalization process, a top-directed situation in which human relations become, as Sartre points out, inert, tyrannical, and inhumane functional relationships), and resistance requires ethics; and both resistance and ethics require the social, for without a social aspect (in one's intention, orientation, and action), both become mere intentionality, desires along the lines of, "If wishes were fishes. . . ." To put it in a more conclusive way, our existence, embedded as it is in a situation of violence and oppression, requires us to orient in certain ways to those who engage in violence against others and those who are victims of that violence. If we align ourselves with those who are the victims of that violence—to my mind, the only authentic manner of existence—then we must necessarily resist through our ethical orientation. And for those who choose to act in a way that makes freedom a value for all, it would seem to me that our choice is one that puts us in a position of resisting both the oppression of others in the current situation and the potential theft of human agency in whatever new ethical social order appears as a result of our action. Our ethics, therefore, is one of resistance, and ultimately, our resistance is one against Ethics as well.

CHAPTER 4

TURNING OURSELVES ON OUR HEADS: HEGEMONY AND THE COLONIZED HABITUS

Chapter 3 detailed the ways in which resistance and ethics are interrelated in existential thought. The embeddedness of individuals in a particular situation of existence also embeds them in a number of social and historical relationships, ones that induce people to act in particular ways (depending upon their position in the social order and their encounter with the situation) and with particular attention to certain others in their situation. Acting in accordance with these "practico-inert" structures, according to Sartre and Merleau-Ponty, leaves people in a situation in which they directly reproduce those structures, which Sartre and Merleau-Ponty held contain either naked aggression or more insidious forms of oppression. And acting in "good faith" requires, to some extent, that one act ethically and resist the mere "circularity" (Sartre 1985 [1960]: 714) and inertia of the social order. The question still remains, though: even though we have seen *why* one should resist, we have yet to see *how* resistance occurs, against what resistance should be or is oriented, or how it can be theorized. That is the task of this chapter.

The act of resistance can be seen as an ethical good, or at the very least as a tool in the process of acting ethically. In order to bolster this claim, though, we need to understand just *what* that act is—how someone comes to make the intentional choice to resist, how someone figures out how they are able to resist, and what that process of decision-making and project formation entails. In order to do this, though, especially in light of the existential claim that resistance is necessary for ethics, we need to first figure out why people *do not* resist—why it is they allow the practico-inert structures of society to overtake their lives and not do anything about it. This task entails that we attempt to understand how it is that the practico-inert infiltrates the individual's consciousness in terms beyond those of Merleau-Ponty's subjectivist reliance on *l'intermonde.* I will do that through Bourdieu's notion of the habitus, one that includes in a fairly phenomenological manner both the experience of practico-inert life and the conceptual structures that suggest how that experience comes to bear on individuals. This, though, requires that we take another step back and bring in Gramsci's idea of hegemony—the colonization of the consciousness by dominant social forces. By pulling these two concepts together, we can see how it is that the habitus is developed, colonized by an outside force for the purposes of supporting a social order, and ultimately can be overturned through the act of resistance.

However, a problem that plagues the theorizing of hegemony, habitus, and resistance to hegemony is a level of analysis question (cf. Collier and Mahon 1993). That is, at what level of social order or action does "hegemony" exist? Is it, as Gramsci pointed out, at the level of consciousness, something to be overcome by working out through revolutionary *praxis* the contradictory conditions of existence in such a way so as to transcend the contradictions, thereby binding theory and practice? Or does it, as Bourdieu seems to suggest, exist at the level of cultural practices that are simultaneously existent in both the physical and intellectual realms? There must be some consideration of Gramsci's analysis of the class struggle as a "war of position," in which both sides tactically negotiate the terms of the conflict at every juncture, thereby making the "hegemonic order" a site of struggle, contestation, and debate, even for people who have no obvious and overt power. Bourdieu's notion of the habitus, as a more sociological extension of Merleau-Ponty's conception of the socially embedded human being and of the Sartrean conception of the practico-inert structures of society as experienced by and embedded in the individual, provides the basis by which we can understand the level at which hegemony and resistance can both take place. An examination of the habitus reveals that it is the site at which the hegemonic inertia of the social structure constructs (or, as I will refer to it later, colonizes) the consciousness of the individual, making it so that the individual serves as the site of the reproduction of the practico-inert. At the same time, though, the habitus also provides the basis by which the "bad faith" existence of the individual as the result of the reproduction of the practico-inert structures of society can be overturned in the process of developing a liberatory project with others committed to developing a situation of concrete freedom.

The habitus, as we will see here, is a crucial concept for the development of a phenomenological analysis of the relationships between resistance and ethics. In fact, the habitus is the combination of two key ideas discussed in chapter 3—Sartre's notion that Ethics, conceived as codified ways of being with others, serves as a form of oppressive inertia; and what could be called an "ethics of the flesh" deriving from Merleau-Ponty's work, one that requires mutual recognition and reciprocity. Its position as the site of socialization, as the site of one's engagement with the world, and the physical marker of one's place in the social order, all make it necessary to examine the development of the habitus in an attempt to develop a counterhegemonic way of being, one oriented to the development of a new way of acting with others in the world.[1] And given that the structural norms of a social order serve to inculcate individuals with the ethical codes appropriate to that order, leaving them unable to do much more than prereflectively reproduce that order, this task becomes much more crucial. As Bourdieu puts it in the interview "Social Space and Symbolic Power," "To change the world, one has to change the ways of making the world, that is, the vision of the world and the practical operations by which groups are produced and reproduced" (Bourdieu 1990c: 137). But, before we can do this, we need to discover just where and how resistance can take place.

The Habitus and Existentialism

For Bourdieu, the key to social reproduction appears in what he calls the habitus—"systems of durable, transposable dispositions, structured structures predisposed to function as structuring structures" (Bourdieu 1977: 72). The habitus becomes a way of organizing the world, relating to the social field, and is the result of past practices and socialization processes, which guide though do not predetermine future ways of being. In other words, the habitus becomes for Bourdieu the embodied locus of the linguistic, intellectual, and cultural attitudes and actions appropriate to an individual's position within a social and cultural field:

> Each class condition is defined, simultaneously, by its intrinsic properties and by the relational properties which it derives from its position in the system of class conditions, which is also a system of differences, differential positions, i.e., by everything which distinguishes it from what it is not and especially from everything it is opposed to; social identity is defined and asserted through difference. This means that inevitably inscribed within the dispositions of the habitus is the whole structure of the system of conditions, as it presents itself in the experience of a life-condition occupying a particular position within that structure. (Bourdieu 1984: 172)

The habitus thereby appears as the embodied and enacted indicator of the individual's position within the social structure, and both reproduces and apprehends all social interactions within the terms given to it by the social structure from which it comes. In this sense, the habitus becomes the site of the dominant social order and its manifestations in the cultural, linguistic, political, and economic realms, and leads the individual social actor to misrecognize the power relations manifesting themselves through interpersonal interactions, that is interactions of habituses, as arbitrary, when in fact they are a direct result of the structuring of society.

While existentialism's concern appears to be primarily with the avoidance of structures in favor of the development of the individual's freedom (or their freedom in concert with the group's freedom), Bourdieu's notion of the habitus appears to be based more in the structure of social and cultural orders, making the individual appear to be nothing more than the product of the structures in which they are born (economic capital) and raised (cultural capital). However, there are in fact a number of linkages between Bourdieu and the existentialism of Sartre and Merleau-Ponty, ranging from their shared participation in *Les temps modernes*[2] to certain political outlooks and forms of *engagement* in political and social affairs, to the foundations of their modes of analysis. As well, the conception of the body as the site of our contact with and inscription in the social order, developed by both Merleau-Ponty and Bourdieu, provides an important theoretical linkage for the development of an existential social ethics. These linkages help make the argument that Bourdieu's notion of the habitus provides us with a concrete way in which to study the embeddedness of the individual in sociohistorical contexts as well as the interconnections between the individual, the social, the historical, and the ethical.

I would argue that despite the distance between Sartre's affinity for Gramsci's ideas and Bourdieu's more structural notions, the two writers have much more in common than is usually attributed for a number of reasons. First, Bourdieu's notion of the habitus contains within it both the idea of structure and the idea of *praxis*. Sartre's discussion of "circularity" (Sartre 1985 [1960]: 714)—the notion that our *praxis* is embedded within and reproduces the structures that have produced us—almost directly parallels the definition provided by Bourdieu of the habitus: "structured structures that are predisposed to function as structuring structures" (Bourdieu 1977: 72). For both Sartre and Bourdieu, our actions are the result of a certain form of structuration, in which an individual perceives their possibilities for action as a result of a formed perception of themselves that their "situation," be it class position, loosely conceived (as for Bourdieu), or place in a set of practico-inert structures (for Sartre), provides for them. The analytic distinction between the two is clear, as Bourdieu himself points out. For Sartre, the primary issue is freedom; for Bourdieu, it is the structures that produce what we *take to be freedom*: "The habitus entertains with the social world which has produced it a real ontological complicity, the source of cognition without consciousness, intentionality without intention, and a practical mastery of the world's regularities which allows one to anticipate the future without even needing to posit it as such" (Bourdieu 1990a: 12). Even though the analytic distinction between Bourdieu's notion of the habitus and Sartre's ideas on action is clear here, Sartre's turn toward a situated form of *praxis* in *Critique of Dialectical Reason* brings the two authors' theories of action closer together. Bourdieu's idea of the habitus explicitly includes the idea that the dispositions that make up the habitus are generative—that is, that there is an aspect of freedom that appears in what many authors (e.g., MacLeod 1987) have argued is complete structuration:

> I wanted to insist on the *generative capacities* of dispositions, it being understood that these are acquired, socially constituted dispositions. . . . But I wanted to emphasize that this "creative", active, inventive capacity was not that of a transcendental subject in the idealist tradition, but that of an acting agent. . . . Constructing the notion of the habitus as a system of acquired dispositions functioning on the practical level as categories of perception and assessment or as classificatory principles as well as being the organizing principles of action meant constituting the social agent in his true role as the practical operator of the construction of objects. (Bourdieu 1990a: 13)

One can see, then, the affinities between the habitus as the formational site of individual action in a sociohistorical context and Sartre's theory of action. The agent is to a large extent socially constructed and has the capacity to be inventive, though this inventiveness is based on the social construction of the agent. As such, Bourdieu's concept of the habitus is not as structural as one might think; the intention behind the concept is to work the middle ground between structure and agency, between structuralism and individualism—just as Sartre's and Merleau-Ponty's work intended to do.

What the idea of the habitus conveys explicitly and in a more experiential way than do the more philosophical existentialisms of Sartre and Merleau-Ponty is the analysis of how we are complicit with the maintenance of systems of domination through our everyday, mundane actions and understandings of our being-in-the-world (instead of the simple philosophical judgment of our complicity). The habitus, in its process of formulating classifications of the world and *praxis* based on those classifications, legitimates certain forms of cultural and social practices while delegitimating others; this is the effect of the doxic nature of the habitus. As well, the acts generated by the habitus are dependent upon legitimation; the actor must discover whether or not their acts are acceptable. As such, the habitus is frequently complicit with the maintenance of a certain state of affairs: "The recognition of the legitimacy of the official language . . . is inscribed, in a practical state, in dispositions which are impalpably inculcated, through a long and slow process of acquisition . . ." (Bourdieu 1991: 50). While Sartre's discussion of circularity does touch on this matter of complicity with dominant social or practico-inert structures, it does not go as far as Bourdieu in attributing this complicity to the form of agency in modern society. Bourdieu acknowledges that people actively *but not intentionally* participate in the maintenance of structures of domination, a position that might also fall under Sartre's term "stupidity" (where people just do not know better than to act in a particular way; see Sartre 1993b: 18–19). But Bourdieu and Sartre are both speaking of the same phenomenon: structures that hierarchize and oppress people are quasi-automatically reproduced by those same people. And as Bourdieu and Sartre both point out, these classifications, both internalized and external, are escapable under the right circumstances, ones that require the development of an extra-habitual awareness of the world.[3] Bourdieu and Sartre thus realize that there is a complicity in acting in accordance with existing social structures and argue that, in spite of their analytic differences, the realm of the "practico-inert" or the automatically reproducing habitus can be escaped under the right conditions—conditions that produce us as *potentialities* for action, as freedom, and as *potential* human beings relating with one another as human beings.

There are many connections between the methodological concerns and the overriding conceptual frameworks of Bourdieu and Merleau-Ponty. Their primary connection appears in the predication of Bourdieu's work on the basis not of the Cartesian split of *en-soi* and *pour-soi*, but rather on the "third term" in between the two—on the "antepredicative unity of the world and our life" (Merleau-Ponty 1962: 61). By basing his work on Merleau-Ponty's notion of the body through which we act on and interact with the world, and arguing that this body is socially constructed, Bourdieu escapes the kind of philosophical solipsism that Sartre's early works, as we have seen, falls into. In fact, as Wacquant argues in his introduction to *An Invitation to Reflexive Sociology*, "I want to suggest that Bourdieu is [Merleau-Ponty's] sociological heir, if one who innovates in ways that are sometimes incompatible with both the spirit and the letter of the phenomenologist's work. In particular, Bourdieu goes beyond the subjectivist apprehension of practical sense to investigate the social genesis of its objective structures and conditions of operation" (Wacquant 1992: 20n35). As such, it would appear that Bourdieu is attempting to incorporate the concerns of the early works of Merleau-Ponty with Sartre's *Critique of Dialectical Reason*: Bourdieu succeeds in incorporating the idea of *l'intermonde* that Merleau-Ponty suggests counters and in fact makes possible the separation, at least in a philosophical sense, of *en-soi* and *pour-soi,* and Sartre's analysis of the processes by which one's *praxis* is converted into the practico-inert by the processes of the group.

Bourdieu has to turn to a study of the objective structures—and in fact, has to emphasize these structures—in order to overcome the perceived subjectivism of Merleau-Ponty's phenomenological perspective: as Wacquant puts it with regard to the example of the soccer game offered by Merleau-Ponty in *The Phenomenology of Perception*, "In short, Merleau-Ponty is silent on the twofold social genesis of the subjective and objective structures of the game" (ibid.: 22). At the same time, though, the habitus as formulated by Bourdieu is, of necessity, slippery: "*habitus is in cahoots with the fuzzy and the vague.* As a generative spontaneity which asserts itself in the improvised confrontation with endlessly renewed situations, it follows a *practical logic*, that of the fuzzy, of the more-or-less, which defines the ordinary relation to the world" (Bourdieu 1987: 96; emphasis in original). In sum, the combination of the objectivity that structures and governs the habitus and the fuzziness of the practical logic that manages the enactment and embodiment of the habitus is such that it becomes the site of the multiple relations described in chapter 3: between the individual and the social, the historical, and, as we will see in this chapter, the ethical:

> In the relation between habitus and field, history enters into a relation with itself: a genuine ontological complicity, as Heidegger and Merleau-Ponty suggested, obtains between the agent (who is neither a subject nor a consciousness, nor the mere executant of a role, the support of a structure or actualization of a function) and the social world (which is never a mere "thing," even if it must be constructed as such in the objectivist phase of research). This relation of practical knowledge is not that between a subject and an object constituted as such and perceived as a

problem. Habitus being the social embodied, it is "at home" in the field it inhabits, it perceives it immediately as endowed with meaning and interest. (Bourdieu and Wacquant 1992a: 128)

Put another way, the habitus is that social aspect of our being that inspires us to action, makes us feel "at home" or not with our social field, and provides us with a fit between ourselves and the world. Seen as such, the habitus would appear to be a conservative mechanism; but as we will see, the habitus can also inspire us to engage in social change once it discerns its ability for this change, what we call here "the overturning of the colonized habitus."

Bourdieu, *la distinction*, and the "Floating Hegemony"

The idea of the habitus as an embodied and yet apparently arbitrary sense of the world draws directly from Merleau-Ponty's conception of the body as the site at which the experiencing individual encounters the social and historical world. Merleau-Ponty's discussion of the body in *The Phenomenology of Perception* deals with the subjective experiences we have of the world through the objective body, and Bourdieu's discussion of the objective social and historical structures in which we exist provides us with the sociological complement to Merleau-Ponty's philosophical depiction of our physical experience. Put another way, both writers axiomatically begin with our presence in the world, and while Merleau-Ponty pursues the subjective experience of our presence, Bourdieu looks to the situation in which we exist as the causative mechanism of our experience, the spontaneity or creativity of our actions in the world, and the reproduction of the practico-inert structures of the social world through our actions.

Consider Merleau-Ponty's discussion of the body; for him, the body is not an organism separate from one's consciousness or from the world (or even separable from either), but rather coterminous with both the individual and the situation (Merleau-Ponty 1962: 105). As such, the body takes on the characteristics of both individual as existent and the situation as reciprocally causal and caused:

> The body is no more than an element in the system of subject and his world, and the task to be performed elicits the necessary movements from him by a sort of remote attraction, as the phenomenal forces at work in my visual field elicit from me, without any calculation on my part, the motor reactions which establish the most effective balance between them, or as the conventions of our social group, or our set of listeners,

immediately elicit from us the words, attitudes and tone which are fitting. (Merleau-Ponty 1962: 106)

This analysis of our reaction to the world establishes two things for us in the consideration of the existential qualities of the habitus. First, it conveys the apparent immediacy and automaticity of the way in which we react to the world; and second, it establishes the potential of our construction of "a certain world" through that reaction. Merleau-Ponty anticipates here the two fundamental qualities of Bourdieu's concept of the habitus—that through our embeddedness with the world as part of a mutually constructive and constructed situation, we react almost unthinkingly, and that our reaction is one that is appropriate to the situation, regardless of the situation. Merleau-Ponty's analysis of the immediate presence of the world to us through the body, then, allows us to begin to comprehend the ways in which the world serves to construct us. Not only does the world present us with a set of stimuli to which we must react and act upon, but it also structures the modes in which we act and react in particular ways—ways that are left unexamined by Merleau-Ponty.

Bourdieu picks up the analysis of our interaction with the examination of the construction of our actions and reactions by the social world. His concept of the habitus, as we have seen here, relies upon the idea that through our socialization processes, we learn how we are to be in the world—not just in a social manner, through the ways in which we interact with others and recognize our positioning in the social field, but also in a physical manner. The habitus, as the internalization and corporealization of social structures, relies at its base upon Bourdieu's notion of the bodily *hexis*. The physicality of our experience of the world provides us with both a habitual way of being in the world (in our posture, our gestures, the way in which we utilize language, and the like) and a physical sense of our place in the world. As Bourdieu puts it, the social realm provides us with "so many reminders of this [social] distance and of the conduct required in order to 'keep one's distance' or to manipulate it strategically . . . in short, 'knowing one's place' and staying there" (Bourdieu 1977: 82). The concept of habitus provides in a sociological sense what the philosophical examination Merleau-Ponty undertakes hopes to do—develop an understanding of "the relation of immediate fit between subjective and objective structures and the elision of its political significance, that is, depoliticization" (Bourdieu and Wacquant 1992b: 74).

The misrecognition, or *méconnaissance*, of the social order as arbitrary by individuals within it, instead of as a direct result of the powered structuring of society by the forces of production, is a result of the social structuring of the bodily *hexis*. Bourdieu notes that "the social sense is guided by the system of mutually reinforcing and infinitely redundant signs of which each body is the bearer" (Bourdieu 1984: 241), signs that provide material guides, manifested in language, cultural, and consumptive practices, that maintain and perpetuate the social structure. By helping to perpetuate the status quo of the social order, this physically manifested sociocultural sense of one's place in the social order, represents the manifestation of the hegemonic social order and therefore makes certain paths of action seem impossible or "out of the question." There is within this notion a sense of the limits of one's possible actions, while at the same time, as these limits are misrecognized as being arbitrary or natural, they are forgotten as limits and misperceived as natural:

> En esta estructuración de la vida cotidiana se arraiga la hegemonía: no tanto en un conjunto de ideas "alienadas" sobre la dependencia o la inferioridad de los sectores populares, como en una interiorización muda de la desigualdad social, bajo la forma de dispositivos inconscientes, inscriptas en el propio cuerpo, en la conciencia de lo posible y de lo inalcanzable. (Canclini 1984: 74)[4]

This consciousness of what is possible given one's social station and corresponding symbolic capital, however, is conflated with the capitalist ideology of what is loosely and inaccurately called "the American Dream"—the idea that one's social position can be improved by getting an education and becoming something more than one's ancestors were. By improving one's symbolic capital, something granted by the recognition of others of the "naturalness" of the possession of this capital (i.e., the misrecognition of the ability of the individual to amass this capital), a person has the ability to elevate their social position and gain the profits that come from this increase in cultural capital. As well, they also begin to take on the cultural, linguistic, and consumptive practices of the group that they are elevated into, and thereby transcend the limits that they originally experienced as a result of their structured habitus. This is the first step in the process that Bourdieu calls "distinction"—the attempt by subaltern classes and class fractions to improve their symbolic capital by entering into social institutions, invariably controlled by and serving the interests of the dominant classes and class fractions, which will enable them to be recognized as being of higher social status than they originally were.

The process of distinction makes more clearly manifest the limits and their subsequent forgetting that characterize the social order. Members of dominated class fractions begin to emulate the cultural, linguistic, and social practices of the class fraction directly above them (i.e., the lower middle class emulates the cultural practices of the bourgeoisie), and attempt through this emulation to increase their symbolic capital so as to appear as members of the emulated class fraction. This does not happen, Bourdieu argues, through the conscious desire of the dominated agent to become a member of the higher class fraction, as the structure of habitus always bears traces of one's "true" social position. Instead, the desire to amass symbolic capital leads individuals to take on the consumptive practices of the class fraction directly above them, as it is through these, as well as through linguistic and cultural practices that symbolic capital is accorded (i.e., playing cricket as opposed to football or speaking proper Oxford English as opposed to a Cockney dialect; Bourdieu 1984: 249; 1991: 54). Again, it is only through the recognition of symbolic capital by others who are authorized to grant this recognition that symbolic capital is actually accorded.

However, the profit that comes through the amassing of symbolic capital depends directly on the absolute number of people who engage in the cultural practices that are being contested. The members of those class fractions that are being contested, who have the ability to grant symbolic capital to members of the lower classes, will not want to be associated with that class fraction. This yields the actual process of "distinction"; that is, distinction only exists through the struggles for the exclusive appropriation of the distinctive signs which make " 'natural distinction' " (Bourdieu 1984: 217–229, 250; 1991: 237). Emulated class fractions, in order to retain their distinctiveness, will move on into "new experiences and virgin spaces, exclusively or firstly theirs" (Bourdieu 1984: 215). In other words, once the consumptive process and the struggles over their symbolic worth are taken into account, the process of distinction becomes one in which the class struggle manifests itself in terms of cultural practices that are variously marked in terms of their profitability within the social field, that is, the worth that they indicate to and is acclaimed by others, which is, then internalized by the individual participants in this class struggle.

At the same time, however, another process occurs within this process of distinction, one that precludes the possibility of assuming that everyone is always emulating the class fractions above them. While this is certainly true for those in marginal class fractions, dominated classes tend, on the other hand, to accept what they are given by the distribution of symbolic capital within the social order. Whereas dominant class fractions work to remain "progressive" in their cultural practices in order to protect their dominant position (Bourdieu 1984: 431,

450), "Dominated agents . . . tend to attribute to themselves what the distribution attributes to them, refusing what they are refused" (Bourdieu 1984: 471). This results in what could be called the "solidification" of lower classes; that is, their cultural practices tend to remain "traditional," leaving very little permeability by those wishing to leave them, as their relative position in the social field becomes increasingly distanced from those who are engaged in the chase for symbolic capital. Hence, the lower classes are left further and further out of the process of distinction, thereby leaving them increasingly powerless within the social field and out of what I would call a "floating hegemony."

While there is within the habitus a site of social practices and dispositions that is structured by a hegemonic order, thereby giving the individual a set of practices and attitudes about the world that structures and delimits possible paths of action, there is also a hegemonic drive that floats toward increased distinction from lower classes (Bourdieu 1984: 215), wherein members of dominated class fractions, eager to increase their symbolic capital, appropriate practices of the class fractions just above them, practices that members of emulated class fractions, eager to maintain their distinction from those who emulate them, discard as being "common": "At each level of the distribution, what is rare and constitutes an inaccessible luxury or an absurd fantasy for those at an earlier or lower level become banal and common, and is relegated to the order of the taken-for-granted by the appearance of new, rarer and more distinctive goods" (Bourdieu 1984: 247–249). This process is a concrete cultural manifestation of the class struggle that in this formulation occurs not at the level of the bourgeoisie/proletariat struggle, but rather at the margins of these classes, as well as the interstices that simplified Marxist formulations neglect. The goal in all of this for the classes involved at this level of the struggle is to secure the exclusive possession of cultural goods or practices at every moment, effecting a permanent revolution in tastes, one that leads to dominant class fractions feeling forced to further distance themselves from lower class fractions. As this floating hegemony spirals ever higher, following the higher class fractions' attempts to further distinguish themselves from lower class fractions attempting to appropriate their cultural practices, dominated classes, especially the lowest classes, fall further and further out of this picture. Bourdieu states that these classes are "at the mercy of the discourses that are presented to them":

> The dominant language discredits and destroys the spontaneous political discourse of the dominated. It leaves them only silence or a borrowed

language, whose logic departs from that of popular usage but without becoming that of erudite usage, a deranged language, in which the "fine words" are only there to mark the dignity of the expressive intention, and which, unable to express anything true, real or "flat," dispossesses the speaker of the very experience it is supposed to express. (Bourdieu 1984: 462)

There is, then, no place for the completely dominated classes within this floating hegemony; the spontaneous discourse, as well as cultural practices, that stems from their lived experience are eliminated or silenced by the dominant language, leaving them no way in which to share their experience with the rest of the social field. At the same time, the dominated classes internalize their position via the refusal of everything that they are refused as a class, and ultimately are left completely out of the class struggle, as it is constituted through contestation over the symbolic meanings of cultural goods. How is this duplicitous process possible?

It is possible in part because the generation and reproduction of the habitus depends on the *doxa* of the social order, leaving it to operate at a quasi-unconscious level. Any social field, Bourdieu argues, delimits three aspects of the social world: *doxa*, or the "realm of the undiscussed"; orthodoxy, a "necessarily imperfect substitute" for *doxa*; and heterodoxy, those aspects of cultural discourse and action that highlight the interstices of the dominant order and make possible forms of social change. *Doxa* is, for Bourdieu, that aspect of the social world that undergirds all other aspects of social and cultural discourse and action. Not to be mistaken for Marx's idea of the economy as the primary aspect of society (though certainly paralleling it), Bourdieu argues that *doxa* is what constructs the habitus and what makes us misrecognize the habitus and its socially reproductive facilities as natural:

> . . . when there is a quasi-perfect correspondence between the objective order and the subjective principles of organization (as in ancient societies) the natural and social world seems self-evident. This experience we shall call *doxa*. . . . Schemes of thought and perception can produce the objectivity that they do only by producing misrecognition of the limits of the cognition that they make possible, thereby founding immediate adherence, in the doxic mode, to the world of tradition experienced as a "natural world" and taken for granted. The instruments of knowledge of the social world are in this case (objectively) political instruments which contribute to the reproduction of the social world by producing immediate adherence to the world, seen as self-evident and undisputed, of which they are the product and of which they reproduce the structures in a transformed way. (Bourdieu 1977: 164)

Doxa is, by this account, the mode by which the status quo reproduces itself, continuing in our society even today, making our understanding of the world and our perceived ability to act in and on that world nearly as quasi-perfect as Bourdieu claims happens primarily in ancient societies. This, though, occurs through the second aspect of the structure of the social field: orthodoxy.

For Bourdieu, orthodoxy is a necessarily imperfect substitute for the power of *doxa*. Orthodoxy is that aspect of discourse that is, for the most part, off limits to controversy and challenge. It is the most traditional aspect of social discourse and practice, delimiting the boundary between the collectively accepted opinion and the individual, challengeable opinion. It marks the boundary between mechanical and organic forms of solidarity: mechanical solidarity, characterized by a strong form of the collective consciousness, is as Durkheim puts it a "solidarity of similarities," in which people are bound together by their adherence to the dominance of the collective consciousness; while organic solidarity, characterized by a weaker form of the collective consciousness and the possibility for solidarity through difference, marks the realm of "competing possibles," or heterodoxy.

Orthodoxy and heterodoxy, in both Bourdieu's and Durkheim's senses of the relationship, are inherently related to one another in a binaristic form. Orthodoxy marks off that realm of social discourse in which there is only one "possible," only one form of discourse or mode of action that is legitimate and accepted by the collective. But societies, ancient or modern, require a certain amount of creativity, appearing in the realm of the heterodox, where some degree of "heresy" is acceptable, so long as it within the bounds of *doxa* (Bourdieu 1977: 169). The relationship Bourdieu lays out between these three aspects of social discourse, then, is this: *doxa*, which circumscribes the entire universe of possible discourse in a social field, allows heterodoxy, its competition, to exist so long as it remains constrained by orthodoxy (ibid.: 170–171). *Doxa* authorizes orthodoxy to act in its stead, constraining the possible realm of competing discourses through orthodoxy's active censorship of heretical discourses and *doxa*'s passive censorship of both orthodoxy and heterodoxy.

Bourdieu's discussion of these forms in the *Outline* leaves them solidly in the discursive realm, save for one apparent sidebar comment (ibid.: 170). Following Marx's depiction of language in *The German Ideology* as practical consciousness, Bourdieu opens the possibility for us to translate these discursive forms into actional forms; in other words, we can make the transition from Bourdieu's sociology of knowledge to a sociology of resistance. Making the linkage to class-based societies, "class" here being tied to one's position in a social field rather than to one's position in the relations of production (Bourdieu 1977: 86), Bourdieu highlights the class warfare inherent in this situation:

> The dominated classes have an interest in pushing back the limits of *doxa* and exposing the arbitrariness of the taken for granted; the dominant classes have an interest in defending the integrity of *doxa* or, short of this, of establishing in its place the necessarily imperfect substitute of *orthodoxy*. . . . If one accepts the equation made by Marx in *The German Ideology*, that "language is real, practical consciousness," it can be seen that the boundary between the universe of (orthodox or heterodox) discourse and the universe of *doxa*, in the twofold sense of what goes without saying and what cannot be said for lack of an available discourse, represents the dividing-line between the most radical form of misrecognition and the awakening of political consciousness. (Bourdieu 1977: 169–170)

And since, for Bourdieu, discourse makes action possible (while *doxa* prevents the possibility of action), we can see that the habitus, dominated as it is by the imperatives of the social order, represents the way that order impels people to serve as practico-inert tools for its reproduction.

Getting beyond the quasi-automatic reproduction of the system, then, requires thinking outside of it. Bourdieu argues that any overturning of the habitus must take place outside the rules of the dominant game, since resisting symbolic domination on its own terms presupposes and in fact demonstrates complicity with the dominating system (Bourdieu 1991: 50–51). This complicity with the dominating system is exacerbated by two separate factors. First, the hegemonic game of contesting the symbolic worth of these practices takes place completely within another hegemonic order, that of the capitalist economic system, which in a Catch-22 way requires that players have capital, be it economic, educational, or cultural, in order to gain capital. Hence, players that might come from lower classes, which by definition do not have capital of any of these sorts, are automatically left out of the game. Second, and much more insidiously, these players from the dominated classes accept being left out of the game, and more particularly reject the game that they are in actuality rejected by. Any conception of the formation of a counterhegemonic order that might lead to liberatory change therefore must take place outside of these two parameters. Problematically, though, these parameters are those that constitute the habitus and govern our relations with the social world. Thus, any formation of a counterhegemonic order must necessarily start with the reconstruction of the habitus in a way that does not perpetuate the hegemonic game; in other words, "To change the world, one has to change the ways of making the world, that is the vision of the world and the practical operations by which groups are produced and reproduced" (Bourdieu 1990c: 137). We therefore need to figure out how this vision of the world is created and made dominant, necessitating a turn to Gramsci.

Gramsci, Hegemony, and the Need for a War of Position

For Antonio Gramsci, being caught up in the Italian Communist Party and its resistance against the national government brought a practical element to his theoretical work. It was impossible to distinguish theory from *praxis* for Gramsci, and this binding of the two inflected all of his thought. Hence, it was difficult to understand why the great mass of the Italian people, living in the conditions of poverty, alienation from the rest of Italy, and exploitation at the hands of the state and corporations, did not rise up against the Italian government. Gramsci surmised that the lack of social transformation as a result of resistance on the part of the Italian working class was due to the implicit consent they gave the ruling organizations as well as the internally contradictory complex of ruling ideas. In other words, the prevailing hegemonic ideology of the time hindered the Italian people from working out the contradictions in the ruling ideology that prevented them from rising up in resistance to the Italian state. Hegemony, then, becomes the way of identifying the condition in which prevailing modes of thought—"the ideas of the ruling class," to paraphrase Marx—conflict with the lived experiences of individuals within the subaltern class.

Gramsci's notion of hegemony, though, started out with a much different focus. Originally, Gramsci meant hegemony to mean the system of alliances the working class must create in order to overthrow the bourgeoisie and establish a proletarian state (Gramsci 1971: 443). Hegemony most clearly means at this point the need for the proletariat to band together with other sectors of society, such as the peasantry, in order to have the means to establish a more just society. Within this, though, are the roots of other aspects of the concept: the need of the proletariat to group together with other segments of the social order implies a concern for the practical, lived experiences of all those who are oppressed; and the need for these cross-class alliances seems to suggest something at the level of thought of these groups that can be linked in order to throw off the chains of the bourgeoisie. In later formulations of "hegemony," Gramsci goes on to elaborate on these two points. By insisting that the doing human cannot be separated from the thinking human, Gramsci notes the importance of the binding of thought and *praxis*. Across classes, we can extend this to argue that there is something fundamental at the level of thought that will help in the class struggle: as every individual carries on some form of intellectual activity, "he participates in a particular conception of the world, has a conscious line of moral conduct, and therefore contributes to sustain a conception of the world or to modify it," what Gramsci calls "common sense," and this common sense appears as "a response to certain specific problems posed by reality," most notably the problems posed by oppression by the bourgeoisie (Gramsci 1971: 9, 324).

The dependence of certain forms of consciousness on their specific temporal, political, and practical settings presented a further problem for Gramsci. If the actual situation of the subaltern classes was one in which they were oppressed, and they knew that they were being oppressed, then why was there not more widespread resistance to the bourgeoisie? Gramsci's argument was that the lack of active resistance on the part of subaltern classes was due to the hegemony of ideas on the part of the ruling classes. In other words, Marx's statement that "the ideas of the ruling class are in every epoch the ruling ideas" (Marx 1978: 172) becomes for Gramsci the foundation for a revised notion of hegemony. Now, the hegemony of the ideas of the ruling classes takes hold in the consciousness of the subalterns, conflicts with their primordial understanding of their conditions of existence, and ultimately prevents subalterns from conceptualizing a social order outside their current one. It is this sense, then, that hegemony exists at the level of consciousness; however, it is always bound up with the practical actions of everyday life in a dialectical and contradictory fashion.

Gramsci thereby argues that members of the subaltern classes follow a conception of the world that is imparted to them by others, and that the contradictions between this conception of the world and the way in which they act in the world on a daily basis provides the mental obstacle that prevents the activities of the subaltern classes from becoming revolutionary, thereby serving to reinforce the power of the state. Gramsci offers two examples of this: the imposition of a unified Italian language upon the country after the Risorgimento, making all spoken dialects socially inferior while forcing members of the subaltern classes to speak a language within which they cannot formulate clear consciousness of their experiences; and the subaltern classes' preference for foreign novels instead of those produced by Italian intellectuals, showing that the national intellectuals' portrayals of experience and feeling do not match popular conceptions of them (Gramsci 1985: 207–208). In sum, the culture of the Italian intellectuals falls away from having anything to do with that of the people's experience, and fails to be the organizing force that Gramsci argues is needed for liberation to occur, leaving the Italian people to "undergo" the hegemony of either the "national" culture or the culture of foreign writers, both of them equally foreign to the conditions of existence of the subaltern classes.

This hegemony of the ideas of the ruling class, then, comes into conflict with the set of ideas that are organic to the lived experiences, practices, and actions of the subaltern classes, which Gramsci argues manifest themselves in the forms of local linguistic dialects, folklore, and other forms of "common sense," the "incoherent set of generally held assumptions and beliefs common to any given society" (Gramsci 1971: 323). These conceptions of the world, which are bound up with the social practices of the subaltern classes, provide a "morality of the people," guidelines for living one's life that are indigenous to that particular set of conditions of existence (Gramsci 1985: 189–190). These ideas are both self-contradictory and contradict those of the ruling hegemony. They are self-contradictory in that they are the accumulated conceptions of all previous experience (as folklore indicates), and are generally not theoretically and critically articulated; and they contradict the hegemonic set of ideas that are imposed by the ruling class. In order to resist this overpowering of the ideas of lived experience by foreign ideas, Gramsci argues that political parties composed of intellectuals organic to (i.e., coming from) the oppressed classes need to begin to critically articulate the ways in which common sense reflects the lived experiences of the oppressed classes, and therefore aid members of the subaltern classes in gaining a "critical understanding of self through a struggle of opposing 'hegemonies'" (Gramsci 1971: 330 f., 333–335). It is through this theoretical articulation of the contradictions between the common sense consciousness that is bound to the lived experiences of the subaltern classes and the overpowering hegemonic ideas foreign to the popular groups that a counterhegemonic social force can be formed.

Hegemony, then, operates in a thoughtful manner—it works to colonize the thought processes of the members of a social order, despite its distance from the lived experiences of those people. It thereby provides a vision of the world, one that requires action to be produced, reproduced, and transmitted. By combining Gramsci and Bourdieu, or rather hegemony and the habitus, we can begin to understand how it is that a set of ideas foreign to the experience of individuals can take such a great hold on their lives.

The Level-of-Analysis Problem: Just Where are We Dominated?

In order to pull this discussion back to the issues of ethics and resistance, we need to see how it is that the concepts of hegemony and the habitus fit together and create perspectives that compel individuals in socially reproductive ways.

Within both Gramsci and Bourdieu's formulations, there is some interplay between the level of consciousness or thought and the level of action or practice. In Gramsci's view, the contradictory consciousness imposed from somewhere else prevents revolutionary action, as what could be considered revolutionary "opportunities" may be passed up due to a lack of awareness of them as "revolutionary opportunities." For Bourdieu, though, hegemony simultaneously affects and effects consciousness and action, and appears to lock one into a particular pattern of beliefs, cultural values, and practices due to one's place in the social field. The set of structured and structuring principles that is the habitus constricts consciousness to consciousness of one's relative position in the social field, and restricts actions to those available to one granted a certain amount of symbolic capital.

I want to argue, with both Gramsci and Bourdieu, that hegemony operates at the level of human agency. Put another way, the hegemony of the social order—or, to return to the Sartrean terminology, the practico-inert structures of the social order reproduced through our everyday actions—operates to construct our entire way of conceiving ourselves on every level of our social lives: our psychological and ontological sense of self; our sense of how we relate to others in our social field, including our conception of the size of that social field; and even our physical sense of being-in-the-world. In the same way that Sartre and Merleau-Ponty argue that our freedom is developed through our interaction with the world, Bourdieu argues that our sense of personhood and agency, wrapped up in the habitus, is developed through our structuration by the objective and subjective structures of the social and historical context. As such, the hegemonic social order constructs our complete sense of self, and in social and historical situations characterized by relations of domination and oppression, it serves to construct a false consciousness of the world and our place in it, giving us a false sense of our agency and freedom. This suggests to us on a daily basis that the proper course of action in our daily lives is not to struggle against the dominant social order in the name of concrete freedom, but rather to continue, in an everyday and mundane fashion, to reproduce the practico-inert structures of society, the very structures that dominate us.

Within this formulation of the habitus as the site of hegemony, we can see that hegemony simultaneously affects and effects both consciousness and action, and that there is a dialectical relationship between the two. As I have described earlier, the educative process by which the habitus is formed is one in which the bodily *hexis* delimits both one's conception of one's place in the social field as well as marks one's actions with the trace signs of one's station, such as accent, body carriage, and the like, which reinforces self-conception. As Bourdieu notes, the anticipated conditions of reception of one's speech, for example, are part of the conditions of production (Bourdieu 1991: 76); and the anticipated conditions of reception also structure one's consciousness of their competence to perform within the social field. Thus, there is a hegemonic imposition at the level of consciousness, most notably in one's consciousness of their position within the social order. At the same time, though, there is also a site of hegemony at the level of action. A person's consciousness of their place within the social order delimits, much in the way that Gramsci notes, possible avenues of action (Gramsci 1971: 268, 326–327). The logic of capital, be it economic, social, cultural, or political capital, governs the possibility for action, in cooperation with and complementary to the bodily *hexis*. At the same time, the desire to amass "profits of distinction" highlights routes of practice that dominated class fractions need to engage in to increase their position, and that dominant class fractions must undertake in order to preserve theirs vis-à-vis their challengers (Bourdieu 1991: 63). Both of these functions of hegemony converge at the site of the habitus, giving one a basis for the improvisation of actions within the limits of what they perceive through their habitus as proper ways of acting. And as we saw in chapter 3, these "*propre* ways" of acting hinder us because they are never fully our own.

The Habitus and Inertial Ethics

It is in the coalescence of the hegemonic order in the habitus that causes us the primary difficulties in working against the system. Because our sense of who we are and "our proper place" are so heavily (though not over-)determined by the hegemonic order, we can rarely begin to envision "something else" or how to get there. We can, as various social movements have done, see what is wrong with the social order and agitate against it. But imagining what a new social order would be like or the concrete steps we can take to develop that social order here and now is made much more difficult for a couple of reasons.

First, the habitus, the "structured structures predisposed to function as structuring structures," locks us into approaching the world around us through these structured structures, through already-existent meaning systems that provide us with a set of lenses with which to see the world. Because we see the world and the possibilities for our action within it through socially constructed lenses, we end up seeing the world and these possibilities for action in ways that are pre-constructed for us, based upon our place in the social order. The habitus thereby takes on an inertial and ethically normative quality; it becomes the translation of the practico-inert social structures into our consciousness of how the world does and should operate. Because the concept of the habitus includes the "structuring structures," those apparatuses enabling us to develop plans of action and see the resources required for carrying out those plans make it a social good to follow these plans of action. And because the habitus operates in a preconscious manner, we essentially do what we are supposed to do; we carry out the imperatives of the society almost automatically. In other words, the social construction of the individual and collective habitus ensures that for the most part, we act "ethically" in the terms of the social order.

For the reasons we saw in chapter 3, then, the habitus as defined by the social order is unethical in the existentialist sense; that is, it prevents us from the free determination of individual and collective projects and compels us to reproduce the existing social order. We are allocated varying degrees of individual agency and the resources for carrying out the plans we develop as a result of that agency, depending on the society in which we exist and our place in that social structure (Sewell 1992: 19). But the fact of the matter, as Sewell rightly points out, is that the habitus, both as a sociological concept and as a way of understanding what we do and how we do it, is geared primarily toward the reproduction of a social order, carrying with it the inertial form of ethics discussed in Sartre's *Rome Lectures*. By ensuring that our actions are more "repetitive" than "evolutionary" (Sartre 1964b: 444), the habitus prevents us from fully realizing our potential.

What would be needed, then, appears to be a dose of "ethical radicalism," to use Sartre's term. The conception of freedom that motivates his discussion of ethical radicalism—"the small movement which makes of a totally conditioned social being someone who does not render back completely what his conditioning has given him" (Stone and Bowman 1991: 77)—implies that individuals automatically, by virtue of their existential freedom, have the capacity for acting in a sovereign and innovative way. The problem, though, has to do with the groups in which we find ourselves; while Sartre clearly recognizes that the imperatives of the group often outweigh the volition of the individual and their capacity for realizing an innovative project, the notion of the habitus seems to suggest that in its usual form, we are prevented from even recognizing the factors that go into preventing us from acting in an ethically radical way. The variety of group memberships; the practical exigencies of our practico-inert daily lives; and the relationship between schemas and resources that is embedded in the habitus—all these things go into preventing us from seeing ourselves as radically ethical actors, let alone as the kind of free beings that an existential social ethics would wish to see in existence.

Ethical radicalism, then, as a counterhegemonic strategy would require a rethinking of the habitus and the norms contained therein. Sartre's comment that the *"[le] but révolutionnaire réel de liquider les limites du Terrorisme"* ("[the] real revolutionary goal of liquidating the limits of Terrorism"; Sartre 1964a: 161) should not go unnoticed here. How would those who are created in the image of Terror eliminate that Terror in themselves? By rethinking their particular habitus in order to create themselves as free beings with others. This comes about, I would argue, as a result of negating the impact of the dominant order on how we think about the world:

> Celui qui—local ou infrastructurel—vient aux hommes du système en partant de structures et celui qui—indéfini dans le temps—indique à chaque homme du système l'humanité comme une *humanité à faire*; non pas dans la construction d'un système (fût-il le *système socialiste*), mais dans la destruction de chaque système. (Sartre, in Contat and Rybalka 1970: 744–745)[5]

This negation of the dominant order is part and parcel of the idea of ethical radicalism; one must, in order to be "radically ethical," figure out a way of acting in a particular situation—and as part of a life project—that is not immediately dependent on or repetitive of the dominant ethical or habitual order. The goal of this kind of action would be to eliminate the repetitive elements of the practico-inert social order for the sake of creating a set of conditions of increasing humanity or increasing concrete freedom. The problem, though, is that one has to radically rethink the ways in which the practico-inert social order has constructed and continues to construct us as inert beings.

Developing Resistant Counterhegemonies

So, then, how do we begin the process by which the habitus, once colonized, can be overturned and rebuilt? That is, how can the habitus be restructured so that it can more adequately effect liberatory change? There are within Bourdieu's definition of the habitus two places at which a Gramscian "war of position" could be waged so as to reformulate the habitus in a revolutionary fashion: the structuring principles of thought and consciousness, and the structured principles of action. First, these structuring principles of consciousness that provide structured principles of action can be engaged in a critical sense, not unlike the way in which Gramsci recommends elevating proletarian "good sense" to a critical philosophy of *praxis*. Gramsci argues that the subalterns' nascent conception of the conditions of existence can be transformed into a revolutionary philosophy of *praxis* through the "organized critical reflection on existing forms of thought and their relation to the actual world that produced them" (Hoare and Smith 1971: 321). By engaging in this sort of reflection on the habitus, I argue that a critical capacity can be brought to the habitus. That is, the individual can come to understand how their experiences within their conditions of existence come to form the ways in which they experience and act within the world, and that these conceptions, which form the individual habitus, are, by a relation of homology, the same conceptions that form a class habitus.

> So it is because they are the product of dispositions which, being the internalization of the same objective structures, are objectively concerted that the practices of the members of the same group or, in a differentiated society, the same class are endowed with an objective meaning that is at once unitary and systematic, transcending subjective intentions and conscious projects whether individual or collective. (Bourdieu 1977: 81)

Radicalizing these tacit conceptions and dispositions by exposing their class-based nature through a war of position with the hegemonic set of ideas and beliefs that provide the bases for these structuring principles of consciousness would begin to show the true nature of the objective structure of the capitalist system, which locks individuals into structural places while convincing them that they can advance out of these stations. At the same time, though, the structured principles of action need to be engaged critically as well. While this would happen partly as a result of the critical exploration of the principles of consciousness that the habitus provides, the principles of action, most notably with regard to the types of actions appropriate to members of certain classes, need to be exposed on their own. Tactically, one could do this by beginning to break class taboos on cultural practices (I leave out consumptive practices here, primarily because of the difficulties that the need for economic capital to engage in them provides here), thereby exposing the structured dimension of cultural practices within a capitalist system. The risk is run, though, of seeming to be "ironic" in the postmodern sense here, that is, that one is merely appropriating, in a pastiche manner (Jameson 1991: 17), the practices of another group for one's own ironic purposes.

Problematically, though, engaging in a war of position gives consent to the rules of the hegemonic game. That is, for one to engage with a hegemonic system on its own terms means to give the system at least tacit consent and legitimacy:

> It is one of the generic properties of [social] fields that the struggle for specific stakes masks the objective collusion concerning the underlying principles of the game. More precisely, the struggle tends constantly to produce and reproduce the game and its stakes by reproducing primarily in those who are directly involved, but not in them alone, the practical commitment to the game and its stakes which defines the recognition of legitimacy. (Bourdieu 1991: 58)

While the war of position is not the same as the emulative struggle over cultural practices in the attempt to amass increased profits of distinction, it is nevertheless a struggle with the hegemonic system in order to expose that system. Here, then, one is forced to face one of the major problems posed for any type of critical theory of resistance or liberation—the problem of immanent critique. That is, with regards to radicalizing the habitus by way of a war of position, we face the problem of continuing to play the rules of the hegemonic game, even if our intention is to overthrow them.

As Scott (1987) has shown, though, actual social movements or "resistance movements" are often not oriented toward radical social change at all, but rather are attempts to call the hegemonic class to follow their own rules. The contributors to *Between Resistance and Revolution* (1997) also show the "level of analysis" problem that current resistance movements face. As the editors to the volume point out, there is a great deal of terrain between small-scale individual acts of resistance (along the lines of Scott's depictions in *Weapons of the Weak* and

Domination and the Arts of Resistance) and outright revolution, a terrain they characterize as "the cultural politics of social protest," a phenomenon they see as ripe for academic study, but which often does not result in direct forms of social change (Fox and Starn 1997: 5–6). The Zapatista referendum of 1999, for example, would fall into this category: it was a direct act of resistance on the part of the EZLN against the Mexican government in terms of forcing the government's hand in approving the peace plan it had helped design; yet, its only direct impact was to get the Mexican citizens to voice their support for the peace plan, which has not resulted in any form of structural social change for the indigenous peoples of Chiapas. (We will devote more space to the EZLN in chapter 6.) So, even social movements that have the benefit of years of the theorization of resistance face the problem we have identified here—that (a) students of resistance movements often have no way to evaluate the efficacy of these movements, and (b) those involved in the movements often have no idea of the degree to which they want to change the prevailing social order and so often attempt to realize goals that fall far short of overwhelming social change. This, in sum, works to dissolve the revolutionary potential of a unified social movement and often leaves them fighting a battle entirely on the dominant social order's terms.

So how can we conceive of, see, and actualize social change through practices of resistance? One way is to begin at the level of the habitus, as this is where the hegemonic social order inscribes itself and the only site at which a counterhegemonic social force can be produced. As we have seen earlier, the habitus is the bearer of the markers of the hegemonic order *as well as* the particularities of an individual's social position and the wholly owned delimitation of the possibilities for social action and perspective. By understanding the practices that are endemic to particular structural positions within society, particularly those in which members of subaltern social groups are engaged, Bourdieu argues that we can understand the habitus of that class fraction. I would extend this in arguing that by understanding the subaltern and colonized habitus, we can understand the hegemonic order as well as the subaltern order that, as Sardar (1998) argues, contains within it the means of resisting hegemony. That is, the means for producing a resistant counterhegemony that overturns the dominated or colonized habitus can create the possibility for developing a concrete situation of freedom. As Sardar points out, in order for "postmodernism's" interpolation and erasure of non-Western cultures to be stopped, these cultures must hold to their authenticity, based as it is on tradition, and begin to construct "cultures of resistance" (Sardar 1998: 273). So how can we do this?

There are, I would argue, three steps through which a resistant counterhegemony can be realized: the assertion of the dominated identity; the assertion of the equal status of the dominated group; and the transcendence of the hierarchy of the situation through the construction of a new way of being. To some extent, the first two steps of this process parallel those identified as being necessary for the development of class consciousness. As Marx and theorists drawing from his legacy assert, it is necessary for proletarians to understand their position as proletarian, and therefore as members of an oppressed class, before the action required to overturn the capitalist systems of domination can occur. This necessary process functions in parallel ways, regardless of the form of domination that characterizes a particular social situation.

The second step in the overturning of what I would call the "colonized habitus" is the assertion of the equal status of the dominated group. The social group that is oppressed by the social system must be in a position to say to the superordinate group, "We are your equal; you will gain from our domination no more." This requires two separate aspects: the act of claiming the power to engage in this assertion, and the ability to realize when one has achieved "equality," whatever that might mean in that particular situation. Remember that for Bourdieu, the habitus is not simply a sociological construct; it is a way of speaking about the deep structures that motivate certain forms of social practice, practices that are embedded in a particular social field and are absorbed by individuals based on their class, race or ethnicity, gender, and other characteristics. It is this situatedness that determines one's habitus, and it is this situatedness that provides the basis for the overturning of the colonized habitus. But habituses are gained from, put into practice by, and overturned through action. We are socialized through our interactions with the social apparatuses that act on us to make us "good members" of society; we reenact our habitus with every action that we engage in; and so it is only through action that the habitus can be overturned. Actions oriented toward overturning the colonized habitus would be those that (a) assert one's equality to a superordinate group through that action, and (b) help construct a new form of social field in which the actions of resistance that lead to the assertion of equality are converted into a new socializing field in which a new kind of habitus— a new way of being with others and for others—can be created.

As I have suggested earlier, this overturning of the colonized habitus is a process that happens through resistance. Bourdieu's depiction of the habitus, when taken in the context of Gramsci's discussions of hegemony and the existentialisms of Merleau-Ponty and Sartre, suggest that the habitus is the way in which the status quo is preserved and that it provides individuals with the means to resist this status quo and begin to establish a new, more just form of society. Granting that our society is one characterized by a variety of forms of oppression, all of which seem to fall within the doxic realm of the social order, we can see that it is our habitus that helps to maintain these various oppressions. Social institutions and practices must maintain themselves, and they can only be maintained insofar as *we* maintain them through our actions and projects and through seeing these actions and projects as meeting existing ethical imperatives: "Le pratico-inerte (impératif) exige le maintien des structures; contradiction mais *non morale*: de fait on peut réorganiser sans cesse en maintenant les mêmes hommes en place" (Sartre 1964a: 153).[6] The inertia of this institutional and social maintenance requires, by the very nature of social structures, our active participation in their maintenance, meaning that the analysis of the habitus as a site whereby our way of being in the world is colonized by the social realm is an important part of the formulation of a project of resistance as well as the creation of an ethical project.

This process of the overturning of the colonized habitus, then, requires the reclamation of our real agency. The institutions of the social and historical situation we inhabit provide to us clear conceptions of the ways in which we are permitted to act, even in spite of the fact that we do not see these possible paths of action as dictated by the social system. These paths of action, in spite of our best intentions, serve to reinforce structures of domination, thereby implicating us in the oppressive social practices these structures perpetuate. For both ourselves and for the development of a situation of concrete freedom, then, it becomes imperative to determine new ways of being in the world and being with others, ways that will bring about a situation of concrete freedom through the reclamation of the inherent agency and self-determining abilities of those with us in our particular social situations. This reclamation of agency becomes an ethical act—an ethics of freedom, one that will become clearer through an examination of the practices of resistance in the Algerian Revolution and the Zapatista movement.

CHAPTER 5

DIRTY HANDS AND MAKING THE
HUMAN: FANON, THE ALGERIAN
REVOLUTION AND AN ETHICS
OF FREEDOM

The fort of the Casauba [sic], all the other forts belonging to Algiers, and the port of that city will be delivered to the French troops at 10:00 this morning French time.

The General in Chief of the French Army pledges to His Highness the Dey to allow him the freedom and possession of all his personal property.

The Dey will be at liberty to retire with his family and his personal property to whatever place he determines; and as long as he remains in Algiers he and his family shall remain under the protection of the General in Chief of the French Army. A guard will guarantee his security and that of his family. The General in Chief guarantees to all the soldiers of the militia the same advantage and the same protection.

The exercise of the Muslim religion shall be free. The liberty of the inhabitants of all classes, their religion, their property, their business and their industry shall remain inviolable. Their women shall be respected. The General in Chief makes this engagement on his honor.

—Conditions for the surrender of Algiers, October 1, 1830[1]

We have sent to their deaths on simple suspicion and without trial people whose guilt was always doubtful and then despoiled their heirs. We massacred people carrying [our] safe conducts, slaughtered on suspicion entire populations subsequently found to be innocent; we have put on trial men considered saints by the country, men revered because they had enough courage to expose themselves to our fury so that they could intervene on behalf of their unfortunate compatriots; judges were found to condemn them and civilized men to execute them. We have thrown into prison chiefs of tribes for offering hospitality to our deserters; we have rewarded treason in the name of negotiation, and termed diplomatic action odious acts of entrapment. . . . In a word, we have outdone in barbarity the barbarians we have come to civilize and complain about our lack of success with them.

—Report of The King's Commission on Algeria, July 7, 1833[2]

Such was the beginning of the French domination of Algeria. What began ostensibly as the honorable surrender of a sovereign ruler and nation quickly resulted in the domination and desecration of an entire population. One hundred twenty years later, this domination was ended through the Algerian Revolution, the longest and possibly most costly of the postwar anticolonial insurrections. The Algerian Revolution provided current social theory with one of its most interesting and informative interlocutors, Frantz Fanon, whose work regarding the real and ontological aspects of anticolonial revolutions has provided insights for much of postmodern, postcolonial, and critical race theory. What has often been ignored, however, are the ethical insights and lessons that Fanon's depiction of the Algerian Revolution provides us. In his work, Fanon not only delivers to us what I would call an ethnographic depiction of the processes by which the Algerian peoples liberated themselves, but also serves as prognosticator for the ultimate success of the revolution in achieving one of its purported primary goals—the creation of a new form of human being. These aspects of Fanon's work—the descriptive and prescriptive—are frequently ignored in favor of depictions of the lingering effects of the colonial mind-set, the impact of these effects on "halfies" (people who live on the border of societal definitions of Member and Other), and the verification of Hegelian and Marxian insights into the dialectics of social relations and political revolutions (cf. Bhabha 1994). This is not to say that these pursuits are not theoretically interesting or socially informative; rather, it is to say that there are other issues raised by Fanon's work of equal importance. Fanon's work carries within it an implicit conception of a social ethics; that is, his work is always concerned with portraying the revolution as transcending the armature of colonial society—as a transforming force upon the human beings within these frameworks in order that the colonial structures themselves be eliminated. In order to do this, though, the foundations for a unity among the colonized must be created, and he argues consistently that this unity should be founded not in terms of some limited cause to which all must sacrifice, but rather upon the project of human dignity, which I see as an ethics of human freedom that can only be manifested through the act of resistance. Unfortunately, the practical implementation of Fanon's ideas—the Algerian Revolution—highlights the dangers inherent in the paradox of a resisting ethics; it is our task to learn these lessons and avoid these dangers.

Here I will utilize a discussion of the Algerian Revolution and Fanon's analyses of colonialism, anti-colonial resistance, and the tensions inherent to that resistance to further develop the theoretical relationship between resistance and ethics I have discussed and to highlight models of social relationships that I believe can inform our own attempts at creating changes in our social world oriented toward the actual, rather than rhetorical, liberation of all peoples. In order to do this, I will first analyze the forms and nature of colonial violence and the construction of what I call the "colonized habitus," arguing that the nature of this violence created the conditions in which the only form of resistance that could be effective against *les colons* was a violent resistance, a radical form of the reclamation of individual agency taken on by those compelled to become and prevented from becoming just like the colonizer. Then, bringing Fanon and some of his critics into the analysis, I will describe elements of the Algerian Revolution itself—the actions taken by the FLN (*Front de Libération Nationale*) against *métropole* France, the French *colons* and Algerians who stood in the way of the FLN's goals; the changes in the habitus of *les colonisés* that made it possible for the Algerian peoples to resist the French; and the success in creating a "new form" of humanity that was seen, by Fanon and others, as the ultimate goal of the Revolution. Working through the tensions inherent in the way the FLN conducted its revolutionary activities, I will then detail the ethics of freedom the FLN stated it wanted to bring about, as well as the ethical implications of the *praxis* the FLN used to achieve its goals. The ethics of freedom present in the Algerian Revolution contains an existential social ethics in its observation of the intimate bond between the individual and the social in every one of our actions; and it provides a clear description of the ways in which the "colonized habitus" (as I have called it), one that forces us into a complicit reproduction of the dominant and dominating social order through our ability to act according to a vision of any other possible path of action, can be decolonized through the reclamation of human agency. And while the elimination of French colonial rule in Algeria was a step forward in the development of Algerian society, sadly, as we will see, the implementation of this ethics of freedom in Algeria was thwarted from the very beginning thanks to the ways in which the FLN fought the Revolution, highlighting the crucial need for the embedding of revolutionary ends in the means used to attain social change.

The Nature of Colonial Violence

Cultural imposition is easily accomplished in Martinique. The ethical transit encounters no obstacle. But the real white man is waiting for me. As soon as possible he will tell me that it is not enough to try to be white, but that a white totality must be achieved. It is only then that I shall recognize the betrayal.

—Fanon, *Black Skin, White Masks*, 1967 (193)

Within Fanon's work, there are many ways to read the violence of the French occupation of Algeria. While Fanon does not often focus on the physical violence inherent in the colonial system, he is particularly interested in the violence to the cultures and the psyches of the Algerian peoples. What I want to argue in this section is that, in the colonial situation in general, and in the Algerian situation in particular, colonial violence takes the form of violence against the humanity of the colonized. This violence works on two levels, and does so insidiously: while the physical violence, which I will not discuss here at length, works against the bodies of the colonized, the violence against the culture, psyche, and human potential of the colonized has their total dehumanization as its goal. An examination of the ways in which the particular form of violence in the colonial regime is necessary in order to understand the ways in which the FLN and Algerians in general responded to this violence; in other words, the presupposition here is that the basis for Algerian resistance to French colonialism lies in the nature of the colonial system itself. For much of this discussion, the ontological elements of the colonial system—those bits that would fit into the *intermonde* described by Merleau-Ponty—are foregrounded for the sake of highlighting the ways in which the practico-inert nature of colonialism is motivated by and motivates the meaning system by which the colonizer and the colonized live their lives. However, it should be noted that in foregrounding ontology as a "causal" element in this analysis, as Fanon seems to do, I do not see ontology as necessarily separable from the economic, political, and military elements of colonialism. Rather, I focus on the ontological because it is within that realm of the colonial system that the ethical implications of resistance and revolution draw forth.

Two additional notes should be made here prior to the analytic work of this chapter. First, I use certain terminology—especially terms such as "settler" and "native"—throughout this chapter, not to universalize the ways in which colonial regimes tended to construct the societal dichotomy, but rather because they are the terms that Fanon, the primary theoretical figure at work in this chapter, utilized in his analysis. The use of the term "native" here is an unfortunate requirement of utilizing English translations of Fanon's work, and current scholarship would certainly not utilize the term in this way. Fanon's use of it—as well as mine—is predicated on playing out the colonial affiliation of the term, developed as a way of categorizing a group of people so that the person or people no longer needed to be attended to or understood in any deeper way. In its use of this method to reduce people to a simple essentialism, the colonial regime can more easily dismiss and avoid empathizing with anything or anyone associated with this essentialism. Those who maintain its usage through scholarship or public discourse maintain this same social distance from those labeled as "native"—and this is certainly not my intention here. Other ways of referring to those people, such as "indigenous persons," are similarly problematic, as the French term *indigène* carries the same baggage that "native" does. My use of the term here should always be taken as in quotations, especially considering the efforts herein to examine the process by which the construction of the "native" is maintained, resisted, and eventually overthrown.

Second, it should be noted that through much of the analysis of the colonial situation, the passive voice is used. This, as some have noted (Anthony 2004), would appear to eliminate the human agency involved in the production and reproduction of the colonial social structure; or, to put this another way, it would tend to foreground and universalize the colonizer's gaze. However, I do not mean the use of the passive voice in this analysis to become implicated in this universalization; rather, it is meant to capture the *processual* aspect of the reproduction of the colonial order. Both colonizer and colonized are produced by and reproduce that social structure, so that while its origin is intentional and agentic on the part of the colonizer, it also continues on through *both* the actions of the colonizer and the colonized. It is that sense of the structural and processual aspect of the maintenance of the colonial regime that I am attempting to maintain through the use of the passive voice. At the same time, I am also working to preserve and present a sense that, following Sartre, Merleau-Ponty, Bourdieu, and Fanon, both colonizer and colonized are trapped within and enslaved by this social order, thereby negating their free human potential.

Violence Against Culture
To begin with, Fanon's thought takes as its fundamental starting point the notion that the French colonization of Algeria reflects the general pattern of the colonial situation in general; that is, the colonial situation is, at the final tally, marked by an attempt on the part of Europeans to elevate "lesser" human beings to the European conception of humanity. It is not, at least in the beginning, marked by racism. Instead, the beginning of the colonial situation is seen as the expansion and protection of European social and political interests. In the beginning, the colonial

situation is only secondarily concerned with the creation of "human beings" in a place where the European conception of humanity is only found in people with white skin; its immediate concern is the exploitation of less-developed societies for labor and resources. As Fanon points out, "Si les expéditions coloniales obéissent à un schéma donné et connu—nécessité de faire régner l'ordre chez les barbares, protection des concessions et intérêts des pays européens, apport généreux de la civilisation occidentale—, on n'a pas suffisamment montré la stéréotypie des moyens utilisés par les métropoles pour s'accrocher à leurs colonies" (Fanon 1964a: 65).[3]

While both military and political domination of the colonized are necessary conditions for the maintenance of colonial domination, this cannot be the only mechanism for the maintenance of the system. The military and political oppression imposed on the "natives" (in Fanon's terms) requires a cultural aspect, namely racism, for the colonial system's maintenance; and in fact, military and political domination precede, make possible, and legitimate racism (ibid.: 45). As Fanon notes, "The fact is that the colonization, having been built on military conquest and the police system, sought a justification for its existence and the legitimization of its persistence in its works" (Fanon 1965: 123). This cultural aspect, according to Fanon, is "racism," the characterization of an outside cultural group based on its skin color. Rather than being the primary motivation for colonialism, racism functions in the colonial situation loosely defined (cf. Omi and Winant 1994) as simultaneously the legitimation of an established situation, the means by which the hierarchies established receive their continued justification, and the tool used to instill the hegemonic order in the minds of the colonized. Most often in historical colonial situations, it is the racism of the more powerful group that legitimates the colonial relationship. In Marxist terms, then, racism could be seen as "superstructural," part of the way in which dominant groups establish, justify, and maintain their dominance, while at the same time serving, through the practico-inert structures of dominance, as a structural aspect of domination (Sartre 1985 [1960]: 714–75; cf. Bell 1992: x).

This racism in itself, for Fanon, is not indicative of the characteristics of the group being racialized; rather, the colonizers (à la Sartre) impose a set of characteristics upon the colonized based on the conception of the latter as "barbarians." The imposition of these racial characteristics, most notably laziness, "pidgin speak," and a "maniacal fervor" for their traditional ways (all ways of evaluating the "natives" in Western terms) places the colonized within a standardized set of relations that make it easy for the colonizers to control these "natives," by dichotomizing the society "in a marked way" (Fanon 1965: 126). This racism, in Fanon's account, is not the enactment of any preconceived notions of another cultural group by that group; it is rather the imposition of a specific, foreign, and imperial form of existence upon the colonized groups. Put bluntly, colonization, instead of being an attempt on the part of Western civilizations to "bring humanity" to the natives, is actually predicated upon racism, and the reality of colonization *seeks to duplicate and perpetuate the conditions which it purportedly desires to thwart*. We can see that the inertia of domination serves to subvert any kind of "civilizing" intention the colonial system may have had; as Sartre puts it, "Thus, in a way, the entire apparatus of violence will have served to constitute a sort of closed field in which practico-inert forces crush the individual enterprise of certain colonialists" (Sartre 1985 [1960]: 728). As such, the colonial system requires for its maintenance a set of conditions in which "good intentions" serve as a superstructural legitimation of the economic order of exploitation, a legitimation that because of the inertial aspects of this order can never serve as a form of *praxis*.

What Fanon's claim requires at this point is an elucidation of his conception of the human subject. To put it briefly, Fanon takes as the fundamental condition of the human being the condition of *action*; human beings act upon the world in ways that satisfy or aid in the project of the human subject's becoming. Paralleling Sartre at most points, Fanon argues that the human state is characterized by its freedom to engage in the project of the person's own becoming—that people are always in the state of acting freely upon the world. What the colonial situation does, however, is to instantly impose two ontologically delimited subtypes of the human species: Whites and Blacks (colonizers/colonized, settlers/natives, etc.). This delimitation is imposed on the basis of skin color, to which "racial" characteristics (which are actually cultural characteristics, and are always evaluated in the terms of White society) are added to give further "definition." In essence, though, this definition imposes a certain form of delimitation upon not only the colonized, *but also the colonizer*. In other words, by imposing a set of characteristics upon a group of people, the colonizer imposes a certain set of possible actions for that group *as well as their own group*, as it is defined in relation to the colonized. This moment of definition in actuality restricts qualitatively (and in existential terms, eliminates completely) the freedom of both Black and White to actualize themselves. As Whites are always expected to behave in ways that are "superior" to Blacks, and Blacks are required to either behave like Whites or be permanently labeled Black, both groups are removed from the condition of freedom and placed in a kind of servitude, in which neither can *act* upon the world in ways that are meaningful to each individual. The inability to act meaningfully upon one's world results in what Fanon identifies as the "devalorization" of the human individual; as the individual in the colonial society can no longer act meaningfully or freely upon their own lives, they no longer have any meaning for themselves (Fanon 1964a: 13). In addition, they no longer have meaning for all others; the human condition of freedom, in the Sartrean model that Fanon adopts, must exist for all humans, or else it exists for none, and those who stand by while the freedom of others is eradicated are complicit with those who steal freedom (Sartre 1963: 24–25).

The process by which the colonial system wreaks violence upon the cultures of the colonized is, in many ways, an insidious one. The presence of Christian missionaries, well documented in much anthropological literature, is one way the colonizers go about civilizing the "natives." Another approach is through language. By requiring the Algerian people to speak French, the colonizer's language, the French gain a number of advantages over the colonized in their attempt to maintain their domination. First, any language carries with it a particular way of seeing the world. Because language references and makes easily translatable a welter of structural oppositions in the world (cf. Bourdieu 1991), language is one way in which the actual conditions of existence are translated into the minds of the members of that situation and are reproduced through discourse. Hence, by imposing a language upon a colonized group, as the French did on Algeria in the 1880s (Ruedy 1992: 75–76), the colonizers have the situationally determined ability to impose a particular worldview on that group as well. The second marked advantage given to the colonizers by the imposition of a language on another group is the ability to determine one's level of "civility" (or cultural capital) by the way in which one speaks the hegemonic language. One's ability to "pass" in the colonizer's world is determined in no small part by their fluency in the colonizer's language. Often, Fanon notes that his acceptance by colonizers, both in Algeria and in France, is determined by the fact that he speaks French; people's surprise at Fanon's linguistic ability—"How well you speak French! How long have you been in France?"—becomes the way in which the colonizer puts the colonized back in their "proper" place. Lastly, the inability of the colonized to speak the colonizer's language often subjects them to another classificatory gesture—the speaking of pidgin by the colonizer—one the colonized generally internalize through a perceived loss of agency. In doing this, the colonizer explicitly, though potentially subconsciously, reminds the "native" that they are not part of the white world (Fanon 1965: chapter 5; Fanon 1967: 18, 32).

Language, though, works as an everyday marker of one's membership in a nation, and it is through this collective consciousness of in-group and out-group membership that the colonizers maintain their subjugation of the colonized. As Fanon notes, culture becomes the first expression of a nation, and culture and language work together intimately to provide markers of membership in this community (Fanon 1963: 244). Hence, the *colons* attempt to "humanize" the natives by giving them both a language and a culture, be it subtly, as through missionary programs, or violently through physical mistreatment not appropriate for even the most unruly beast. For the colonized, it is only through the assimilation of this language and culture that their apparent structural position within the colonial situation can be ameliorated; for the colonizer, this is the sign that their work of "civilization" progresses. Here, I say "apparent" structural position for one reason and one reason only: the native's real position within the colonial situation is permanent and immutable; any changes that appear to take place in this, such as the apparent amelioration of one's position through the acquisition of the colonizer's language, are only that—apparent.

Another aspect of the colonial process of the dehumanization of the "natives" is through the replacement of native traditions, cultures, and social practices with those of the colonizers. The imposition of language that I have described here is only one way of doing this. Another is by imputing new, Western, "civilized" (read: inferiorizing) meanings to the stories of the colonized. The Br'er Rabbit stories of the plantation-era South of the United States are cited by Fanon as an example of this. While for the colonized these stories mark off a pattern of resistance (what has been called a "narrative of liberation": Taylor 1989: 3–6; cf. Scott 1990), the colonizer sees them as displaying the natives' low level on the evolutionary scale (Wolfe, in Fanon 1967: 174). By marking these stories with the meanings (and psychical issues, if one takes Wolfe seriously) of the Whites, the colonizers find yet another way of maintaining their superiority through culture. By reinscribing subaltern (or what Gramsci would call "folk") discourses with dominant meanings (i.e., the animalistic nature of Black consciousness), these tales attempt to transmit these dominant meanings to the consumers of these ways of seeing the world. In other words, the cultural justification for the hegemonic colonial system (Gramsci 1971: 80ff., *inter alia*) becomes a matter not of trying to figure out why the colonized are "naturally" inferior, but rather of constructing the social world of the colonial system in such a way that the "natives" are *made* to be inferior and naturalizing this construction in the minds of colonizer and colonized alike.

The imposition of French culture upon Algeria, perpetrated through the imposition of the French language, French medicine, French radio, French newspapers (to cite the many examples given by Fanon), works in such a way so as to structurally classify the Algerian peoples as inferior beings—nonhumans. But this cannot only happen by offering up colonial culture to the "natives." Instead, there must be a well-structured plan of attack on the culture of the colonized for this to work. The world of the colonizer must be laid out over every aspect of the world of the colonized, and this layering must be enforced with such vigor as to force the colonized to either submit to the colonizer's world or to disappear. As Fanon writes,

> Colonialism obviously throws all the elements of native society into confusion. The dominant group arrives with its values and imposes them with such violence that the very life of the colonized can manifest itself only defensively, in a more or less clandestine way. Under these conditions, colonial domination distorts the very relations that the colonized maintains with his own culture. (Fanon 1965: 130)

This distortion of the relationship between the colonized and their own culture occurs only through the imposition of a new form of collective unconscious, in which the colonized are now forced, under threat of censure, imprisonment, or death, to evaluate themselves in a foreign set of terms, those of the colonizers. In this set of terms, the colonized are labeled through their use of language, their cultural practices and traditions, and fundamentally by the color of their skin. This is primarily due to the imposition of a culture to which conformity is both mandatory and impossible for the colonized. Hence, it is given the character of a war against the form of existence of the *colonisés*, a war that is bent on total annihilation of the "native" as an existential subject. The attainment of these imposed conceptions of "humanity" is impossible for one unfortunately simple reason: those who, in the colonial situation, are deemed to be subhuman are subhuman because they have dark skin. This dark skin serves as the primary marker of subjugated humanity within the colonial situation; it serves to show all of the colonizers that a particular individual, regardless of their linguistic, intellectual, or any other ability, is below the Whites, and can therefore never become White. This tension between the mandatory conformity to colonial culture and the impossibility of attaining a non-marked status insinuates itself, as Gramsci identified, into the psyches of the colonized, so that this racial drama takes place most insidiously at the level of the individual consciousness.

Psychological Violence

The structuration of the colonized's place in the colonial situation is thereby translated into a form of psychological violence. That is, the Black soul or psyche is always already given a particular place within White society, colonial or not; this structural place is, to be loose about it, at the bottom of the barrel, and in particular it is a "white man's artifact" (Fanon 1967: 14). Given this premise, as well as the cultural impetus of the colonial system to attempt to "civilize" the "native" through their acculturation, we can see that in Fanon's analysis, dead on through all estimations, the native, prior to the act of resistance, is stuck in a structural double bind: either the native attempts to "become" white, and loses contact with their culture and people, while becoming "accepted" by white society; or they resist assimilation, and are *refused* a place within white society. Fanon puts this most poignantly: ". . .*turn white or disappear*" (Fanon 1967: 100).

In the colonial situation, as in the social situations discussed so far, meaning preexists *colons* just as it does *colonisés*. In Fanon's words, "And so it is not I who make a meaning for myself, but it is the meaning that was already there, pre-existing, waiting for me" (Fanon 1967: 134). What characterizes the colonial situation as different for Fanon is that, unlike in the colonizers' realm, the colonized do not have the ability within the colonial situation to construct their own life-meanings with the materials they are given. The meaning that preexists the native is constructed through the imposition of the *colon*'s system of values upon the colonized society. Within this system, the black person is constructed as "immoral" and it is impossible, from the *colon*'s point of view, to bring the black person up to the whites' level of "morality."[4] In other words, the White has constructed the moral aspects of the colonial situation so that the Black has two options: either achieve White standards of morality, or remain an "immoral nigger." Both of these options are supported externally to the individual by the military, political, and social practices of the colonial regime; the former by the rewarding of the Black, who is "no longer Black," the latter through their constant inferiorization by others (Fanon 1967: 192).

It is through these external reinforcement mechanisms that this drastically serious life choice, as well as the structural double bind in which *les colonisés* are placed by the mere existence of this life choice, that the dilemma "turn white or disappear" works its way into the collective unconscious of *colonisé* society. Because any sort of validity is violently stripped from native culture, its members are constantly forced into seeing themselves as inferior. However, this inferiority complex is not played out at the subconscious level. Instead, for the native it is played out at the level of the conscious; because this inferiorization is made manifest in the political, social, and cultural realms of the colonial situation, the colonized has no time to make this "unconscious"—their survival depends on adjusting to this (Fanon 1967: 149–150). The "native" is forced at every moment of their existence to choose whether or not to "turn white or disappear," to be apparently accepted as an equal (knowing full well that the color of their skin prevents them from ever becoming an equal to the White) or to be ignored, structurally categorized, or killed.

It is in this structural double bind that the psychological violence of the colonial regime comes to the fore. Because of this structural double bind, the colonized are forced to maintain a neurotic relationship with their own; that is, the desire to have one's humanity recognized by White society forces one to turn away from all that could make one Black in the colonizer's eyes. As the Black is constructed by the White to be lazy, stupid, and immoral and, in Fanon's words, the bearer of "the burden of the original sin" (Fanon 1967: 192), and the Black is deemed not to be human, the Black is forced to choose between inhumanity and humanity. In the colonial situation, this is the only choice; and choosing the latter forces "the native" to escape their people:

> Quite simply because—and this is very important—the Antillean has recognized himself as a Negro, but, by virtue of an ethical transit, he also feels (collective unconscious) that one is a Negro to the degree to which one is wicked, sloppy, malicious, instinctual. Everything that is the opposite of these Negro modes of behavior is white. Thus must be recognized as the source of Negrophobia in the Antillean. In the collective unconscious, black = ugliness, sin, darkness, immorality. In other words, he is Negro who is immoral. If I order my life like that of a moral man, I simply am not a Negro. (Fanon 1967: 192)

In the second step of the double bind, the escape from "Negritude" is limited by one's skin color. For Fanon, this leads to a collapse of the ego through an insidious path: (1) the "Negro" is culturally constructed as the root of all evil and subhuman; (2) those deemed to *be* "Negroes" see their humanity stripped away from them; (3) in an attempt to regain their humanity, they take on the characteristics of "the humans" (Whites) and try to leave behind those sociocultural qualities that made them "Negro"; (4) once they embark on this process of "turning White," they find that they no longer belong to their own culture or society; (5) they also find that, because of their skin color, they can *never* belong to White culture or society. If ever anything resembled the proverbial "Catch-22," this double bind would be it. The imposition of this required form of distinction, to use Bourdieu's term, forces those who choose to "turn white" to distinguish themselves from their primary group, and are made unable to fully achieve this distinction; they are thereby left in a middle ground, without classification, without a class, and without a sense of the humanity for which they struggled.

This collapse of the ego that comes through the inability to turn white leads, for Fanon, to the "death" of the "actional person" (Fanon 1967: 154). The self-image of the native, torn in two through an ontological process by which the "carrot" of membership in the *colon*'s version of the human race is yanked away and the "stick" of being identified as subhuman is constantly struck upon their body and soul, inevitably undergoes a collapse when this "stick" becomes the colonizer's club or rifle-butt. This collapse is doubly reinforced: the native, who has chosen to escape their status as "Negro" by throwing off all that the Whites said made them "Negro," also has their new identity as "white" taken away in the moment of the recognition of one's skin color. In other terms, the colonized takes the Other, the colonizer, as the sole object of their actions and desires; this Other, the only one who can give the native "worth," rejects the native, leaving them separated from the worlds of both the colonizer and the colonized (loc. cit.). It is at this point when Fanon argues that his task as psychoanalyst is to bring this unconscious destruction of the colonized individual to the fore in the native's consciousness. I would argue, though, that we need to take the analysis one step further, as this all-out assault that constitutes the colonial situation is not simply one against a particular culture or mentality; it is one against *an entire way of existence*, upon the humanity of the colonized.

Violence Against Humanity
Fanon's most important insight into the nature of the colonial regime and into the resistance it engenders is that the regime is constituted on the elimination of an entire mode of human existence. Instead of being predicated upon the conversion of "native" subjects into "good Christians," the colonial regime is bent on the reconstitution of natives in one of two ways: "human" in the European sense, or dead, either metaphysically or in reality. There are no ambiguities here; for the "native" in Fanon's analysis, there are only two choices—"turn white or

disappear"—and these two choices are made virtually if not actually at gunpoint. The violence of the colonial system exists both as an actual threat against one's life and as a structural condition of existence. Violence, in other words, transcends each of these realms toward a set of social conditions in which violence is both actual and ontological. This is, Fanon argues, a result of what Sartre calls the mistake of Western European humanism—the taking of the élite, in this case the French, for the genus (Sartre 1963: 26). In other words, the epistemological foundation for the European colonial regime (and by extension, Western culture) is that only "the *colons*," the white hegemony, is human; all else is out of place in this epistemological model. In this sense, then, the goal of any colonial regime is to humanize or destroy—either "create" humans where there once were only "savages" (read: impose Western conceptions of "humanity" onto other cultures), or eliminate the onto-logical existence of the "savages" from the face of the planet.

For Fanon, this category of "humanity" imposed by the colonial élite carries with it a more punitive edge than modern conceptions of Otherness. Whereas modern North American cultures are at least on the surface taking a more "inclusive" view of those they determine to be Others, the colonial regime categorically refuses to admit the human existence of its Others, the colonial "natives." It is not a matter of epis-temologically establishing categories of Human Subjects and Non-human Others; there simply are no non-humans—they either convert or disappear (Fanon 1967: 140; cf. Sartre 1985 [1960]: 720). This onto-logical denial of the existence of Nonhumans is not motivated by hate; as Fanon points out, "*Hate demands existence, and he who hates has to show his hate in appropriate actions and behavior; in a sense, he has to become hate.* That is why the Americans have substituted discrimination for lynching" (Fanon 1967: 53; emphasis mine). In the colonial ontol-ogy, this is tantamount to an epistemological revolution. For the White to hate the Black, the White has to grant the Black's existence, something completely contrary to the covert goals of the colonial regime. Where the colonial regime succeeds in conveying what I would call the image of hate is in the establishment of the hegemonic order of the colonizers' superiority, the very goal of the colonial regime. In this attempt, the colonizer posits their superiority, and therefore the colo-nized's inferiority. It is only here that "*the racist creates his inferior*" (Fanon 1967: 93); through the categorization of people on the basis of skin type, the White in fact asserts a negative identity: the White is defined only through their definition as being superior to the Black. This becomes the site for what becomes the double bind of the colonial regime: the fact that through this hierarchization, the colonizer inextricably binds them to the colonized, and therefore puts them into a position of dependence upon the colonized for their sense of identity (Fanon 1967: 96–97).

This set of relations becomes the defining conception of the colonial regime and its violence against the humanity of the colonized. The colonizer chooses to negate the existence of the Black, yet is completely bound up in their relationship to the Black. This double bind has only one conceivable conclusion for the colonizer: take the path of least resistance and follow the original goal, to negate the Black's existence by imposing the choice of "assimilation or death" onto the Black (Fanon 1967: 109–110). As the Whites have the ontological power to impose the relationship between settler and native onto the native, and military power to back up this imposition, there is only a one-way relationship, and no ontological way out of it for the Black. Hence, we can see that Fanon's assertion that "[L]'objet du racisme n'est plus l'homme particulier mais une certaine forme d'exister" stems precisely from the ontological negation of the natives' existence, and results in "le déjà célèbre appel à la lutte de la «croix contre le croissant»" (Fanon 1964a: 40).[5] The "cross against the crescent"—Christianity versus Islam, White versus Black—converts the colonial process from civilization to cultural annihilation, a process in which the creation of the "doubly alienated" *colonisés* highlights in terms of its effects on potentially actional and free beings.

The results of this epistemic violence, contrary to the merely academic perspective taken by some (cf. Bhabha 1994), are felt in the psyche of the "native," in that the native no longer becomes the object of their own action. Instead, the colonial double bind of turning white or being erased forces the native to orient their actions toward the colonizer, who will always reject them (save in the case of "token" admissions to the group, who generally serve as legitimation of the possibility for "turning white"). In other words, the victims of the colonial situation are compelled to turn to the victimizers for any sort of validation, be it real or epistemological, of their existence as a human being (Fanon 1967: 98). Because of the always incomplete nature of the human being and the need for recognition *qua* human that Fanon (through Hegel) posits, the native is forced by the epistemic violence of the colonial situation to turn to the colonizer for that acknowledgment, as the ontological terms of this acknowledgment have been forcibly reset by the Whites. But, as I have noted earlier, even as the Black is forced to accept White society as its object of orientation and its totality, the Black is refused their goal, to "become" White: "Cultural imposition is easily accomplished in Martinique. The ethical transit encounters no obstacle. But the real white man is waiting for me. As soon as possible he will tell me that it is not enough to try to be white, but that a white totality must be achieved. It is only then that I shall recognize the betrayal" (Fanon 1967: 193). Through this betrayal, the Black realizes that they do not "in actuality"—and I put this in quotes because the overwhelming violence of the colonial situation makes this realization moot—require the acknowledgment of the White that they are human; they are human beings first, and Black second (Fanon 1967: 97). This realization, coupled with the everyday violence of the colonial system, leads to a dramatic collapse of the Black ego, in that the colonized cognitively realize the following path:

- the White has imposed a conception of humanity onto the colonized society, a conception that forces the colonized to "turn white or disappear," as there is no room for Blacks/nonhuman Others;
- becoming White/"human" is a totality in the colonizer's ontology;
- becoming White/"human" is also a totalizing impossibility, due to the colonized's skin color;
- because becoming White/"human" is impossible, and to refuse to become White (i.e., assimilate) leads to epistemological, and possibly physical, extermination, one is unable to do anything to gain recognition as human by the colonizers.

The ego of the colonized collapses, on Fanon's analysis, because of the realization that the acknowledgment on the part of the colonizer that the colonized who has opted to "turn white" has "become human" can never come; hence, the colonized can never be seen *by their Others* (the colonizers) as human. All along, the object of the natives' actions has been the settler, in the hopes of regaining their "humanity" (in the settler's terms); yet this form of cultural capital can never come, because the terms of the settler's ontology can never permit it. Hence, because of the paradoxical realization on the part of the native that they are humans before they are Black, yet their humanity is denied by Whites because they are Black first in their ontology, the Black ego collapses. The result of this collapse of the ego, for Fanon, is that the colonized person ceases to be an *actional* person; that is, they stop acting upon the world (Fanon 1967: 154).

While this analysis would make it seem that in the colonial situation both colonizer and colonized feel corresponding effects of this devalorization process, this is not the case. Because of the physical violence that lies behind the epistemological attacks on the humanity of the colonized, the "natives" feel their dehumanization more profoundly.[6] As I have shown earlier, these effects appear in many guises (the erasure of indigenous cultures, the neurosis of being forced to struggle in vain to be recognized by foreigners as a human being, etc.), but all are rooted in the will toward the destruction of the indigenous lifestyle, culture, and practices by those who come in the name of Civilization. The question arises, then, whether there exists the possibility for the colonized to reclaim their freedom. The answer is yes, but only through the physical reenactment and reversal of the violence wreaked against the humanity of the natives. Their revolution, for Fanon, is the only tool by which they become human.

The Nature of Colonial Violence and Colonial Hegemony

Given this depiction of the varieties of colonial violence, what then can we say about the *nature* of this violence? This question becomes essential for understanding both Fanon's work and the work of the resistance. The question leads us to deal with how these explicit policies combine with the implicit intentions of the colonial regime to create a kind of violence against subaltern groups peculiar to the colonial situation in the first instance, but, by extension, endemic to all social groupings characterized by structural hierarchies and inequalities.

Sekyi-Otu provides the first insight into the peculiar nature of the colonial situation. In *Fanon's Dialectic of Experience* (1996), he argues that the colonial regime maintains the imposition of a radical and violent bifurcation upon an already-existing society. This bifurcation, based entirely upon the racialization of its subjects (both colonizer and colonized, White and Black), is particularly violent in its refusal to allow any kind of interaction between subordinate and superordinate:

> The "originality of the colonial context," says "Concerning Violence," resides in the adamant bipolarity of the positions of colonizer and colonized, in this peculiar institution of difference lived as absolute contrariety. Therein lies the "totalitarian character," the *violence*, of colonial domination as racial bondage: the extraordinary tyranny of a form of social division and human intercourse permitting of no reciprocal exchange between the opposing agents, no ironic substitutions or transformations of their places, positions, properties. A language of separation and subjugation unrelieved by irony—such is the story of the social world which "Concerning Violence" is constrained to tell. (Sekyi-Otu 1996: 158–159)

It would seem, then, as if there were an epistemological wall between colonizers and colonized, made real on a daily basis (cf. Tillion 1958; Bourdieu 1958). If this were indeed the case, though, then the obvious first move of the revolution would be to tear down this "wall" and attack those directly on the other side.

This presumes, though, that the colonial situation is truly Manichean, a presumption that our earlier discussion of the nature of colonial violence belies. The "bipolarity" that Sekyi-Otu finds in Fanon's depiction of the colonial situation (1996: 158–159) is really, I would argue, a *tripolarity*.[7] There are, *from the point of view of the colonized*, at least three groups in the colonial situation: *les colons*, with their riches, political power, and the ability to grant recognition of one's humanity; *les colonisés*, the disenfranchised Algerians who were subjected to the colonial regime; and a third group, relegated to an ontological "no-man's land."[8] This group, which I would call "doubly alienated," is constituted by those members of the colonized peoples who, believing that they could indeed "turn white," attempted to gain recognition of their humanity and took on the habitus of the colonizers, only to be refused admission to this group because their skin color prevented them from ever "becoming white." This group appears to me to be the group that originated the FLN's insurrectionary activities, despite the differences in their particular backgrounds and the ways they came to this political realization (Quandt 1969: 74). Maurice Viollette, in a 1926 letter to the French Minister of the Interior, wrote that there were 100,000 *évolués* (economically and socially "advanced" Algerians) who felt as if they had no homeland:

> Six out of ten of these are ready to adopt the French fatherland without second thoughts, but if the French fatherland rejects them, raises itself so high that they cannot reach it, they will make their own fatherland, and we will have willed it. (Viollette, quoted by Ageron, vol. 2 of *Histoire de l'Algérie contemporaine*; in Ruedy 1992: 144)

Viollette's premonitions came true, and while by most accounts this group was less well-educated than the liberals who were working the French government for reforms in the Algerian colony, many of the original 22 members of the FLN had been political candidates whose ambitions had been frustrated by election-rigging (most likely intended to keep young Algerians out of prominent political offices), and nearly all were veterans of the French Army. As Talbott notes (1980: 27), these veterans took the knowledge they gained from fighting for the French, as well as the manifestoes of Colonels Rémy and Passy, heroes of the

French *Résistance*, and utilized them against French rule in Algeria. One could say that the origins of the FLN indicate a clear use of using "the master's tools" to tear down "the master's house"; and without attempting to inductively reason their psychological state, I would argue that the characteristics Ruedy, Talbott, and Quandt claim that the revolutionaries shared (most notably, their desire to elevate themselves to the level of the colonizers) indicate a parallel with the "doubly alienated" I have described here.

So, how does this indicate the nature of colonial violence? I have said above that the trifurcation of the colonial regime involves a third group not necessarily invoked by Fanon or his readers as crucial for the revolution, this "doubly alienated" group; and the indications are that this group was the one that created the FLN and began the insurrection, since an entire subjugated population does not rise up *en masse* to fight against the tyranny of the colonial situation:

> But 8,500,000 people do not simultaneously initiate any enterprise. On November 1, 1954, all but a few thousand Algerians still accepted the inevitability of the colonial situation even if they despised it. Even one year later, though the revolution was spreading, the men and women willing to make the dangerous leap into revolutionary activism still constituted a small minority of the population. (Ruedy 1992: 156–157)[9]

Since it was but a small group who began the insurrection, and the primary goal was to construct in revolutionary action the unity of the Algerian nation, I would argue that the nature of colonial violence is the *enforced alienation from both one's social group and oneself* that results from the apparent offer to grant humanistic recognition to the colonized subject if they turn away from their "uncivilized" ways, and the subsequent refusal, through the racialization of conceptions of humanity, to grant this recognition because of one's skin color. The subsequent double alienation ends up leading, as Fanon's psychoanalytic works reveal, to the loss of human agency and the freedom to act upon one's own life, and ultimately to the acceptance of revolutionary violence as the tool to regain this freedom.

"The carrot and stick of recognition": this implies, not entirely incorrectly, that the sole motivation for the Algerian Revolution, as well as other anticolonial struggles, is primarily ontological—that the revolutionaries merely want to be the recipients of an ostensibly universal form of recognition, but have been denied this based on characteristics that are out of their control (in this case "race"). This is indeed a powerful motivation for revolution, and some revolutions have been fought for less (tax revolts, e.g.). Remember, though, that in the colonial situation in particular, ontology and the empirical world mutually reinforce one another: governmental policies intended to maintain the separation between *colons* and *colonisés* have this ontological basis (the denial of the universality of "universal human rights"), and the effects of these policies (which range from the double taxation imposed by the *impôts arabes* to prohibitions on the taking of French citizenship by Algerians who refuse to give up their Muslim civil status) are felt on the existential level for those on the wrong end of the laws.

The Algerian Colonial System, Political Culture, and the Colonial Habitus

Those laws, though, are the sociological manifestations of the ontological issues we have examined thus far. In the case of the Algerian Revolution, both the governmental policies (such as the *impôts arabes*; Ruedy 1992: 90; Horne 1977: 63) and the ontological directions Fanon identifies work together to construct the paths by which social change can come about—or rather, to hegemonically prevent possible paths of resistance for the subaltern group. As we have seen, *colon* and *métropole* governmental authorities severely limited the possibilities for participation by Algerians in governmental affairs and commerce. Explicit limitations on who could become French citizens in the Algerian colonial regime (i.e., European settlers and those Algerian Muslims who chose to attempt to "become white" through the renunciation of their Muslim civil status) enforced a direct limitation on those who could participate in governmental affairs above the level of the civil service. And in the cases of those Algerians who did attempt to run for government office, even in the mixed communes, election rigging worked to ensure that they could not win political power (Talbott 1980: 27; cf. Quandt 1969). Until 1947, when all people living in Algeria were granted French citizenship, there had been separate electoral colleges for *colons* and *colonisés*, with *colons* having on average a six-to-one ratio of political power. The Organic Statute of 1947 that brought Algeria into France in the same manner as a Canadian province, while granting political participation rights to all in Algeria, maintained a three-to-one power ratio between *colons* and *colonisés* in the Algerian Assembly that replaced the *Délégations financières*. Subsequent elections up to the start of the Revolution in 1954 were delegitimized through arrests of Algerians, ballot rigging, and other forms of political machinations (Ruedy 1992: 151–153; cf. Quandt 1969). In sum, without the ability, legal or practical, to engage in governmental affairs at a one-to-one ratio with the European contingent in Algeria, the colonized subjects had no legitimate political means by which to effect change in the Algerian polity.

Economically, the characterization of Algerians as "pauperized" is fairly accurate (Horne 1977: 63; Ruedy 1992; Talbott 1980; Tillion 1958). But, as Ruedy points out, there was at the same time as the overall pauperization of Algerian society a concomitant stratification amongst Algerians, with the rise of a "middle class" of landowners. The colonial government used this group as an example, arguing that over time, all of non-European Algerian society would come to resemble this group. However, this middle class appears on closer examination to be a statistical construct; contemporaneous with this rise in landowners of mid-sized properties was an increase in the percentage of rural unemployed workers (to nearly 50 percent by 1954) and studies reporting that some 65 to 75 percent of the rural population was "poor" or "very poor" (Horne 1977: 62; Ruedy 1992: 123). Other statistics show the proletariat amounting to nearly 1.2 million people (including the Algerians who moved to *métropole* France to find work) (Ruedy 1992: 125). Three hundred thousand of this proletariat were those who had moved to France and rotated in and out of the workforce; the majority of these, according to Ruedy, were bachelors, and probably contributed little to the colonial GNP. So, combining the fact of the expropriation of family wealth at the start of the occupation, the transfer of the majority of lands from Algerian to *colon* hands, and the proletarianization of the Algerian population, we can see that the only people who could have possibly had a significant economic influence on the Algerian colonial situation were the five to six thousand bourgeois Algerians at the top of the colonized economic scale—Algerians who had no intention of sacrificing their profit for the freedom of their people.

Cultural factors also limited the possibility for social change to be gained through legitimate means. The colonial and *métropole* governments had virtually bankrupted the Islamic education and cultural system and had, to a large extent, taken control over those elements that survived the financial attrition. Furthermore, the dueling French discourses of Catholic religious dominance and Enlightenment rationality meant that any moves made by the Islamic establishment to effect some kind of social change would most likely have been ignored or treated as examples of the need for further "civilizing" measures. Reforms within the Islamic establishment did occur, but these were primarily oriented toward the development of the Algerian nationalist movement (Ruedy 1992: 136). In sum, then, attempts through cultural institutions such as the Islamic institutions to engage in a process of social change would have been futile.

This is not to say that reforms did not happen in the Algerian colony. They did; they just happened because of French *métropole* initiative, not because of either Algerian or *colon* initiative. The seizure of control of the colonial education system by the mainland government in 1944 is one example of direct *colon* opposition to the expansion of educational opportunities to Algerian Muslims (Ruedy 1992: 126; Horne 1977: 43). Another example is the series of events that surrounded the Blum-Viollette bill of 1938, a bill that would have implemented a policy of "assimilation" and granted about 25,000 Algerian *évolués* full citizenship. Opposition to the bill was such that most of the *colon* mayors struck against the bill, and French Prime Minister Blum refused to support the legislation (Ruedy 1992: 144; Horne 1977: 37). *Métropole* officials knew the risks of this kind of strategy of social reform; as Maurice Viollette wrote as early as 1926, 100,000 *évolués* felt as if they had no homeland, and would choose France or, if refused the position they felt they deserved in France, would create their own nation (Ruedy 1992: 144). Relations between the *colons* and the *métropole* government were nearly as strained as those between Algerians and *colons* and Algerians and France; and as such, *colons* strove to enact the kind of control they wanted to hold over Algeria, not the kind metropolitan France or the Algerian people themselves did.

Following this analysis, we can safely argue that the Algerian people were on the whole disenfranchised politically, economically, and culturally. The means by which this disenfranchisement was imposed upon them by both the *métropole* and colonial governments was such that there were no politically acceptable avenues of redress for the colonized subjects. Through the socially constructed absence of legitimate paths by which the Algerian people could make claims for the enactment of policies designed to bring the same kind of equality and freedom to the Algerian majority that the European minority enjoyed, the *colons* found it relatively easy to maintain their dominance. Those in the Algerian colonial situation with a colonized habitus, which had at its root the realization that Algerians had no power within the colonial society, could not but produce and reproduce a situation in which the expression of consent was impossible and the expression of dissent was inconceivable without risk to one's life. This is the "black resignation" Tillion noticed in her early 1950s study of Algeria (Tillion 1958: 41), as well as the deprivation of the agency of the colonized Fanon sought to redress throughout his works.

Without opportunities for any type of "legal resistance" to occur, the Algerians were left with only one option: armed rebellion designed to expel the colonizers and with them, all vestiges of the colonial regime, be they political, economic, cultural, or at the root of all these, onto-logical. The situation in which *les colonisés* found themselves, then, is one that worked to dehumanize the colonized. By defining "humanity" in terms of the colonizer, the colonial system dangled the carrot of recognition as "human" in front of the colonized by offering them the chance to make themselves like the colonizer. Almost immediately, though, that carrot was taken away by the reimposition of the brute fact of the colonized's skin color; the fact of blackness was brought against the colonized as a marker of the impossibility of being recognized as human. In the case at hand, the negative valuation of anything tradi-tionally Algerian—Islam, Arabic as the language, any traditions that people might practice—compelled Algerians to attempt to purge those traits and attributes from their habitus. At the same time, though, the refusal of the *pieds-noirs'* (French citizens born in Algeria and often descended from colonists) to recognize what they themselves defined as "civilization" in Algerians reinforced for both *pieds-noirs* and Algerians the mandatory division between them, one that, as we have seen, every-one's actions and reactions reproduce on a daily basis.

This is not to say that *all pieds-noirs* were racist in their actions, or to say that *all* Algerians experienced the colonial habitus as described by Fanon, Tillion, and others. Rather, it is to say that the overwhelming force of the colonial situation compelled people to act as if this was the only way to act. Algerians were supposed to act as if French *colons* were the paragon of humanity; *colons* were supposed to act as if Algerians were either their "little brown brothers and sisters" who were in need of civilizing, or as cheap labor that was to be exploited as much as possible. As Bourdieu puts it,

> La société coloniale est un système dont il importe de saisir la logique et la nécessité internes du fait qu'il constitue le contexte en référence auquel prennent sens tous les comportements et en particulier les rapports entre les deux communautés ethniques. Aux transformations résultant inévitablement du contact entre deux civilisations profondément différentes tant dans le domaine économique que dans le domaine social, la colonisation ajoute les bouleversements sciemment et méthodique-ment provoqués pour assurer l'autorité de la puissance dominante et les intérêts économiques de ses ressortissants. (Bourdieu 1958: 106)[10]

Given the compulsion exerted by the colonial system, one would expect that Algerians' habitus would be remarkably conflicted, exposed to both the *liberté, égalité, et fraternité* of revolutionary French culture and the impossibility of ever attaining those ideals, thanks to the colonial social situation.

It is not surprising, then, that the political culture that developed in Algeria would be one in which competition between individuals for colonialist crumbs would arise. This political culture was not necessarily developed solely under French colonial rule, but rather pre-existed the 1830 occupation of Algeria; the colonial system, however, seems to have worked to perfect it as a mode of orientation to others. Much in the same manner as Marx described the competition among proletarians for low-paying jobs in a capitalist system, Algerian political culture was motivated by what Quandt describes as *boulitique*: "'I try to get you to do something stupid so that I can take your place.' It is no surprise, then, that Algerian leaders often behave, *and expect others to behave*, as if they are constantly maneuvering and scheming to acquire more power" (Quandt 1969: 266–67). When one has been socialized into a system in which crumbs of dignity, economic resources, and other social goods are scarce, one internalizes the need to compete, sometimes to the proverbial death, for those resources. The additional Algerian political concerns of honor and demands for equality, as well as the concomitant *méfiance* or "mistrust" that characterizes relations between political actors, went hand in hand with this habituated response to scarcity (ibid.: 265–268, 270). Given the nature of the violence inhering to the Algerian colonial situation, the obvious inability of Algerians to participate in changing the situation through their own political participation, and the twinned responses of depression and neurosis and the competition over the scarce resources delivered by the colonial system, we can see then that the potential for some kind of violent explosion was high, to say the least (Beckett 1973: 8).

The Necessity of Anticolonial Violence

On dit volontiers que l'homme est sans cesse en question pour lui-même, et qu'il se renie lorsqu'il prétend ne plus l'être.
— Fanon, *Pour la revolution africaine*, 1964a (13)[11]

From the preceding discussion, we can see that for Algerians living under French colonial and *pied-noir* rule, the situation was intolerable. The majority of the Algerian population was in poverty; the civilizing mission of French colonialism offered Algerians something the *pieds-noirs* and the *métropole* were unwilling to fulfill; and Algerians were left struggling against one another to attain the few benefits of French rule that were distributed to them. It is no surprise, then, that November 1, 1954, saw a general insurrection begin against the French colonial government. The question for us at this point is: What sorts of ethical issues manifest themselves in the ways in which the Algerian Revolution in its practical context was carried out?

This discussion must begin with the issue of how it is that a rag-tag group of militants were able to mobilize large sectors of the Algerian people in its anticolonial struggle. A phenomenology of the daily experience of colonial oppression as a basis for that revolutionary motivation becomes the logical starting point. In the Algerian case in particular (and the colonial situation in general), there is no mutual recognition between colonizer and colonized. As such, each is construed by the other as "seriality"—one of many of its kind, replaceable by any of the Others and serving as an obstacle to one's freedom. To the colonizer, each and every Algerian is the same factical entity, and prevents the colonizer from the full and free exercise of their ability to exploit the colony for all it is worth. To the colonized subject, imbricated in a system which conveys daily that the world is "cut in two" (Fanon 1963: 38), each and every *pied-noir*, regardless of their political affiliation or fondness for the rewards of colonialism, represents the oppressor and shows to the colonized both the impossibility of achieving the colonizer's conception of "humanity" and the impossibility of doing anything but trying to gain their recognition. This in itself would appear, according to Merleau-Ponty, to be enough to try to overturn the colonial situation; for him, others are supposed to be the means by and with which one enacts their freedom rather than obstacles preventing the free exercise of human potential. This phenomenological analysis of colonialism and justification for anticolonial violence may be enough to infuriate Algerians; however, it does not directly address the practical tactical issues of carrying out a revolution (such as garnering materiel and personnel to actually fight the revolution), leaving that decision as a secondary factor that would be addressed by actually getting people to support the movement. So how is it possible for the FLN's *Comité de 22* (the leading members of the revolutionary movement) to argue to the remaining eight-and-a-half million Algerians that revolutionary violence is necessary?

One way—and I would argue that this is in part the path that the FLN, and Fanon as its chief interlocutor (some would say propagandist)—would be to *universalize* the ontology of the doubly alienated. Remember here Viollette's 1926 comment that of the 100,000 *évolués* in Algeria who felt they were without a "fatherland," six of ten would choose France unless France rejected them. Taking this example, we can see that those who began the modern nationalist movement, be they these 100,000 *évolués* or *La Comité de 22*, exemplify Fanon's analysis of the colonized's psyche. Put another way, this group of people are those who strove to have their humanity recognized by the colonizer by attending *their* schools, speaking *their* language with *their* dialect, and partaking of *their* cultural and economic practices at the risk of alienating themselves from their fellow *ratons* (the French slang term for native Algerians), and were rejected by both the colonizers and the colonized.[12] In order to get the entire colonized population moving in the direction of revolution, then, the FLN had to show that all Algerians—be they the multiply alienated *Beni oui-oui* or the peasant in Kabylia—were in the same situation. Furthermore, Fanon's writings in the FLN journal *El Moudjahid* go far to give *les colonisés* a language for the experiences they have already had of colonial oppression, a way of seeing that each individual Algerian lived their lives in the same colonially constructed way that other Algerians did.

In other words, a *national collective consciousness* had to be constructed, one whose resonances could be felt by every Algerian. This national consciousness, I would argue, occurred, in Fanon's work at least, through the universalization of the double alienation felt by the *évolués* and other leaders of the nationalist movement. Following Sekyi-Otu's analysis of the political dramaturgy of Fanon's work, we can see how Fanon argues that the analysis of the colonial psyche is a result of *the colonial situation in toto*, rather than just the experience of a particular segment of the colonized population.[13] In a discussion of the assimilationist practices of the colonial regimes, Fanon writes:

> Cet événement désigné communément aliénation est naturellement très importante. On le trouve dans les textes officiels sous le nom d'assimilation.
> Or cette aliénation n'est jamais totalement réussie. Soit parce que l'oppresseur quantitativement et qualitativement limite l'évolution, des phénomènes imprévus, hétéroclites, font leur apparition.
> Le groupe infériorisé avait admis, la force de raisonnement étant implacable, que ses malheurs procédaient directement de ses caractéristiques raciales et culturelles. (Fanon 1964b: 46)[14]

We know, though, that it was predominantly only urban Algerians who were directly under the force of "assimilation"-oriented policies and procedures (Talbott 1980: 43; Ruedy 1992; Tillion 1958), even though during the 30 years prior to the Revolution urban populations grew as a result of migrations into cities and from the migration of many Algerians to mainland France for work. So which group of Algerians is Fanon describing? The "doubly alienated," I believe. But—and this is the important point—*to which group* of Algerians is Fanon describing them? The remainder of the colonized subjects. In essence, Fanon's writings offer to colonized Algerians a way of understanding the commonalities of their experience under colonialism, even if that model of understanding is predicated on the experience of a certain type of experience of colonialism, that of the "doubly alienated." It is through the prognostication of the coming of this kind of consciousness, in conjunction with feelings that Fanon's audience must have already had about their loss of agency under French rule, that this collective consciousness is developed.

There are, then, two aspects of Fanon's depiction of the structural formations of alienation in the colonial situation that are important here: the phenomenological description and analysis of the structural formations for those who have been imbricated in the colonial double bind of "turn white or disappear" and find themselves further alienated from both themselves and any particular social reference group to which they might have belonged; and the prognosticatory aspect, in which Fanon presents the process of alienation as an inevitable continuation of French colonial rule in Algeria. For his readers, though, Fanon's work must have conveyed this dual perception—that if this process of the denial of humanity is occurring for those who have actually attempted to "turn white," then it can only continue for everyone. As such, while one could see Fanon's work in this dual sense as setting out the "doubly alienated" in the position of an existential vanguard, the important aspect for my argument is that Fanon's work provides a phenomenology of Algeria's alienation as well as a phenomenology of the path of their resistance.

By arguing that all of non-European Algeria is coming to the same lack of agency that the "doubly alienated" group already felt, Fanon made it possible for the colonized subjects to see themselves as part of a dispossessed minority, an Algerian national unity that was in preparation for the reassertion of its humanity. It is in this way—making known and knowable what one already "feels"—that Fanon's work functions as a tool of the creation of class consciousness. Fanon's descriptive and theoretical work strikes an intuitive chord within the colonized: they know intimately the psychological distress Fanon identifies, the insults suffered, the existence racialized. The inferiorized group in the colonial situation knows *through their existence* the fact of being oppressed;

Fanon's work merely gives it "a name," as it were:

> The originality of the colonial context is that economic reality, inequality, and the immense difference of ways of life never come to mask the human realities. When you examine at close quarters the colonial context, it is evident that what parcels out the world is to begin with the fact of belonging to or not belonging to a given race, a given species. In the colonies the economic substructure is also a superstructure. The cause is the consequence; you are rich because you are white, you are white because you are rich. (Fanon 1963: 40)

Because of this "originality of the colonial context," the everyday realities of the colonial situation are felt by every colonized subject: the spaces within which they can legitimately live, work, move, and exist are clearly defined, almost always in racial terms, and these abject limitations on their potential life projects, to return to the Sartrean term, are felt as part of the colonized's habitus. By universalizing and showing the acute effects of the colonial situation, Fanon highlights the structure of the colonized habitus, one that is constructed to know, consciously or unconsciously, what is for "the likes of us." And through this highlighting process, Fanon makes the argument for the necessity of anticolonial violence—the overturning of the colonial situation, the radical assertion of the humanity and equality of the colonized, and the claiming of "universal human rights" for the rest of humanity.

One of the more important tasks Fanon's work achieves is informing the world at large about the actual situation on the ground.[15] As such, in this kind of writing characterized by the dual movements of reportage and advocacy, what could be called "embellishment" of the situation is often called for. And as Sartre says about Fanon's *Les damnes de la terre*, "If he demonstrates the tactics of colonialism, the complex play of relations which unite and oppose the colonists to the people of the mother country, it is for his brothers; his aim is to teach them to beat us at our own game. In short, the Third World finds *itself* and speaks to *itself* through his voice" (Sartre 1963: 10–12). In other words, Fanon's work has as its primary intention *the development of the unity of the Algerian peoples in the struggle against French colonial rule*; it is only as a secondary benefit that we have Fanon's reportage of the revolution. The embellishment that one might find in Fanon's writings, especially in *El Moudjahid*, functions, following Sekyi-Otu (1996: 103), as political dramaturgy intended to provide a phenomenology of oppression and to unify the Algerian people in the first instance, and the colonized peoples of the world in general, in the struggle against colonialism.

By universalizing the experience of colonial oppression and the betrayal that "Western humanism" wreaks on *les colonisés*, Fanon's work is able to show the process by which colonial violence was enacted and the toll it took on all levels of individual and collective existence—existential, social, psychological, cultural, and ontological. Its inculcation into the habitus of all who existed in the colonial regime is not difficult to notice. The fact that only a few thousand Algerians chose to surrender their Muslim civil status in favor of French citizenship; the self-imposed exile of hundreds of young men in the face of possible conscription into the French Army; the "fanaticism" of the colonized professed by the colonizers; the implementation of measures intended to deny the colonized the possibility of economic, social, or political advancement in spite of protestations that these measures were intended to "civilize" Algerians—these issues and many other policies I have cited here show that everyone understood the practico-inert rules of the colonial game. Those who chose to tempt fate and transgress the status assigned to them by the colonial regime—members of the group I have called the "doubly alienated"—found out in brutal ways that in spite of the ideological and discursive claims to the contrary, escape from this system could only take two forms: "black resignation, or unconditional revolt: there are no other alternatives in the world they are offered" (Tillion 1958: 41).

The Development of Anticolonial Resistance

> The existence of armed struggle shows that the people are decided to trust to violent methods only. He of whom *they* have never stopped saying that the only language he understands is that of force, decides to give utterance by force. In fact, *as always*, the settler has shown him the way he should take if he is to become free. The argument the native chooses has been furnished by the settler, and by an ironic turning of the tables it is the native who now affirms that the colonialist understands nothing but force.
> —Fanon, *The Wretched of the Earth*, 1963 (83–84)

From the beginning of the French conquest of Algeria, resistance had characterized the Algerian response to French troops. After the capitulation of Algiers and the surrender of the Dey, Algerians were left to fend for themselves against the rapacious attack of French armed forces who engaged in a general process of "rape, pillage, and burn" (Ruedy 1992: 50, 55; Horne 1977: 30–31). Between 1830 and 1871, Ruedy notes, there was only one year (1861) in which major armed attacks on colonial forces did not occur, and revolts took forms ranging from Algerian elites militarily organizing their personal entourages to uprisings organized by religious brotherhoods (ibid.: 55–58). Abd al-Qadir, a young religious man who was made head of the resistance just after the French invasion of Algeria, was one of the early prominent resistance leaders and attempted in 1833 to organize areas of Algeria not controlled by France into an independent Algerian nation-state, free from the control of both the Ottoman Empire and France. In 1834, though, al-Qadir signed a treaty with French Minister Desmichels that granted him, temporarily as he would find out soon enough, control over the interior of Algeria, save for the Constantinois (ibid.: 57–62). In 1837, though, France moved away from its policy of restricted occupation, conquered the Constantinois, and eventually held all of Algeria. Over the next 34 years, as French control over Algeria extended from the coastal cities into the Saharan plains and the mountains of Kabylia and as colonists followed the troops, Algerian resistance retreated with it. By 1871, we could say that all effective wide-scale resistance to French colonial rule had disappeared. During this time, though, I would argue that the resistance was not yet motivated by the ontological issues raised by Fanon's work in conjunction with the Algerian war of independence, but rather was sparked by a combination of loyalty to Islam (and therefore to Islamic rule) and antipathy to rule by foreigners, be they Arab or European.

It is not until the twentieth century that Algerian resistance began to take on the ontological motivations that Fanon identifies in his analyses. Prior to the uprising at Sétif on V-E Day, resistance when it occurred took the form of a *quid pro quo*—we resist the colonizers, they attack us, we attack them back. The Sétif insurrection, timed to occur with the victory of Allied forces in World War II, served notice that, now that the war was over, it was time to deal with Algerian issues in Algeria. The insurrection began as a demonstration, and after *Parti Populaire d'Algérie* protestors unfurled "forbidden" nationalist flags and banners, the police attacked, leaving 40 Algerians and Europeans dead. As word went out about the conflict, people in the rural interior attacked police stations, *colon* settlements, and other sites of French colonialism. French colonial forces went on the offensive; and in contrast to the 100 or so Europeans who died as a result of the uprising, somewhere between 1,500 to 45,000 Algerians were killed (Ruedy 1992: 149–150). While the explicit intentions of the original demonstration may have been to call attention to the plight of Algeria, the ultimate impact was to link up the rural and urban populations, making it possible for a widespread nationalist movement to begin.

Demonstrations of anticolonial sentiment continued to occur between 1945 and the start of the Revolution in 1954. After the Organic Statute for Algeria was passed in 1947, which integrated Algeria into France in the form of a province, the MTLD (*Mouvement pour le triomphe des libertés démocratiques*) won control over a total of 110 municipal councils and, barring the *colon* election-rigging that eventually prevented this from happening, had the potential to control the new legislative assembly created by the Organic Statute. The result of the extension of French control over Algeria and *colon* interference with the democratic rights the Algerian people had finally been granted was the rise of nationalist parties: the MTLD, the PPA, the OS (*Organisation spéciale*), and ultimately the FLN came into being as direct protests of the further colonization of Algeria (Ruedy 1992: 151–155). Problematically, though, these parties lacked the internal cohesion that other nationalist parties in North Africa had: questions over inclusivity ranged from nomenclature regarding the terms "Arab," "Berber," and others; and the demographic base of Algeria's nationalist parties did not have the class basis or cohesion of parties in Tunisia and Morocco, both of which had won their battles for independence. It is at this point that the mobilization of Fanon's insights into the psychology and ontology of colonialism makes possible, at least in part, the unification of the people in revolutionary struggle.

Revolutionary Strategy and the 1954 Declaration[16]

> The war, by merely setting the question of command and responsibility, institutes new structures which will become the first institutions of peace.
> —Sartre, Preface to *The Wretched of the Earth* (1963: 23)

The FLN developed out of the last attempt at forming a unified Algerian party, the CRUA (*Comité révolutionnaire d'unité et d'action*) and French attempts to quash the Algerian "terrorists," the MTLD (Talbott 1980: 37). Their manifesto, issued just before the start of hostilities on November 1, 1954, drew from the lessons of the Tunisian and Moroccan wars for independence as well as French discourses of *liberté, égalité, et fraternité* and liberal notions of the universality of citizenship (Ruedy 1992: 160; Talbott 1980: 27). The terms of the manifesto are those one would expect from documents such as the American Bill of Rights or the French Declaration of the Rights of Man and the Citizen—and from a people who had been exposed to and simultaneously denied these same rights by a colonial power. Focusing on attaining the goal of "National independence through: 1. restoration of the Algerian state, sovereign, democratic, and social, within the framework of the principles of Islam; 2. preservation of all fundamental freedoms, without distinction of race or religion" (FLN, in Horne 1977: 95), the FLN utilized the discourses of "equality," "mutual respect," "liberty," and "sovereignty"—all commonly accepted discursive and philosophical ideas within the world community, as the United Nations Charter points out—as a way of demonstrating to Algerians and to the world that their interest is in the liberation of the Algerian nation through the elimination of the vestiges of colonialism (Gillespie 1960: 112–113). As Gillespie notes (174), "Algeria's nationalists now speak of 'Liberty, Equality, Fraternity' with all the fervour that must have inspired Frenchmen in 1789." It is interesting to note, too, that these notions, at least in principle, were carried through to the end of the Revolution in 1962—though as we will see, they were problematically betrayed by the time of the official declaration of Algerian independence.

It is clear from the way in which these demands and goals are put in the FLN manifesto that this at least partially exemplifies Scott's notion that resistance is often intended merely to get the ruling powers to play by their own rules (Scott 1990: chapters 2, 7). The discourses of equality, rights, and the respect for "French cultural and economic interests honestly acquired . . . [and] persons and families" (Ruedy 1992: 160; Horne 1977: 95) all echo documents with which the French colonial powers had dominated Algeria for 120 years. As well, the FLN Manifesto does exemplify the core of what Fanon was saying: the stated desire to reclaim the humanity of the colonized from the colonial power. In declaring Algeria's intention to be treated as an equal partner in the determination of its relationship with France, and its claim to be the sole determining force for Algeria's own future, the FLN's Manifesto shows that not only were the rebels trying to get the hegemonic powers to play by their own rules, but that they were going to obtain the recognition of their humanity through whatever means necessary. At this stage, this humanity is still the colonizer's conception of "humanity": the vision of human rights and dignities portrayed by the Manifesto are indeed those of Western humanism, though they are written with an eye toward determining their own direction in the world. Yet, this Manifesto did not necessarily capture the experience or imagination of many Algerians, or even really inspire the concern of *pieds-noirs* or French colonial or metropolitan authorities. As Ruedy (1992: 156–157) reports, the majority of Algerians accepted as inevitable the dominance of the French colonial regime at the start of the revolution. Only somewhere between 900 and 3,000 fighters made up the entire revolutionary army. So how is it that, after a very short time, all of Algeria seemed to rise up against the French and the *colons*?

Revolutionary Tactics and Tactical Goals

There are two ways in which the FLN so quickly expanded its support base. The first, as we have seen, is what I have argued to be the universalization of the experience of alienation that Fanon's writings perform. By making the experience of "the colonial psyche" known—in other words, by highlighting the aspects of the colonial habitus that made it impossible for Algerians to determine the paths of their own lives— Fanon's work creates a form of collective consciousness, one that exemplifies both what is resisted against (the system that imposes this lack of agency upon its people) and the means with which to resist (the reversal of colonial violence against the colonizer). As such, the FLN worked to show to the mass of the Algerian people that *they did exist as a potentially unified and actional people* and that the FLN existed as the voice of the Algerian people: "The task of the revolutionary leadership was first to convince the Algerian people of its existence, then to give it confidence in its capacities, and finally to create structures through which those capacities could overcome French power and within which the people could begin to express its nationhood" (Ruedy 1992: 157). This process occurred through the presentation of a phenomenology of their oppression, intended to serve as the basis for the Algerian people's resistance, via the writings of Fanon, the broadcasts of Voice of Fighting Algeria, and other means, all of which were designed to inspire and elicit the writing of individual Algerians into the Revolution.

The second means by which the FLN expanded its support base in the early phase of the Revolution was not directly the result of FLN actions. Reprisals by the colonial army against Algerian "rebels" were not, at least in the beginning, directed against the FLN. Instead, members of other groups, such as the more moderate MTLD, were rounded up and imprisoned, mostly because the colonial government did not really know of the existence of the FLN; and upon their release these more moderate activists fled to the FLN. But more importantly for the average Algerian was the extreme nature of French reprisals against *them*. Mass arrests, military sweeps through the countryside, and attacks by crack paratroopers and counterinsurgency troops against entire villages where acts of sabotage or "terrorism" had occurred—all these indicated the French notion of "collective responsibility" for the resistance movement, one that held noncombatants as responsible for attacks on the colonial government (Ruedy 1992: 161; Horne 1977: 113–115, 117, 119, 123–124). Algerians generally flocked to support the FLN as a result of these reprisals. The national unity needed by the revolution for its success was created by *demonstrating the violence of the colonial regime*. For every Algerian arrested, attacked, or killed by colonial forces, more anticolonial revolutionaries—their family, friends, and fellow townspeople—were born.

Phase 1: Fighting the Colonialist Regime (in Everyone)

At the start of the revolution, Algerian resistance operations took two forms: attacks upon *métropole* institutions, and attacks upon Muslim collaborators. Police and military detachments, federal office buildings—these were the colonial targets the FLN focused against. *Colons* themselves were not targets in the first months of the war; targets included infrastructural elements, such as petroleum depots, factories, and electrical substations, causing nearly 200 million francs in damage (Horne 1977: 88–94). The FLN from the start of the Revolution through the Soummam conference in 1956 had prohibited any kind of attack on European civilians; and save for two accidental *pied-noir* casualties, the FLN mostly held to this prohibition during the early phase of the Revolution (ibid.: 91–92; Hutchinson 1978: 42).[17] The point of this phase of anticolonial violence was to strike at those elements considered by the FLN as most oppressive against Algerians—the police, the military, and the capitalist economic infrastructure, which ensured the continued proletarianization of Algerians. It had as a secondary intention the amassing of a larger cache of weapons that could be used for further operations against the regime, a goal that seemed at least early on to be a massive failure (Horne 1977: 94, 96).

In the midst of fighting a revolution, and beyond the initial transition from a small number of conspirators into a real "revolutionary movement," a movement has to figure out some way to elicit the support of the population, with secondary goals (of decreasing immediate desirability) of ensuring their compliance with the revolutionary movement's goals and aims, and the prevention of betrayal of the movement and its personnel to the government and its authorities. The revolutionary movement needs support; it needs to be able to count on the compliance of the population; and it needs to ultimately win the battle for the "hearts and minds" of the population in its struggle against the government. In the early phase of the Algerian Revolution, the FLN, directed by the CRUA, worked to build its numbers by coercing a form of support and/or compliance that was, as Hutchinson notes (1978: 40–41), directly related to the failures of the November 1, 1954, insurrection. The fact that a spontaneous uprising *à la* Fanon's predictions (Fanon 1963: 120, 131; Beckett 1973: 14) did not happen as a result of the 1954 Toussaint uprising meant that the FLN had to find other ways to mobilize the population. The phenomenological depiction of the experience of colonialism was not—but would become—a large part of this mobilization process; but additional tools needed to be found. The FLN chose violence.

Starting with what Hutchinson calls "compliance" tactics,[18] the FLN chose to respond to France's refusal to negotiate with political violence intended to ensure that the rebels could consolidate their hold on the Algerian populace. The institution of the OPA (*Organisation Politico-Administrative*) at the local level, coupled with the enforcement of rules reflecting "a certain Islamic puritanism, a desire to boycott French products, and a means of asserting its authority over the population" (Hutchinson 1978: 44), all gave the FLN the ability to enlist villagers as auxiliaries (*mousseblin*) or as actual ALN fighters. Frequently, violations of the rules instituted by the OPA resulted in mutilations of Algerian violators. As well, the acts of sabotage against French-Algerian infrastructure carried out by the ALN and *mousseblin*, with the resulting and brutal retaliation by French soldiers, paratroopers, and the *gendarmerie* against villagers, ensured that villagers were likely to respect the authority of the FLN in their region (especially when and if the FLN could combine this tactic with a form of vengeance for particularly brutal French reprisals; ibid.: 57–59). Also subject to compliance-oriented forms of violence were "rivals for political authority and any 'traitors' who disobeyed the FLN" (ibid.: 45). In an attempt to consolidate its own authority and position as the ultimate voice of Algeria, the FLN would regularly attack members of the Algerian elite created by the colonial administration, as well as members of the MNA, whose political program was ideologically similar, and with whom French President de Gaulle had offered to negotiate instead of the FLN (ibid.: 45–46).[19] Practically speaking, compliance tactics worked to ensure that the members of the general Algerian population, fearing attacks or reprisals against them, would respect and obey the authority and political dominance of the FLN, as failing to do so was seen by the FLN as treason to the revolutionary cause. As Hutchinson points out, "The FLN invariably insisted that the victims of compliance terrorism, whether elite or mass, were 'traitors.' There were frequent warnings of the fate reserved for traitors, and the killers often pinned notes explaining this motivation to the bodies of the victims. Anyone who was not actively pro-FLN risked being labeled a traitor since the FLN did not feel that mere neutrality was sufficient after a certain point" (Hutchinson 1978: 47–48). Even beyond this, the FLN viciously attacked those Algerians who "collaborated" with the colonial regime, either because of their economic or political status, their participation in the colonial system of affairs, or because they paid taxes and thereby helped to maintain the colonial regime. At some points during the first two years of the war, entire villages that cooperated with or tolerated the occupying colonial forces were decimated; on average, the first 30 months of the revolution saw the FLN kill six Muslims for every French soldier it killed (Ruedy 1992: 164).

However—and it is important to note this, especially with regard to compliance and "endorsement" tactics—it is difficult to truly identify the motivations for the extent to which the Algerian public became involved in the Revolution; the actions of the FLN, especially with regard to satisfying a need for vengeance against French repression, were seen by many as honorable, giving membership in the organization a particularly positive status and members a great deal of pride, in addition to the fear that crossing the FLN would inspire (Hutchinson 1978: 48–50). This crossover in terms of the perceived motivations of Algerians who supported the FLN and the particular tactics used to elicit or coerce that support is apparent in the notion of endorsement tactics, which were designed to inspire "admiration and respect in the 'resonant mass,' " "provoke repression from the government," and satisfy "Algerian demands for vengeance against those whom they considered their persecutors" (ibid.: 49). In some respects, the FLN was willing to sacrifice members of the Algerian public (or to take advantage of their willing sacrifice) in order to further galvanize their support base; hence, by attacking French targets, eliciting a swift and brutal repression, and responding to the public's call for vengeance, the FLN could show itself to be the speaker and caretaker of the people. Especially during the exchanges between FLN and French forces in the Constantinois in 1955, with their resulting mass casualties (an estimated 12,000 Algerians were counted as either dead or "disappeared" in August-September 1955; ibid.: 51), the FLN decided that, as a response to the "collective responsibility" the French used as a justification for brutal repression and torture against Algerians, they would pursue "collective reprisals against Europeans, military or civilian, all responsible for the crimes committed against our people" (FLN, in Hutchinson 1978: 50). After 1956, with the change in its responses to French attacks and its inclusion of French civilians in its potential target list, it became clear that the FLN had become "the representative of the Muslim population" (Hutchinson 1978: 51).

Phase 2: Internationalizing the Insurrection, Ensuring FLN Dominance

The Soummam Declaration of 1956, while working to develop the first revolutionary institutions within the FLN, including the *Comité de Coordination et d'Exécution* to ensure the programmatic and tactical unity of the FLN over and against the autonomy granted to the regional *wilayas* (Horne 1977: 145), dealt with two key programmatic points important for our analysis here. The first of these is the internationalization of the Revolution; that is, the Revolution needed to be more widely addressed in the international media and by allies of France, both inside and outside the UN. The second key point is the statement by the FLN that they would henceforth be seen as the only legitimate representative of the Algerian nation and its people. The intersection of these programmatic issues with the use of revolutionary violence represents, as we will see, the crux of the problem when looking at the ethical implications of the FLN.

One need not think long and hard to imagine how the Algerian Revolution, especially in the early years, would have been reported in the international media; examples of similar kinds of political issues abound. The fact that during the first two years of the Revolution most of the attacks engaged in by the FLN were against either Algerians or French soldiers, with the concomitant retributive acts by the latter, would not have merited much notice in the international media. However—and the FLN knew this—attacks on French civilians would compel the world to notice the Algerian problem. By this time, two key factors must be noted, more for contextual reasons than as justifications: the reciprocal violence between Algerians and *pieds-noirs* and French forces had ensured that there would be no way to keep European Algerian civilians neutral; and that after 1955, this polarization of the two communities ensured that "neither side made distinctions among individuals" (Hutchinson 1978: 53, 69).

By the start of the Battle of Algiers in 1956, both sides were almost indiscriminate in their use of violence against the other. The use of "isolation" tactics (ibid.: 62), focused on increasing the separation between Algerians and *pieds-noirs* in all aspects of life, in conjunction with "disorientation" tactics (68), worked to further the goal of making life for *colons* in Algeria intolerable, assuring that the French government would eventually negotiate sovereignty with the FLN. Violence used against members of the *pied-noir* community worked to demoralize and terrorize members of this community; and large-scale attacks, such as that on the Cafétéria and the Milk-Bar in Algiers in 1956, ensured that coverage of the Algerian conflict made the front pages of newspapers around the world (ibid.: 57). In addition, further fuel to this effort was given by the *pied-noir* community itself, as the French colonial admin-istration gave them the right to "defend themselves" against Algerian violence, which often meant either preemptive attacks on random Algerians or retributive attacks for acts of violence against the commu-nity. Eventually, the 1961 establishment of the OAS (*Organisation de l'Armée Secrète*), which was dedicated to enacting "counterinsurgency measures" against Algerians, whether members of the FLN or not, certainly did little to inhibit the tendency for reciprocating violence between the communities and virtually assured that the Algerian Revolution would make the news (ibid.: 55, 70–71; Heggoy 1972: 243). By the end of the war, the implementation of OAS *Instruction no. 29*, which pronounced the rejection of "any idea of defence in favour of a generalised offensive," and essentially declared war on both Algerians and the French government, ensured the continuation of bloodshed on both sides, and the final consolidation of FLN authority through vengeance tactics, through to the declaration of self-determination (Horne 1977: 516).

The precipitating act of the Battle of Algiers, a failed general strike by Algerians in 1956, was actually timed to match the UN General Assembly's discussions on the Algerian situation and the right of colo-nized countries to attain the self-determination granted to all peoples by the Universal Declaration of Human Rights (Horne 1977: 247). In part, this was a result of the increased international attention given to the FLN's claims; even the United States and United Kingdom became involved in the debate, forcing France at one point to withdraw from the North Atlantic Treaty Organization and stultifying relations between France and its traditional allies (ibid.: 315–316). Even the 1960 passage of UN Resolution 1514(XV), the "Declaration on the Granting of Independence to Colonial Countries and Peoples," can be seen as increasing the international motivation to solve what could more gener-ally be called "the colonial problem." The added pressure on the French government, especially after the failed *putsch* against de Gaulle and the establishment of the Fifth Republic, served to force France to legiti-mately deal with the FLN's demands for independence for Algeria, and is in part what ultimately caused France to accede to the FLN's demands. The internationalization of the conflict through the use of anti-European violence, though motivated almost equally by the counterviolence of the European community, was a large factor in bringing the Revolution to a politically successful conclusion for the FLN.

As well, the Soummam Declaration posited the FLN as the sole legitimate voice for Algeria. This was not simply a propagandistic statement by the FLN; by that time, the FLN had won the intra-Algerian struggle for dominance among the nationalist movements. Through the use of endorsement (eliciting an explicit statement of allegiance) and compliance (ensuring mere obedience, with or without a statement of allegiance) tactics, the FLN had virtually ensured that no other organization would challenge its authority as the representative of Algerians; however, it still had to work to maintain both internal control of its fighters and of members of the Algerian community within the areas under its control. The Soummam Conference itself had as one of its intentions the solution of internal conflicts within the FLN, namely between the internal and external leadership (those within Algeria, who handled the day-to-day direction of the Revolution, and those who were outside Algeria—in Tunisia, Morocco, Egypt, or imprisoned in France—who were supposed to make important materiel connections with other Arabic and supportive nations) (Heggoy 1972: 162–164). We can see, then, that just because the FLN had no external competitors for power, it still sought to consolidate its control in areas it governed and maintain its dominance. It did this through the continued use of endorsement tactics, ensuring that it could continue to recruit new members through people's outrage at French repression; through the use of violent attacks as a kind of "safety valve" for FLN soldiers who may have been getting bored; and through the use of obedience-inducing tactics for FLN soldiers, generally when the de Gaulle government made overtures of peace to *wilaya* leaders or to the FLN in general (Hutchinson 1978: 76–81). The FLN would also use violent tactics as a bargaining chip during the negotiations with France, as well as a tool with which *wilaya* commanders could remind the GPRA that the troops in the field were suffering. Violent attacks by segments of the FLN that were not necessarily authorized by the CCE or the GPRA served, in some sense, as a form of *boulitique*, working to ensure that the party from whom control was trying to be wrested did something stupid (Quandt 1969: 266–267). Rivalries among the FLN factions indeed continued and were exacerbated during the last three years of the Revolution, during which time violent attacks were used as a way of undercutting the position of the GPRA, or to punish *wilayistes* for these undermining moves (ibid.: 81–84). And even the massacres at Mélouza and Wagram in Kabylia, in which FLN soldiers killed nearly 350 Algerians who were suspected of being part of a new armed faction of the MNA called the *Armée Nationale du Peuple Algérien* (and therefore represented a threat to the control of the FLN over the revolution), worked as a macabre version of *méfiance*, and actually created the possibility for a "truce" between the FLN and MNA and a further consolidation of the FLN's dominance (Le Sueur 2001: 166–168).

Of course, the use of violence against individual threats to the FLN continued. Algerians who were "compromised" by their association with the French were frequently threatened and/or attacked, and "traitors," those who worked actively with the French—either as *harkis* (Algerian members of the French *gendarmerie*), as *bleus* (Algerian agents working with the regular French forces), or who reported on FLN activity to French forces—were regularly found with their throats slit or, in one instance, were massacred for their suspected involvement with the French (Hutchinson 1978: 64–67, 80). In some respects, this does not differ from what regular national armed forces do in the event of finding double agents or traitors during wartime, for which the usual punishment is execution; the difference here has to do with the element of proof—more often than not, the people executed by the FLN were merely suspected or were selected to intimidate others who might be considering similar kinds of actions. Yet, it does indicate the extent to which the FLN was willing to utilize Algerians as a kind of "cannon fodder"; to the FLN, the Algerians were—or rather, to use Sartre's terms, were made into—tools for revolutionary *praxis*. The problematic element here, though, was the extent of this habituated violence against suspected enemies to the cause.

Phase 3: Postrevolutionary Violence and the Delimitation of Democracy

As Horne points out, the principles described in the FLN's 1954 Declaration—the insistence that France deal with Algeria as a sovereign nation, the decision that all who remained in Algeria after independence would have the option of becoming true Algerians, and the demand for equality and liberty for the Algerian people—were held to throughout the Revolution (Horne 1977: 95–96). However, the problem with a revolution is that once a movement has won, they *really* have to win, meaning that the power they have won must be consolidated. And given that the FLN did not militarily win the Revolution, but rather that France decided it could no longer hold Algeria and gave it up, the FLN felt further pressure to consolidate its power over what was left of the competing nationalist parties and movements so that it could ensure its rule over postindependence Algeria.

Thus, after the conclusion of the negotiations at Évian and on the eve of the referendum confirming Algeria's independence from France, the power struggle between Ahmed Ben Bella, just released from a French prison, Ben Yousef Ben Khedda, head of the *Gouvernement Provisoire de la République Algérienne* (GPRA), and Houari Boumedienne, head of the ALN, blew into a nearly six-month-long civil war, a result of the tensions throughout the revolution between the internal FLN and the "army over the fence." In a classic instance of both *boulitique* and *méfiance* (Quandt 1969: 264–267), the personal rivalries between these three leaders, all clamoring to become what Lewis (1969: 328) calls "Algeria's paramount political mandarin," blew into an all-out power struggle, with the lives of Algerians caught in the middle. Ultimately, somewhere on the order of 15,000 Algerians lost their lives during the first summer of independence (Horne 1977: 537), all over the positions that each of the three leaders would hold in the new Algerian government—a government that had to be created *de novo*, since Algeria had not inherited a governmental apparatus, save for one that had been in exile during the entire Revolution.

Even beyond the postindependence civil war, the FLN enacted vengeance tactics against survivors of the war who had betrayed the revolutionary cause. The primary foci of these attacks were the *harkis*, Algerian members of the French *gendarmerie*, on whom France had turned its back. As Cohen points out, "But once De Gaulle accepted the Algerian nation, proclaiming it the inevitable result of the forces of history, their presence was an embarrassing reminder of the war, and France's failure to protect those Moslems it had rallied to the French flag and who had been the object of much sentiment in France" (Cohen 1980: 108). Of the nearly 200,000 Algerians who had served France as *policiers*, only about 52,000 ever made it to France, many of them secreted away by French officials (ibid.: 107; Talbott 1980: 246–247; FARAC 2001, para. 29). The rest, as Horne graphically describes, were brutally murdered in revenge for their actions during the war:

> Hundreds died when put to work clearing the minefields along the Morice Line, or were shot out of hand. Others were tortured atrociously; army veterans were made to dig their own tombs, then swallow their decorations before being killed; they were burned alive, or castrated, or dragged behind trucks, or cut to pieces and their flesh fed to dogs. Many were put to death with their entire families, including young

children.... Estimates of the numbers of Algerians thus killed vary wildly between 30,000 and 150,000. (Horne 1977: 537–538)

The fact that the French government mostly abandoned those who had worked for them under threat of death (and because it was one of the few paying occupations for Algerians during the war), and that the new Algerian government massacred them in revenge for their wartime activities for *raisons d'état* ("reasons of state," specifically the need to consolidate the state and to exact revenge against those who had worked against the FLN during the war; FARAC 2001, para. 43), indicate the lengths to which the FLN was willing to go for the sake of controlling Algeria and France was eager to put the war behind them. For France, the use of Algerian *harkis* (and its later rejection of them after they were no longer of use to France) against Algerians had continued the colonial logic of "divide and conquer"; for the FLN, the vengeful obliteration of those who had made their choice, whether out of fealty to France or the need for income during the Revolution, showed that the FLN was willing to ensure its dominance against all perceived threats to its newfound power, even if those threats were merely memories of the failure of revolutionary solidarity.

Furthering the FLN's dominance in the new Algeria was the extension of its Revolution-era insistence that it be the sole voice of Algeria. Despite the programmatic insistence that the Revolution was fought to bring democracy to Algeria, the FLN ensured that it was the only legitimate political party in the country. Working the heroic position of liberators of Algeria, the FLN was partially able to consolidate its position as the head of a one-party government based solely on the fact that it "won" the Revolution. In addition, the power struggle between Ben Bella, Boumedienne, and Ben Khedda, and the civil war it brought about were expanded to include purges of FLN members opposed to the personal authority of Ben Bella, and actions against individuals attempting to form other political parties (Horne 1977: 540). Despite the fact that the FLN itself did not have a coherent political program or ideological consistency, and was thereby unable to transition from "an eclectic wartime movement into an effective governing party" (Lewis 1969: 328), it was also unwilling to tolerate the existence of competing political parties. The FFS (*Front des Forces Socialistes*), headed by Aït Ahmed, was one of these parties that attempted to form, and included former *maquisards* and FLN members, including the leaders of *wilayas* III (Kabylia) and IV (Algérois) and Boudiaf, Khider, and Krim, all high-level FLN leaders (Heggoy 1969: 120–123). The 1963 border war with

Morocco led the FFS to declare a "truce" with the FLN to preserve the integrity of Algeria; however, on completion of that war, the FFS attempted to reorganize, an attempt that was quashed by its internal disorganization and the use of the ALN as a tool of repression (ibid.: 125; Lewis 1969: 334). In large part, though, the FFS, characterized as "the most important challenge to the system established by Ben Bella," failed because "the Algerians were too tired of war to care enough to risk anything substantial" (Heggoy 1969: 126), an apathy that enabled the FLN to institute itself as *the* government, succeeding in what may very well have been its goal all along.

The Colonial Situation, the Use of Violence, and the Colonial Habitus

Given the extreme measures the FLN took to win national liberation and to implement the program described in the 1954 Declaration, it would seem odd that at the end of everything, it would end up contravening its own goals. Much of this, though, has to do with the particularities of the situation in which it found itself fighting France.

The use of political violence in ways that could arguably be called "terrorist" (depending of course on one's definition of the term) seems on its face to be an utterly irrational choice. To pick a fight with a much larger military force; to attack troops and civilians with full foreknowledge of the repression to come; to attempt to bring about a great nationwide uprising with only about 3,000 troops at one's disposal—all these seem to be the mark of some kind of insanity. Yet the choice to use "terrorist" tactics is perfectly rational within the colonial situation as described by Fanon. As Hutchinson notes,

> In the case of the FLN, the dominant reason for choosing terrorism appears to have been its expected utility in achieving the insurgents' goals, despite the unquestionable influences of psychological, social, and organizational factors. [. . .] The key motivation for terrorism in a context in which the normal means of access to government (elections, political parties, interest groups, strikes or demonstrations) were denied was a willingness by the FLN to accept high risks and a considerable inequality of power between the revolutionary movement and the French regime. (Hutchinson 1978: 133–134)

The FLN found itself in exactly this situation: the means of political participation in the liberal sense were unavailable to Algerians; the disparities in the military materiel available to each side were huge; and it was becoming clear in the international realm that colonial countries were becoming less willing to maintain their hold on their colonies. Furthermore, the makeup of the colonial situation "provided the FLN with an emotional reservoir of mutual suspicion and a ready-made cleavage—social, cultural, religious, racial, economic, and above all political—to exploit" (ibid.: 131). And the colonial habitus, the sensibilities driven into Algerians by the colonial social order, made the goals the FLN had developed not only appealing, but also eminently viable, to Algerians. Offered a lifelong meal of *liberté, égalité, et fraternité*, yet denied the right to sit at the table and sup on Western humanism, Algerians had clearly sensed that they needed to be in charge of their situation; and the inferiority imposed on them by French colonialism in social, political, and economic terms ensured that they were ready to explode against their colonial oppressors. Fanon's phenomenological depiction of the effects of colonialism on the colonized provided confirmation of Algerians' suspicions of the nature of things. All Algerians needed was a catalyst, and the FLN provided that (Beckett 1973: 10–11). Given the tools the FLN had at their disposal, the choice of low-level political violence was rational.

The choice of political violence as a means to national liberation, then, should not be in question given the focus of this work and Fanon's analysis. What becomes problematic—and what will serve as the basis for the forthcoming ethical analysis of the Algerian Revolution—is the way in which the FLN deployed this tool in the pursuit of its goals. The deployment of political violence in the cause of national and social liberation can most definitely be understood, with certain exceptions, as ethical; the use of violence against the people on whose behalf a movement fights for independence, and for reasons of maintaining political dominance rather than ensuring a wide-scale social transformation, most certainly is not. Ultimately, where the Algerian Revolution fails in an ethical sense is in this latter use of violence. As we will see, in the notion of liberation Fanon's writings present as the *leitmotif* of the Algerian Revolution (and anticolonial violence more generally), there can be an ethics of violence twinned to an ethics of freedom; however, the one must be used in the furtherance of the other, and the FLN failed in this important respect.

Ethical Radicalism and the Algerian Revolution

To understand the import of the Algerian Revolution, particularly for the purposes of developing a resisting social ethics, we need to explore the ethical implications of the Revolution, both in terms of its goals and in terms of the means utilized to attain those goals. Following from the discussion in Chapters 2 and 3 about the makeup of an existentialist resisting ethics, the remainder of this discussion proceeds to evaluate the ethics present in the Algerian Revolution. There are to my mind two forms of ethics present in the historical track of the Revolution, as in any revolutionary moment: an *ethics of freedom*, in which the development of a situation of practical freedom for all by necessary means is a crucial good; and an *ethics of violence*, in which the use of violence as a means to attain a situation of concrete freedom can be ethically justified. This examination proceeds along the lines of measuring the "theory" of the revolutionary situation in Algeria—the ethics of freedom that motivated the ends posited by the FLN and Fanon—against the *praxis* of the Revolution as carried out by the FLN.[20]

Starting With an Ethics of Freedom: Decolonizing the Habitus
The first ontological shot of the Algerian Revolution, the Declaration of November 1, 1954, provides us with a starting point for developing the ethics of freedom I see as present in the plan of the Algerian Revolution. This declaration, as we have seen above, is steeped in the Western humanistic rhetoric of self-determination; claims to national sovereignty and independence, democracy, and equality of persons work to demand the construction of a situation radically different from that of French colonialism. This would also imply—nay, demand—the construction of a new kind of human being that would build and foster the continued construction of a new Algeria. The FLN, through its declarations and through the theoretical work of Fanon, made this at the very least the propagandistic reason for pursuing the Revolution. The overt goals of the Algerian Revolution would suggest, then, the idea of an ethics of freedom as motivating the movement toward liberation and would motivate Algerians to remake themselves, to destroy the colonial habitus in favor of building a new way of being in the world.

But what would be this "new kind of human being" that is the result of this clearing of the colonial habitus? For Fanon, the goal of the anti-colonial revolution is the creation of human beings who feel in a visceral way their interconnectedness with others. They are those who have known the oppression of the colonial era, the inequalities that colonialism forced upon them, and the sense of being both part of the revolutionary whole and of encompassing the entire Algerian nation within themselves through their action, and who no longer want to live without that whole. They are also those who know the experience of an absolute lack of freedom. The fighting of the Revolution signifies the elimination of a type of "interference" with Algerians' affairs—the elimination of a class that interferes with the self-determination of the Algerian peoples. And yet, as Berlin rightly points out, freedom can mean nothing if it is not discussed in the context of the pauperized nation. Without more-than-adequate food, clothing, shelter, education, and resources for the development of the people as people, freedom is a purely academic concept: "It is true that to offer political rights, or safeguards against intervention by the state, to men who are half-naked, illiterate, under-fed, and diseased is to mock their condition; they need medical help or education before they can understand, or make use of, an increase in their freedom. What is freedom to those who cannot make use of it? Without adequate conditions for the use of freedom, what is the value of freedom?" (Berlin 1969: 125–126). So it is, then, that during the revolutionary struggle land and dignity are the highest priorities (Fanon 1963: 44–45); but after independence is won, the goal of developing a new kind of human being by developing a new kind of freedom has as its first practical step the development of a standard of living in which "freedom" would actually mean something. If we take Berlin's words as having a direct bearing on the Algerian situation, the depauperization of Algeria would be as important as the decolonization of the country and its people. The development of freedom in the decolonizing society, following this logic, would then depend on the development of a society in which every individual has adequate means to make use of the kind of freedom they as a people decide upon.

In other words, the development of freedom for all requires a fundamental change in all levels of our conditions of existence: existential, economic, social-ethical, and political. Existentially, the development of a new kind of social freedom requires changes in the way in which one exists with others. Economically, one must have adequate resources to take advantage of and enact the kind of freedom brought about by the people. Socially and ethically, interpersonal relations must be such so that the condition of freedom can be maintained. And politically, freedom must be ensured for all through injunctions against the amassing and exercise of arbitrary state or individual power. In sum, the development of a situation of practical freedom for all would require the decolonization of the colonial habitus.

The first step in the decolonization of the colonial habitus as described earlier in this work would be manifested in social and existential terms the transition from seriality to the pledge group. The universalization of the experience of revolution; the transport of the radio listener to the Revolution and vice versa; the terroristic Third that is the constant threat of French attacks on the revolutionaries and on the radio listeners—all these create the conditions that allow for the necessary transition of the serial individual into a member of the pledge group. Recalling the earlier discussion of the pledge group, we can see that this step is necessary in the creation of a revolutionary movement. As Ruedy put it, "8,500,000 people do not simultaneously initiate any enterprise" (1992: 156), but it is necessary in the revolutionary context to get as many of them as possible *involved* in the enterprise. And once this mobilization is afoot, the consciousness that the one is part of the many is inescapable and necessary: "The practice of violence binds them together as a whole, since each individual forms a violent link in the great chain, a part of the great organism of violence which has surged upward in reaction to the settler's violence in the beginning" (Fanon 1963: 93–94). The radio network *Voice of Fighting Algeria* (Fanon 1965: 84, 89, 93), in conjunction with Fanon's writings in *El Moudjahid* and the FLN's attacks on "Muslim collaborators," helps to construct this pledge group through the collectivization of the experience of colonial victimization, of fighting in the Revolution, and the delivery of messages regarding the necessity of one's participation in the Revolution (through the execution of proven "counterrevolutionary collaborators").

The second step in the colonized subject's changing of their habitus is the enactment of the reversal of their "structured structures" that tell them that their place in the colonial order is "the last" rather than "the first." This second step, I would argue, amounts to the assertion of the hegemonic habitus within the colonial situation. By asserting the *particular* form of humanity that characterizes the colonizer, the colonized begins the process of developing a counterhegemonic habitus. The colonizer's version of "humanity" means violence against us, the colonized subject says; so in order to assert our "humanity" as we know it (from the wrong end of colonial violence), we will redirect colonial violence against the regime and its perpetrators in all of us (Beckett 1973: 9). This is Fanon's "first step" in overthrowing the colonial regime: "The well-known principle that all men are equal will be illustrated in the colonies from the moment that the native claims that he is the equal of the settler. One step more, and he is ready to fight to be more than the settler. In fact, he has already decided to eject him and to take his place . . ." (Fanon 1963: 44–45). Once the colonized decide to assert their equality to and their humanity from the colonizer, they have committed themselves to revolution. Since the ontological background for the colonial system is one of "humans versus nonhumans," for the purported "nonhumans" to rise up in defiance of this, it is necessary to realize that this will incur violence against them by the hegemon, and in turn, that *les colonisés* must resort to violence to back up their claims of equality.

The third step in the clearing of the colonial habitus would be to go past the old hegemonic order, that is, to find a new conception of humanity to hold to, one that is better than the former conception of "humanity" that enabled exploitation, institutionalized violence against the people, arbitrary arrests, beatings, torture, and death. It is on the issue of torture that this becomes most clear in Fanon's writings. The torture and subsequent murder of Ali Boumendjel, a Paris-trained Algerian lawyer accused of distributing literature for the FLN, made clear that French forces, especially the paratroop divisions, were practicing torture against arrested Algerians and refusing to turn them over to the *procureur général* office for prosecution (Talbott 1980: 90; Maran 1989: 170; cf. Aussaressess 2002). The public outcry in France against this event and other instances of the torture of Algerian prisoners showed that French paratroopers especially, but French forces in general, were engaged in an excessive campaign against the Algerian population, rebel and civilian alike. Groups ranging from the Catholic *Comité de Résistance spirituelle* to Sartre and Merleau-Ponty's journal *Les temps modernes* decried the excesses of the French troops, critiques often supported by eyewitness or participant accounts of the torture. Against this so-called "Gestapo in Algeria" (Talbott: 1980: 91–96), the FLN decided that rather than engaging in the same kinds of excesses against French troops, they would refrain from the use of torture in an effort to be better than the colonizer. As Fanon reports,

> In a war of liberation, the colonized people must win, but they must do so cleanly, without "barbarity." The European nation that practices torture is a blighted nation, unfaithful to its history. The underdeveloped nation that practices torture thereby confirms its nature, plays the role of an underdeveloped people. If it does not wish to be morally condemned by the "Western nations," an underdeveloped nation is obliged to practice fair play, even while its adversary ventures, with a clean conscience, into the unlimited exploration of new means of terror. . . . (Fanon 1965: 24–25)

This is quite obviously a tactical move, intending to ensure that the image of "Algeria" as a barbaric, uncivilized nation would be countered through the absence of torture on their part, thereby making them look "better" than the French. As well, the use of torture against the French would confirm the French mode of recognition—that the Algerians were an uncivilized people that only understood violence (cf. Maran 1989: 157, 159; Horne 1977: 134). But more important than that,

I would argue, is the *prima facie* intent behind this move: to really bring about a new kind of humanity, one who in the face of the violent reprisals of the French refused to engage in a *quid pro quo* with regard to torture. The FLN directives to not use torture against its enemy, and its condemnation (and even execution; see Fanon 1965: 25) of those who engaged in torture against the French, show that the *quid pro quo* that characterized past resistance to French rule should no longer have a place in a situation dedicated to the creation of this new kind of human being. As we will see later, the emphasis on the righteousness of the war against the French did not carry over to the means used to ensure the compliance of Algerians with FLN rule.

So how does the exposure of the colonial habitus translate itself into what I would call an ethics of freedom? The colonial habitus is that set of structures that make possible the colonized subject—the Algerian who sees themselves as the colonizers claim to see them, as someone who could potentially be brought up to the "human" level through exposure to the "civilizing" process that is colonialism. The colonized subject's success, in this view, is dependent upon their ability to "play along" with their subaltern role without even realizing how they have been subordinated; their failure would be to realize how they have been subordinated through their habitus and act against it. What begins as a micro-level analysis of the functioning of the colonial habitus translates into the exposure of the macro-level impact of that habitus; put another way, the success of the hegemonic order in maintaining the colonial habitus within individuals results in the maintenance of the status quo, while its failure resulted in the overturning of the colonial order.

It is the work of the FLN and its universalization of the colonial habitus that makes possible the transition to the next stage of clearing the colonial habitus—the assertion of the colonized subject's equality to the colonizer. This step, I would argue, is necessary both for the development of the revolution in a practical sense (i.e., the development of the collective consciousness of oppression) and for the development of an authentic decolonization. As Gordon points out, "authenticity" (using Sartre's term) is the realization of the bare fact of a person's choice to hold to certain beliefs in order to construct and identify their "true" self (that of a free, active, choosing being): "Authenticity is a form of 'self-recovery of being which was previously corrupted.' It is a form of taking hold of existence from a choice of bad faith. . . . To provide a theory of authenticity therefore requires a prescription of 'therapy' for the serious man" (Gordon 1994: 61). In the Algerian context, this "'therapy' for the serious man" is the Revolution. The state of "bad faith" the colonized subject was in prior to their engagement with the Revolution was *imposed* on them by the colonial situation. The colonial situation, which held Algerians out to be proto-humans, able to be "civilized" yet at the same time refusing them this move toward "civilization," kept the colonized subject in a state of bad faith by demanding of them that they "allow themselves" to be "civilized" by the colonizer, something that was refused to them through their situatedness in the colonial context. Hence, this form of bad faith was a demand on their existence, one that, if satisfied, eliminated their existence to both parties in this bifurcated world. In essence, the colonial situation removed the possibility of choice from the existence of the colonized subject; it made it impossible to choose to meet this "colonial demand," and it made it impossible not to meet the demand.

The first stage of clearing the colonial habitus is this realization that choice has been removed from their sphere of existence. The picking-up of arms by the revolutionaries oriented them to the fact of their existence as choosing beings. The assertion of the stance of the dominated—showing how Algerians as a whole were made less human by what the colonizer says they are—puts them in a position of being able to choose to be less or more than they are through their engagement in the Revolution. By giving back to the colonized subject their choice about the path of their existence, the second stage of the clearing of the colonial habitus can occur through their decision to engage themselves in the war against the colonizer. It is the choice of the colonized subject to resist that shows them that they have the possibility to choose their own way of life. This choice, though, is not made for the sake of "being authentic"; rather, it is a choice made to have the power to determine a new path for the colonized. This second stage of the clearing of the colonial habitus is not yet authentic, though, because even though it is *of* the situation (i.e., it is an "immediate" choice to revolt against the colonizer, to assert one's equality with them, to struggle to rid one's country of them), it is still *defined* by the situation. The goal of the choice (to get rid of the colonizer) and the means of the action (the use of violence against those who have used violence against us) are both still defined by the situation and only exist because of the situation, not because of our human reality. They are demands from our reality, to use Gordon's words, but they are also demands on our reality.

Following this reading of Fanon, it would be in the third stage of the decolonization of the habitus that the actions of the formerly colonized could become "authentic." Once the war for independence is won, the possibility is there for the world to exist anew for the decolonizing subjects. Neither the means nor the goal of the establishment of a postcolonial society are defined by the situation; the Algerian people should be enabled to choose for themselves how their social relations should be. Gordon's "demand from our reality" is this: the decolonizing subject needs to choose for themselves how they will be among others; they must choose the beliefs that will, once enacted, order their society; they must choose between recreating the colonial regime's *ethos* based on a presumption of difference through negation or a presumption of the similarity of all human beings *qua* human beings; and they must choose their orientation to this choice of belief system (Gordon 1994: 153). But rather than the "radical freedom" attributed to Sartre, this kind of freedom to attempt to create anew the Algerian social order stems from the realization of the humanity of the decolonizing subjects in the second stage of the clearing of the colonial habitus, and would need to authentically work in concert with that humanity. The value system by which decolonized Algeria could recreate itself needed to be one that was authentically chosen by the people and actualized through the party, rather than one imposed by the party upon the people. So, we can see that what I have called the clearing of the colonial habitus, on closer examination, would be a move by the decolonizing subjects toward an "authentic" existence that is freely chosen on their own. The three different stages of the clearing of the habitus reflect the moves that would be needed to make the transition from an existence lived in "bad faith," albeit a bad faith that is imposed on the colonized subjects by their situatedness in the colonial context, to an authentic existence in which the decolonizing subjects realize their ability to choose their own path freely.

This attempted move toward an authentic existence embodies the development of an ethics of freedom in the language and the theory of the anticolonial revolution. There is, in the first instance, an "ethics of recognition," to use Honneth's (1995) terms: the attempts by both the group that I have called the "doubly alienated" and the resisting Algerians constitute a struggle for the recognition of their humanity by the colonizer. The primary focus of this struggle is the ethical call by the colonized subject for the colonizer to see them as human in the colonized's own terms rather than the ontological terms of Western humanism. Through this struggle, especially after its universalization within the colonial context, the colonized subject both realizes and asserts their humanity. They realize it in the moment in which they choose to no longer tolerate the oppression of the colonial context, and they assert it in the moment at which they say, with words or bullets, that they are equal to the colonizer. This movement constitutes an ethics of recognition because it has as its focus the recognition of two separate aspects of colonial life: the recognition of the true nature of colonial violence, its alienation of the colonized subject from themselves and from others in the same situation through the construction of them as mere factical beings; and the struggle to obtain the recognition of their humanity from both the colonizer and other colonized subjects. The move made in the act of revolutionary violence was not to have been just a political one, in the sense of replacing one form of government with another or one ruling party with another; it was also to be an ethical one, replacing one kind of human being and one mode of social relations and interactions with an entirely new one. It is this struggle that appears parallel to the first two stages of the clearing of the colonial habitus.

Beyond this struggle for an ethics of recognition, there lies an ethics of choosing. Recognition is, in this view, only the first step in the transition to an "authentic" existence on the part of the decolonizing subjects. Their authenticity lies in realizing that the only fact of human existence must be the fact of choice—that is, the fact of the freedom on the part of both individuals and collectivities to choose their own life-project given the material that they are provided with through their situatedness—and that requires a situation in which this fact of choice can be realized through the exercise of individual and collective agency. In the colonial situation, the material provided to the colonized subject prevents the free choice and active development of a life-project; all aspects of the colonial situation exclude the possibility for the free choice of a life-project on the part of the colonized subject and, to a similar extent, the colonizer. For the colonized subject, the choice is, as Fanon poignantly put it, to "turn white or disappear"; for the colonizer, the choice is to be the master or to betray one's race (Fanon 1967: 100; cf. Sartre 1976 [1948]). In either case, the possibility of an authentic existence is denied by the colonial situation; for both colonized and colonizer, the necessity of the reproduction of the colonial situation makes it impossible to do anything but act out the role preassigned to the individuals on either side of the line by the fact of their skin color. This can be seen in Sartre's preface to *The Wretched of the Earth*:

> . . . we in Europe too are being decolonized: that is to say that the settler which is in every one of us is being savagely rooted out. Let us look at ourselves, if we can bear to, and see what is becoming of us. First, we must face that unexpected revelation, the strip tease of our humanism. There you can see it, quite naked, and it's not a pretty sight. It was

nothing but an ideology of lies, a perfect justification for pillage; its honeyed words, its affectation of sensibility were only alibis for our aggressions. (Sartre 1963: 24–25)

If we too are being decolonized, it is because the colonial situation had colonized all of us in the first place. The colonial situation—and even beyond the colonial situation, any sociohistorical situation characterized by exploitation, domination, and unfreedom—puts us all in the position of both victim and executioner: victims, because we have been put into a situation in which the only possibility for existence was one characterized by "bad faith"; and executioners, because we refused to act to eliminate the colonial situation and therefore, by leaving ourselves in the situation of "bad faith," became complicit with the oppression and murder of people far across the globe.

Taken together, these aspects of the anticolonial revolution can be seen as exhibiting an ethics of freedom: its purpose, the elimination of the colonial regime and the concomitant creation of a new version of humanity, would free us all. As Fanon points out, the decolonizing subject wants to know the humanity of all, even that of the colonizer: "The new relations are not the result of one barbarism replacing another barbarism, of one crushing of man replacing another crushing of man. What we Algerians want is to discover the man behind the colonizer; this man who is both the organizer and the victim of a system that has choked him and reduced him to silence" (Fanon 1965: 32). The anticolonial revolution has as its existential outcome the possibility of a return to an "authentic" existence—that of the possibility of a free choice, made from the materials provided by the decolonized situation, that is oriented to as a free choice for all. This return to authenticity creates the existential conditions within which freedom has a real meaning, one created by the people who fought for this freedom. Rather than merely inverting the social structure of the colonial regime and thereby refusing the dialectical transcendence of the "master/slave" narrative, as some critics have argued (Alessandrini 1995: 65), I would argue that the liberation effected by the anticolonial revolution is one in which the constructedness of the postcolonial situation is laid bare and one in which all people *should* have the socially structured opportunity to help create a new world in which the stratification, bifurcation, and oppression of the colonial situation no longer has a place. In Gordon's words, this liberation is our freedom from an existence characterized by pure *presence*—that is, characterized by being-in-itself (Gordon 1994: 134); the move in the third stage of the clearing of the colonial habitus, that stage which parallels the move toward authentic existence, would require that our being-for-itself, our free, choosing, and creating (and destroying) being, work in the situation to build anew.

The essence of freedom, though, lies in our interconnectedness with others. In the colonial context, the situation is one in which everyone—colonizer and colonized alike—is forced by the nature of the social situation to see every other human being as facticity, as being-in-itself. In the postcolonial context, the humanity of all has been revealed, sought out, and enacted through the violence of the revolution. This situation, in which it is *possible* to create a new social situation out of and beyond the meanings of the old, is one in which the freedom of others becomes of prime importance. During the Revolution, the social lived through the actions of the individual, and hence the act of resistance taken on by an individual was done for the sake of Others; in other words, the freedom of the individual to engage in anticolonial resistance became the embodiment of the freedom of all others to engage in revolutionary acts. The postcolonial era, I argue, should be no different: the freedom of the decolonizing subject to help create a new social situation is *and must have as its primary concern* ensuring that this act of creation is one in which the possibility for others to participate in its creation is maintained. The bond of freedom that Merleau-Ponty identified as being dependent upon the freedom of others means that the construction of a new society requires that the freedom of others to pursue their own paths *within the postcolonial situation* be ensured through every action.

Put another way, an ethics of freedom lies in the reclamation of human agency over and against practico-inert social structures and practices and those who maintain them. The maintenance of these oppressive and/or dominating social structures require either active participation in the associated practices or a bystander position with regards to them, both of which leave one with "dirty hands"; if one chooses not to act against oppression, one is involved in the oppression, be it in their backyard or across the world. To act against them, of course, leaves one with dirty hands as well—resistant actions always require the sacrifice of one's good standing in the dominant social order—but in this resistance, the actor reclaims their agency and works to reclaim the agency of all through their action. And, as this existentialist analysis of the Algerian Revolution has shown, this agency is the heart of freedom; one cannot be free, after all, only in one's mind or outside of history. It was the enactment of this ethics of freedom and of this call for the reclamation of the agency of the people that motivated the pursuit of the Algerian Revolution; but, the development of the idea of this ethics of revolutionary ends requires the counterpart of the ethicality of the means to implement this ethics of freedom.

Developing an "ethics of violence"?

Within the colonial situation, or any situation characterized by exploitation, oppression, and unfreedom, the possibilities for reclaiming this agency through the practice of an ethics of freedom are limited if not non-existent. When life is oriented to survival, when all those on your "side of the fence" have been reduced to soulless, non-actional people, the chances for enacting this kind of ethics are slim to none. Eliminating the social structures and interactions that impose this mode of inauthentic existence on people becomes paramount to making oneself "human" again. Hence, the enactment of an ethics of freedom would, in this kind of situation, mandate the pursuit of an *ethics of violence*, one that has liberation as its goal and, following Sartre's words in the *Rome Lectures*, contains the end it works for within the means used to get there.

All revolutions—indeed, according to the existentialists, all political and social orders—are predicated upon violence. And since all forms of social change, revolutionary or otherwise, are constructed by the social order from which they spring, violence can be *and needs to be* ethically legitimated as a means of social change if one is working from within a context of violence. In the concrete case of Algeria, the ontological violence of the status separations between "colonizer" and "colonized" were reinforced through a daily violence against the colonized subject's ability to freely determine their life, their ability to make a standard of living that allows them to become more than they are, and against their person. The construction of the colonial situation through violence, then, begets the violence against the colonial situation in the Revolution's efforts to liberate the Algerian people, to decolonize them, and to make them "human" again (Beckett 1973: 9–10). For Fanon, it was essential that the reclamation of the colonized subject's humanity take place through violence: "He of whom *they* have never stopped saying that the only language he understands is that of force, decides to give utterance by force. In fact, as always, the settler has shown him the way he should take if he is to become free. The argument the native chooses has been furnished by the settler . . ." (Fanon 1963: 83–84). Violence was, as Beckett reminds us (1973: 9), to be both an instrument for the elimination of French colonial rule over Algeria and a solution in itself for the unification of the decolonizing colonial subjects with the nation in formation as a whole. The instrumental element raised by

Beckett is satisfied; the French give up their control over Algeria as a result of the Revolution. The question for us becomes whether or not the latter element, the *ethical* element of this violence, actually occurs.

The Ethics of Violence Against the Pieds-Noirs

Unlike other colonies around the world, the situation in French-controlled Algeria can best be described as a form of "settler colonialism," in which control over a colony is deepened not by injecting increasing numbers of military personnel into a country, but instead by sending large numbers of settlers as a way of furthering the economic and political ties between mother country and colony (Good 1976: 597–601). By deploying large numbers of settlers, what starts off as a purely military situation becomes more complex and multifaceted, so that by the end of this phase of development, the colony is essentially controlled by the settlers more so than the mother country. For the mother country, settler colonialism, as the French Minister of War put it in 1843, works "to sanction, to consolidate, and to simplify the occupation we achieve by arms" (ibid.: 601). This form of colonialism works to transplant a much more vicious version of the capitalist class structure into the colony, so that the settlers effectively serve as a version of the bourgeoisie, leaving the colonized as a proletariat class worse off than that the settlers left at home. The power the *pied-noir* community exerted against the metropolitan French political system gives a sense of the importance of the maintenance of this kind of colony for France; that is, the fact that multiple French governments abandoned radical reforms of the colonial system in Algeria in favor of placating the *pieds-noirs* is a testament to the extent to which the settler community could influence the political process.

As such, it is a bit facile to see the *pieds-noirs* in Algeria as merely "civilians" and any kind of violence against them as ethically unjustifiable. To be sure, many French Algerians were sympathetic to the nationalist claims of the FLN, MTLD, and MNA at the early stages of the Revolution; they felt that France did not necessarily need to be in control of Algeria any longer, or at the very least believed that Algerians deserved to be treated as equal to the French in all spheres of social life. In large part, this group of potential sympathizers with the FLN cause is the reason why attacks on Europeans were prohibited during the first two years of the Revolution; however, as the Revolution became more entrenched, mobilizing that support for the FLN cause became more difficult, and eventually this group was lumped in with the rest of the *colons* (Hutchinson 1978: 53). That larger *colon* community—those who employed and exploited Algerians, worked to consolidate their control over Algerian land (in 1954, 1,000 *colons* owned one-seventh of the arable land in Algeria; Good 1976: 603), and who resisted any and all calls to view Algerians as equally human and deserving of political, social, and economic participation—was not at all empathetic with the nationalist cause. The eventual unification of these two groups in opinion, attitude, and action merited in the FLN's eyes their treatment as "the exploiting class," as well as the ensuing attacks on them.

Crenshaw's criteria for evaluating the ethicality of the choice of targets of political violence claim that individuals who "are harmful . . . because they are decision-makers or uniformed agents who are responsible for the state of injustice" can be ethically legitimized as targets, whereas "citizens of the state, with no public role . . . are harmless, although passive obedience to the rules of an unjust regime incurs some moral responsibility" (Crenshaw 1983: 4). In the Algerian case, we can at least understand the FLN's position that *colons* were directly harmful to Algerians, that they were responsible for the state of injustice, and that they held a public role (namely the control they wielded over colonial policy); all of the different ways in which the violence that inheres to the colonial system discussed earlier in this chapter indicate to us the reasons for this argument. This position, especially in its post-1956 formulation that all *colons* were enemies to the nationalist cause, ignores the possibility that individual settlers were sympathetic to or supportive of the FLN's agenda, and in its lumping-together of sympathizers with oppressors makes anyone into an object of revolutionary violence. But as we saw in Merleau-Ponty's analysis of French life under German control, life under occupation leads those under the occupation to view the occupiers as merely markers of their position in a system so as not to validate the control (Merleau-Ponty 1964: 142). This is why, when Camus calls for a truce and cessation of attacks on both French and Algerian civilians because, as he puts it, "les armes ne distinguent plus l'homme de la femme, ni le soldat de l'ouvrier" ("weapons neither distinguish between women and men, nor soldiers from workers"; Camus 1958: 174), neither side can do it (cf. Aronson 2004a).[21] For the FLN and French forces (and after 1961, the OAS), people on the "other side," regardless of efforts to see them as sympathetic or even contributing to the cause, are simply the other side, and their particularities no longer matter. The *pieds-noirs*, just like the French armed forces and *gendarmerie*, do not distinguish between individual Algerians; given the nature of the colonial system and colonial habitus, it would be difficult to ethically require, or even to envision, that Algerians do the same in their attacks, regardless of their efforts to do so in the early years of the Revolution. It is thus not impossible to see why it is that attacks on "the French," regardless of their position within the colonial system, were ethically justified for the FLN. To the mind of Algerians living under French rule, every *colon* was a sign that Algerian liberation had not yet been won.

The Ethics of Violence Against Algerians
As we have seen, the FLN used violence against fellow Algerians in a variety of positions for a variety of reasons that fit into the different aspects of their revolutionary agenda, reasons that can roughly be grouped, following Sartre, into "fraternity" reasons and "terror" reasons. It is important to use this approach at this point because it enables us to examine the paradoxical and ultimately ethically self-defeating ethical aspects of this element of the FLN's revolutionary practice.

Fanon's argument about the effects of revolutionary violence, namely that it enables the unification of the colonized people in pursuit of their liberation, constitutes the "fraternity" element of this revolutionary conduct. By picking up arms against the French, individual Algerians became coupled with the rest of the Algerian nation, and worked to eliminate two victims of the colonial system—the French colonizer, and the colonized subhuman within the Algerian. Given this phenomenology of revolutionary experience, we can see why steps taken by the FLN to inspire, induce, or coerce the participation of Algerians in the Revolution can be seen as ethical. Acts of violence against the French regime, intended to ensure a swift and brutal reprisal by French forces against innocent Algerians, were a sure way to highlight the violence inherent in the colonial system. By calling out French forces and compelling them to attack Algerians, the FLN could make sure that it had a steady supply of volunteers for the revolutionary forces, thereby enabling the sense of national solidarity Fanon describes in *The Wretched of the Earth*. This, though, required the use of violence; and while the FLN did not directly wield this form of violence against Algerians, was designed to ensure that they would suffer the impact of French colonial violence more clearly than they did prior to the Revolution. In increasing the population that directly understood how violent French colonialism could be, the FLN was sure to foster some degree of national consciousness.

Other acts of violence used against Algerians, though, blur the line between "fraternity"-oriented violence and sheer terror. Violence used to eliminate parties competing with the FLN for dominance in the revolutionary movement, such as the MNA and MTLD, is one form of this ethically tense violence. In attacking members of other nationalist organizations, the FLN could be seen to be fostering a form of nationalist solidarity among these opposition parties; tactically speaking, in the revolutionary context the colonized need to have a unified voice with which they speak and act, and the existence of multiple and competing organizations can—and at some points during the Revolution, did—serve to fracture the movement by providing alternate groups for negotiation and by continuing the colonialist tactic of "divide and conquer." In pursuing this tack, though, the FLN makes clear one of its key goals, namely positioning itself as the dominant party in the post-revolutionary era. It is this goal that taints the ethical possibilities that inhered to the way the FLN went about developing a nationalist consciousness and solidarity; after all, when the message the FLN sends out through its actions is "join us or die," it is hard to see the kind of voluntarism and spontaneity Fanon saw as necessary to the success of the anticolonial revolution.

Attacks on members of rival nationalist organizations, such as the MNA and MTLD, display the terroristic aspect of this duality. If the goal of the FLN was to unify the Algerian people in revolutionary fraternity, then the best way to approach the existence of other nationalist organizations was simply to work with them; as it was, surviving members of the MNA and MTLD, among other groups, ended up joining the FLN because they felt that the FLN was the only legitimate voice of the Algerian people, which appears *ex post facto* to obviate the need for attacks on these organizations. In the heat of the revolution, perhaps some degree of bullying might be in order; the need to motivate millions of people to rise against a system that had dominated their lives for years might justify some degree of arm-twisting. And yet, the FLN pursued an ongoing struggle, often using means that could easily be called "terroristic," to consolidate its position of leadership of Algeria even from the first days of the Revolution. It did this, as many scholars have noted, solely to take control of Algeria after the Revolution, thereby ensuring that "the last shall be first" without giving those who were truly last in colonial Algeria—ordinary Algerians—the opportunity to decide this for themselves. Beyond the effort to consolidate its own post-revolutionary position through attacks on other nationalist organizations, the FLN also attacked the people it was supposed to be mobilizing in the revolutionary effort. The kinds of attacks discussed earlier—the elimination of villages that supported or tolerated French troops, retributive attacks on those who informed on the FLN, and even the use of ordinary Algerians as "cannon fodder" for the legitimation of vengeance attacks on the *gendarmerie* and the *pieds-noirs*—indicates the fundamental tensions in the ethics of violence the FLN used during the Revolution.

This ethics, I argue, has two aspects. First, it involves the prioritization of the Algerian nation over the particular persons of Muslim "collaborators." By attacking those Algerians who would participate, for whatever reason, in the maintenance of the colonial system, the FLN was sending a message to all Algerians: your participation in the colonial system will kill you; whether by our hands quickly or by French hands in a slower manner, the result is the same. The ethical perspective at work here is one of a historically oriented consequentialism: from the point of view of the development of the nation and therefore the potential fruition of concrete freedom, Algerians who continue to participate in the colonial system are for the FLN as harmful to the development of a free Algerian nation as the French paratroopers who captured and tortured Algerians. The claim of Algerian collaboration, it would appear, stems directly from the admonitions of Sartre regarding one's position vis-à-vis resistance: "Very well then; if you're not victims when the government you've voted for, when the army in which your younger brothers are serving without hesitation or remorse have undertaken race murder, you are, without a shadow of a doubt, executioners" (Sartre 1963: 24–25). While Sartre's words, in this case, are directed at the French readers of Fanon's *The Wretched of the Earth*, they are the same words he and Merleau-Ponty have used elsewhere in their criticisms of Camus's decision to not support the Algerian nationalists, for example, to express this sentiment: if you do nothing to increase the human freedom in the world by resisting, in whatever form you can, the oppression of others, then you are the oppressor because you allow this to occur.

Second, from the point of view of the FLN, these attacks work to consolidate their control over the Algerian population, making easier the transition to its solitary political rule after the Revolution. By eliminating those Algerians who continued to maintain the colonial system, even if it is through their decision not to revolt against it, the FLN eliminated those it constructed as collaborating with the colonial order, if not as outright maintaining the oppression of Algerians. Muslim maintenance of the colonial system, even if it is through such seemingly innocuous means as paying one's taxes, is, by this reasoning, the perpetuation of the "natives' " existence, *but this time by the natives themselves.* In addition, the requirements of any revolutionary movement, including the mobilization of an entire population, require the transcendence of the "divide and conquer" mentality of the colonial regime, a mentality the existence of these "collaborators" shows quite clearly, as they are part of the oppressed supporting the oppressors: "Violence is in action all-inclusive and national. It follows that it is closely involved in the liquidation of regionalism and of tribalism. Thus the national parties show no pity at all toward the *caids* and the customary chiefs. Their destruction is the preliminary to the unification of the people" (Fanon 1963: 94). So, the deaths of "collaborators" at the hands of the FLN were, from the FLN's point of view, the deaths of colonizers within the bodies and minds of the colonized. Sadly, the overall message of the FLN's efforts to elicit and ensure compliance with its goals ended up being "join the FLN or die."

The message of FLN attacks on Muslim "collaborators," then, is twofold. First, it is the clearest statement of the principle of collaboration: by not actively resisting oppression in whatever way you can, you participate in that oppression and therefore open yourself up as a target for the resistance movement. It simultaneously blurs and clarifies the lines between the positions (rather than the actual personages) of colonizer and colonized. The attacks blur the lines between "colonizer" and "colonized" in two ways. First, the invocation of Western "humanism," with both its civilized and violent aspects, against humanists has led, as we have seen, to extreme forms of violence enacted by Algerians against Algerians. This would seem to put the FLN in the same category as the French colonial forces—those who would engage in acts of violence against the Algerian people for their own gain. The second way in which these attacks seem to blur the apparently clear status differential between colonizer and colonized is by putting the "Muslim collaborators" in the same status position as the *colons*, that is, by implicating Algerians who, wanting to live the life they knew without any apparent desire to perpetuate the colonial system, go "through the motions": they pay their taxes, humbly serve their *colon* bosses or masters, and live their lives without any apparent risk because they are not "rocking the boat." Without intending it, then, those Algerians who are not yet part of the anticolonial revolution end up replicating the system that makes it impossible for them to live their lives as they would want to live them. There are many different ways to speak of this group of people—for Sartre, they would be in "bad faith," unaware of their own human potential because they are "stuck" living out their "seriality," their inertia, and their "facticity"; for Bourdieu, they would be reenacting their habitus, structured as it is by the colonial system and structuring their lives so that they replicate the system, because they were unable to see a way out of this cycle.

FLN attacks on this group of Algerians, from this point of view, would seem from this perspective to be misplaced and ultimately exerting the same kind of coercion as the *colons* over the people who simply want to live their lives. These attacks, to those who survive them, might appear to serve notice that all who do not cooperate with the FLN die, and would ultimately exact this cooperation out of simple fear for one's life. But, these attacks also clarify the lines by effectively identifying all those, Algerian or French, Arab or European, who perpetuate the oppressive colonial system, and all those who do not actively resist are perpetrators, regardless of the color of their skin.

It is this messy aspect of any resistance movement that I argue provides us with the kinds of lessons to further our task of developing a resisting social ethics. What this conundrum identifies for us is an important issue—that of intentionality versus consequentiality. Which of these aspects of the analysis and practice of ethics is more important? Put simply, both are important. Let us take an "intentionality/consequentiality" comparison of these two perspectives on these attacks. In the intentionality column, we would see that for the FLN, the stated intentions behind this intra-Algerian violence are two-fold: it wants to mobilize the entire population in its struggle against French colonial rule so as to create a set of social conditions in which Algerians can freely and *en toto* determine their own future and path; and they want to draw the lines between "colonizer" and "colonized" as ontological (rather than practical) categories so that the Algerian people can "choose sides." For the "collaborators," their intention would be to assure their security vis-à-vis the colonizer by following all the rules, both those codified in the form of law and those that appear in the colonial habitus. Ruedy's comment (1992: 157) that the bulk of the Algerian population was "resigned" to the dominance of the French colonial system at the start of the Revolution should not be taken as an indication that this group necessarily wanted the continuation of the colonial regime. Some, to be sure, may have if they had profited from the system personally; but for those whose lives had been demeaned under colonialism, this may not have been among their highest priorities. In the consequentiality column, we would observe in the revolutionary moment that the FLN viciously killed the very people on whose behalf and with whom they were resisting French colonial rule. The ultimate result may have been the cooperation on the part of the population with the FLN, or even the Algerian people's active participation in the Revolution, but the means that were used could not necessarily be seen as "just." For the "collaborators," the consequence of their continued participation in the colonial system, either through apathetic contributions to the means by which colonialism maintained its hold or through active collaboration, is the continued reproduction of the colonial system and thus their continued oppression within that system. Yet the execution of these "collaborators," especially when they are merely suspected of collaboration, violates the very goals the FLN tries to bring about through their murder. So which of these ethical considerations carries the most weight in the final analysis?

Merleau-Ponty's words in *Humanism and Terror*[22] bring light to the empirical and philosophical contradictions that the foregoing analysis provides. Alternately, though not in a contradictory fashion, he says:

> The irony of fate drives us to do the opposite of what we think we will do; it forces us to doubt our senses, to impugn our proneness to mystification, and brings to light not just the terror which each man holds for every other man but, above all, that basic Terror in each of us which comes from the awareness of his historical responsibility. (Merleau-Ponty 1969: 92–93)

> The Revolution takes on and directs a violence which bourgeois society tolerates in unemployment and in war and disguises with the name of misfortune. But successful revolutions taken altogether have not spilled as much blood as the empires. All we know is different kinds of violence and we ought to prefer revolutionary violence because it has a future of humanism. (Merleau-Ponty 1969: 107)

The attacks on Algerian collaborators with the French colonial system would appear to contradict the revolutionary program (and hence the apparent ethicality of the revolution in the first place); however, the reconciliation of these attacks with the ethical sensibility of the revolution is one that can only occur through the recognition of the impurity of everyone involved in liberatory social action. For Merleau-Ponty, the site at which these ethical questions can be answered is not one that is "in the moment," but rather is at the site of history: the revolutionary party or actor cannot take into account any apparent conflict between the goals of the revolution and the means required to enact it; and so long as the goals of the revolution are the creation of a new, free humanity able to be its sole determining force over its future, the means utilized to reach this goal are necessary and therefore ethical (Merleau-Ponty 1969: 129). In other words, so long as the goal of the revolutionaries is the achievement of free humanity, one that is better than the kind before it, the means are ethical *but impure*, implicating everyone involved—revolutionary, oppressor, bystander, and collaborator—in the ambiguities of historically and ethically oriented action. The question of whether or not these attacks on "collaborators" were ethical can only be answered by looking at the *consequence* of the attacks *in combination with the intention* behind the acts.

From this historically oriented standpoint, then, the deaths of Muslim civilians wanting simply to "live their lives," even though those lives were constructed by and reinforced the colonial system, can be partly seen as historically ethical because the FLN, who stated their desire to destroy the French colonial system in order to create a new version of humanity, won the independence of Algeria, and these civilians, through their "bystander" position, were a tactical obstacle to the liberation of Algerians. Because the Algerian Revolution was a war designed to assert the individual and collective agency and humanity of the Algerian people; because to assert the French version of "humanism" required that the revolutionaries assert the collective agency of Algerians and demand for the recognition of their humanity through the same violent means by which they were taught it; and because the tactical exigencies of ensuring that the Algerian population participated in, cooperated with, or complied with the revolutionaries required the death of those who did none of these—all these things combine to ethically justify to the FLN these attacks on "Muslim collaborators" in the name of the Revolution. From the standpoint of *the revolutionaries*, this set of actions is ethical because it is a necessary step in the process by which the Algerian people could decolonize themselves. The intention behind this form of social action is singular and crucial: to convey the historically and ethically oriented message of the impending demise of those who continue to support and maintain the colonial regime. As Merleau-Ponty put it, "History has a meaning only if there is a logic of human coexistence which does not make any event impossible, but at least through a kind of natural selection eliminates in the long run those events which diverge from the permanent needs of men" (Merleau-Ponty 1969: 153–154). The meaning created by the entire historical *praxis* known as the Algerian Revolution would appear to eliminate this event in favor of the permanent needs of humankind, namely the freedom the Revolution intended to bring to the Algerian people.

At least this is how the FLN would attempt to justify this form of violence. Violence used in the cause of eliminating French colonial control over Algeria is easier to justify, even if it did involve civilians who, by virtue of the nature of the economy and polity of Algeria and the actions of the OAS later in the Revolution, were more clearly implicated in the attempts to either preserve French control or destroy

Algeria on the way back to the *métropole*. But the violence used by the FLN against fellow Algerians—those who were supposed to be both comrades and beneficiaries of the Revolution—is less easy to justify. The combination of Merleau-Ponty's discussion of the direction of revolutionary violence, Sartre's notion of ethical radicalism, and the concept of the colonial habitus developed from Bourdieu's work all highlight one particular problem with intra-Algerian violence—namely, that it became habitual over the course of the Revolution. Charges of collaboration and treason, used frequently throughout the Revolution against obstacles to the FLN's goals, became less substantiated over time and more a bloody instantiation of the principles of *boulitique* and *méfiance*. Any Algerian not controlled, not turned into a tool for the furtherance of the FLN's revolution, became an obstacle in the FLN's satisfaction of its own goals, namely making the last in the colonial order "the first." And to put the final nail in the coffin of the ethicality of *how* the FLN carried out the Revolution—not the ethicality of the Revolution, but rather its particular practical implementation—is the elimination of both competing political entities after the referendum on independence and the vengeance exacted on the *harkis*. If the FLN were truly committed to a revolution that would create a new version of humanity and would bring about a concrete practical freedom for all, settling these kinds of scores would have been inconceivable acts, set aside in favor of reconciling all Algerians in the pursuit of sovereign self-determination. Instead, in an ironic twist to Sartre's preface to *The Wretched of the Earth*, leaving aside the end of French colonial rule in Algeria, the state of Algerian freedom after the Revolution is the same as it was before 1954, in large part because the revolutionary practice of the FLN indeed instituted "new structures which will become the first institutions of peace" (1963: 23).

It is in large part because the stated ethical goals of the Revolution—the bringing of equality, democracy, socialism, and freedom and self-determination to all the Algerian people—were never implemented that we can say the types of violence enacted against Algerians, whether proven or suspected collaborators or simply civilians who became cannon fodder, by the FLN are ethically unjustified. If the Revolution had been a success; if the FLN had not worked from November 1, 1954, to recent years to ensure its continued position as the only political party; if the state of Algeria today was better than the state of Algeria in 1962, or even 1954; if we could speak of a situation of concrete freedom and a transition from colonized "subhuman" to decolonized "human"—then we could see that, while tragic, those sacrifices might have brought about a more beneficent situation for the Algerians who survived and came after the Revolution. If the stated revolutionary ends of the FLN had been present in the *praxis* used to fight the Revolution, then we might be having an entirely different discussion about Algeria (cf. Santoni 2003: 141–144). But those things did not come to fruition, leaving us to recall the more heartrending aspect of Merleau-Ponty's statement in "Sartre and Ultrabolshevism": "Those who will be shot *would understand* tomorrow that they did not die in vain; the only problem is that they will no longer be there to understand it. Revolutionary violence insults them most grievously by not taking their revolt seriously . . ." (Merleau-Ponty 1973b: 130).

The Ethical Failure of the Algerian Revolution

Leaving aside the fact that explicit French rule over Algeria ended as a result, we can see that from the standpoint of a resisting social ethics such as that developed here, the Algerian Revolution truly was a failure. The result of the Revolution was the replacement of the *pieds-noirs* and metropolitan rule over Algeria with FLN rule of Algeria—a switch of personnel more than a switch of a social order. At this point, it should be clear that the ethics of freedom that was the stated intention of the FLN on November 1, 1954, was never fulfilled through its revolutionary *praxis*. It may never have been a true intention of the movement at all. It is not simply that the goals of the 1954 declaration were never implemented; every revolution, from the American and French revolutions of the late eighteenth century to many of the recent anticolonial, "communist," and even "post-communist" revolutions, has failed to implement at least some of the ideas it holds forth at the start of the war, simply by virtue of the nature of revolutions—namely that once the revolution is won, the first thing that must be protected is the victory of the revolutionaries. What is more troubling in the case of Algeria is that the ethics of freedom it put forth—and held out as a model for other anticolonial revolutions, particularly in Africa—was betrayed in the moment where the FLN's "revolutionary" *praxis* violated the stated revolutionary goals.

First and foremost was the FLN's quest to dominate post-revolutionary Algeria. From its attacks on rival nationalist organizations during the early years of the Revolution, to the civil war that followed the referendum on independence, to the prevention of the establishment of rival political parties during the years of the consolidation of the new Algerian state, the FLN has continuously worked to ensure that it remains the power center in Algeria. Beckett (1973: 26–27) argues that one of the causes of the failure of the Algerian Revolution was the element of spontaneity among the oppressed classes that Fanon identified as crucial for the revolution; however, on the analysis developed here, the problem was not with the revolutionary spontaneity of the masses, but with the ways in which that spontaneity was mobilized—or rather, turned against Algerians—by the FLN. Fanon's notion of the position of the mass party was that it should not be "a tool in the hands of the government. Quite on the contrary, the party is a tool in the hands of the people; it is they who decide on the policy that the government carries out" (Fanon 1963: 185). In Algeria, either during the Revolution or after, *this never happened*; not only did the FLN never become an authentic expression of the people, but it never seems to have intended to be such a party. Its efforts to quash rival nationalist groups and to eliminate rival parties during the post-revolutionary consolidation of the state makes clear that the ruling concerns of Algeria are the concerns of the FLN, regardless of the bloody consequences.

From the discussion developed here, it should be clear that all the factors in the Algerian Revolution combine into a situation that displays its real revolutionary weakness: the FLN fought a war for national independence instead of social liberation, for Algerian sovereignty over Algerian territory instead of the sovereignty of Algerians over their collective social project. The former involves the change of leadership and ruling political structures; in this, the FLN achieved its objectives. In the latter, in which the entire social order is shaken up and rebuilt from its roots, and in which the entire collective has the opportunity to participate in that rebuilding of a new, human social order, the FLN has remarkably failed. Consider Fanon's words on the matter:

> Nationalism is not a political doctrine, nor a program. If you really wish your country to avoid regression, or at best halts and uncertainties, a rapid step must be taken from national consciousness to political and social consciousness. The nation does not exist in a program which has been worked out by revolutionary leaders and taken up with full understanding and enthusiasm by the masses. . . . The work of the masses and their will to overcome the evils which have for centuries excluded them from the mental achievements of the past ought to be grafted onto the work and will of all underdeveloped peoples. (Fanon 1963: 203)

This one key point—the involvement of the people of Algeria in building Algerian society anew—is enough to damn the FLN. But it also highlights one of the key complications of the Revolution, namely that by aiming for national liberation and independence (with the FLN taking the helm after the Revolution), the FLN eliminated the possibility for a real, autonomous reconstruction of Algerian society and the creation of Fanon's "new kind of humanity," and ensured that the necessary decolonization of Algerians, or the clearing of the colonial habitus, would never come to fruition.

The execution of "Muslim collaborators," the vengeance attacks on *harkis* and *bleus*, and the kinds of repressive tactics used to maintain post-revolutionary domination, all go to show the lengths to which the FLN aborted the kind of revolution Fanon saw as necessary for the true elimination of colonialism. In taking on these tactics, the FLN violated the ethics of freedom they themselves laid out; they showed that despite protestations to fight a clean war in order to attain the kind of humanity the *pieds-noirs* had denied them for so long, they were only willing to go as far as needed to ensure their dominance. The Algerian Revolution could very well have served as the model for all anti-colonial and decolonizing revolutionary projects. Its stated goal of bringing about a situation of humanity, characterized by the lessons they had learned from 132 years of French colonialism as well as the desire to eliminate the colonial system (and not necessarily the colonials themselves), does contain the kind of ethics of freedom developed above. Unfortunately, in attempting to bring about the revolutionary end of national independence, the revolutionary *praxis* utilized by the FLN ensured that this ethics of freedom could never come to fruition. And in this sense, for most Algerians it might not really matter whether a French government in Paris or an indigenous government in Algiers ruled over them; they are still ruled over by those who have no interest in enabling them to be truly free.

Lessons Learned: Freedom and "Making the Human"

One might question at this point what it is that would make this lengthy case study of the Algerian Revolution worthwhile, especially forty years after its conclusion. The situation in Algeria nearly forty years after the Revolution is, put baldly, rather desperate. Following Roberts's (2003) long-term analysis of Algerian politics, we can see there is no effective mode of governance and remarkably little in the way of political institutionalization (168, 207). The formal constitution of Algeria places national sovereignty in the hands of *le Peuple*; yet control over Algeria and its politics lies firmly in the hands of the ANP (*Armée Nationale Populaire*, the inheritor of the ALN) (204). The FLN still works to ensure its dominance over Algeria, going so far as to regularly extend the "state of emergency" in the country and its suspension of open elections, despite its licensure of other political parties and organizations in a form of "managed pluralism" (168, 211n1, 263–264, 270). And the regime is still notoriously unsympathetic to the needs of Algerians, particularly in rural areas such as Kabylia, where riots in 2001 were the expression of resistance to *al-hagra*, the legal deprivation of political participation and the arbitrariness of governmental actions toward the citizenry (293, 302). Despite efforts by the FLN to make it seem as if Algeria were moving toward a democratic political and social order—and despite some economic successes over the last forty years that marginally improved the situation for individual Algerians—the society seems little better off now than it was at the end of the Algerian Revolution. It would appear that Fanon's prognostications about the "Pitfalls of National Consciousness" (1963) and the taking of power by an unresponsive, isolated, incoherent political body have come true. It would seem that all the promise of the revolution has disappeared. So why this attention to the intricacies of how a failed revolution was carried out?

It is the act of revolutionary agency that best characterizes the importance of the Algerian Revolution (or really, any revolution that is intended to aid in the cause of human freedom). Given the concern throughout this book with the creation of a set of conditions in which the potential existential freedom inherent in all individuals can become the concrete basis for a state of affairs, it should be clear that the kind of "ethical radicalism" inherent in revolting against an oppressive regime is designed to bring about such a state of affairs. But how is it that this kind of agency comes through in the taking-up of arms against such a regime? Or, to put it another way, how can the apparently unethical act of revolution *be* ethical?

The notion that it would be unethical to resist against an existing social order relies on two assumptions: first, that the ethical values and imperatives present in that social order are universal and apply without regard for the particular social and historical situation; and second, that the social order genuinely operates in accordance with those values. Yet, existing social orders are not created by the values of those who live within them by their own volition, but rather continue through time and history, echoed by the actions of those in our current situation repeating them as the basis for their *praxis*. They are historically determined, but not of our determination; they preexist us, and we repeat them in a doxic manner, thereby reproducing the social order that creates these values and requires us to maintain them in order to maintain the social order. Further, we can see that the majority of existing societies do not live by their own ethical maxims. For freedom or democracy in their genuine, intended forms to exist in societies claiming to be characterized by them would require drastic changes in the social order. So the idea that resistant social action is unethical is one perpetuated by the social order for the sake of preserving that social order, not for the sake of ensuring the collective weal of a society.

But, resistant action itself runs a paradoxical course as well, one well-demonstrated by this examination of the Algerian Revolution. It is not simply the resistant action that begins to create an ethical social order; instead, it is also the results of resistance that continue the process of developing a situation of concrete freedom in the world. The individual resister, once they engage in the process of ethical radicalism and act against the dominant order, in essence pledges themselves to the resisting group. But once this is done, then the group, especially if it wins any kind of revolution, must consolidate its control over its members or the members of society. In order to do this, though, they must in essence violate the ethical values they wished to bring into action by looking on the members of the group as tools for the perpetuation of the "victory of the revolution" and must crush any opposition to the revolutionary regime. In doing so, the cause of freedom for which the people fought is crushed, whether temporarily or permanently. How is it possible to manage the paradox inherent in the fact that fighting for the cause of freedom so often leads to a new kind of oppression and inequality?

Sartre's *Cornell Lectures* discussion gives us the phenomenological basis for understanding the ethical paradox inherent in revolutionary action:

> Mais déjà l'objet de valeur est homogène au moment d'inertie de la praxis: parce que, dans l'unité synthétique d'une praxis, je me fais inerte pour combattre l'inertie du monde, l'inertie de l'objet et son unité de fausse intériorité me renvoient condensés et passivisées ma propre inertie et son unification pratique. En fait je me fais instrument (contre-inertie) et l'objet c'est moi-même me faisant instrument. Ainsi ce premier temps de la valeur—objet implique sourdement l'idée de moi-même comme valeur en tant que pouvoir, c'est-à-dire inertie forgée. (Sartre 1964b: 479)[23]

Under the already-existing practico-inert system, we are made into instruments. Sartre's discussion of both social groups in general (in *Critique of Dialectical Reason*) and the pauperization of the Algerian people in particular shows the ways in which we are made into instruments by the dominant social order, whether for the sake of producing profit in a capitalist order or the normative state of society. In the resistant act, though, we reclaim our agency by making ourselves into instruments designed to liberate others and ourselves. We objectify ourselves, make ourselves into "revolutionaries," in an attempt to struggle and eliminate the practico-inert structures of the original social order and to create a new social order. Thus, the act of taking up arms against an oppressive regime becomes, for Sartre, Fanon, and for us in facing structures of unfreedom and oppression, an ethical act. When we passively participate in the social order, simply reproducing ourselves and that social order, we deny our responsibility for that order and for our objectification by others within that social order. Turning ourselves into tools designed for the particular purpose of liberation is the first step in bringing about a situation of concrete freedom; even though we are still objectified, we take responsibility for this objectification and the purposes for which it is taken on. In pursuing any kind of resistant action within a pledged group, we make the move from bad faith to authenticity, and begin the process of transforming ourselves from subhumanized human beings into genuine human agents.

What is necessary is that people are willing to make this first step on this humanization process *and* are willing to encourage the continuation of this process. We can make ourselves willingly into tools for the sake of our liberation, both individual and collective; however, that choice must continue to be our own, over and against the crushing force of the practico-inert social order. Sartre realized that taking on a certain morality in the service of revolutionary action also ran the risk of turning us into victims of that same process:

> De fait la contradiction de la morale révolutionnaire c'est qu'elle est la seule à se déterminer en fonction de l'homme intégral; mais qu'elle limite son but, *en elle même*, en fonction des exigences de la lutte, *et* produit n'entant que praxis-processus des morales d'estime-urgence qui sont aliénées au processus.
>
> Le problème est donc de savoir comment produire le mouvement dialectique qui font en posant ces *morales* aliénées conteste leur limite en fonction du but même qu'elles veulent atteindra. (Sartre 1964a: 147; cf. Bowman and Stone 1992: 167–168)[24]

Anyone committed to the development of "integral humanity" must ensure that they do not take the limited victory of the revolution or resistant action as the entire victory or the full liberation of humankind. The practico-inert social order and its accretion into the individuals who make up that order does not readily fade away; the creation of integral humanity is not an overnight process, and cannot be achieved only by winning battles and taking political power. Instead, the morality they create to win the battle, the willingness of individuals in the group to make themselves tools for the revolution, must be furthered and extended in the postrevolutionary period, even if it requires what could be called "counterrevolutionary" activity.

Sartre's discussion of his dialectical morality in the 1964 manuscripts gives us the sense that this is the necessary process to engage in—that we *must* question, analyze, and correct the alienation inherent in the revolutionary group as soon as it becomes an oppressive, practico-inert force.

> En un mot la possibilité éthique ou norme (c'est-à-dire l'action produisant ses propres moyens) est le *sens* de la praxis historique: celle-ci, corrigeant sans cesse ses déviations, paraît comme pénétrée; en effet d'une sorte . . . d'elle-même qu'elle soutient et nourrit, quel que soit l'objectif, et par rapport auquel elle semble se contrôler sans cesse elle corrige ses déviations et remanie sans cesse son champ pratique, pose le dépassement par l'invention et refuse les limites pratiques de l'invention en réorganisant celle-ci perpétuellement comme si par ce développement temporel (perpétuel remaniement d'elle-même) elle devait atteindre au bord du temps historique ce type *a priori* de praxis, c'est-à-dire l'action incondi-tionnée ou si l'on veut la fin faisant par l'invention libre surgir ses propres moyens. (Sartre 1964b: 411–412)[25]

Once a liberatory movement makes the transition from being "histori-cal *praxis*" to the practico-inert and from the ethically radical to the rule-bound Ethical, the movement no longer serves its purpose, instead bringing "the Terror" to bear on those who worked to bring about liber-ation. The "Terror," in this case, prevents individuals and collectivities from creating their own ends with their concomitant *moyens propres*, prevents the reshaping of the practical field to further develop the inte-gral humanity Sartre sees as so important, and, in effect, revisits the oppressive forces upon those who fought so hard for their liberation. Thus, what is needed is a constant critique of the new revolutionary order. Or, to put it another way, we need to resist the Ethics of the new order in much the same way that resisting the Ethics of the old order would make possible this liberation: "*la lutte contre le système révolution-naire risque de détruire la force révolutionnaire . . . mais le renforcement aveugle du système risque de soumettre l'homme à une aliénation non pas d'exploitation mais d'oppression*" ("the struggle against the revolutionary system risks destroying the revolutionary force . . . but the blind rein-forcement of the system risks submitting man to an alienation not only of exploitation, but of oppression"; Sartre 1964a: 164–165; cf. Bowman and Stone 1992: 187–188).

And in large part, why the Algerian Revolution never succeeded in its mission to be a truly liberating force—and, in part, why most twentieth-century revolutions have failed to achieve what we would consider "human freedom"—is due to its failure to ensure that the contestation of the alienated colonial morality willingly constructed by the revolutionary group in order to achieve its aims continues to be contested once it alienates its members. The need to consolidate the revolution, already established when the FLN embarked on its plan to establish itself as the only speaker for the Algerian people and continued through the decisions it made on its tactical approach to fighting for the demise of the colonial system, ensures that any challenge to what the FLN decides is *the* Algerian Revolution is going to be fought off as fervently and furiously as the FLN fought the OAS. What Sartre, Fanon, and others saw in the Algerian Revolution, and in the process of revolutionary violence in general, was a way of reclaiming the humanity of the colonized through the elimination of all vestiges of the colonial system. When the situation in which a group finds itself is characterized purely by violence, violence may very well be what is needed to create a humane social order; to borrow from Santoni,

> Although Sartre's Preface [to *Les damnes de la terre*] appears to share the *Notebooks'* view that counterviolence *presents* itself as a "recuperation of a right" and is a "demand on Others," it seems to allow, in the name of re-creating human self-respect and bringing about a new higher-level humanity, a counterviolence by the oppressed that—at least temporarily —can transcend the antidialectical, non-coexistential, anticommunitarian dimensions of violence. (Santoni 2003: 74)

This glorious revolutionary end, one that we can agree is a desirable state of human society, is one that the revolutionary violence of the FLN ensured would not be developed in Algeria. It is not so much in the dirtied hands of the FLN with regard to the killing of French colonists; while ethically ambiguous, the independence of Algeria was a valuable goal, one that can be partially justified through these kinds of violent tactics (even more so after the OAS, involving both disgruntled French soldiers and *pieds-noirs*, began its attacks on Algerian civilians in 1961). As Gordon points out, "From the standpoint of the colonizer, his place in the colony is not an unjust one. To replace him is to replace the innocent. For the colonized, his previous place in his society was not an unjust one. The fact that he has been replaced reflects an injustice. The former faces the threat of violence; the latter is already living it" (Gordon 1994: 77–78). However, it is in the ways the FLN used violence against its own people, both inside and outside the FLN, that the consequences of the "antidialectical, non-coexistential, anticommunitarian dimensions" of violence were transferred from the hands of the French colonists into the hands of the FLN. The means the FLN used to attain its goals—national liberation and its own political dominance — violate any notion of ethical radicalism as developed here. And it is in that sense that we have a crucial lesson about the ways to develop a resisting social ethics; sadly, this lesson is only in the negative.

For us to develop a "resisting ethics" predicated on our commitment to social justice and our orientation to others, we need to understand and exemplify the goal of others' experiences while avoiding their pitfalls. The major pitfall here, to use Sartre's formulation, is that the means used to attain revolutionary goals do not already embody the revolutionary ends to be achieved. For a true ethical radicalism to come about, and for a social order to be built that allows for the kind of sovereign, autonomous self-determination Sartre and Merleau-Ponty both wanted to see in the world, the path toward that state of existence must already contain elements of that state. And though the Algerian Revolution could have been the violent "midwife" (to borrow Sartre's term) of a new form of humanity, the way the FLN decided to achieve their ends prevented this from ever coming into being; as Santoni notes, "although still allowing that the 'violence of the colonized' against the colonialist oppressors 'could be called just,' Sartre would not maintain [in *Hope Now*], as he did in his Preface to *The Wretched*, that the colonized 'have become men' " (Santoni 2003: 81). From the beginning of the Algerian Revolution, the structural organization of the FLN prevented any kind of integral humanity from coming to the fore; the consolidation of power by the revolutionaries-turned-politicians after the Revolution ensured that its stated goals were not to coming into being any time soon. Yet, we have learned a great deal from this examination of the Algerian Revolution; however, we need a more positive case study of the unification of means and ends in resistant *praxis*. Exploring the revolutionary activities and organization of the Ejército Zapatista por Liberación Nacional (EZLN) will provide us that example.

Chapter 6

"For Everyone, Everything": Social Ethics, Consent, and the Zapatistas

Our discussion of the ethics of freedom present in the Algerian Revolution might lead us to pose a crucial question for the development of a social ethics predicated on the practice of resistance, namely the question of its relevance for Western societies. After all, one might ask, how could Western societies adopt the same kind of ethics when there is already a well-entrenched individualized *ethos* at work here? How dramatically would such a change in ethos affect our social structures and our daily lives? And would we face the same dilemmas here that Algerians did after the consolidation of the Revolution—namely, the loss of the freedom for which the revolutionaries stated they fought, the civil war and institutionalized terror people faced everyday, and the uncertainty of ever changing the situation?

These are, of course, entirely valid questions to pose at this point of the work. In particular, the issues regarding structural changes in Western societies are a crucial one to consider, especially if we *do* want to bring about the kind of ethics I am developing here. The ethics of freedom discussed earlier, one that can appear only in the form of resistance, would have to be dramatically adapted in order to be brought about within the relative comfort and security of Western societies. How we can do that, though, seems to be a problematic issue. If that ethics of freedom only appears in a revolutionary moment, in which the oppressed take up arms against their oppressors, then its appearance in a nonrevolutionary society seems highly suspect; the historical situations simply are not parallel. In part, this has much to do with the particular means used to attain revolutionary ends, which usually have no corollary in neoliberal Western societies. However, choosing different means, ones more appropriate to our particular historical situation, might make this paralleling process more suitable. In other words, translating the ethics present in a revolutionary situation into a nonrevolutionary moment, as the "extreme case study" approach does, is a valuable process.

In a similar manner, we can look elsewhere for insights into the mode of social organization that might foster the version of ethics I argue for here. This is, of course, a necessary step; after all, even a cursory examination of alternative modes of social organization such as the anarchist collectives of the nineteenth century and the hippie communes of the twentieth century shows that an alternative ethical *praxis* may very well be practiced at the micro or local level without ever impacting the larger social order. We need to think about how our social order can be reorganized to foster the development and enactment of a socially oriented ethics, as well as the kinds of social structures that would support such a way of being. For this, I turn to the Zapatista National Liberation Army (*Ejército Zapatista por la Liberación Nacional*, or EZLN) and an examination of the structural elements that make this resistance movement unique in the twentieth and twenty-first centuries. In particular, it is the absence of any disjuncture between revolutionary means and revolutionary ends that makes a case study of the EZLN's writings and actions a beneficial case for figuring out how to deepen the existential social ethics we are working to develop. It is this intimate linkage between revolutionary means and ends, as well as the EZLN's willingness to follow through on their own organizational principles through the 2003 establishment of "Committees of Good Government," that demonstrates to us the way past the blockages the FLN were never able to surpass—namely, the blockage represented by the reinstitution of a colonized habitus at the level of the social-structural order.

While there have been many others who have looked at a variety of aspects of the Zapatista movement,[1] ranging from their popularity in the developed world to their impact on the anticapitalism movement and the discursive aspects of EZLN communiqués, only a few have explored the essential structure of the EZLN and its relations with larger indigenous communities and movements. With regard to the issues under discussion in this work, this is the crucial element of the EZLN. It is in the Zapatista mode of social organization that we can see if the EZLN "practices what they preach" as well as how it is that we can draw on the lessons the movement has had to learn in terms of its organization and the practical implementation of their goals. It is to this that I turn now.

From the Base to the Base: Social Structure of the EZLN

> ... in moments of rest they hear another voice, not the one that comes
> from above, but rather the one that comes with the wind from below and
> is born in the heart of the indigenous people of the mountains, a voice
> that speaks of justice and liberty, a voice that speaks of socialism, a voice
> that speaks of hope ... the only hope in this earthly world.
> —Subcomandante Marcos, *Shadows of Tender Fury* 1995 (45)

January 1, 1994, was the first day the world knew of the Ejército
Zapatista por la Liberación Nacional. Timed to coincide with the implementation of the North American Free Trade Agreement, the EZLN
attacked and took a number of villages in the Mexican state of Chiapas.
In what became known as the usual manner of the EZLN and its representative, Subcomandante Insurgente Marcos, the EZLN announced
the attacks a number of days prior to the New Year, only to have those
warnings ignored by Mexican authorities (Marcos 2001: 76). Later, a
series of communiqués—the signature of the EZLN—were issued, stat-
ing the claims the EZLN was making against the Mexican government,
including the triptych of "justice, freedom, and democracy" (Marcos
1995: 62). These communiqués were sent not only to Mexican presi-
dents Carlos Salinas de Gortari (until 1994) and Ernesto Zedillo Ponce
de Leon (until 2000), but also to U.S. President Bill Clinton, the U.S.
Congress, and (more regularly) to "the peoples of the world" (Marcos
1995: passim). Shortly after the taking of San Cristóbal de las Casas by
EZLN forces, the Mexican Army responded, leading to a series of military conflicts, cease-fires, and standoffs that continue even today. For
nearly ten years, the EZLN, by virtue of both military force and the
attention from intellectuals and activists from around the world, has
held off the incursion of the Mexican Army into EZLN-held territory.

This altogether too brief history of the EZLN does not tell the entire
story. There are two additional historical aspects to the decade-long
struggle of the EZLN. The first happens much earlier than the implementation of NAFTA, when Subcomandante Marcos, the product of a
self-described middle class and literary upbringing (Marcos 2001: 77),
first went into the jungles of southeastern Mexico to foment revolution
in 1983 (McManus 2002: 4). Taking with him a standard issue
Leninist/Maoist perspective on the revolutionary potential of the proletariat, Marcos tried to convince the indigenous peoples of Chiapas that
they *were* proletarians—and they had none of that. Their experiences,
Marcos reports, did not match anything Marcos told them; and rather
than leaving the jungles to find more willing revolutionaries, Marcos

and his colleagues stayed in the jungles to learn from the Mayan descendants (Marcos 1995: 84). Don Antonio, one of the elders in the Chiapas village Marcos lived in, is the prototypical teacher; one of Marcos's books, *Zapatista Stories*, is a compilation of the indigenous stories Don Antonio told Marcos to awaken Marcos's revolutionary consciousness. Thus, one of the aspects of the EZLN story left out by more conventional historical treatments is the inversion of the usual vanguardist model—namely, that the "vanguard" who went into the jungles to foment revolution were taught by those they expected to teach.

The second aspect of the EZLN story has to do with the conditions in which the EZLN was developed. Finding themselves in a situation not unlike that Algeria faced under French colonial rule, those Tzeltal, Tzotzil, Chol, Tojolabal, Mam, and Zoque peoples who eventually formed the EZLN existed in a desperate state of impoverishment. Moved from region to region in southeastern Mexico, the indigenous peoples of Chiapas had been systematically dispossessed of their land and disenfranchised since the colonization of Mexico by Spain in the sixteenth century. Forced labor, a continuing trend in the region, combined with the consolidation of arable land into *caciques*, large farms and ranches held by powerful local landowners (Ceceña and Barreda 1998: 56–57). And even into the 1970s, forced dislocations, including one series in order to build hydroelectric dams on the Grijalva River that removed 90,000 people from some of the most arable land, took its toll on the remaining lands of Chiapas (Burbach 1994: 119). This continuing impoverishment and disenfranchisement provides the impetus for one of the basic elements of the EZLN political agenda, namely land and freedom: control over the land in southeastern Mexico by the rightful indigenous inheritors, and the ability to utilize it in the best interests of the community (Marcos 1995: 45). Forces other than the merely material conditions also played a part in the development of the EZLN: the material conditions combined with the work of "liberation theologists, independent peasant organizations, growing social and economic differentiation within the Indian and peasant communities, and the use of violence by ranchers, *caciques*, and governors of the state," and changes in other Central American guerrilla movements also impacted on the development of the EZLN movement (Burbach 1994: 119; Leyva Solano 1998: 38). In sum, the formation of the EZLN, in common with numerous other situations on the planet today (EZLN 1996a: 39), depended on a complex of material, intellectual, and cultural forces that made possible the construction of a revolutionary movement.

It would seem, then, that the conflict between the EZLN and the Mexican government would be a limited one, oriented to attaining land reform and increased political enfranchisement, or at the very least protection against further dislocations and enforced labor. Or, it could be understood as a defensive battle against neoliberal governmental and economic policies; as Gilly suggests, looking at it in that light, the Zapatista rebellion and other indigenous people's movements appear to be "movements in defense of traditional society and its bonds with the land, against the invasion of modernity incarnated on one side in the world of mercantile exchanges and money as mediators and vehicles for all human relations; and on the other, in the modern nation-state and its juridical order as a guarantee of the universality of these exchanges" (Gilly 1997: 17; original in Spanish). But the EZLN saw the parallels between the situation of Chiapan indigenous peoples and other groups around the world, ranging from other groups of indigenous peoples to oppressed minority or immigrant populations. The EZLN struggle is much broader; the Zapatistas see their enemy, the Mexican government, as one player within and manipulated by a much larger system, that of neoliberalism, and all its concomitant ills: "impoverishment, unemployment, the dismantling of social rights, privatization of public goods and services, ecological destruction, disarticulation of social organizations, authoritarianism, ideological regimentation, social atomization, and subsumption of that is human to the logic of money and the market" (EZLN 1996a: 39; original in Spanish). Given this awareness, it only seems logical that the EZLN struggle is not just against the inhuman conditions of their existence, but rather the inhuman conditions of existence faced *by all of us*; if we are all trapped by the logic of the market and money, and if we all face the societal ills described here, then we all find ourselves in the same proverbial boat. It is no wonder, then, that the person of Subcomandante Marcos and the movement of the EZLN see themselves as the voice of disempowered peoples from all over the world—not in a vanguardist way, as constructing the new path to human liberation for all, but as the interlocutor for millions of voiceless, powerless people from North and South, East and West. It is this, combined with the particularities of the EZLN social structure, that make the Zapatista National Liberation Army a strong model for new forms of social organization.

Relations Between the EZLN and the Larger Social World

This solidarity with others in similar situations is most clearly manifested in what has become almost a slogan for the EZLN: *todo por todos,*

nada por nosotros, "for everyone, everything, for ourselves, nothing."
Seeing themselves as bound together with all those who struggle against
injustice, the EZLN has put themselves in the position of fighting *for*
and *with* the subalterns of the world. As the CCRI-CG (*Comité
Clandestino Revolucionario Insurgente-Comandante General,* the central
command of the EZLN) puts it in an April 1994 communiqué:

> For whom do these men and women walk? Who drinks their blood? For
> whom is the light of their words? For whom do they change their death
> to life? One-hundred days, ten years. Who will join hands with these men
> and women who cannot be with you here today, and take the flag that
> their blood snatched away from the hands of the powerful? . . .
> You, our brothers and sisters. For you, our blood. For your dark night,
> our timid light. For your life, our death. Our war for your peace. For
> your ears, our words. Your pain, brothers and sisters, will find relief in our
> fight. For you, brothers and sisters, everything; for ourselves nothing.
> (Marcos 1995: 199–200)

In large part, the EZLN does not see itself as only fighting the Mexican
government, or even the rearrangement of the bases of American hegemony and neoliberal economic and political policies (Ceceña and
Barreda 1998: 57). Rather, it sees its struggle as a struggle for *national*
and *social* liberation, that nation being the entirety of Mexico, defined
both as the "homeland" or *patria* of Mexico *and* those elements opposed
to the Mexican state—namely civil society (Holloway 1998: 167).

In fact, it is this reliance on civil society as the basis for the Zapatista
rebellion that makes it unique among twentieth-century revolutionary
movements. First and foremost, the EZLN has no plans for taking political power for itself. The Zapatista perspective on revolution is one that
sees the necessity of power "but not *the power*; it is necessary moreover
to think of ideologies, but not *the ideology.* . . . Zapatismo is the best
example of new revolutionary thought; it doesn't need to convert itself
into the new 'official ideology' of revolutionaries, nor does it need to
institutionalize itself" (EZLN 1996a: 52; original in Spanish). Rather
than engaging in a winner-take-all battle between ideologies or hegemonies, the EZLN sees that traditional conception of revolution (either
take power or be destroyed) as a way of taking power without changing
the nature of power—and this violates the point of the revolution
(Marcos 2001: 70). The EZLN's vision of itself from the beginning of
the insurrection was as a "plough," intending to provoke a bottom-up
transformation of Mexican society by bringing the population's discontent with the Mexican political order to the surface for the sake of

returning power to the people as guaranteed by the Mexican Constitution (Marcos 2001: 71–72; Burbach 1994: 113). By emphasizing civil society as the basis for revolutionary action, the EZLN sees an opportunity for "thinking outside the box": by avoiding the typical contest between two armed parties for an already-existing system and conception of political power, the move into civil society achieves some of the fundamental goals the EZLN has set for itself, in particular that of reclaiming political power for the people, not just in Mexican society but in *every* society.

To further the restructuring of the social orders, the EZLN has put itself in the position of relying on forces outside the armed faction of the New Zapatismo Movement (Leyva Solano 1998: 42) for its success. Quite explicitly, Subcomandante Marcos states its reliance on others outside the actual armed force of the EZLN for the success of its revolutionary goals: "Today we are not expressing what we were before 1994, or in the first days of 1994 when we were fighting; we are acting on a series of moral commitments we made in the last seven years. . . . In every town square, we told people: 'We have not come to lead you, we have not come to tell you what to do, but to ask for your help'" (Marcos 2001: 72). Indeed, like many other indigenous and Indian people's movements of the late twentieth century, there has been a dramatic reliance on social formations outside of the local; international assistance, ranging from the UN to other resistance movements, has been of significant importance for the expansion of movements and the addressing of indigenous goals (Brysk 1996: 44–45). This internationalization of social movements, which derives from the international support offered to some movements and is translated into larger bases of support for other movements, constructs the kind of solidarity the EZLN sees as its basic tactical need. The building of international solidarity, evinced in the EZLN-convened Intergalactic Conference for Humanity and against Neoliberalism in 1996 ("The 'Intergalactic'"; Löwy 1998: paras. 33–34), combined local, national, and international groups and issues into a unified conference addressing the common concerns of resistance groups around the world.

The "Intergalactic" provided but one of a number of opportunities the EZLN has taken to engage in discussion and debate about issues of common concern to the wide variety of what could be called "pro-humanity" movements (including anti-globalization and anticapitalism movements). When discussing his "average day" (if such a thing can be said about someone who is both revolutionary leader and political and cultural icon), Subcomandante Marcos includes "discussions with various of the groups I have mentioned: a large number of worlds or sub-worlds—the difference depends on how they are persecuted or marginalized—that have been affected by our message" (Marcos 2001: 74). These discussions draw particular focus to the EZLN emphasis, ethical to its core in the way we have discussed throughout this work, on both an intentionalist and consequentialist perspective of the tactics to be used: "We do not believe that the end justifies the means. Ultimately, we believe that the means are the end. We define our goal by the way we choose the means of struggling for it. In that sense, the value we give to our word, to honesty and sincerity, is great . . . " (ibid.: 76). By having as a stated goal the unification of human civil society in the pursuit of justice, liberty, and democracy, the EZLN sees itself as limited in the choice of means to achieve that goal—namely, the use of justice, liberty, and democracy as means to achieve them as goals.

The point of the EZLN rebellion and the associations they have developed with other organizations and movements committed to the revolutionary triptych (some 60 that are included in the broader Mexican network of the New Zapatista Movement [NMZ]; Leyva Solano 54–55) is to develop in conjunction with others an entirely new conception of how power should be organized, distributed, and exercised. The *Segunda Declaración de la Selva Lacandona* (Second Declaration of the Lacandon Jungle) put it this way:

> En este sentido, esta revolución no concluirá en una nueva clase, fracción de clase o grupo en el poder, sino en un espacio libre y democrático de lucha política. . . . Una nueva política cuya base no sea una confrontación entre organizaciones políticas entre sí, sino la confrontación de sus propuestas políticas con las distintas clases sociales. . . . (EZLN 1994: para. 17)[2]

To the EZLN, Article 39 of the Mexican Constitution, which accords all political sovereignty to the people, is to be taken at face value; and given the lack of genuine democracy in Mexico—and in other countries around the world—the creation of a set of conditions in which actual direct democracy and popular sovereignty can be exercised is the most important goal of the rebellion. Once that is achieved, and once members of society have the capacity for genuine self-determination (Vera 1997: para. 2), then the "real" revolution begins. The EZLN, by its own admission, is merely "the revolution which makes possible the revolution" (Lorenzano 1998: 131). By pursuing their revolution, the EZLN only wants to bring about the conditions in which others can contribute to the creation of a more just social order through their own revolutions, whether violent or not. And to that end, as Subcomandante Marcos puts it, "We are all base communities of support in great struggle for humanity and against neoliberalism" (EZLN 1997: para. 12).

It is, of course, on this front that the EZLN has been most successful in drawing attention to the plight of indigenous peoples around the world and to the Zapatista struggle for justice and dignity. From the very first communiqué sent out on January 1, 1994, the EZLN has relied upon and utilized, quite successfully, a variety of communication technologies to develop a base of support and to convince the developed world that we are all, at least potentially, "base communities of support." From faxing communiqués to a variety of Mexican newspapers, to the use of satellite telephony, to the wide variety of Internet-based communities that have sprung up around the EZLN rebellion, the place of technology in fostering the world as a base community of support has been not only a huge boon to the rebellion (even going so far as to rely on "National and International Civil Society" to convince the Mexican Army to abandon a 1999 planned series of attacks; CCRI-GC 1999: paras. 3–4), but also a model for organizing other organizations and movements, including the anticapitalist and anti-globalization movements (McNally 2002: 16–17, 25). The use of communication technologies to foment support for the Zapatista rebellion (among other resistance movements) has become so pervasive that the U.S. Army commissioned a study on the practice of "Netwar," the use of communication technologies to develop support networks for liberatory and/or terrorist movements (Dubar-Ortiz 2002: para. 12; cf. Arquilla and Ronfeldt 2001), resulting in a simultaneous furtherance of the use of these technologies for resistant purposes and an infiltration of these movements via those technologies. This ironically should be taken as a sign of the success of the EZLN's use of these modes of communication and as an indication of the extent to which there is the potential for a worldwide base of support (cf. Hellman 1999).

Through the use of communication technologies, the well-fought-for position of the EZLN as a loudspeaker through which the impoverished and oppressed of Chiapas and the rest of the world speaks, and through the willing sacrifice of the EZLN for the sake of creating a situation in which the *real* revolution, the revolution of "civil society," can take place, we can see that the Zapatistas have struggled to build strong connections with other groups with parallel goals. This in its own right is worthy of valorizing. However, the real test is whether or not the EZLN "walks the walk" of its liberatory discourse and its characteristic calls for direct democracy, a reinvigorated civil society, and the return of sovereignty to the people. For that, I turn to a discussion of the structure of the EZLN.

Structure of the EZLN

> We hope you understand that we had never run a revolution before and that we are still learning.
> —Subcomandante Marcos, *Shadows of Tender Fury* 1995 (217)

In the first instance, the EZLN is the military front of a group of Mayan-descended indigenous peoples living in the southeastern Mexican state of Chiapas. This description seems simultaneously obvious and trite for some of the reasons described earlier. However, it is crucial to remember this as the unifying motif of the Zapatista movement—it *is* a movement that utilizes ethnicity as an organizational category and as a political instrument for making claims against the Mexican government. The use of ethnicity as this tool by the inhabitants of the Las Cañadas region of Mexico in fact coincides with the announcement of the EZLN's attacks on San Cristóbal (Leyva Solano 1998: 45), though it is somewhat unclear whether that relationship is causal or not. However, by positing the claims made by the EZLN and the larger Zapatista movement in terms of ethnicity and an ethnic identity, the movement was able to position itself vis-à-vis the state of Mexico and the world at large differently than it could have if it were a Marxist or Maoist movement; put another way, the deployment of ethnicity as the key tool for claims-making parallels the work of new social movements, which posit an identity and a form of consciousness as the unifying core of the movement (Brysk 1996: 41). Had the movement been based on an objective class position, it may very well have been less successful precisely because it would not have been able to capture the proverbial imagination of the world. In placing identity and consciousness at the core, indigenous movements like the EZLN were able to turn "indigenousness" into a "modern vocabulary of nationalism: the hinge between tribe (or empire) and a modern state system" (ibid.: 48).

In putting identity at the core of the movement, the EZLN was able to dramatically expand its realm of potential support in two key ways: by having a fuzzy concept as the organizing principle, enabling other potential supporters to see what they needed to in the movement; and to make the movement as much about issues that face subaltern persons outside of Mexico as it is about the mountain inhabitants of Chiapas.

The fuzziness of "indigenous" identity greatly increases the power of the movement, in part because the identity is predicated on "cultural and racial difference" and alterity, enabling different readings of the core identity (Brysk 1996: 46). For policy-makers, the identity is one that is hierarchized, marginalized, and essentially ignored, which enabled the EZLN to build its support network secretly before announcing itself as a wide-scale social movement. For supporters, the concept of the nation that is included in the notion of indigenousness is a broad one, especially when the EZLN announces itself as a national liberation army; for the EZLN, nation can and does include the *patria* or homeland, the category of membership of "nationhood," that which is counterposed to the state, and even, as Holloway notes, "the idea of struggling wherever one happens to live, fighting against oppression, fighting for dignity" (Holloway 1998: 167). The openness or fuzziness of the concept of nation makes it so that anyone interested in supporting the movement can see themselves within that concept. It also ensures that other issues facing potentially aligned groups, such as the issue of dignity that pervades EZLN communiqués, are issues that can speak to a broader public, ensuring that what begins as a movement of the weak, focused on local issues and identity politics, becomes a stronger movement with a larger base of support (Brysk 1996: 39).

This use of identity as a core organizing principle of the movement, however, is not the only basis for the movement; material concerns and claims share center stage with the fuzzier concepts of "indigenousness," alterity, and dignity. Given the inhuman state of existence in Chiapas and the powerlessness of the indigenous peoples of Mexico, the EZLN developed an agenda comprising demands in the political, economic, social, and cultural realms, including: land redistribution; fair pricing for agricultural goods; the development of an infrastructure of care (the alleviation of malnutrition, medical facilities and physicians, and veterinarians to take care of livestock, among others); the cancellation of indigenous debts; cultural autonomy, including an indigenous press; full and free education; the end of discrimination and racism; an end to evictions and police repression of indigenous peoples in the name of wealthier landlords; dramatic electoral reform, both in Chiapas and Mexico; and rural electrification (Marcos 1995: 221–224). Beyond these demands regarding the material conditions, other conditions relating to the identity-based issues, such as those regarding the equal valorization of indigenous peoples and cultures, and issues regarding the position of women in indigenous communities and Mexico in general were put forth in order to fully ensure the equitable treatment of all peoples in Chiapas and the nation of Mexico and to, as Lorenzano put it (1998: 131), "to contribute to a vast movement which would return power to society, understood as a dense and complex network of horizontal forms of solidarity."

These demands, in part, are bound up with the fundamental forms of organization in the EZLN. The military force and its parallel political organization, to which the armed force is subordinated, are drawn from volunteers from Las Cañadas and other areas of EZLN-controlled Chiapas, meaning that the "base of support" of which the EZLN often speaks is actually "liberated territory/self-organised population/regulation of daily life/organs for 'people's power'/the militias and the army" (Lorenzano 1998: 138–139). Beyond the efforts of Subcomandante Marcos and his colleagues in the mid-1980s, the EZLN fighting force has by all accounts become an organization of "communes of workers," the "material basis of the armed political commune; their federation (in Indigenous Revolutionary Clandestine Committees) under a unified, collective and military–political command (the General Command) is the Zapatista Army of National Liberation (EZLN)" (ibid.: 139). There is, therefore, no real separation between the EZLN army and the communities they govern; those communities provide the material and political support for the activities of the EZLN, regardless of the form those activities take. The political and military structures of the EZLN are organized in a directly representative format: both the political organizations and armed forces in this case are built from and organized around grassroots members; the CCRIs are representative communities, with delegates from local committees representing those committees to the regional committees, and so on with regard to the General Command, the highest authority in EZLN-controlled areas (Leyva Solano 1998: 46–47). By organizing on the basis of direct and grassroots-based representation, the EZLN is able to ensure that its activities represent the majority will of the communities in its sphere of control.

While this mode of organizing an armed revolutionary force may seem contradictory to our usual conception of how the military should operate (hierarchically, clearly defined chain of command, martial discipline and orders carried out from above), it makes sense given the EZLN's overall goals. Subcomandante Marcos first gave insight into this organizational principle in discussing the reasons why he, the first "face" of the EZLN, is the Subcomandante: "I have the honor to have as my superiors the best men and women of the various ethnic groups. . . . They are my commanders and I will follow them down any path they choose. They are the collective and democratic leadership of the EZLN, and their acceptance of a dialogue is as true as their fighting hearts . . ." (Marcos 1995: 84). Drawing from traditional indigenous modes of social organization, in particular majority rule and continual discussion about the direction of a social order, the EZLN has preserved these indigenous forms of social structure in its revolutionary command while at the same time ensuring its commitment to not becoming institutionalized, seeing its decision-making process as a methodology more than a proposal: "Es un solo cuerpo discursivo que se relaciona más con una metodología de construcción que con una propuesta tipo, es decir, se trata de una invitación hecha a todos los espacios de la otredad para manifestar su existencia y empezar a tejer una red mundial de resistencias que permita a cada punto discontinuo fortalecerse frente al poder . . . "[3] (Ceceña 1999: para. 34). This methodology is in large part the implementation of the twin claims that the EZLN is not a revolutionary vanguard, but rather a plough to bring people's discontent to the surface, and that the ends of any revolutionary action are not what justifies the means used to attain the goal, but rather the goal is determined by the means chosen to attain it (Marcos 2001: 72, 76). If the goal is to deepen democracy, nondemocratic means cannot be used to attain that goal; and if the EZLN is not a vanguard bringing revolutionary enlightenment to the people but rather a tool for the people's expression of their own needs, then this mode of social organization makes perfect sense—it becomes an organization designed to enable the people to enact their own plans, their own goals, and to engage in processes of self-determination.

In enacting this revolutionary methodology, and in structuring the EZLN as the executor of the people's will, the self-declared experimental nature of the Zapatistas becomes more comprehensible. Marcos himself apologizes on a number of occasions for the seemingly haphazard beginnings of the EZLN, reminding his readers, "we had never run a revolution before" (Marcos 1995: 217), and making it clear that the identity of the EZLN was under construction, "creating an identity as we go along" (Marcos 2001: 76). The EZLN rebellion is, in large part, a "conscious work of building," in which "discussion of projects, implementation, evaluation of achievements and shortcomings . . . lays the very foundations of social life" (Lorenzano 1998: 134). The "permanent interrogation" (ibid.: 135) that characterizes EZLN decision-making serves two important functions: first, it enables the continual contribution of the membership of the EZLN and aligned groups and communities to the project and activities taken on by the movement, returning decision-making power to the people; and second, it enables the expansion of the base of support by virtue of seeing the potential contribution they can make to their liberation and that of others (ibid.: 131, 138).

The enlargement of the Zapatista project—what has also been seen as the formation of a separate New Zapatismo Movement (NMZ) or Zapatismo—has been the result of this kind of permanent interrogation and conscious work of building. Realizing that engaging in dialogue with only the Mexican government was fruitless, both in terms of practical outcomes and the Zapatista discourse, the EZLN began to create an "alternative national project," the National Democratic Convention (CND) (Leyva Solano 1998: 48–49). This convention, a collection and ongoing dialogue between groups in Mexican civil society (and elsewhere; ibid.: 48), was created to provide a space for the discussion of important national and international matters. By doing this, the EZLN broadened the base of support, diversified its activities, and made more realizable the goal of reinvigorating civil society as a political force by eliminating the dividing line between the two. In convening and participating in the CND, the EZLN made clear that their viewpoint and perspective was not to be imposed on the convention; rather, the CND was to develop its own set of goals and agenda for the attainment of true democracy in Mexico:

> Yes to the first steps in the construction of something greater than Aguascalientes, to the construction of peace with dignity. Yes to the beginning of an effort greater than the one that has produced Aguascalientes. Yes to the effort for democratic change that includes freedom and justice for the forgotten people, the majority of our country. Yes to the beginning of the end of this long, grotesque nightmare that is called the history of Mexico.
>
> Yes, the moment has come to say to everyone that we neither want, nor are we able, to occupy the place that some hope we will occupy, the place from which all opinions come, all the answers, all the routes, all the truths. We are not going to do that. (Marcos 1995: 248)

In beginning the transformation from being the Zapatista National Liberation Army to the central convening figures in the New Zapatismo Movement, the EZLN has attempted both to ensure that its goals of deeper democracy and social justice for the people of Mexico can be met and to concretely address the needs of a population that has been warred against, whether militarily or not, for the whole history of Mexico.

We can see, then, that the agenda the EZLN set forth in 1994—the satisfaction of both the material needs of the indigenous peoples of Chiapas and the development of a deeper democratic society for all of

Mexico, as well as beyond—manifests itself hand-in-hand with the tactics the organization has used to satisfy that agenda. By drawing from indigenous experiences of the "invasion of modernity," particular elements of indigenous identity, "the persistence of old forms of command, and the accumulation of collective experience and the formation of their own leadership" (Gilly 1997: 68–70), the EZLN has built an organization that simultaneously pursues a set of goals that has the enhancement of human dignity at its core and, by the EZLN's standards, has organized itself around the principles it wants to enact. In linking the goals and means used to attain those goals (Marcos 2001: 76), the EZLN has in large part found a way to avoid the kind of postrevolutionary Terror Sartre warned against; and despite the fact that the revolution is not over, the EZLN seems well on its way to avoiding the problems that faced Algeria after its war of independence. It is in these structural elements of the EZLN's organization that we find the means by which this has been achieved.

Mandar obedeciendo and *preguntando caminamos*: "to command obeying" and "asking while we walk"

In pursuing this path, the EZLN has drawn upon and transformed particular organizational traditions of post-Mayan indigenous peoples as tools for making decisions about the activities of the EZLN. These traditions, which go hand in hand, are *mandar obedeciendo*, "to command obeying," and *preguntando caminamos*, "asking while we walk."

The essential notion behind the structural organization of the EZLN is simultaneously simple and complex: those who would appear to lead an organization or social grouping are actually not the leaders. Rather, the "leaders"—perhaps "representatives" or "delegates" would be better, though no more accurate, terms—are the executors of the general will of the people. Representatives of the people who hold leadership roles are, by virtue of their position, beholden to the communities they represent, and their leadership is immediately revocable if they do not satisfy their duty to "command obeying the community" (Holloway 1998: 164). The community here is the social organ that provides the basis for all decision-making, and is the ground on which the leadership and any kinds of structures of power are built. Those who are selected to occupy positions of authority in a society are put there for the sake of satisfying the needs of the collective. As the CCRI-CG put it in a 1994 communiqué, "We see that the lack of reason among those who command by commanding is what causes our pain and deepens the sorrow of our dead ... And we see that there must be change, and that those who command should obey, and we see that this far-away word, 'democracy,' which names government with reason, is good for the many and the few" (Marcos 1995: 151). The invocation of some of the essentials of American democratic theory here, especially calls to protect against the tyranny of the majority, is particularly stunning in light of the critique leveled at nonrepresentative forms of government—in the communiqué, Mexico, but by extension, the United States. In any case, the assurance of "the good for the many and the few" is the primary reason for the existence of any kind of social order; and the EZLN holds that at the core of its social structure through the use of *mandar obedeciendo*.

This principle of *mandar obedeciendo* ensures that the essential power basis in a society, the essential sovereignty of a sociopolitical order, remains with the people. By creating a social structure in which the leadership is revocable for, as Marcos puts it, not having "the will of the majority ... in the hearts of the men and women who command" (Marcos 1995: 151), the Zapatistas have in essence constructed a structure that inverts the currently existing sociopolitical order of hierarchies and power relations between one segment of society and the majority. As the *Cuarta Declaración de la Selva Lacandona* puts it,

> Por el otro lado, el proyecto de la transición a la democracia, no una transición pactada con el poder que simule un cambio para que todo siga igual, sino la transición a la democracia como el proyecto de reconstrucción del país; la defensa de la soberanía nacional; la justicia y la esperanza como anhelos; la verdad y el mandar obedeciendo como guía de jefatura; la estabilidad y la seguridad que dan la democracia y la libertad; el diálogo, la tolerancia y la inclusión como nueva forma de hacer política. (EZLN 1996b: para. 46)[4]

This new "guide to leadership" (*guía de jefatura*) essentially decenters the existing political structure by removing government and governmentality from the core of a political order. In reconceptualizing the sociopolitical order of things, *mandar obedeciendo* works to ensure that "power is neither the essence nor the center of politics" (Nolasco 1997: para. 9; original in Spanish). It goes even further to create a situation of compatibility between governors and the governed by removing the vertical structures of power and the "professionalization" of political activity in the form of parties and "inherited" presidential power (Ceceña 1999: para. 46).

In this joint decentering of politics by removing the government from the center and the transition to an order in which the base of society has the power to recall their leadership, what is gained—and relied upon for its success—is the collective participation of the people in decision-making processes. When the EZLN declared war on the Mexican government in 1994, it did so only as a result of discussions with all the communities within its area of influence, ensuring that *they* were the ones to make the choice to go to war; the EZLN only suggested this particular course of action to be considered among others (Holloway 1998: 164–165). Further organizational developments, policy changes, and amendments to the Zapatista agenda, including the inclusion of the Women's Revolutionary Law (developed as a result of claims made against the CCRI-CG by women participating in the EZLN; Millán 1998b: 67, 70), were made along these lines as well: if the community wanted something done, the leadership of the EZLN had to do it (Holloway 1998: 165). This mandating of power to civil society ensures that it remains "the true protagonist of democratic politics, the true 'controller' of the 'controllers'" (Rojo Arias 1997: para. 49; original in Spanish). The way to ensure that the leadership is responsive and responsible to the people, of course, is to ensure that there is a continual dialogue between representatives and the people and that the voices of both the few and the many are heard (Marcos 1995: 151).

The additional structural concept at work here is *preguntando caminamos*, literally "asking while we walk." Increasing the involvement of the people in the collective decision-making processes of a society subjects the social order—not just the policies of the leadership (however defined) of that order, but the *entire* social structure itself—to a "permanent interrogation . . . of social life as a whole, which [the EZLN] address and question as to its capacity for self-organisation and self-transformation" (Lorenzano 1998: 135). The only way to bring about a situation where to command is actually to obey, the Zapatistas argue, is not to impose the "party line," but to do it "through opening up spaces for discussion and democratic decision, in which they would express their view, but their view should count only as one among many" (Holloway 1998: 175). Seeing one of the crucial problems with current pseudo-democratic political orders as being the separation of political society and civil society (*à la* Marx's critique in *On the Jewish Question*), the use of dialogue and conversation about what is to be done by a social order completely deconstructs that separation by making civil society political. In other words, with politics deprofessionalized, with the "leadership" of a social order instantly recallable if they fail to obey the mandate of the people, and with the key decision-making body being the collective rather than the leadership, those elements outside the state apparatuses become *the political body par excellence*. Further, this deconstruction of the barriers between political and civil society ensures that the content of politics—the decisions that are made, the processes that go into making those decisions, and the benefits of those decisions for the population as a whole—are prioritized over the insulation and protection of political persons (Rojo Arias 1997: para. 48). The furtherance of *mandar obedeciendo* and *preguntando caminamos* as principles for governance and structuring society means that politics is no longer a matter of implicit or explicit force or the distancing of the political apparatuses from the people, but rather becomes a matter for the "force of reason and the heart" (Rojo Arias 1997: para. 70) and a continual confrontation of leadership, political parties, and the population as a whole, which ultimately has the authority to change the entire system if it no longer works for them (Nolasco 1997: para. 39).

What is contained within this form of social organization governed by the twinned conceptions of *mandar obedeciendo* and *preguntando caminamos* provides us with a deeper insight into how the EZLN social structure can serve as a model for social structures outside that context. First, these two principles imply a greater concern for dignity than appears in currently existing "democratic" social orders. Dignity, as many authors have pointed out, is the lynchpin of the EZLN critique of "occidental" thought. Posited in the sense of "that which rises against humiliation, dehumanization, marginalisation" (Holloway 1998: 184), dignity for the Zapatistas becomes a "radical, open-ended class category" (Paulson 2001: 280) that encompasses the absence of humanity under a neoliberal capitalist system. Dignity as a concept works to provide the EZLN with a way of capturing the plurality and diversity of human goals and humankind while at the same time eliminating the hierarchization that comes with the notion of alterity (Ceceña 1999: para. 51). The world the EZLN wishes to bring about is one that has the possibility of containing multiple worlds; or rather, "The praxis of dignity, as relational, as tending towards openings, as irreducible plurality, is an enactment and a performance of utopia-as-process. It is a reconfiguration of the world in political practice and thought, which changes the whole conceptual structure and modality of theorising from a mode based on the given, and closing the present (as legislative, authoritative)" (McManus 2002: 11). The conceptual framework of dignity, just like the structural concepts of *mandar obedeciendo* and *preguntando caminamos*, ensure an open-endedness to revolutionary action: The world must be made as the people who live in it see fit; those structures created to make that world must always be subject to revision and reconsideration; and the people who lead these social groups must always be recallable if they no longer lead with these two issues at their heart. The discussions that produce this action and its necessary open-endedness are those that ensure the reciprocal recognition of "multiple dignities" or projects (Holloway 1998: 179) and value those projects for their contribution to the collective well-being. The collective will, from a Zapatista point of view, will through this practice and these goals regain its moral authority (Nolasco 1997: para. 68), and it is through that moral authority that the "we" of the community is constructed through each decision it makes (Millán 1998a: para. 10).

Thus, in constructing a social organization that has taken on both the ends of creating a fully democratic social order characterized by justice and dignity and the means of having a directly democratic revolutionary organization (where direct democracy has become "la forma de la vida"; EZLN 1996a: 54–55), the EZLN has built for itself a social order in which the will of the people and of the base communities of support is both the basis of political power and the recipient of the good of political actions. It receives this good in two ways: the direct results of policies and decisions made by the collective will; and the capacity for participating in both individual and collective projects of self-determination. As such, it provides us with at least one model for organizing a social order around the principles we have discussed throughout this book—a socially oriented ethics, predicated on the practice of resistance, that takes as one of its primary goods an ethics of freedom.

Social Structure and Social Ethics in the EZLN

> La particularidad del discurso zapatista es que pone en cuestión *disciplina moral y definiciones* desde otra ética y otras definiciones basadas en unas sociedades no "anteriores" o pasadas, sino actualmente vivientes dentro del territorio mexicano. A partir de esa existencia, no proponen el regreso a ningún pasado sino que abren la disputa sobre el contenido y la definición de esta modernidad presente en la cual ellas también existen.
>
> —Gilly, *Chiapas: La razón ardiente* 1997 (96)[5]

Much as we saw in at least the ethically positive aspects of the project motivating the Algerian Revolution, the ethics of freedom present in the structure of the EZLN and the structure they work to see in all societies has three key components: freedom as its goal; freedom as a process; and the value of sacrifice through resistance in the name of freedom.

The first component, taking freedom as the goal of resistant action, is a key element in the EZLN agenda. The restatement of the EZLN agenda in a mid-January 1994 communiqué includes the economic, social, and political demands that would have to be met in order for the overall goal of increased freedom for the indigenous peoples of Chiapas and the people of Mexico to be attained. In particular, these include solutions to the "grave material conditions of life which we, the indige-nous people of Chiapas, suffer"; "racism, marginalization, lack of respect, expulsion from our land, attacks against our culture and tradi-tions"; and "the lack of legal space for real participation by us, the indigenous people of Chiapas and all Mexicans, in national political life" (Marcos 1995: 88–89). This set of demands indicates a genuine desire not just for the amelioration of the poor standard of living in Chiapas in mate-rial terms, but also the yearning for the capacity of self-determination on the part of Chiapans and all Mexicans. This quest for self-determination, a characteristic of many indigenous movements, goes beyond the usual "framework of local autonomy, cultural survival, and 'ethnodevelop-ment': empowered and informed self-management of cultural and social change" (Brysk 1996: 41–42), and instead encompasses autonomy for *all* Mexicans, cultural survival for *all* peoples of Mexico, and self-management for everyone. Reflected in a letter from Subcomandante Marcos to Leonard Peltier, in which Marcos writes, "knowing oneself with history impedes one from being tossed around by this absurd machine that is the system" (Marcos 2000: para. 23), the notion of self-determination at work in the EZLN political agenda and social structure is one where the collected members of the social order are able to integrate their past, present, and future in ways they see fit. As Millán puts it, the EZLN conception of freedom as a goal comprises

> una plataforma de compleja interacción entre derechos ciudadanos modernos y antiguas concepciones del mundo, corazón que puede revi-talizar a occidente guiándolo por una modernidad distinta, una que ponga coto a la idea-fuerza de progreso a toda costa, de univocidad y homogeneidad del "desarrollo," imponiendo límites racionales (en térmi-nos humanos) a la razón instrumental. (Millán 1998a: para. 17)[6]

It is this complex interaction of ancient and modern conceptions of social membership and freedom that the EZLN works to preserve in structuring its organizations along the lines of *mandar obedeciendo* and *preguntando caminamos*; by ensuring that the leadership is beholden to the collective membership of the organization *on the collective's terms*, these structural precepts ensure that the collective makes its decisions based on the extent to which *it* wishes to imbricate itself in the moder-nity it faces down. Put another way, the dignity of the membership is maintained by giving the membership the decision-making authority with regard to participating in the conflict between the humanity they wish to see and the negation of that humanity as present in the larger social order (Holloway 1998: 183–184). In this way, the version of freedom the EZLN holds as its goal parallels the notion of positive freedom as developed by Isaiah Berlin: "Liberty as a right encompasses the notion of human self-development and of dignity, where that would include the enjoyment of the rights and duties of citizenship" (Rojo Arias 1997: para. 74; original in Spanish). This liberty, which must appear in both living and acting (ibid.: para. 86), will be the key marker of the eventual success or failure of the EZLN.

The structural norms of the EZLN's political and military organization also work to ensure the second element of an ethics of freedom, namely freedom operating as a process instead of a signifier of some end state of affairs. A large part of the EZLN agenda demands self-determination, which as we have seen elsewhere in this work cannot be a one-time deal, but rather an ongoing process of self-actualization. In discussing the flexibility of EZLN forms of social organization, Vera Herrera argues:

> Son prácticas surgidas de la vida en comunidad y abarcan sus formas de organización, conformación política, impartición de justifica y otras muchas de relación humana. Juntas son lo mejor de los pueblos indios y coinciden con las búsquedas de organizaciones ciudadanas, rurales y urbanas en su atención al tejer procesos. Coinciden también con el viejo sueño autogestionario, con las previsiones de los anarquistas, o con los planteamientos radicales de Deleuze, Foucault o el mismo Ivan Illich. (Vera 1997: para. 2)[7]

As well, Rojo Arias claims that the EZLN's primary valuation of freedom as a core element of their agenda is in part a reaction to an understanding of the currently existing legal system as a form of coercion and their view of a deeper form of democracy as "the condition *sine qua non* for the exercise of liberty" and personal and collective self-determination and development (1997: paras. 135–138; original in Spanish). Linking democratization, liberty, and individual and collective self-determination in this way ensures the processual aspect of freedom. By seeing these three aspects as intertwined and making them not only revolutionary goals but also means to achieve those goals, the EZLN works to reinvigorate the ethical aspects of political life by creating both the descriptive and normative conditions required for collective decision-making, making the situation one characterized by both the practice of collective decision-making and the prescriptive goodness of collective participation in the social order (Ceceña 1999: para. 47). Ensuring the practical implementation of this notion of freedom as processual, as embodied in the practices of self-determination and collective participation in decisional processes, creates the situation the EZLN looks to attain: the fostering of relations between individuals, not objective (i.e., class, race/ ethnicity, or gender-based) positions in society (EZLN 1996a: 61, 117).

Finally, the EZLN's recognition of the need for solidarity with others and sacrifice for the sake of freedom in a social order is clear. The linking of the Zapatista struggle to other similar struggles for democracy, justice, and freedom is made clear throughout their communiqués; the EZLN sees their situation paralleled in other contexts around the world, sees themselves as providing some form of example of the possibility of struggling for dignity, and works to ensure that their struggle is not the primary one, but rather one that occurs in conjunction with those others with similar ends. As the CCRI-CG put it in a February 1994 communiqué,

> We saw in these words that if our struggle was alone again, once again it would be useless. So we directed our blood and the path of our dead to the road that other feet walked in truth. We are nothing if we walk alone we are everything when we walk together in step with other dignified feet.
> [. . .] We have little to offer you since the poverty of our lands is still very great and our place in the history of Mexico is still very small. But walking in step with you and with all the good people of this world, we will have to grow and finally find the place that our dignity and our history deserve. (Marcos 1995: 139)

That sense of solidarity, captured in the Intergalactic Conference for Humanity and against Neoliberalism in 1996, sees the particular struggle of the EZLN as having to occur in conjunction with other struggles, "national in their form, popular and international in their content," and needed to be "accompanied by forms of solidarity and resistance on the part of the dominated and excluded in the countries of the center" (EZLN 1996a: 41; original in Spanish). That struggle, following the Zapatista model of *mandar obedeciendo* and its positioning of representatives as the executors of the collective will, is one the EZLN takes on willingly, to its potential and/or probable detriment and for the benefit of others: "Para nosotros el dolor y la angustia, para nosotros la alegre rebeldía, para nosotros el futuro negado, para nosotros la dignidad insurrecta. Para nosotros nada" (EZLN 1996b: para. 10).[8] In understanding their position as one of struggle on behalf of others—and note, this is not the vanguardist approach of saying "we know better than you," but rather an approach oriented to solidarity with others as expressed in their willingness to take up arms—the EZLN gladly sacrifices itself in the name of a better, more just social order for all. It is this that, almost above all else, signifies the ethics of freedom present in the EZLN; in the name of both bringing about freedom as a goal and increasing freedom as a processual means for attaining that goal, the EZLN gives up its own freedom for the sake of ameliorating others' conditions of existence.

It is a result of this ethics of freedom that we can see the implications of the EZLN's actions and structural organization for a larger existential social ethics, the one we work to develop here. The first element of an existential social ethics displayed here is a radical revision of the power relations in the social order. Moving from the vertical, hierarchized conception of power present in Western societies to a more horizontal form of social relations is one of the crucial elements for both the creation of this form of social ethics and for its perpetuation and expansion over time; the EZLN approach to social structure is a key way to do this. First and foremost, the EZLN knows that its revolution cannot institutionalize itself or else it violates its own goals and agenda: "A juicio de muchos, el zapatismo es el mejor ejemplo del nuevo pensamiento revolucionario; no debe ni puede convertirse en la nueva 'ideología oficial' de los revolucionarios; no debe ni puede institucionalizarse" (EZLN 1996a: 52).[9] It has to avoid the self-institutionalization of the Terror described by Sartre precisely because of its commitments to opening the world to further revolutions and to fostering better relations between individuals as persons, not examples of objective positions or tools for the revolution (ibid.: 61). This falls in line with Subcomandante Marcos's claim that thinking in terms of whose hegemony will win betrays the revolution (Marcos 2001: 70). It also comes through in the notions of *mandar obedeciendo* and *preguntando caminamos*, which work to ensure the development of horizontal forms of social solidarity and to foster a deepening of democracy and democratization (Lorenzano 1998: 131; Millán 1998b: 67). By structuring the Zapatistan forms of social organization in such a way that there is continual interrogation of both the policies and the organizational forms themselves, then, the EZLN has modeled a significant change in the form of power relations.

Concomitantly, this change in the forms that power takes also foster an increase in discussion and collective participation in decision-making processes, another key aspect of the form of social ethics developed here.

Providing a "bottom-up" transformation of Mexican society (and hopefully outside of Mexico as well), Zapatista social organization can preserve and foster collective discussion and consensus building as modes of making decisions for a community (Burbach 1994: 113). The ongoing discussion created by and needed for the success of *mandar obedeciendo* and *preguntando caminamos* as organizational forms works to continuously reinvigorate the revolutionary project (Lorenzano 1998: 135, 143). Two significantly ethical elements of social life are constructed and reconstructed through the encouragement of dialogue and discussion, through *la fuerza de razón*. First, the construction of horizontal forms of social solidarity—bonds between and among equal individuals not seen as examples of hierarchized positions in *le champ du politique* (to borrow Bourdieu's term)—occurs through the valuation of everyone's contribution to collective decision-making processes. This process of "encountering" other members of a society is one that can only further the sense of solidarity created by involving everyone in the work of a society. As Vera puts it,

> Esta forma imaginativa de hacer política no está exenta de riesgos. Se necesita fuerza y seguridad para incluir posiciones muy dispares en su seno, todo con tal que el debate y la discusión sean asequibles. . . . La propuesta zapatista de ser generosos e incluyentes—de ubicar el poder como útil si tiene el diseño repartido y articulado de un tejido—tiene un potencial enorme porque remite al proceso de conformación y continuidad de la organización: el orden no se impone, se encuentra, se descubre, se teje: "juntar los momentos en un solo corazón, un corazón de todos, nos hará sabios, un poquito más para enfrentar lo que venga. Sólo entre todos sabemos todo"—dijo un *marakame huichol*. (Vera 1997: paras. 62–63)[10]

This form of group-based discussion and debate, wherein clear spaces for collective participation are created by the social order to foster collective participation, further has the result of more direct bonds between members of that social order, increasing the solidarity felt among people, the comfort in expressing one's views, and eliminating the feeling of oppression that derives from a clear lack of capacity for participating in the social order (ibid.: para. 36). In sum, the transformation of vertical relations of power into horizontal bonds of solidarity and the fostering of discussion among inhabitants of a society become mutually reinforcing social forces, preventing the institutionalization of any kind of postrevolutionary Terror and ensuring the continued capacity for participation in the group.

The more direct bonds constructed through these discursive processes can also create a sense of solidarity in the collective project of building a new social order, another integral element of an existential social ethics. Self-determination, one of the key components of the EZLN agenda, requires a set of social conditions that enable individuals and collectives to engage in processes of *autogestionario*, to use the Zapatista term. The construction of such a set of conditions by the EZLN through *mandar obedeciendo* and *preguntando caminamos* results in forms of political articulation that make possible the enactment of a collective project, one that is collectively determined through these very forms (Holloway 1998: 175–176). And as we have seen, the EZLN sees itself as working *in solidarity with* other groups struggling to attain the same goals of democracy, justice, and freedom; even the EZLN's proposal for continued discussion after the 1999 plebiscite on peace talks with the Mexican government indicates as much:

> We believe that allowing the network we strengthened through the Consulta to fade would be a serious error. We would like to continue a dialogue with everyone who participated in the Consulta, in whatever capacity. Yet, we must first ask, IS IT NECESSARY TO CONTINUE TO BUILD UPON THIS WORK? HOW WOULD WE RE-DEFINE AND REGENERATE IT?
>
> The following themes could serve as guides for our dialogue:
> 1. THE NEED for the organization of a local and national relationship that understands the importance of our voice in the struggle for justice, democracy and liberty in Mexico, while also understanding the demand for struggle here.
> 2. THE NEED for a process that identifies principles that unite us.
> 3. THE NEED to develop struggles that engage us as members of a civil society conscious of its role nationally and internationally.
> 4. THE NEED for the organization of people, a movement, which like the wind, spreads the seeds and pollinates the flowers of struggles locally, nationally and internationally.
> 5. THE NEED for the organization of a web that binds us to a practice that aspires to reclaim self-governance, in the establishment and defense of social norms and relationships while building an international political norm that demands that those who govern, "govern by obedience."
> 6. THE NEED to ask, dialogue and answer the following question: What is resistance to us? (Marcos 1999: paras. 14–21; capitalization in original)

The development of the organizations Marcos outlines; the call to practice *mandar obedeciendo*; the request to discuss the meaning of resistance—all these indicate the extent to which the EZLN works to foster solidarity in the project they have taken on along with and parallel to others. In pursuing this form of collective work, the EZLN strives to integrate efforts at the local, national, and international levels of social life, thereby expanding the solidarity that characterizes their efforts beyond national borders and beyond the local struggle in Chiapas (Löwy 1998: para. 34). This collective project—one that the structural norms of *mandar obedeciendo* and *preguntando caminamos* allow for extension into other types of projects that may or may not be less resistant—is one that is enabled by these structural norms and is furthered by the forms of discussion and debate these norms foster and reproduce.

This struggle for collective solidarity in the revolutionary project, whether one sees it as limited to victory in the quest for autonomy and self-determination or the continued building of new and ethical social forms, is one that does not operate like "really existing socialism," which is "disciplinary and bounded" (Vera 1997: para. 24; original in Spanish). Rather, this form of collective solidarity and bondedness in furtherance of a collectively determined project also creates a set of conditions that fosters and encourages the development of individual projects that are in line with and help to further the collective project of democracy, justice and freedom. *Un mundo donde quepan muchos mundos* ("A world that includes many worlds"; Millán 1998a: para. 4): this is the point of self-determination in the EZLN agenda. What would be the point, after all, of building a new social order in which only the collective has agency and requires its members to pursue only those paths of action decided on by the collective? Would this social order be as inhuman—or perhaps even more inhuman—than the one struggled against? For the EZLN, the revolution is supposed to be the one that *brings about* the revolution, which they see as "self-creative, a revolution created in the process of struggle" (Holloway 1998: 165–166). By putting the notion of dignity at the center of Zapatismo, the EZLN has constructed a collective project that has to ensure the dignity not only of the group-in-revolt, but also of all those individuals who are in struggle within the group-in-revolt (loc. cit.). The task of the revolutionary movement, then, is to create a set of conditions that can reclaim the importance of humanity for everyone concerned:

> Ampliar nuestro mundo defendiendo el derecho a la existencia de otros mundos implica modificar rasgos sustanciales de nuestra propia cultura. No sólo relativizarla, tomar distancia crítica ante ella, sino también, por ejemplo, preguntarse acerca de las formas del conocimiento humano. De alguna manera, se trata de construir un conjunto heurístico que nos

permita conocer sin evadir la responsabilidad del conocimiento en el estado actual de las cosas del mundo, planteándose como problema el de generar nociones que desestructuren paradigmas cognitivos dominantes al abrir espacios para experiencias vivénciales diversas, la de los muchos mundos que habitan el mundo, y que hoy, queremos, resignifiquen la humanidad. (Millán 1998a: para. 20)[11]

To include these many worlds and diverse life experiences within our collective conception of the world simultaneously enables the pursuit of different life-projects by members who also contribute their diversity to the collective project, and construct the EZLN's ideal vision of a demo-cratic social order, that of "a 'common house,' a space of the free taking of decisions where it would be possible to be manifested in distinct opinions, including [distinct] visions of the world" (Rojo Arias 1997: para. 68; original in Spanish). By recentering politics around the issue of dignity for both the collective and the individuals within the collective, the EZLN's agenda can encompass projects oriented to the good of both aspects of the social group without privileging the needs of the one over those of the other.

In this way, the social ethics present in the EZLN's political agenda and organizational norms can also address what may be a large part of the cause of the plight of indigenous peoples, both in Chiapas and around the world: the issue of Otherness or alterity. By working to develop a democratic social order that represents the unity of dignities (Holloway 1998: 179), the EZLN agenda allows for the integration of a wide variety of ways of life within a larger umbrella of democracy, justice, and freedom. In doing so, the focus is moved from alterity and deciding who counts as a fully participating member of a society to valorizing the diversity of modes of existence within that society: "En el discurso zapatista la emancipación humana supone la eliminación de la alteridad pero no de la diversidad. Todos los mundos son posibles porque ninguno se impone sobre los demás, porque cada uno ocupa su espacio, porque respetando la diferencia es como se alcanza la igualdad" (Ceceña 1999: para. 51).[12] And in validating and respecting the differ-ences in people's individual and collective life-experiences and projects, the hierarchies present in the notion of alterity can be eliminated, thereby eliminating the need for the Other (ibid.: para. 39). Integrating all these different ethical aspects of the EZLN agenda, then, would yield a social order in which dignity and freedom are normative values, put into practice through the establishment of sociopolitical structures that enable and encourage the participation of all in collective decision-making processes, and yield a society characterized by equality and the capacity of individuals and collectives to pursue projects that expand the concrete freedom of all.

Ethical Radicalism and the Zapatistas: The *juntas de buen gobierno*

> You are in the autonomous territory in rebellion of the Zapatistas. Here the people command and the government obeys.
>
> —Sign at the entrance to the Caracol at Oventic,
> San Andres Larrainzar

Given the kind of existential analysis we have used throughout this book, it would seem clear what an examination of the organization of the EZLN offers for the development of a resisting social ethics. The combination of their stated goals and the way in which the Zapatistas have arranged their collective decision-making processes ensures that instead of the mere "national liberation" that appears to have been the goal of the FLN, the project of Zapatismo is rather a form of social liberation, one that works toward a situation of concrete practical freedom for all, both individually and collectively. Yet, the ever-surprising Zapatistas have gone even beyond this valorous goal in transforming their social organization again, highlighting the practice of processual consent and freedom described thus far.

The Aguascalientes—the meetings held regularly between the EZLN and the rest of civil society that could make it to Chiapas—provided the Zapatistas with the opportunity to regularly consult with those who were engaged in parallel struggles for dignity and democracy in the face of the expansion of neoliberalism. After the 1995 destruction of the original Aguascalientes by the Mexican Army, more sites were established to hold these meetings, ensuring an ongoing dialogue between partners in the movement for which Zapatismo was merely a microcosm, or what Marcos called the "spaces for *encuentro* and dialogue with national and international civil society" (Marcos 2003: para. 26). What had transpired in recent years, however, were two parallel notions of "charity" from the larger international community: the provision of goods not needed by the Zapatista communities (Marcos has recently joked about carrying in his backpack a single pink high-heeled shoe received from an NGO), and the insistence by some NGOs that they, and not the Zapatistas, control projects they provide. Rather than remaining the world's resistant "Cinderella"—the term is Marcos's—the EZLN decided to reconsider its path heading into its second decade.

As a result of nearly two years of silence and discussion, the EZLN announced in August 2003 that the Aguascalientes were "dead," and that an entirely new form of Zapatista social organization was to be developed. Taking seriously the San Andres Accords and the COCOPA Laws, which had claimed to implement "indigenous autonomy," the EZLN declared that it was implementing what *La Jornada* called "Autonomy Without Permission" and establishing new forms of self-governance in Zapatista communities. These new institutions were designed to ensure a greater degree of autonomy for Zapatista areas, both from governments and from NGOs bent on deciding what projects the indigenous peoples needed without their consultation; to moderate and negotiate relations between Zapatista and non-Zapatista communities; and to serve as a gateway or bridge between Zapatista communities and the outside world. The twinned institutions, *juntas de buen gobierno* (committees of good government) and *caracoles* (literally translated, a conch shell, but also the Mayan symbol for speaking and the local tool for calling communities together), were to implement the spirit of indigenous autonomy that had been betrayed by the Mexican government. As well, Subcomandante Marcos announced that the EZLN was no longer to be the spokesperson for the Zapatista communities, as the notion of an army governing a region was completely anathema to the goals of Zapatismo.

The *juntas de buen gobierno*, five committees made up of delegates from the Autonomous Councils of the various Zapatista-held zones of southeastern Mexico (and thereby including all thirty Zapatista Autonomous Municipalities in Rebellion, or MAREZs), have as their primary function the management of affairs common to the various MAREZs and to neighboring non-Zapatista communities, and report only to the CCRI-CG. In particular, their duties include attending to the "inequality of development" between MAREZs due to the differential allocation of NGO projects through the determination of needed projects and the collection of a "brother tax," which redistributes development monies to localities unnoticed by NGOs but in need of development; mediating conflicts between MAREZs and between MAREZs and "official municipalities" (i.e., government-controlled towns); monitoring reported human rights violations and inconsistencies in the application of policy; ensuring that projects pursued in the MAREZs are completed in ways agreed to by the communities; monitoring the implementation of laws developed and agreed to by the MAREZs; attending to civil society members that visit the communities or pursue projects in the area; approve Zapatista activities in official municipalities;

and "care for Zapatista territory in rebellion that it manages, which it manages by obeying" (Marcos 2003a: Part 6, paras. 3–13; SIPAZ 2003: paras. 4–11).

In serving as both a conduit between MAREZs and between MAREZs and official municipalities, the *juntas* effectively democratize intercommunity relations. By involving direct representation from the autonomous municipalities, including those that may very well have conflicts with another MAREZ, the *junta* extends the consensus-building decision-making processes with the EZLN into relations between communities; as well, by having the *juntas* negotiate with non-Zapatista municipalities with regard to issues arising between them, this consensus-building process can extend outside of the communities. This latter issue has become particularly important in recent years, when official communities have claimed that the EZLN has tried to impose Zapatismo on them. As Comandante David put it at the inauguration of the *juntas* in 2003, "It is not necessary to be Zapatista in order to be served and respected by the Autonomous Municipalities in any part of our territory. By being a member of the community or of the municipality to which you belong, you have the right to be served. . . . We, the Zapatistas, are not going to attack anyone, nor impose anything on the brothers who are not Zapatista. We will be respectful with all our indigenous brothers, without regard to their organization, their party or their religion, always and as long as they respect us and respect our communities . . . ." It is in the shared experience of "discrimination and humiliation . . . hunger and poverty . . . marginalization and ignoring by the bad government" that their problems arise, Comandante David continues; therefore, in the spirit of indigenous autonomy, a solution agreed to by all parties within this situation should be the one developed (Comandante David 2003: paras. 4–7). As well, the establishment of the *juntas* as the interlocutor between Zapatista communities and international civil society further extends the radical form of democracy practiced within the EZLN into relations with the outside world; while the *juntas* are charged with serving as this conduit with the outside, they do not have the ultimate decision-making authority, being as restrained by the principle of *mandar obedeciendo* as other Zapatista institutions, thereby ensuring that the communities represented by the *juntas* decide on the implementation of development projects, the pursuit of research in the area, and other activities involving NGOs. The *juntas* are also charged with ensuring the elimination of inequalities between communities as a result of receiving NGO and civil society assistance by determining themselves where development funds most need to be directed and reserving 10% of project seed money for redistribution to "less favored *autonomías*" (Ross 2003: para. 7; Marcos 2003a: Part 6, para. 21). As one of the fundamental issues of the entire Zapatista movement has been the structural inequality between the center and periphery of the neoliberal world economy, the Zapatista communities argued that there should not be those same inequities within Zapatismo. In establishing the *juntas* as managing bodies, then, the EZLN avoided the inertial repetition of the Mexican government structure by ensuring that the Aguascalientes did not become new *cabeceras* (county seats), dominating the rest of the Zapatista communities (ibid.: para. 6). The *caracoles*, technically the "Houses of the *Juntas de Buen Gobierno*," provide the actual physical site of the *juntas*, as well as a welcoming center for members of outside organizations. Inheriting the tradition of the Aguascalientes as the meeting place for peoples from within and without Zapatismo, the *caracoles* also concretely manifest the principle of indigenous autonomy, serving as the site of intersection between the Zapatista movement, neighboring communities, and, as in the case of Oventic, which hosted the inauguration festival, the outside world.

The second large-scale transformation of the EZLN involved its structural relation with the rest of the movement. Since the start of the insurrection, the EZLN has been the representative of the movement, the voice through which the CCRI-CG spoke to the broader world (personified in Subcomandante Marcos); and even though the principles of *mandar obedeciendo* and *preguntando caminamos* governed how the CCRI and EZLN operated, there was some suspicion that Marcos was actually the person "in charge." (In Marcos's August 2003 communiqués, in fact, he joked that in addition to the sign at the entrance to Oventic, he wanted one that said, "Here the Sup governs, and everyone can do whatever they like"; Marcos 2003a: Part 7, para. 2). Commencing with the *juntas de buen gobierno*, though, the EZLN became even further subordinated to the collectives in the Zapatista movement, and in particular to the *juntas* as the instantiation of the new form of the collective. From the beginning of the rebellion, the EZLN served as the primary face of the movement and its executive body, ensuring the implementation of decisions made by the communities and the CCRI-CG and protecting the communities from outside threats.

Over time, though, the institutionalization of Zapatismo in the form of the EZLN, and in particular the personification of it in Subcomandante Marcos, had tended toward granting the EZLN more power than the people it obeyed. As such, after the MAREZs requested that the CCRI-CG serve temporarily as their representative while the restructuring of the EZLN was effected, the EZLN decided that it could only contribute to the further democratization of Zapatismo through stepping aside as the face of the movement. As Marcos put it (2003b: paras. 8–9, 11),

> And so we are now handing back the ear, the voice, and the gaze. From now on, everything having to do with the Rebel Zapatista Autonomous Municipalities will be spoken by the authorities and by the Good Government Juntas. . . .
> The Zapatista Army of National Liberation cannot be the voice of he who governs, or the government, even if he who governs, governs obeying and is a good government.
> The EZLN speaks for those of below, for the governed, for the Zapatista peoples who are their heart and blood, their thought and path.

Further, Marcos reported that the *juntas* would have no recourse to the *Votán-Zapata* (the Zapatista Army) for the purposes of governing; the army could only be used to defend Zapatista territory from military or paramilitary threat (as it did in December 2003, when supporters of the PRI, spurred on by a Mexican senator, threatened to attack the *caracol* at Morelia; Edinburgh-Chiapas Solidarity Group 2003: paras. 2–5).

In reframing the relationship between the armed elements of the EZLN and the governing bodies of the communities and MAREZs, and in removing the possibility of using the armed EZLN as a tool for governance and conflict resolution, the Zapatistas in effect deepened the democratic elements of the movement. Marcos himself argued that in retaining the final decision-making capacity in Zapatista territory, the armed EZLN essentially worked against their own commitment to the furtherance of democracy; as he put it, "The military structure of the EZLN in a way 'contaminated' democratic traditions and self-government. The EZLN therefore constituted an 'antidemocratic' element within a communal system of direct democracy" (Marcos 2003: Part 5, para. 11). The commitment of the EZLN to distributing power "democratically, horizontally, and on a rotating basis" (SIPAZ 2003: para. 14) was in essence counteracted by the existence of a body—especially an armed organization—that held final decision-making authority. In removing itself from that capacity, the armed elements of the EZLN freed up the democratic distribution of power and ensured that all elements were more fervently able to participate in collective policy decisions.

In pursuing this large-scale reconstruction of the structure of the Zapatista movement, the EZLN and its member communities have reflected upon the extent to which the means it uses to attain its revolutionary goals match the ends it wants to attain. In seeing that the development of the institutions of Zapatismo had begun to betray the original goals set forth in the rebellion, the EZLN did what the FLN was never able to do: to step aside as the front line of the revolution in favor of granting greater autonomy to the people with and for whom they fought. Rather than preserving its position of pre-eminence in the movement (as well as its international popularity), the armed EZLN chose to further advance the revolution it helped to start by eliminating itself as the leadership of that movement. Fanon argued that the post-revolutionary political leadership needed to be the interlocutor for the people, and that its voice needed to be the voice of the people, who had been enabled to decide their own collective affairs. This aspect of social liberation, for reasons discussed in the previous chapter, was never allowed to occur, in large part because the FLN chose to rule over a free nation rather than be the catalyst for the people to lead themselves into their future. The EZLN stated from the very beginning of the rebellion that they never wanted to rule, but rather to merely be (to borrow from Che Guevara) the element that makes possible the revolution: " 'our function is not even that of the detonator. You are the detonator. We are much less. We are the primer, the thin layer of fulminate of mercury inside the detonator covering the explosive which merely activates it— helps it to fire better. That's all' " (Guevara, in Debray 1975: 15). In this radical restructuring of the movement, the EZLN ensured that it would remain merely the primer for the indigenous rebellion and the institution of local autonomy.

In doing so, of course, the EZLN more closely represents the kind of liberatory social structure Sartre was envisioning with his notion of ethical radicalism. That notion, which relied on the ability of members of a group to rethink not only the project of the group, but also its ability to reorganize the group for the sake of bringing about its originating goals, is directly reflected in the restructuring of Zapatismo. The preservation of a social grouping is carried out through the transformation of *praxis* into the practico-inert, and ensuring the repetition of those practico-inert social structures through the transformation of human acts into *exis* and the habitus (Sartre 1964b: 427). The refusal to acknowledge where things "went wrong"—where practical action became historical, ossified repetition—and to fix those issues is the one sure way to ensure the death of a resistant social group; if the preservation of the group takes precedence over the enactment of the state of freedom to which the group dedicated itself, then both are done for. Or, as Lévy puts it, "To restore meaning to the idea of revolution, if it's possible, one must

do away with the concept of fraternity-terror. . . . Against the illusion—
and this one is in no way poetic—that human unity has been achieved
in current social conditions, a revolt raises the real and profound issue
of unification . . . " (Lévy, in Sartre and Lévy 1996: 96). In order to
attain that unification of humankind, whether in the microcosm of the
set of worlds contained in Zapatista-controlled Mexico or in the larger
world the EZLN wishes to see created, the armed EZLN had to get out
of the way and let the people work to build their future. In doing so, the
EZLN shows us that their commitment to a processual and concrete
freedom, unlike that of the FLN, is real and genuine.

Lessons Learned from the EZLN

> And so make an effort and put yourself in our place: entire years prepar-
> ing ourselves for firing weapons, and it so happens that it's words which
> have to be fired.
> —Subcomandante Marcos, "Chiapas, the Thirteenth Stele,
> Part Two" (2003a), para. 21

For these reasons, it should be clear that the Zapatista National Liberation
Army and its political organizations have much to offer those of us wishing to create a more just and ethical social order. The affinity that some in
the overdeveloped Western world have for the EZLN may be based on a
pop revolutionary ethos, in the same way that the figure of Che Guevara
has become a popular and commodified icon for displaying one's dissatisfaction with the social order. However, for many others, whether in
indigenous rights movements, anti-globalization or anticapitalism movements, or those who simply want to see a more just social order, a closer
look not just at the figure of the EZLN, but at how the EZLN works to
attain its goals of democracy, justice, and freedom, is warranted. In particular, those of us in the North can emulate a number of elements present
in Zapatista forms of social organization to bring about the existential
social ethics we have discussed throughout this work.

Modes of Social Organization

The organization of the EZLN's political and military branches,
governed by the norms of *mandar obedeciendo* and *preguntando caminamos*, was not developed arbitrarily, as if it were chosen out of thin air.
These structural norms are grounded in the traditional practices of
the indigenous peoples of Chiapas (Millán 1998b: 66). However, it was
not simply because these were traditional practices that they were

chosen; rather, they were selected precisely because they fit in with the political agenda of the EZLN. Given the geographically and historically limited goal of autonomy the EZLN, like many other indigenous people's movements, held to, the articulation of a traditional practice as an ideal form of social organization makes sense; after all, it would be theoretically inconsistent to develop an organizational form that matched that of the oppressing society. As well, the taking-on of a form of social organization that maintains some kind of hierarchy within the society—military leaders over civilians, selected political figures over "voters," or some other form—would continue the implication of the dominant overdeveloped Western model of social organization that, if traced back far enough, is much of the reason the Zapatistas are rebelling against the Mexican government (McManus 2002: 8). So the positioning of these structural norms as the norms to be practiced in a revolutionary organization dedicated to fighting for indigenous autonomy makes perfect sense.

This, though, is not the only reason these structural norms were chosen. Rather, the selection of *mandar obedeciendo* and *preguntando caminamos* as the primary organizational norms matches the larger and more universally applicable goals of justice, democracy, and freedom. Seeing democracy as appearing more among the oppressed than the oppressors (McNally 2002: 16–17), the EZLN chose to foster a form of democracy that relies upon the oppressed for decision-making in the organization rather than being the ones to decide policies, military actions, and the substance of the revolutionary laws for the people in whose name they rebel. As McManus reminds us, Subcomandante Marcos is actually the sub-commander of the EZLN; the people of the Zapatista communities and members of the organizations are the ones who command via *mandar obedeciendo* (McManus 2002: 5), thereby ensuring that the collective membership of these communities maintain their control over the path the whole takes and they take within it. Democracy, therefore, becomes a situation in which everyone participates in the collective self-determination of the social; it relies upon the participation of all precisely by creating a space within which all are able to participate.

In large part, the bond between the structural norms and the political goals of the EZLN thus relies on a link between revolutionary means and ends. In choosing to pursue a particular set of ends, ones that include a deepened sense of democracy and full collective participation in that social order, the EZLN had to refuse the use of any other set of means to achieve that goal, at least vis-à-vis the members of Zapatista communities in rebellion. With regard to the Mexican government and army, other potentially unethical means could be—and needed to be—used to attain the goal of justice and dignity; as we saw in chapter 5, claiming dignity against an oppressive social group is a difficult thing to do through negotiations, and often requires an ethical return of the violence in the oppressive social order against the oppressors. Unlike the Algerian Revolution, in which the means used to "mobilize" the Algerian population to support the revolution were unethical in the sense of not being completely wedded to the ends being pursued, the EZLN's structural organizing principles, being bound together, serve as a more acceptable mode of resistant conduct in societies not prone to revolution or rebellion. But *within* the revolutionary group, as Marcos points out (Marcos 2001: 70), one cannot use unethical means to attain ethical ends; because the ethicality of the means are defined *by the ends*, a set of means that contradict those ends would simply be the return of oppressive violence, albeit executed by different persons. This is why the EZLN insists on pursuing a form of direct democracy in the pursuit of a society characterized by direct democracy—because it simply *must*.

What makes it possible for us to uphold the Zapatista structural norms as the basis for a social organization in the overdeveloped West is precisely the linking of revolutionary means and ends the EZLN engages. If the EZLN chose means that were particular to the fighting of a revolution, it would be nigh impossible to extract those means or other elements from their mode of social organization for use in other societies. But, since the EZLN has chosen an internal set of means that have more to do with the conduct of the organization internally—how it organizes its members, its decision-making processes, and its reproduction as a group—and that match its sociopolitical ends, it becomes an easier matter to see the value of emulating their structural norms in our own social order. North American and Western European societies are able to take on *mandar obedeciendo* and *preguntando caminamos* as structural norms and organizational principles for their social orders in part because these norms as both means and ends of the Zapatista revolution are hermetically bound together and fall in line with social and political values we in the North/West see as our own. As McNally points out, "On the face of it, [the EZLN's communications] were not particularly radical words—echoing, as they did, the rhetoric of the American Revolution of 1776, or the French Revolution of 1789" (McNally 2002: 16). And given the commitment of members of the social justice movements to "democracy, justice, and freedom" and to the dignity of all peoples, pursuing a set of means parallel to that of the EZLN to bring about these ends seems to be a fairly obvious thing to consider.

Processual Consent and Freedom

One of the additional benefits of taking on the EZLN's structural norms as our own is the construction and solicitation of consent on a regular basis. As we have seen earlier, the EZLN relies upon and fosters the participation of all the members in its constituent communities precisely so that the actions it takes on are those of the community. What is contained within this is an active mode of consent (cf. Schaffer 1997), one that representative democracies have failed to maintain over the years. Consent in a social order characterized by "commanding by obeying" and "asking while we walk" is an ongoing process, not a one-time deal; any action that emanates from the collective in these conditions is the action of the collective, not of a small group within that collective who pursues a line of action everyone has not consented to. Decisions made in Zapatista communities are consensual; everyone has participated in the taking of that decision; and everyone agrees to be bound by the decision made. Hence, the people's consent to not just the policies made by the collective, but *to the structure of the collective itself*, is reinforced and reinvigorated on a consistent and ongoing basis. As Lorenzano reminds us, "the Zapatistas are a permanent interrogation . . . of social life as a whole, which they address and question as to its capacity for self-organisation and self-transformation" (Lorenzano 1998: 135). Without this ongoing interrogation of the beneficence of the current social structure, the structure would ossify and become a mere replacement for the old social order, which neglected its members' wishes and served to reproduce itself and satisfy the desires of its leadership. The structural norm of *preguntando caminamos* prevents that from occurring by ensuring continual consultation with all others in the movement, and guaranteeing a processual consent to the policies and the organization itself.

In ensuring the maintenance of consent as an ongoing aspect of the social structure, the Zapatista mode of social organization also ensures a continued preservation of concrete human freedom. Since the leadership of the organization—nay, the entire social structure—is revocable (and has already been substantially altered) should it fail to meet the needs of its members, the preservation of the organization cannot outweigh the preservation and enhancement of its members. As we saw in the Algerian case, the FLN, once it gained the independence of Algeria, worked to consolidate its power in the name of furthering the revolution. In doing so, it ended up enacting the postrevolutionary Terror described by Sartre because its emphasis was on preserving the *structural form* of the revolution, not the *content* of what the revolutionaries fought for. *Preguntando caminamos* and *mandar obedeciendo* as structural norms ensure that what is preserved throughout the existence of the organization (or its reconstruction, if need be) is the *content* of the political aims for which the revolution was fought. The form is irrelevant, Marcos continually reminds us, if the content of the political order is not enacting the ends of justice, democracy, and freedom. As such, these structural norms serve as a continual check on the authority of the leadership and ensure that the projects of the collective, both taken as a whole and as a sum of the individual aims of members within it, are still front and center of the political agenda. In doing this, the freedom of the individual members and the collective are preserved, and the projects that both take on are able to contribute to the development and improvement of all concerned. If nothing else were to be the enactment of the kind of freedom discussed so far in this book, this would be it.

But beyond this preservation of the freedom of individual members and collectives, the Zapatistas have ensured that the social structure of the revolutionary movement is appropriate to the continuing development of that freedom and the material conditions to support it. In transforming the relationship between the armed elements of the EZLN and the MAREZ communities through the establishment of the *juntas de buen gobierno* and the further subordination of the military to the civilian governments, all the while maintaining the structural norms of *mandar obedeciendo* and *preguntando caminamos*, the Zapatista movement and its membership have shown themselves to be willing to reconstruct the social order in which they operate. The reflection of Sartre's notion of ethical radicalism in this move is unmistakable; the EZLN gave up its position of leadership in the Zapatista movement for the sake of furthering the expansion of democratic participation and self-determination, thereby showing its commitment to implementing the liberatory ends it proclaimed in 1994 through the means it uses in the struggle against the Mexican government and the neoliberal economic order in 2004. In following through on its promise to fight for the liberation of all peoples through means that reflect the ends it wishes to implement, the EZLN represents a resistance movement that sees resistance not simply in the practical achievement of its goals, but also in the way in which it goes about attaining those goals.

What we have with the EZLN, then, is a model of social organization that is dedicated to the preservation of human freedom through a variety of means. The first has to do with the concrete political agenda the EZLN developed a decade ago: a dedication to freedom from oppression, the increase of individual and collective capacities for self-determination, autonomy in determining how the collective's affairs would be organized, and the material conditions necessary to support these goals. The second has to do with the means used to achieve these ends, namely the deployment of the very goals the EZLN wanted to achieve as means for organizing its constituent communities in a movement to achieve those goals. The structural norms of *mandar obedeciendo* and *preguntando caminamos* were from the outset designed to represent both the utopian ends of the EZLN *and* the "utopia-as-process" of the means the EZLN uses to achieve those ends (McManus 2002: 11, 13, 14). In deploying the ideal ends of the organization as means to attain those ends, the EZLN's future orientation (loc. cit.) is made a part of the present, demonstrating both to the members of its constituent communities and to other affiliated parties that these ends can be attained. Finally, in setting itself up as only a part of the revolution in the name of dignity, as only a sliver of the work to be done, and "as the revolution that will make possible all other revolutions," the EZLN has, in positing its own futility as a "permanent revolution" *à la* Trotsky, ensured that the ultimate determination of what is needed for human improvement lies with its membership and not with any overriding institutional prerogatives that would conflict with or outweigh the preservation of human freedom as an active process. In doing so, the EZLN has shown its worthiness, not just as a valid and just resistance movement for the indigenous peoples of Chiapas, but also as a model for emulation by others who work in other contexts to bring about democracy, justice, and freedom.

Radical Democratization
In constructing a mode of social organization that exemplifies a practical and tactical commitment to the expansion of human freedom in the ways we have explored here, the EZLN has simultaneously provided a model for a truly radical democracy. Many studies of radical democracy[13] have as their goal the deepening of democracy as a process within a given social structure; however, once the social structure is established and the process is in place, few acknowledge, or even address, the potential need for the revision of the structure in order to continue to meet the needs of its members. The EZLN agenda and practice does precisely this: the structural norms of *mandar obedeciendo* and *preguntando caminamos*, taken together, require that the representatives of the social order continually ask their constituents, "Is this social order meeting your needs? If not, how can we change it so that it will?" Given that those

needs are in line with the overall collective project (whether it is the EZLN's or some other collective's project), these principles of social organization ensure that the order *must* change in order to remain legitimate, just, and ethical in its members' eyes. If democracy is seen as a form of social organization that is designed to simultaneously better the individual and the collective, then one cannot argue with the claim that a radical democratic social structure must be able and required to change if it no longer fulfills its purposes. The EZLN has designed and implemented a form of social organization that is both democratic and radical in its goals for individuals and collectives and in the development and enactment of social actions.

The Ejército Zapatista de Liberación Nacional, therefore, offers us a unique example of a resistance movement that captures both the popular imagination and the attention of those who are committed to furthering the causes of social justice and the quest for a social ethics. Much as we saw in our examination of the Algerian Revolution, there is a strong ethics at work in the Zapatista movement, one that builds on the ethics of freedom present in the way that Fanon and the FLN described the motivations for the Algerian Revolution and extends it to its logical and pragmatic conclusion. Different from the path the FLN took, though, the EZLN's actions show its commitment to the building of a new social order, precisely because it took its commitment to revolutionary ends more seriously than it took its position as the revolutionary means. In providing a social structure in which the existential freedom of the people can be actualized, one governed by founding principles that ensure that the institutions are expendable for the sake of the ethics of the movement, the EZLN has given us a notion of social liberation unavailable to us from the case of the FLN. The utopian social structure and practice of the EZLN (McManus 2002) is one that can be emulated in the development and furtherance of an existential social ethics. I now turn to a discussion of what that kind of ethics would look like, how it would operate, and how we can develop it.

CHAPTER 7

TOWARD A RESISTING SOCIAL ETHICS

. . . we have gone beyond the point where the subject of suffering can be examined as a single theme or a uniform experience. That an abiding concern about an interpersonal process also contributes to the definition of what being human is about means that suffering is profoundly *social* in the sense that it helps constitute the social world. That this social process carries an existential resonance today means that it is part of the constitution of *our* world. Social suffering possesses these meanings, among others. . . . To engage human problems, we hold, is to engage this moral, political and cultural nexus.

—Kleinman, Das, and Lock, *Social Suffering*
1997 (xxiv–xxv)

"Do you really want to go to Stanleyville?" I ask. "Who knows how long Gizenga can hold out against Mobutu? The whole thing could collapse any day."
"I know," she says, "but I have to go."
"Why do you have to go?"
She closes her eyes. She says, "The world divides in two and sometimes I wish I could be in your world, James, where you don't care about politics, where you can see all points of view."
"What's so wrong with that?"
"There's nothing wrong with it. But few people have this privilege. When you are on history's losing side, to accept your enemy's point of view is to accept starvation and slavery."

—Bennett, *The Catastrophist*, 1997 (294)

The State of Affairs: Requiring Resistance

In *Social Suffering*, Kleinman, Das, and Lock collect a wide variety of essays analyzing the ways in which social suffering is constructed, represented, and dealt with by national, international, and nongovernmental bureaucratic organizations. The texts collected range from depictions of the responses of Holocaust survivors to the constant presence of their wartime experiences, to depictions of AIDS and starvation in far-off lands, to terror wreaked by Maoism in China and the *apartheid* regime in South Africa upon their own populations. The topical list of forms of suffering dealt with by this book is short, as one would expect from an edited volume, and painful for anyone who has a modicum of empathy and compassion. Their dominant points, however, are most illuminating. First, they argue that what is not represented to us in the media does not exist, and that which is represented is manipulated in order to maintain a certain Western, separated, and individuated way of understanding the world. As they put it, "What we represent and how we represent it prefigure what we will, or will not, do to intervene. What is not pictured is not real. Much of routinized misery is invisible; much that is made visible is not ordinary or routine. The very act of picturing distorts social experience in the popular media and in the professions under the impress of ideology and political economy" (Kleinman, Das, and Lock 1997: xii–xiii). Seen in this light, human misery is made real to us only when necessary and only in ways that are readily consumable; and even then, the ability to witness the forms of suffering in the world, be it personally or through the media, is dependent wholly upon our willingness to see it. If we choose to, we can change the channel away from CNN when they show hacked-up corpses from some civil war or beaten POWs; if we so desire, the homeless man and his dog at the end of a freeway offramp are no longer visible.

Yet—and this is the second point of *Social Suffering*—whether or not we see suffering in the world, whether it is thousands of kilometers away or on our doorstep, it forms the basis for our social life today. While the AIDS crisis in Africa may seem to us to be playing out on another planet and to be the fault of those who are unaware of Western disease-prevention methods, we are implicated in how it is "handled" and by whom. Homelessness—something which, depending on what part of town we live in, may never be visible to us—is produced by an economic system in which the inability to "keep up" is severely punished, a social order in which the right to free speech is guaranteed while the right to food, clothing, and shelter are not, and a moral system in which "normalcy" however defined gives kudos to the society while "abnormalcy" is the fault of the individual. Sydney, Australia, the site of the 2000 Summer Olympic Games, proclaimed that homelessness would not be a problem during the games; it does not take a critical eye to realize that this was not because homelessness as a social problem was solved before July 2000, but rather because the homeless were rounded up and "deported" from the visible areas of the city. As Kleinman, Das, and Lock put it, the examination

of any kind of social suffering "makes the moral and the political inseparable . . . the cultural processes of global social change . . . are also trans-
muting subjectivity, so that what we have, perhaps naively, taken to be
panhuman existential conditions are changing too" (Kleinman, Das, and
Lock 1997: xviii). Of course, this presupposes that we are aware of the
wide variety of suffering in the world; but even if we try to remain in the
dark about the world's suffering, we are implicated in it.

These forms of suffering do not simply exist in the world; many are
also being struggled against in a variety of ways. The demise of the colonial era, for example, was not simply the result of the colonial powers
waving their hands and granting liberation to their colonies, but rather
was the outcome of years of struggle against the expropriation of the
abilities and the dehumanization of colonized peoples. Those problems
that are the consequences of capitalism—alienation, the physical disin-
tegration of workers through their labor, the theft of people's productive
power, the expulsion of those who will not comply with the requirements of the capitalist system, and the enslavement of those who are
least able to protect themselves against the all-mighty profit motive—are
fought against in a variety of ways, ranging from the efforts of labor
unions to protect workers to the "Battle of Seattle," in which tens of
thousands of people protested against the World Trade Organization, to
the EZLN and parallel movements around the world. And "development" programs, intended to more fully integrate non-Western developing countries into the world economy by ensuring that the path of
capitalist development is followed according to Western dictates, are
being fought against by a variety of groups, ranging from environmen-
talists struggling against the destruction of the rain forests by American
corporations to groups of Indians who threaten to commit mass suicide
if hydroelectric dams that will destroy their homes are built. Put another
way, *resistance exists*, and it constructs and is constructed by the same
social field that causes a multiplicity of sufferings in the world—the one
that makes our lives so much easier.

The main contention of this work has been that the examination of
the simple premise "resistance exists" shows us that regardless of our positioning on the matter, we are implicated in both the cause and the fact
of resistance. Regard Sartre's words on the matter just before his death:
"Against the illusion—and this one is in no way poetic—that human
unity has been achieved in current social conditions, a revolt raises
the real and profound issue of unification; the unity of the human enterprise is still to be created. . . . the revolt is an appeal to an ethical order:
the forgotten are making themselves heard" (Sartre and Lévy 1996: 96).

The question Sartre implicitly raises in this passage is this: since it is we of the hegemonic nations who have forgotten many of the peoples in the world, what will we do about it? This is not the ahistorical question of more traditional conceptions of ethics. We are the ones who continue to bolster the social forms that result in the types of suffering we have briefly described here, if only through our inaction and apathy; and these forms of human and social suffering generate resistance movements whose work helps to structure the social field in which we live. If there were no resistance, if there was no one who found the current social order utterly intolerable, then we might be justified in not aligning ourselves vis-à-vis anyone else. But there are those, both globally and locally, who find the world intolerable and who put themselves at grave risk to try to change it. And it is because of this that we are compelled to align ourselves for or against those who do resist, and that we can no longer ask the Kantian question "what should I do?" in abstraction from existing sociohistorical situations. For those who might continue to hold to an abstracted notion of "right action," Eagleton's words should be heeded:

> If there is one moral certainty in all this, it is surely that people will rise up against the system the moment it is rational to do so. That is to say, the moment when it becomes tolerably clear that there is nothing any longer in the system for them; that the perils and discomforts of disaffection outweigh the meagre gratification of conformism; that sheer apathy is no longer materially possible; that even an obscure, untested political alternative would be better than what they are landed with; and that anger at the unjust way in which they are being treated is more powerful than fatalism and fear.
>
> Such moments don't of course come often, since it is rational not to rebel against a social system, whatever its grave deficiencies, as long as it is still capable of delivering you just enough gratification to outweigh the risk and laboriousness of seeking an alternative. Once it is not capable of this, however, men and women will take to the streets as surely as night follows day. (Eagleton 1999: 37)[1]

For those who think this unlikely, the fact of resistance—the fact that people *do* resist, that they *do* find it rational to risk everything in the name of reclaiming the power to build a better life for themselves and with others, and that the crumbs thrown to them by the hegemonic social order are no longer what they need—shows that it already happens. And we are not far from being put in the same position.

Now, the social-ethical question must become: do we support those who resist on behalf of the expansion of human freedom, or even contribute to this resistance? Or do we allow the continuation of the intolerable situation in which others in our world find themselves, thereby betraying all the values we claim exist for us by ensuring that these values continue to exist *only for us*? Given the ethics of freedom I have developed throughout this work, this is the only ethical question we have left to ask—and then we must act on it, for our failure to act on behalf of human freedom means to act against it and ourselves.

The Project of Concrete Freedom: Developing a Social Ethics

From the outset of this work, we have explored the variety of ways in which resistance and ethics are linked, finding that in not only a theoretical sense, but also in a real, practical sense, the two are inextricably intertwined. From here on, I presume one thing—that we willingly align ourselves with those who struggle for liberation, both for political emancipation and for a new conception of "humanity." The prime reason for this presumption is the claim made at the end of the preceding paragraph; namely, that if we are not on the side of those who struggle for their liberation, we are against them, even if we do not actively take a stand on the issue, and we are thereby against ourselves. This resistant existential social ethics is intended to help those of us who intend to bring about a situation of concrete freedom in conjunction with those who already struggle for it, this being to develop and redevelop a practice of an ethics of freedom in the world and with others in the world. The question thereby becomes, how do we begin to orient more ethically to and with those who resist?

First, we must work to actualize the possibility for genuinely *human* relations with others, be they our neighbors or those clear across the world. We have already seen that we who see ourselves as outside the world exist in bad faith: we see ourselves as outside society, coming to it only when we need to and seeing ourselves as radically independent of one another. Since we can see that social interaction is possible and desirable, given the right circumstances, we can also recognize "the possibility of human contact, albeit recognized with a critical eye" (Gordon 1994: 181). This "critical eye," I would argue, is dependent on our conception of what "human contact" is. We can no longer see it in the traditional Western humanist/liberal-individualist manner, for as we have seen in the preceding chapters, this is the manner that leads directly to structures of oppression, be they as radicalized as the Algerian colonial situation or as mundane as poverty and social stratification at home. Rather, we must realize that those who resist are compelling us to renegotiate our conceptions of human and humane relations. Instead of merely taking it for granted that all of our needs, wants, and desires are the same as everyone's around the world, social movements are struggling to develop new conceptions of relations with others and with us; and our alignment with those who struggle for freedom requires us to participate in the renegotiation of these forms of social relations.

The alternative I have developed here requires that we understand our positioning vis-à-vis others in the world and the practico-inert structures that regulate and mediate our social relations. This second aspect of a social ethics, what we have called "orientation," has been clearly stated a number of times: if we are not acting with those who seek to liberate themselves individually and collectively, then we act against them, even if we choose not to act at all. By our repetitive action and/or inaction, as we have seen, we inadvertently and unreflectively reproduce structures of oppression, whether or not we see them locally or on CNN. As such, in order to truly identify and act upon newly negotiated ways of being with and toward others, we need to acknowledge our responsibility for the position they are put in and we find ourselves in. Our privilege is such that our approach to others may very well be rebuffed; as Sartre noted in his preface to *Les damnes de la terre* with respect to the French Left's support of the FLN, they do not need our support (Sartre 1963: 21). However, we cannot claim to support the cause of concrete freedom without acting to provide this "support"; we must acknowledge our positioning in structures of domination and must collectively identify ways in which these structures can be eliminated. Without this, we will continue to be complicit in the oppression of others and, by the analysis developed here, with our own oppression.

But the recognition and elimination of our complicity in these structures requires what I have described as the decolonization of the habitus. The set of "structured structures predisposed to function as structuring structures" (Bourdieu 1977: 72) that govern the ways in which we relate to one another in our current situation is such that we are left *not* relating to one another. We exist in a social order predicated upon structures that serve to serialize, separate, and individuate us and make impossible the conceptualization of what genuine social relations might be. As such, our habitus has been colonized by the practico-inert structures of utilitarian egoism, and in order to learn to act ethically, we need to decolonize ourselves. In the Algerian case, the revolutionary project enacted by the Algerians against the French served to decolonize them; in the North American case, we must decolonize ourselves or else it will be done for us. As Sartre puts it in his preface to *The Wretched of the Earth*, "This book had not the slightest need of a preface, all the less because it is not addressed to us. Yet I have written one, in order to bring the argument to its conclusion; for we in Europe too are being decolonized: that is to say that the settler which is in every one of us is being savagely rooted out" (Sartre 1963: 24). If we do not begin the process of becoming new people in conjunction with freedom-seeking others in the world, then those who are the victims of our current social forms will work to see that we are decolonized as they take back their agency and freedom through a revolutionary project.[2] This, then, is a crucial aspect of an existential social ethics—being with others through *praxis* intended to decolonize the existing social system and us.

In developing new ways to be with others and how others need us to be, we will also be embarking on the next step in an existential social ethics—the reclamation of our agency. As we saw in our examination of the social structure of the EZLN, it is entirely possible to construct a social order in which the preservation of the agency of the collective *and* the individuals is preserved. The structural norms of *mandar obede-ciendo* and *preguntando caminamos* enable individual and collective agency in the development of collective projects and the preservation of spaces within that collective project to pursue and develop individual projects, even going to the extent of allowing for the dismantling of the social order if it will further the cause of the expansion of human freedom. Yet within our current social order, our "agency" is tolerated only as long as it supports the unspoken collective project—the extension of Western forms of social order across the world, regardless of their appropriateness to the economic, cultural, and political aspects of the society being colonized. We are unwitting "commissars" for the hegemonic social order, and we are granted our freedom and agency as long as we continue to fulfill our function. Part and parcel of this functionality of our lives is that we are not supposed to orient to others, be they our neighbors or members of a distant society. In figuring out how we *can* orient to others and how they need us to orient to them, we reclaim our agency to be *with and for* others. Being with others, as we have seen earlier, is an integral part of the development of a collective project, but this development process requires that we reclaim our agency. In the Algerian case, the reclamation of agency occurred when the *colonisés* took up arms against the French. In our case, we must build a different path in which we can reclaim our ability to act autonomously and with others. This reclamation of our agency is only one aspect of the problem; we must also reconceptualize what agency should be.

The importance of this should be clear: in a world where the majority of people are not able to pursue the life-paths that expand their freedom, we are also left unable to fully act as self-determining freedom-seeking agents in the world. This has a great deal to do with our colonized habitus; but it has as much to do with our inability to fully act in ways we would want to in order to enact the kind of social change we would want to see occur in the world. For example, those who would want to see a state of distributive justice are constrained by practico-inert social structures (i.e., not having the sort of political power to enact this kind of change) from acting in a way that would bring distributive justice into the world. Those who would want to see all the peoples of the world treated with the same respect and concern as we claim to treat one another in Western societies are restrained from working with or compelling others to display this same kind of respect. This is the problem with "liberatory social theories" such as Fraser's (1997); because her dual call for redistribution and recognition leaves the fundamental structures of Western society in place and attempts solely to reform them, she leaves those within her society without the agency to act in ways that might violate the norms of those structures. In addition, the reclamation of agency is not a one-time event. It is entirely possible, as Sartre shows in *Critique of Dialectical Reason*, to reclaim our agency through a group project only to see it taken away from us by the transferal of our sovereignty to that of the group. As such, we need to work to ensure that agency becomes a permanent, processual aspect of our existence through developing and enacting projects that ensure that we and others are able to continually develop and enact our projects.

The reclamation and reconceptualization of agency, too, will be involved with another aspect of an existential social ethics—the reactivation of consent. Because our existence is such that we find ourselves in a world that is not of our making, we are from the very beginning prohibited from consenting to the dominant social order or to any other version of it. Against the social contract theorists such as Hobbes, Locke, and Rousseau (and the early Sartre), we are not individuals first who only later consent to becoming members of society; this "origin story" of the beginnings of a social formation is one that in any case grants the right of consent to the mythic forms of the social order to the "first generation," those who are party to the original social contract. The generations that come after this one, though, are forced to comply with the hegemonic social forms; this is so even if we follow Locke in his claim of tacit consent (1988: §119) in which subsequent generations' continued presence in a society or inheritance of a previous generation's property determines that they continue to consent to the social order. Without this ability to consent to the project, we are even less free than

Sartre's pledged group members; at least in that formation, the individuals who decide to join the revolutionary group have the ability to make that decision. Instead, we reenact the existing set of repetitive norms in the hopes of maintaining our own security and comfort, only to see those two things fade in our time. In order to enact an existential social ethics, though, we must reclaim the ability to consent to the social forms that mediate and embody our relations with others. This goes hand in hand with the reclamation of our agency; and, like the reclamation of our agency, the reclamation of consent requires that we struggle to enact it as a processual aspect of our social existence. Put another way, we must collectively ensure that there are means through which everyone has the ability to consent to the dominant social forms that mediate our lives. This means we must ensure that everyone has the freedom and agency to actively participate in the development of the collective project that results in the social order. In order to do this, though, the populace must recognize that the freedom of all depends upon our individual ability to decide with others how our social lives are to be lived.

To raise the problem of consent in this way is to raise the problem of democracy. It is a central claim of liberal democratic theory that we live in a system whereby our collective interests are adequately represented and in which we have the latitude to pursue our own interests, goals, and life-paths. This, though, is a misrecognition of the nature of modern liberal democracy. As Wood rightly points out, the idea of democracy (which we presume to be the result of some form of social contract) has contracted in the time since the Glorious Revolution, and certainly since the American Revolution. Rather than being a government "of the people, by the people, and for the people," in every election, be it local or federal, we instead surrender our power of self-determination to an oligarchical representative caste that, instead of governing for us, rule over us. In sum, then, liberal democracy involves a shift from democracy as the exercise of popular power to passive participation—or, put more baldly, requires a transition from a spontaneous collective self-determination process to little more than life in an ant farm. As Wood puts it,

> In an age of mass mobilization, then, the concept of democracy was subjected to new ideological pressures from dominant classes, demanding not only the alienation of "democratic" power but a clear dissociation of "democracy" from the "*demos*"—or at least a decisive shift away from popular power as the principal criterion of democratic values. The effect was to shift the focus of "democracy" away from the active exercise of popular power to the passive enjoyment of constitutional and procedural

safeguards and rights, and away from the collective power of subordinate classes to the privacy and isolation of the individual citizen. (Wood 1995: 227)

Put another way, we have been convinced that our "passive enjoyment" of constitutional protections and rights has, through the act of voting, remained an "active exercise of popular power." Yet, the removal of our agency is part of the link between "liberal democracy" and market capitalism (ibid.: 228–236), which in effect allows the dominant classes to ensure that a concept of freedom that belonged to an era "where privilege was the relevant category" was "applied to a world where privilege is not the problem" (ibid.: 233).[3]

The reclamation of agency through an existential social ethics would do much to ensure that those of us who struggle to develop a situation in which human freedom is greatly expanded have the agency to determine collectively what our mediating social structures would be based upon. To use a different term, an existential social ethics would *radicalize* the idea of democracy (seen in the ancient Greek ideal of "rule by the people") and extend it into all areas in which groups of people interact—the polity, the society, and the economy. Rather than attempting to socialize the economic market, or to reform campaign finance rules so that political candidates have more accountability to their constituents, this form of ethics seeks to ensure the active collective participation of people in all areas of their life. The only way to do this, of course, is to ensure that everyone has the ability to participate in the democratic processes that create rules to mediate human interaction.

This kind of radical democratization of social life necessarily entails resistance. First and most obviously, a social order, despite its claims to be democratic, that inhibits everyone's ability to participate in collective decision-making processes must be resisted in order to bring about a democratic social life. Beyond that, though, Sartre's insights into the difficulties of postrevolutionary life—namely that revolutionary social orders are characterized by practico-inert structures and ethical codes—make it clear that even the postrevolutionary practico-inert must be resisted as well. *The ethics of resistance, in other words, require us to resist those Ethics in the name of the very values embodied in that code.* This processual resistance, or even a processual consent as the EZLN maintains in its revolutionary organization, is the only way to ensure that the values of humanity can be maintained without turning them into mere commodities or slogans for propagandistic purposes. Instead, we must maintain an ethically radical stance, not just with regard to the system that surrounds and constructs us, but with regard to how it is we live our own lives. Otherwise, the existential sovereignty that should inhere to the individual and the collective ends up remaining the mere repetition of past social orders that have no concern for those who live in it today. An existential social ethics that has this processuality embodied within it is the only way to ensure this state of affairs.

An existential social ethics therefore requires that we individually develop projects that advance the primary concerns of this ethics—namely, the development and furthering of both individual and collective freedom in the establishment and maintenance of a state of concrete freedom. As we have seen in this work, our freedom is bound up with others' freedom, and we bear responsibility for the impact of our actions and projects on those others. In this way, the free development of our own project—a development which requires that we have the agency to enact the "potential freedom" indicated by the thoughtful formulation of our project—can have one of two impacts on others, neither of which are immediately perceivable to us: either we act in order to expand human freedom by concretizing a social situation in which agency, consent, and responsibility hold; or we act in order to extend our own "freedom" to the detriment of all others in our situation. Our project and the acts that bring it into the world, whether we like it or not, explicitly position us in this way—we either serve or hinder the cause of freedom. As Gordon reminds us, "The rejection of the social world is a form of bad faith" (Gordon 1994: 180), and the pursuit of an egoistic project, one that benefits us at the cost of others, serves as a rejection of the social world. The extent to which, though, we are able to formulate a project that serves both our freedom and the freedom of the collective,[4] is at present limited at best and nonexistent at worst. As such, the development of freedom and ethics as prime characteristics of social and individual lives, requires a form of resistance.

As we have seen earlier in this work, resistance movements in their very acts against the status quo engage all of these aspects of an existential social ethics: they struggle for the ability to develop social forms that require their consent; they battle to reclaim their individual and collective agency, not just from the practico-inert structures of colonialism but also from themselves and their "bad faith" existence; and through their participation in revolutionary *praxis*, they become one with the group and take the social into themselves. In addition, resisters also fight for new ways of being with others—not simply those on their side of the struggle, but with *everyone* in their social field:

> No, we do not want to catch up with anyone. What we want to do is to go forward all the time, night and day, in the company of Man, in the company of all men. The caravan should not be stretched out, for in that case each line will hardly see those who precede it; and men who no longer recognize each other meet less and less together, and talk to each other less and less. (Fanon 1963: 314–315)

The revolutionary decolonization movements are not the only social movements to do this; one has only to think of the American Indian Movement (AIM), Food Not Bombs, ATTAC, and the anti-WTO protests around the world, among countless others, to see that these changes in ethical relations through liberatory *praxis* happen within our own sociohistorical context.

Paradoxes of a Resisting Social Ethics

> "You always want to be left out of things, Gillespie," he says scornfully, "but you're involved in this. I don't mean just because you have connections with the people we're looking for. You're involved in the same way we're all involved. People like you don't like the dirty games people like me play, but you benefit every time we play and win. You won't admit it, you'd probably deny it even to yourself, but you want me to win, because if I lose, then so do you. You lose everything. All your privileges. Writing, publishing, journalism—to mention only the things of particular interest to you—they're only possible in a certain context, and my job is to make sure that context continues to exist. Sometimes that means doing unpleasant things, sometimes it means associating with unpleasant people."
>
> —Bennett, *The Catastrophist* 1997 (270–271)

While this selection from Bennett's novel *The Catastrophist* illustrates the perspective of the CIA agent who struggles to have the leaders of postliberation Belgian Congo serve as puppets to the U.S. government, the sentiment conveyed by the quotation is clear: those who envision the world in a particular way—and here, I reclaim this quotation from the interests of imperialism, even if that interest is only in this fictional context—must play "dirty games." This, then, is the first paradox of this ethics: in order to begin to act in a socially ethical way, we must first begin to resist the status quo ethical imperatives that dictate our own lives to us and, to a large extent, ourselves by actualizing our potential freedom within our own project. This requires, though, that we act against the practico-inert structures that have informed our lives to date;

or, put another way, this actualization of freedom requires the decolonization of our habitus. We have been trained to act in ways that perpetuate systems of inequality, exploitation, and oppression. In order to change the social order so that these systems no longer exist, we must act against inequality, exploitation, and oppression in our own forms of *praxis*. This, then, goes back to the first linkage between resistance and ethics, wherein the desire to enact an existential social ethics requires a form of resistance. Acting for the liberation of others and the corollary of acting against oppressive social structures and practices is not an egoistic matter. It requires that we in privileged positions in the hegemonic social order realize the potential sacrifice of our position in the social order and embrace that sacrifice as a result of our ethical act. In addition, when we do act against structures of exploitation and oppression, we act not to only benefit anyone who is close to us (i.e., friends, family, lovers, all of whom could be harmed through our act), but also people who may not exist in proximity to us; as such, we develop an orientation at a distance to those we wish to work with for our collective liberation.

The second paradox of this kind of resisting ethics, though, is a trickier one: in acting ethically toward others and with a historical sensibility, we may be forced by the exigencies of the situation and this new project to engage in seemingly unethical acts. The essential ambiguity of the meaning of any act, resistant or not, means that our hands are often dirty regardless of the result. When moved into the realm of resistance, though, the specter of complicity looms large: "Political action is of its nature impure, because it is the action of one person upon another and because it is collective action" (Merleau-Ponty 1969: xxxii). As such, the ambiguity inherent in *praxis* requires us to take responsibility for the acts in which we engage—and this provides the second linkage between resistance and ethics. The responsibility we are required to take on because of the ambiguity of action yields a necessary resistant orientation to others. In our *praxis* against structures of oppression, our actions can often turn against our intentions, and we are responsible for this result because our project is potentially the cause of deleterious effects. We must, then, plan our actions so that to the greatest extent possible (given the exigencies of the situation and our knowledge of the possible ramifications of our action) the effects of our action do not boomerang on the intentions of the action, either in the short term or in the longer term. The case of the FLN serves us well here: while their intentions may have been to liberate Algeria and Algerians, their actions led them to betray not only those good intentions, but Algeria itself. As such, our responsibility closely binds us to others; our acts need to emanate from a positive ethical orientation to others, one that embodies our desire to see a situation of concrete freedom come about in the world. As Merleau-Ponty puts it, "The right to defend the values of liberty and conscience are ours only if we are sure in doing so that we do not serve the interests of imperialism or become associated with its mystifications" (Merleau-Ponty 1969: xxiii). In this way, we can see what Sartre means when, in one of his last interviews, he says:

> By "ethics" I mean that every consciousness, no matter whose, has a dimension that I didn't study in my philosophical works and that few people have studied, for that matter: the dimension of obligation. "Obligation" is a poor word, but to find a better term you would almost have to invent one. By obligation I mean that at every moment that I am conscious of anything or do anything, there exists a kind of requisition that goes beyond the real and results in the fact that the action I want to perform includes a kind of inner constraint, which is a dimension of my consciousness. (Sartre and Lévy 1996: 69–70)

Sartre's point here is clear and important for our argument: every act is motivated by an other, and we feel the requisition (a much better term than "obligation") that these others exert on us in our action. The issue becomes, then, a matter of *how* we orient to that requisition, and this becomes a matter of the practical requirements of the situation in which we operate and of the project we wish to bring about. In this light, we can see we would negatively orient to those who would oppose our project and presents us with "a problem to be solved," while we would orient positively to those with whom we struggle.

There is one additional paradox of a resisting social ethics: no existential social ethics can be *or become* a "rigid," rule-governed ethics. A particular act made necessary by the situation and the project at hand may require that we violate the very principles of the ethical order we wish to bring about. Or, as Merleau-Ponty puts it, "Does not every action involve us in a game which we cannot entirely control? Is there not a sort of evil in collective life? At least in times of crisis, does not each freedom encroach upon the freedom of others? Forced to choose between action and respect for consciences which are mutually exclusive and yet solicit one another, if the respect is to be meaningful and the action humane, is not our choice always good and always bad?" (Merleau-Ponty 1969: xxxviii). Merleau-Ponty's response, is that the *sens* of the apparently unethical act as it unfolds through history may legitimate *though not excuse* the act. To put it another way, following Sartre's logic, an unethical act in our time, if intended to bring about an "integral humanity," is in itself ethical, though treated as "unethical" by the order against which this person is resisting. As such, even in the ethical act, we are not pure; we have committed ourselves to a sequence of events that, once started, are no longer under our control but for which we are wholly responsible. We can, in fact, *never be ethically pure*: acting in a resistant manner that is ethical is unethical in the here and now; and failing to act against an unethical social order—or worse, specifically acting to support an unethical social order in the name of "acting ethically" in the here and now—leaves us in the position of acting unethically with regard to the furtherance of our collective human potential.

The linkage with resistance here is clear: any act intended to bring about a new conception of justice is one that may need to violate *though must not betray* the very idea of justice we intend to actualize. The ethical act, which is also a resisting act, is one that leaves us no way to stand outside the historical process. In a manner similar to Sartre's condemnation of Camus for taking the wrong (i.e., ahistorical) stand with regard to the Algerian Revolution (Sartre 1965), we can see that acting in an ethical manner embeds us within a situation that unfolds despite us, and failing to act ethically embeds us in the perpetuation of an unethical situation (Aronson 2004: 209, 218–19, 221, 224, 232). In other words, we are fully complicit in any case; it would be more desirable, in this sense, to commit oneself to the "immoralism" that has the potential to lead to a better social world (Merleau-Ponty 1969: 107; cf. Sartre 1965: 67–68). Again, this paradox of ethics is one that cannot be solved in a purely theoretical manner; the question it poses must be decided in the practical field. It is the *sens*, the future orientation of our project, the needs of the others with whom we act, and the *praxis* by which it comes into being, that will answer the question.

Recipe, Not Method: Outline of a Resisting Social Ethics

Now that we have examined the immediate path laid before us by our current situation, it is necessary to present some vision of why this path of a resisting social ethics has become necessary. Following Geras's notion of a "minimum utopia" (Geras 1999), by which only the barest outline of the minimal characteristics of a social order to be developed through liberatory *praxis* is detailed, we can see that the development of a situation of concrete freedom is paramount. In this kind of situation, freedom as a process is actualized; or, to put it another way, the primary characteristics of my minimum utopia are actual social freedom, consent, agency, and a social solidarity through a multiplicity of individual projects working in concert to ensure the continued processual characteristic of social freedom. As I have argued, the prescription given here is intended to provide a vision of a social order in which *everyone* has the ability to work out these collective problems and to *collectively* determine the social forms that will mediate our lives.

The primary issue presented by the fact of our serialized existence in the here and now is that ethics is, at least to start with, an *individual matter*: the individual is the one who has to deal with the orientations, exigencies, paradoxes, and ambiguities discussed in this work in the formulation of their project. After all, it is with the individual that any ethics has to begin and it must work outward, resisting the serializing tendencies of our individualistic social order. Moreover, the inherent sociality Merleau-Ponty and Sartre attribute to our existence emphasizes that we do not exist outside of society, but rather within a social group. This sociality does two things for us: first, it reminds us that our ethical orientation is always toward others, even though we might not intend this to be the case; and second, that the balancing of the liberation of the group and the freedom of the individual is a necessary concern, both in the individual's orientation to others and in the group's orientation to the individual. Indeed, Sartre's primary concern in *Critique of Dialectical Reason* is with reminding us of the need to guard the individual's freedom over and against the practico-inert tendencies of the social institution (even the revolutionary institution). The protection of the individual against the "fraternity-terror" involved in the formation of groups is, as I have argued, not necessarily the taking of the individual's freedom as superior to that of the collective, but rather with the group itself guarding against the oppression of the individual through the group's need to institutionalize itself as the basis of power:

> Through the undertaking of the pledge and through the concrete determination of the future, through pledged inertia, it *actualised* the power and sustained it in the milieu of freedom—thereby producing common freedom as constituted freedom—and, through its mediation (between the group and the object) it produced the common, here, as individual. On the other hand, freedom, conceived as a common transcendent subject, denies individual freedom and expels the individual from function; function, positing itself for itself, and producing individuals who will perpetuate it, becomes an *institution*. (Sartre 1985 [1960]: 600)

In this way, Sartre's observations on the buildup and dispersion of the pledged group shows both the danger to individual freedom that the institutionalization of the pledged group poses and the necessity of preserving individual freedom *simultaneously* with collective freedom. Sartre's words here provide us with more of a warning than with a hard-and-fast diagnosis: the individual is not free when the group attempts to freeze its form and requires individuals to bend mechanically to its will. This diagnosis of the tendency for groups to ossify their functional requirements, then, is one of the more important issues raised by this examination of existentialist thought. To boot, Merleau-Ponty's discussion of the "yogi and commissar" problem (Merleau-Ponty 1969) is oriented toward ensuring that individuals have some agency in their choice of how they orient to the group; put another way, Merleau-Ponty's concern here is that the inertia of the group does not allow only two orientations to the group, that is, traitor or mindless enforcer.

This, then, is the major problem with which we have to deal now. If freedom is the ultimate value we should work to attain, and our freedom entails the freedom of others, then the construction of a balance between individual freedoms and collective freedom, where freedom is *taken as concrete, actualized freedom in the practical field,* becomes the problem a social ethics has to contend with. How are we to conceive of this balance? Does this balance require that either the individuals involved or the social group sacrifice something of themselves, and if so, what and to what extent? Is there a reductionism involved here, one that values certain freedoms at certain levels of social life more than others? What is the conception of "freedom" that our work should bring into being?

The first issue we should deal with is the notion of "freedom" we are taking as our goal. Potential freedom is the type Sartre describes in *Being and Nothingness*, in which we are always able to "synthesize" the field or situation in which we find ourselves into a coherent orientation to that situation. This is the kind of freedom that enables an individual to develop though not necessarily implement a project, a slave to be free in chains, or an individual to live in "bad faith": it is an internal freedom, one that grounds the second type of freedom but, because it remains internal to the individual, never appears to us in *praxis*. It remains "potential" because the situation in which one finds themselves may not, or in situations of unfreedom *does not*, permit the individual to enact the project they develop. Actual freedom, though, is the freedom that allows us to act upon a project. It is this kind of freedom that brings us to act in and on the world and which forces us to become what we would want to be. It is not a limited freedom as was Sartre's early conception of potential freedom, but one that develops a project, works to actualize it through *praxis*, and then bears sovereign responsibility for the effects it has after its conversion into the practico-inert: "I call it sovereignty because it is simply freedom itself as a project which transcends and unifies the material circumstances which gave rise to it and because the only way to deprive anyone of it, is to destroy the organism itself" (Sartre 1985 [1960]: 578).[5] Actual (or what we can call "concrete") freedom is such that it motivates a particular form of *praxis* oriented to bringing about a project and dialectically results in the potential for more free *praxis*. The tension between these two versions of freedom raises one of the crucial issues for this work: the degree to which individuals and collectives have the agency to consent to the forms of social and political relations, and the extent to which this consent is actualized as a process rather than an event. In Sartre's discussion of group formation, the individual joining the group has the opportunity to pledge themselves to the project of the group; but once pledged, the collective exacts a kind of terror against the individuals, leading to the elimination of their freedom and agency in favor of that of the group. And, as Merleau-Ponty points out, this emphasis on group sovereignty over the individual means that the only two positions individuals can find themselves in with respect to the group are the "yogi" and the "commissar": in the position of being either a rebel against or traitor to the group, or a tool for the group to reinforce its terror. Neither of these positions, though, is satisfactory, and to my mind, the way in which to ensure that these reenactments of the terror of the institution do not recur is to develop a process of consent. We need a version of freedom that ensures that potential freedom is consistently and continuously actualized into concrete freedom.

This brings us to the second aspect of our understanding of freedom. We should also recall that, as Dufrenne put it, "freedom fails to take itself as its own end" (Dufrenne 1998: 282); that is, freedom should not be seen as an "end state" that characterizes a social order and that signifies the "end of history" once it is achieved. Instead, freedom is to be taken as a "good" because once actualized, human freedom brings about a set of conditions in which freedom can continue to be actualized. Put another way, freedom is a process as well as a characteristic of an action; freedom is an aspect of an action that, if actualized, provides the basis upon which it can continue to be brought into existence, concretized, and continued *ad infinitum*. Taken together, these two aspects of freedom—the concept of concrete freedom, and the processual aspect of freedom as it is brought into the world through our projects—show us that the free enactment of projects through freely intended *praxis* should, assuming that one acts in "good faith," result in the continuation of the process of freedom, thereby allowing the individual to concretize their freedom, that is, to make the expansion of human freedom the overarching historical result of all their projects.

As such, we need a conception of social freedom that does not privilege some at the cost of oppressing others; or, put another way, we need a version of freedom at the social level that limits the ability of those who would harm others through the exercise of their freedom to develop those projects so that everyone can exercise their freedom. This is not an invocation of Berlin's "negative" conception of liberty, nor even a turn to his "positive" liberty (in which the question becomes "What, or who, is the source of control or interference that can determine someone to do, or be, this rather than that?"; Berlin 1969: 150–151). Rather, it draws directly from Merleau-Ponty's discussion of the balance between historical accountability and the radical freedom that appears to be exercised in our society, in which everyone attempts to out-freely-act everyone else. His discussion of the necessity of violence in Marxist philosophy highlights this perfectly:

> He who condemns all violence puts himself outside the domain to which justice and injustice belong. He puts a curse upon the world and humanity—a hypocritical curse, since he who utters it has already accepted the rules of the game from the moment that he has begun to live. Between men considered as pure consciousnesses there would indeed be no reason to choose. But between men considered as the incumbents of situations which together compose a single *common situation* it is inevitable that one has to choose—it is allowable to sacrifice those who according to the logic of their situation are a threat and to promote those who offer a promise of humanity. (Merleau-Ponty 1969: 110)[6]

Merleau-Ponty's claim here is that, in spite of the fact that the revolution's success can only be experienced by those in the future (and that those of us in the epoch all experience it as failure, whether we kill, are killed, or are bystanders complicit with whichever side is the worst; Merleau-Ponty 1969: 107–108), some freedoms and even individuals can, if the situation absolutely requires it, be sacrificed for the sake of human liberation. Even then, though, we can never know if their sacrifice is beneficial or detrimental to the revolution until it has been completed; as such, the ambiguity inherent in our choice to either pursue the revolution and the necessary sacrifice of some or to languish in the current state of affairs, and our freedom to act in either case, are balanced with the historical responsibility we hold for our actions. The point of evaluation of this "willingness" to use violence to bring about social freedom, though, is whether or not it is "capable of creating human relations between men" (ibid.: xviii), in other words, the *sens* that the violence we exercise takes on.

What would these "human relations" be, though (since this is the question of what social freedom would look like)? I believe that this

262 / RESISTING ETHICS

form of human relations entails the following aspects of social life. First, individuals would be free in a concrete sense to formulate and actualize projects in order to create themselves as members of a free collective. Documents such as the Universal Declaration of Human Rights ostensibly ascribe these rights to every citizen of the countries who are signatories to the declaration (though, not so surprisingly, the United States has not signed the complete document). But, because of the intersections of the individual, the social, the material, and the historical sets of conditions in which we all exist, our ability to *enact* the freedom we are supposedly guaranteed is severely constrained. Interpersonal, intrasocial, material, and historical circumstances prevent most of us from actualizing any sort of genuine project of freedom we can envision for ourselves. Sartre's claim that even in a state of slavery we have to engage in a free synthesis of the practical field (Sartre 1985 [1960]: 578n68) shows us the necessity of some sort of free action. The goal, though, is to create a set of conditions in which necessity is no longer the primary motivating factor of this type of "free" act, but *praxis* results from the choice of a project, having the consequence of augmenting human freedom. So as opposed to a radical, unchecked freedom that results from an individualistic pursuit and creation of meaning in the world, one that results in the historical sense of our continued oppression and the historically ethical demand for resistance, we need to conceive of a model of freedom that allows for the pursuit of individual projects within a *larger, collective project of the construction of actual freedom for all.*

To create this situation, though, we must ensure that freedom is not a commodity in the way that many people conceive of it—that is, it is not a state of affairs to be attained once and for all, but rather is a *process* to be continuously carried out. Sartre's conception of the goal of liberatory movements—the development of a sovereignty of individuals *over* themselves and *with* others—requires that the creation and maintenance of a state of freedom be an active process. As he describes it,

> La morale est un certain rapport de l'homme avec l'homme. Mais ce rapport n'est pas à l'origine une inerte relation d'intériorité. C'est un rapport actif de réciprocité qui se passivise et s'éternise (éternité de l'instant) par la médiation de la matière ouvrée. La morale change dans la mesure où la matière ouvrée change et où (comportement) nos rapports changent avec la matière ouvrée. (Sartre 1964b: 476)[7]

There is an emphasis on change and flexibility in Sartre's concept of a human morality; allowing the social order, our relations with worked matter, or our relations with others to ossify, thereby allowing the inertia of the world to outweigh our capacity for evolutionary *praxis*, would subvert any kind of liberatory movement by ceasing both the liberation and the movement. Thus, the social order to be created in the future, through a process started by the baby steps encouraged by ethical radicalism, would have to be one that was consistently and processually subject to revision by the members of that social order, through means that are *propre* to the goals and projects of that order, to ensure the furtherance of a state of concrete freedom.

In order to envision this process, we must also recall Sartre's discussion of the problematics of the formation of social ensembles. The most problematic aspect of the transition from seriality to collectivity (in the form of the pledged group) is the aspect of institutionalization. Once the pledged group, seen as the resisting or revolutionary group, has solidified itself, it remains in fear of its demise and enacts simultaneously the "fraternity terror" that is intended to maintain the bonds between its members and the institutionalization of members' functions within the group. As Sartre puts it, "In a degraded group, to sum up, every proposal is 'divisive,' and its proposer is suspect—because he offers a glimpse of his freedom—and a divider; and any local regroupment, provided it is determined in interiority by the individuals present rather than by *the others*, elsewhere, who hold power, is a faction, because the inertia of the Others will make it into a separate group inside the group rather than a subgroup . . ." (Sartre 1985 [1960]: 602). Here, we can see in clear terms the essential tension between individual freedom and group freedom; once a social ensemble struggles to maintain its cohesion, those who suggest alternate paths as an expression of their individual freedom are seen as a threat to the freedom of the social. And as the state of dissent politics shows us, this is the condition in North America today: the freedom of the social is seen as the status quo, even though it does not amount to the freedom of the individuals who make up the social; and the assertion of individual freedom and agency over and against the status quo is liable to be seen as a threat to "social stability," "law and order," or as "domestic terrorism" and the like.

We are today in a world where violence and resistance to that violence exists, and these two forms of social practice are such that they create the field in which we exist and must therefore align ourselves. As a result, there are three steps to the development of the sociohistorical situation in which we can develop a social order based on concrete freedom and an existential social ethics: the recognition of the necessity of the decolonization of the habitus; a collectively constructed project intended to liberate the populace as a whole; and the avoidance of the postrevolutionary Terror so that freedom as a basis for and characteristic of individual and group action can continue to be brought into the world. We must realize the ways in which our social order constructs us as means for the preservation of its practico-inert social structures, and we must figure out if that social order creates us as we wish to create ourselves. If not, we need to develop individual and collective projects that bring about a state of affairs in which we *can create ourselves*, both individually and collectively, in the ways we wish. But that process cannot be a one-time or even a one-era event; instead, it must be a continual process, one that ensures the freedom of future generations even in the exercise of our own freedom. If not, we will find ourselves in a new version of the Terror we face today.

One way to transcend this process by which Terror becomes the hegemonic form of social and political relations is that described by Fanon with regard to what the postrevolutionary Algerian political situation should have been. As Fanon points out, the postrevolutionary political and social order must maintain the same kind of "fighting spirit" that characterized the revolution, since winning the war of liberation is only the first step in the process of developing a free society. As such, the postrevolutionary leadership cannot manage the society's affairs in the same way that the colonial regime did—through obfuscation, confusion, and dissimulation meant to ensure the colonial bourgeoisie's position vis-à-vis the populace (Fanon 1963: 152–153, 180). While this is clearly what happened in postindependence Algeria, Fanon's cautionary words to the Algerian national leadership in "The Pitfalls of National Consciousness" show us another path. This path is one in which all the "governing" structures of a social order are the expression of the will of the people. Put another way, the postliberation society should be managed in a "bottom-up" fashion, in which the political and social structures that are introduced serve as a conduit for the wishes of the people:

> But we who are citizens of the underdeveloped countries, we ought to seek every occasion for contacts with the rural masses. We ought never to lose contact with the people which has battled for its independence and for the concrete betterment of its existence. [. . .]
>
> For these reasons, the political bureau of the party ought to treat these forgotten districts in a very privileged manner; and the life of the capital, an altogether artificial life which is stuck onto the real, national life like a foreign body, ought to take up the least space possible in the life of the nation, which is sacred and fundamental. In an underdeveloped country, the party ought to be organized in such fashion that it is not simply content with having contacts with the masses. *The party should be the direct expression of the masses.* (Fanon 1963: 187; emphasis added)

Instead of maintaining the existing political, social, and economic structures (Fanon 1963: 152–153), the postliberation society needs to construct its own regimes by which the will of the populace—not some hackneyed "public" opinion poll, but the collective's actual will—is expressed. What is needed is a social order characterized by its continual and processual receipt of the consent of the people, one in which those to whom the task of the management of social affairs is delegated are continuously in touch with *and dependent upon the populace* for both the authority to manage social affairs and for the ways in which social affairs are to be managed. The EZLN principle of *mandar obedeciendo* enables us to envision this kind of order. In developing a system in which the people's will is actualized through the projects taken on by the collective's leadership, the EZLN has in essence developed a radicalized form of democracy. This serves both as a model for us and as a way to avoid the problems faced by post-revolutionary Algeria.

Fanon's call for a bottom-up, more clearly democratic leadership style by which the people actively and directly participate in the construction of a social and political order and in its management provides us with a good example of how social freedom, agency, and consent can continue to be maintained throughout a society's existence. This state of affairs, though, is not an immediate occurrence for Fanon; rather, this process takes time, something that both politicos and peoples rarely appreciate. This is the historical aspect of this process of liberation; it is only through the "immoralism" (to use Merleau-Ponty's term) of the liberatory movement that we can realize how much the structures of the *ancien régime* have accrued in our habitus, our consciousness, and in our sense of safety and security. Fanon's words on this matter, while focused primarily on the underdeveloped countries, also hold true for the ideas developed here of how best to change things:

> In Algeria, we have realized that the masses are equal to the problems which confront them. In an underdeveloped country, experience proves that the important thing is not that three hundred people form a plan and decide upon carrying it out, but that the whole people plan and decide even if it takes them two or three times as long. The fact is that the time taken up by explaining, the time "lost" in treating the worker as a human being, will be caught up in the execution of the plan. People must know where they are going, and why. (Fanon 1963: 193–194)

What undergirds Fanon's propositions about the proper form of the relationship between the social and the individual as it should be constituted in a postliberation society are the conjoined ideas of solidarity and self-determination (in other words, the development of a free collective project through the free projects of the members of the society). Solidarity appears here in the integration of individual experience and projects into the national experience and project, and sees the individual as "a link in the chain of national existence" (ibid.: 200) and the national in the individual. The liberatory project itself is a project of collective self-determination, of finding a new way in which the social order is "open to all, in which every kind of genius may grow" (Fanon 1965: 32). And both can, if enacted properly by all members of the social, lead to the enactment of both individual and social freedom.

This form of solidarity, though, is not akin to either the mechanical or organic forms of solidarity discussed by Durkheim (1997), in which the structural requirements of a society determine the ways in which individuals pursue their relations with one another and their conceptions of who they are. This is how things already are: as most introductory sociology students know, North American societies are characterized by a combination of mechanical and organic forms of solidarity that surface at various points in time depending upon the needs of society. Rather, the concept of solidarity at work here is one in which individuals experience themselves as part of the collective because their free action is in concert with others in the group, while at the same time the individual has the ability to actively help in the construction of the group's project, thereby more fully integrating the individual into the development, enactment, and continual critique of the collective project and vice versa. As we can see in our own time, this is not the case: those who are against the globalization of Western capitalism, for example, have in recent decades found themselves left with only two options, either succumbing to "the juggernaut of modernity" (Giddens 1990) or being marginalized within the system while at the same time being forced to participate in the system. One of the goals of the existential social ethics being developed here, though, is the elimination of this compulsion to participate in the collective project; instead of being forced to succumb to the force of the collective, individuals, through their *praxis*, are able to see their own project as contributing to the furtherance of both individual and collective freedom. This form of solidarity, of course, is dependent upon a number of aspects of the existential ethics we have discussed here, most notably responsibility: whereas in our current situation we do not feel responsible for the exploitation of peoples halfway around the world, under this new model we would be responsible for both the construction of the project (one that should not include the exploitation of anyone, be they neighbors or citizens of a far-off country) and for the consequences of this project. The ultimate goal, though, would be to ensure that individuals would be able to pursue a project whose *sens* ran against the ossification of social institutions so that both the vibrancy of the group's freedom and the individual's agency and ability to pursue their own complementary vision of themselves would be preserved, thereby ensuring the continued solidarity of the collective.

This concept of solidarity, too, ensures that both the individual and the collective are able to reclaim and retain the agency to engage in freedom-seeking projects of self-determination. We have already examined the need for the individual to reclaim and retain their agency. The exigencies of the North American habitus, developed as it has been within a social form that is highly serialized and individualistic, inhibit us from realizing our agency both to pursue projects that go against the status quo social order or to even envision an alternative to the hegemonic social order, and are such that we are in essence trapped into reproducing quasi-automatically the practico-inert structures of society. Within this context, the need for individuals to reclaim their agency is clear. But how does this translate into the realm of the social?

Recalling Merleau-Ponty's argument that we are inherently social by virtue of our existence in the world, we can see that there are two ways of being in the world: in competition with others, thereby reducing both our freedom and that of others; or in cooperation with others in an attempt to construct a situation of concrete freedom. In addition, by virtue of our ability to act in the world, we are immediately positioned in an ethical manner in relation to everyone else in our practical field. As such, our choice to act against others displays our desire to destroy their freedom, thereby locking us into a cycle of reproducing the structures of oppression through our egoistic project (since the practico-inert structures of our social order are already predicated upon egoism). However, our choice to act with others for the sake of bringing about a situation of concrete freedom is one that displays both our desire for solidarity and our realization that our freedom and our ability to act in the world is wholly dependent upon that of others. Because we are embedded in a situation and dependent upon that situation for the construction and enactment of our project, if we find ourselves in a situation of oppression we are only able to freely draw upon a field of meanings characterized by collective unfreedom—both an actual and an existential contradiction in terms. Of course, any project we develop in this historical moment is characterized by this contradiction. However, in acting with others for our collective liberation, we can transcend this initial situation of collective unfreedom with the intent of bringing about a project dedicated to the establishment and maintenance of a situation of concrete freedom in which we all can develop projects that continue the processual aspect of freedom.

So, our choice to act in solidarity with others in the first instance represents our choice to "pledge" ourselves to the project of the group. This, though, is where the issue of ambiguity appears to us in an existential social ethics. Once we pledge ourselves to the group, we are compelled to continue the project of the group, even when the completion of the project violates the intentionality of that project (namely, the establishment of concrete freedom for the group and for the individuals who comprise the group). How do we deal with this ambiguity? One way is to ensure that "freedom fails to take itself as its own end" (Dufrenne 1998: 282). Freedom is itself processual; there is no end to freedom because once freedom does take itself as its own end, it is no longer free, but institutionalized, objectified, and a slogan—in other words, *inert*. As such, the decision of individuals to integrate themselves into a collective project of self-determination is such that it *must become processual*; the pledge must always be freely given, and can only be given insofar as the group continues to ensure the freedom of the individuals within it and as long as the group is something to which individuals can freely pledge themselves. It is only in this way that the potential violence of the group against its members can be counteracted. Another way to deal with this ambiguity is to recall the issue of responsibility, discussed earlier, in which we are all responsible for the impacts of our actions on and in the world; as such, the group's theft of its members' freedom for whatever reason, including the maintenance of the group's sovereignty, would be horribly unethical, as it would defer its responsibility collectively and, due to the makeup of any social group, individually in an act of bad faith. So the responsibility brought to the group by the individuals who comprise it provides us with a second way to keep account of the ambiguity of any collective project of liberation.

Another way of keeping account of the ambiguity in any collective project—and this is another important aspect of ensuring the liberation of the collective—is to ensure the continued and processual consent of the members of the group to the project at hand. This is, after all, the point of any kind of resistance as we have defined it here: to allow all the peoples of a social grouping the ability to develop and to consent to the forms of social relations that mediate their everyday lives. Liberation is about the reclamation of agency and the ability to freely give one's consent. In order to avoid the ossification of the group, then, the ability to consent to the dominant social forms must be maintained at all times;

this is, after all, the highest form of freedom we can envision, as it is the ability to consent to the hegemonic field of meaning from which every project arises, be it collective or individual. In addition, any form of social relations can be renegotiated; and following Merleau-Ponty's claim that any form of violence can be tolerated and ethical so long as it brings about a more human and humane society (Merleau-Ponty 1969: 107), we can argue that a temporarily anarchic situation can be tolerated because it may very well lead to a new, more humane situation in which consent as an expression of agency and freedom continues to exist for all.

These, then, are the goals of a social ethics: to bring about a socio-historical situation in which freedom exists concretely for all, in which we are able to individually and collectively engage in a freedom-seeking process of self-determination, and in which the highest expression of our freedom and agency is the ability to consent to both the dominant collective project and the way in which that project is to be pursued. These are, though, the very characteristics of resistance; that is, key resistance movements in the late twentieth and early twenty-first century are oriented to the very potentialities of social life I have identified here as the goals of an existential social ethics. Put another way, the aspects of resistance that draw people to them so that they can liberate themselves and "their people" are those self-same aspects of the ethical project I see operating in the works of Sartre and Merleau-Ponty. Both men (and, I would argue, Bourdieu as well; cf. Bourdieu 1998) tried in their philo-sophical works and in their engagement in everyday political affairs to outline and to exemplify the kind of resisting ethics I have developed here, one that resists both practico-inert structures of oppression and the ethics' own tendency to institutionalize itself socially. Sartre's disaffec-tion with the PCF ultimately revolved around the Party's unquestioned support for Stalin; and the main problem with this support had to do with the fact that the Soviet "revolution" had become the entire *raison d'être* of the Soviet regime rather than the liberation of its peoples from the throes of either tsarism or capitalism. And, as their support for the FLN in the Algerian Revolution showed (as misplaced as it may be seen in hindsight), both Sartre and Merleau-Ponty felt that the development of a more humane historical path was more important than the tempo-rary discomfort of a lack of a clear social order. An existential social ethics thus requires our willingness to sacrifice our safety, security, and dominance in the world for the safety, security, "infinite unity of our mutual needs" (Sartre 1963: 27), and equity of all the peoples of the world. If we are willing to do this, then we should be willing to forego our secure way of being in the world for the good of us all; if we are not, this way of being may be taken from us in the name of freedom, for then we are the executioners of whom Sartre and Fanon speak, and we *will* be called to task for it.

Closure

> I have another story. A fantastic story, better than the killing of the ANC colonel. Zoubir Smail, Lebanese-born diamond merchant, Communist Party member, close associate of deposed prime minister Patrice Lumumba, widely rumoured to have organized and facilitated the secret Soviet funding of the ANC, murdered by Mobutu's secret police. Eyewitness account of tortured body in Léopoldville's Central Prison. I can use all of this—along with my own arrest and beating—for novels, stories, plays. It can be the dramatic set-piece around which my work will turn. I will be able to make something of this. Yes. As long as I can make the deal with Stipe. I gaze at Smail. *Does a man die at your feet, your business is not to help him, but to note the color of his lips.* I must gather my wits. I must note the color of his lips.
> —Bennett, *The Catastrophist* 1997 (268)

Bennett's protagonist Gillespie, having just been arrested for collaboration with "the enemy" in the Belgian Congo and beaten bloody, realizes what I have spoken of all along—that we are implicated in the world, both in its oppressive and liberatory moments. For most of *The Catastrophist*, Gillespie struggles to keep himself separate from the decolonization struggle going on around him, claiming that his sole purpose for being in the Congo is to be with his lover, Inès, a correspondent for the Italian Communist newspaper *L'Unità*. His primary claim: his journalistic "objectivity" will protect him from the involvement Inès bears at the core of her being. As the novel progresses, though, Gillespie finds himself increasingly implicated and involved in the revolutionary struggle, going as far as to evacuate (as an expression of his love for Inès) one of the ANC leaders who has become Inès's lover. As the book ends, Gillespie realizes he has lost Inès because he could never be where she was—in the thick of the struggle for liberation:

> I had to look in a place where sceptics like Stipe and doubters like me, like Grant, like Roger, like most of us, do not believe anyone really wishes to be—anyone sane, adult, mature, reasonable. It's a place we laugh at, we scorn, and we sometimes say does not exist at all. But I caught sight of it at the Sankuru when Patrice stepped on to the *barque* to recross the river, and again on my last day in Léopoldville when the silent crowds followed Pauline down the boulevard and Charles picked me up from the road. . . . I was always too much a watcher, too much *l'homme-plume*;

> I was divided, unbelieving. My preference is the writer's preference, for the margins, for the avoidance of agglomeration and ranks. (Bennett 1997: 312)

As I have argued throughout this work, we may claim that we are "too much *l'homme-plume*," but we are fully implicated in the sociohistorical situation we seem to inevitably reinforce through our lack of desire to transform it, and we need to figure out how to orient to and work with those who do struggle to transform the world. An existential social ethics, one predicated on the lessons learned from the practice and experience of resistance, provides us with the needed tools to work out our mutual co-implication in the practico-inert structures of oppression and the practices of resistance, and to conceive of a world in which social freedom, individual and collective agency, and consent as a processual aspect of social life would be brought into fruition.

We have seen here, though, that this process is a difficult one, both to envision and to enact. Most of us are comfortable with our lives, fairly happy to be educated, work, marry, reproduce, retire, and pass on. Yet, as any careful review of the world press can show, by this very contentedness we ensure, either unwittingly or intentionally, that others are not able to decide for themselves how their lives will be led. We are implicated in and causative of the sorry state of affairs that characterizes the early twenty-first century, and as the events of the early part of this century have shown, that implication will be made explicit and revisited upon us whether we like it or not. Many people already have this sense that things need to change but are unable to see how or where they can start that change. The path of this work—from a theoretical examination of resistance and ethics, to the linking of the two in understanding Ethics as we know them as inertial, to envisioning how we can change ourselves to see our responsibility for the state of the world, to the analysis of the errors of the FLN and the innovations of the FLN—has attempted to lay out a possible starting point for this change.

The goal of this work has been to challenge the implicit social norms of apathy and the experience of impotence that characterize much of modern life in the West. Most rule-based concepts of ethics prevent us from legitimately acting in any way that challenges the status quo. Yet, we *can* change the ways in which we operate in and with the world. Since we are already oriented to others because of our embeddedness with them in the world, through changes in how we conceive of our relations with others and ourselves we are able to enact positive, liberatory change in the world. Our hands are already dirty; the question

I leave here is whether our hands will be dirtied through action intended to bring concrete, actual, enacted freedom into the world, or through our choice to preserve ourselves at the cost of all others in the here and now and in the future. There is no Lady Macbeth-like way out of this situation, and we cannot wish these dirty hands clean; the spot can only disappear if we struggle for it to disappear.

NOTES

Chapter 1   Complicity, Ethics, and Resistance

1. Throughout this work, the use of the term "ethics" will be premised on this definition. Starting in chapter 2, however, two variants of this term will be used to highlight the distinction between currently existing concepts and the one I work to develop here. "Ethics" (capital E) will be used to refer to this kind of rule-bound morality captured in philosophical and religious discourses that contain within them a clearly defined set of prescriptions of rules of conduct. "ethics" (lower-case E) will be used to refer to the notion developed throughout this work, namely that of a practical mode of conduct intended to attain a particular state of affairs rather than merely fulfill the requirements of a set of rules. I apologize for any confusion on this matter.

2. Other thinkers take a variety of approaches to deal with these kinds of criticism of Ethics and ethical thought and deal with issues paralleling those dealt with in this book, including: Martha Craven Nussbaum, *Cultivating Humanity* (1998: Harvard University Press) and *Sex and Social Justice* (2000: Oxford University Press); Ted Honderich, *After the Terror* (2002: Edinburgh University Press); Onora O'Neill's *Constructions of Reason: Explorations of Kant's Practical Philosophy* (1990: Cambridge University Press) and *Bounds of Justice* (2000: Cambridge University Press); and Peter Singer's *How Are We to Live? Ethics in an Age of Self-Interest* (1995: Prometheus Books) and *One World: The Ethics of Globalization* (2002: Yale University Press).

3. Some examples of these paradigmatic approaches to resistance (and this list is by no means exhaustive) include: Giorgio Agamben, *Homo Sacer: Sovereign Power and Bare Life* (1998: Stanford University Press); Judith Butler's *The Psychic Life of Power: Theories of Subjection* (1997: Stanford University Press) and *Gender Trouble* (1999: Routledge); Nick Dyer-Witheford, *Cyber-Marx: Cycles and Circuits of Struggle in High-Technology Capitalism* (2000: University of Illinois Press); Michael Hardt and Antonio Negri's *Empire* (2001: Harvard University Press); John Holloway, *Change the World Without Taking Power: The Meaning of Revolution Today* (2002: Pluto Press); Antonio Negri's *Time for Revolution* (2003: Continuum Publishing Group); Theda Skocpol, *States and Social Revolutions: A Comparative Analysis of France, Russia and China* (1979: Cambridge University Press); Amory Starr, *Naming the Enemy: Anti-Corporate Movements Confront Globalization* (2001: Zed Books). These are certainly not the only perspectives on resistance, rebellion,

and revolution; however, I see works such as these as being indicative of the general approaches taken by scholars of resistance.

4. Fraser (1998), however, in *Justice Interruptus* is able to grapple with the intersection of Butlerian post-structuralist resistance and the "redistribution project" of Marx. However, Fraser's primary difficulty in that work is her reliance on groups subordinated on the basis of identity (i.e., nonwhites, women, etc.) as the norm, without realizing that this reproduces dominant social structures precisely through their "resistance." While I do not have the space to fully detail what groups in the world merit the term "oppressed peoples," I can suggest that there is a wide range of forms of oppression, and depending upon the particular exigencies of a sociohistorical situation, certain groups will be brutally oppressed in one situation and "relatively free" in another.

5. Noam Chomsky would be an obvious exception to this claim; his *Manufacturing Consent* is devoted specifically to the examination of the ways in which "consent" has been constructed in a way that actually eliminates the possibility for us to positively agree to the rules of our social order in any meaningful way.

Chapter 2   As Fragile as Glass: Balancing the
Individual and the Social

1. This same idea of "existence precedes essence" appears, in mutated form, in the works of Lyotard, Harvey, Butler, and many others, all of whom claim that as a result of the "death of metanarratives," all "essence" is gone, left to the individual to remake at will—exactly what we will see in *Being and Nothingness*.

2. "Our review would like to contribute, on its modest part, to the constitution of a synthetic anthropology. But it finds itself not only . . . preparing progress in the domain of 'pure knowledge': the long-term goal upon which we are fixed is a liberation."

3. "*The pure future* of the imperative is neither knowable or predictable. Its character as pure future, that is to say as the future that no one has prepared, that no one can help realize, is in fact *a future to be made*."

Chapter 3   Methods, Not Recipes: Rethinking Ethics
In (and Through) Resistance

1. "To say it better, he does not oppose—as if it were a value to other values— that is his need that is opposed to the order of things in reclaiming *for men against things* the reality of man. On the one hand, *the mutilated man*, subordinating men to things; on the other, the oppressed man subordinating things to man as a means to restoring the human."

2. In the case of the African National Congress, though, this is *precisely* what was hoped: the ANC called on Western trading partners of South Africa to divest from and boycott the country's economy in order to bring the country

to a standstill. The ANC, in other words, realized the importance of a short-term sacrifice in the name of the destruction of the *apartheid* system.

3. Unlike other forms of ethical thought, such as contractualism and utilitarianism, the types of evaluations one might make in an existential ethics are not those of a cost/benefit analysis based upon a set of first-order moral rules. First, contractualism and utilitarianism seek to formulate rules to be applied at all times in all situations, such as "in conflict, the rule should be to minimize human casualties at all costs." In many cases, this is historically inconceivable and might actually be subverted by one's enemy. Second, if first-order moral rules are not formulated, then the cost/benefit analysis can be utilized without an ethical basis in some larger project. This is necessarily a slippery issue, one that to my mind utilitarianism in particular often tries to avoid, while an existential ethics explicitly takes it into account.

4. The discussion here contains, at least to my knowledge, the first English-language sociological treatment of the unpublished *Conférence à l'Institut Gramsci* (the *Rome Lectures*, as it is known to English-language scholars) and *Notes for the Cornell Lectures*, prepared for a conference at Cornell University in 1965, but canceled in protest of America's involvement in the Vietnam War. Neither manuscript has been published due to the wishes of Arlette El-Kaïm Sartre (his adopted daughter and owner of the copyrights); however, sections have been published (see Contat and Rybalka 1970, e.g.).

5. "Morality is a certain relation of one man to another. But this relation does not have as its origin an inert relation of interiority. This is an active relation of reciprocity that is passivised and made eternal (an eternity of the instant) by the mediation of worked material."

6. "In the imperative of the custom, the content of the norm fixes a destiny for me: I must produce myself through my action. The interiority is from time to time the subject of my possible act and the possibility that I could produce myself as a subject, in a word, the possibility of an indifferent determination from my past having no relation with my act. One echoes the past and the imperative is a discovery of the future as much as it is a disqualification of the past.

   But, simultaneously, this future that poses the unconditional possibility that I produce myself as interiority, poses as well as the imperative that has already been respected by individuals in preceding generations. For the men of the past, this was a future. In reality, this future is for them also a *future anterior*: for the moral agent that I am today, it announces itself as *my future* as well as a repeated fact."

7. "The imperative is therefore the thing dictating its laws to praxis while it is maintained by *the action of others*. If one wishes, *praxis crystallizes and congeals in the sense where the same human is imprisoned by the manufactured product*."

8. "Every particular and dated ethic is historical in its content.

   Every particular and dated ethic presents itself as an overtaking of history.

   Every particular and dated ethic is a stoppage of history and maintains a society by repetition.

   Every particular and dated ethic is overtaken by history.

   Every particular and dated ethic is alienation (man as the product of his products, man as the son of man). . . .

Every particular and dated ethic radically takes hold of and locally explodes history from a double point of view: the future (integration with death); the past (repetition against evolution)."

9. "Ethics as *alibis*: 'one must, when one loves, etc.' In this sense, superstructures, but they are . . . disguises for real conduct, only these real conducts are themselves ethical (e.g., an ethic of austerity or generosity can hide a practical interest. But *the interest* can be as well an imperative, one could say a moral (as a simple verbalism) in hiding another (. . . the reign of simple fact)."

10. "One understands that past praxis, inscribed in the inertia of exteriority, dissolves itself if it is not maintained by those who profit by it. It is therefore *through* the class struggle (because they maintain it against those who frustrate it) and *in the same movement of history* that is *the imprisonment of the unconditioned and conceivable ethical future.*"

11. Many thanks to David McNally for helping me clarify this position.

12. Interestingly, Alexander claims the existence of an opposition of violence to reason in twentieth-century thought, arguing that Aron's *History and the Dialectic of Violence* is the only work to really deal with the theme of violence in *Critique of Dialectical Reason*, a theme he takes as a philosophical truth of existentialism. Alexander argues that the philosophical justification of violence is something that most thinkers are unwilling to pursue, partly because of its opposition to reason, and partly because of "the omnipresence of violence in this century's life" (Alexander 1995: 86n7). I would argue, though, that Alexander's desire to maintain the dominance of reason goes farther to explain his characterization of the *Critique* as an "apologia for violence" (loc. cit.) than does the antirationality of Sartre's work. On the contrary, I would argue that this aspect of Sartre's work—this claim that violence can be and often is ethical—is not apologetic, but rather aware of the historical exigencies of the situation. Sartre's point is not to argue that violence is the only means to liberation, but rather one that is frequently a necessary consequence of the situation one finds oneself in (Alexander 1995: 72).

13. Merleau-Ponty, in fact, went so far as to help draft the final version of the "Manifesto of the 121," the French intellectuals' statement against the institution of conscription for the Algerian War, and elicited Raymond Aron's signature on the manifesto. See Whiteside (1988: 233).

14. The details of the very public debate between Sartre and Camus, in which their friendship was ended because of Camus's refusal to take a stand with regard to the Algerian Revolution, are well documented elsewhere. To provide the short version: Camus stated that both the French colonial forces and the *Front de la libération nationale* were engaged in an unjust fight, and that negotiations between the two sides were necessary. Sartre's critique, issued in *Les temps modernes*, was predicated on Camus's book *The Rebel*, in which he argued that oppressors, oppressed, and all those who stand "on the sidelines" were implicated in the historical situation; further, Camus's call for negotiations was an attempt, according to Sartre, to abdicate his own historical responsibility for the Algerian war. See Sartre 1965.

15. By now, it should be clear that there are two ways in which ethics have been discussed in this chapter, one in the present, and one in the future. The present "ethics," better indicated as "morality" save for the polemic overtones of the term, is one that prevents the full potential of humanity from being developed, as it requires that our action be oriented to the reproduction and maintenance of the status quo. The other, a more future-oriented conception of ethics, is the one that Sartre and Merleau-Ponty wish to see brought into the world through ethical radicalism, revolutionary liberatory action, and whatever other means necessary to create the possibility for a genuine "humanity."

16. "Or, if one prefers, the unconditioned future or *the human future of man* and the identification of morality in the sense of history cannot be produced as such by the class that denies history. This rigorous norm is produced by the exploited classes inasmuch as their human project of producing humans is in contradiction with the inhuman conditions that make them facts."

17. "We have seen the contradiction of ethics. We have seen the proper motif for ethics: the will of sovereignty in reciprocity" (Sartre 1964b: 445).

18. "The fraternal man can demand *negatively* in looking backward (suicide), [or] positively by revolutionary praxis, by really being in their birth the product of man. . . . That is to say, a society where the practico-inert is unceasingly dissolved to the extent that it is formed by a union of men against the mediation of the inert; society without structure, an economy producing man without institutions (the State) or alienated morality."

19. "The unconditional normative is *here also* the foundation of the imperative. The transformation of the fundamental structures of the system . . . by making terror useless does not suppress its means but the unconditioned end is discovered anew and praxis takes it as goal, starting with the real revolutionary goal of liquidating the limits of terrorism."

Chapter 4   Turning Ourselves on Our Heads: Hegemony and the Colonized Habitus

1. Sartre's notion of *exis* and Bourdieu's concept of *hexis* are, in essence, the same concept, differing only in the use of the sometimes-silent *h*. Both concepts work to convey the notion of the habitual aspects and actions of the human body and one's sense of the *propre* (both "proper" and "one's own") place in the social order.

2. The connection between Bourdieu's work and existentialism hearkens back to 1962, when one of Bourdieu's first articles, "Les relations entre les sexes dans la société paysanne," appeared in *Les temps modernes*. As Davies reports in his history of *Les temps modernes*, this article, along with "Les sous-prolétaires algériens" that appeared in August 1962, shows Bourdieu's work is close to both the methodological concerns of Sartre (and, if one can attribute concerns posthumously, to those of Merleau-Ponty) as well as to Sartre's projected development of a "synthetic anthropology." Bourdieu

relied upon a phenomenological approach to these studies, which gave these pieces the fieldwork-oriented content that the journal needed in light of its concerns with the interconnections between sociology, ethnography, and colonialism (Davies 1987: 98). As *Les temps modernes* began its move toward a more structuralist perspective under the editorial leadership of Jean Pouillon, Bourdieu's work continued to play an important part in the development of the journal's project, though Bourdieu's structuralist emphasis leans away from Sartre's chosen emphasis on *praxis* (ibid.: 143). And Bourdieu's later work in the sociology of education helped develop *Les temps modernes'* analysis of the position of intellectual vis-à-vis the student movements of the mid- to late 1960s; Bourdieu's pieces deriving from his move into the sociology of education analyze the "phenomenology of need, shared by staff and students, to imagine that communication takes place between them" (Davies 1987: 187), showing that the engagement that members of the French academy professed contained within it a type of "terror" that is enacted upon the students, a terror that in some way reproduces the form of the relationship of "*le 'bon colon' à des 'indigènes'*" (Bourdieu and Passeron 1965: 441; in Davies 1987: 187). As such, Bourdieu's work contributed a great deal to the development of *Les temps modernes* and provides a useful counterpoint to the developing work of Sartre; as Davies points out, "Sartre predictably holds closer to the Gramscian concept of hegemony than to Bourdieu's ideas on habitus and cultural legitimation" (Davies 1987: 182–183).

The posthumously published collection of Bourdieu's essays from *Les temps modernes* and other forums, *Interventions 1961–2001*, includes a number of Bourdieu's contributions and commentaries on the relationship between his work and that of Sartre. In particular, Bourdieu argues that Sartre served more as a model of the ideal intellectual than as an intellectual comrade; however, in later years, it was Sartre's contribution to the myth of the "free intellectual" that Bourdieu found annoyance with: ". . . même s'il est encore beaucoup trop grand pour les plus grands des intellectuels, le mythe de l'intellectuel et de sa mission universelle est une de ces ruses de la raison historique qui font que les intellectuels les plus sensibles aux séductions et aux profits d'universalité peuvent avoir intérêt à contribuer, au nom de motivations qui peuvent n'avoir rien d'universel, au progrès de l'universel" (". . . if he is still the most grand of the grandest of intellectuals, the myth of the intellectual and of their universal mission is one of these ruses of historical reason that makes it so that the intellectuals most sensitive to seduction and to the profits of universality can have an interest in contributing, in the name of motivations that can have nothing universal, to the progress of the universal") (Bourdieu 2002: 47).

3. To quote at some length from Bourdieu and Sartre regarding the possibilities for "escape" from what I call the colonized habitus:

> In short, to the great despair of the philosopher-king who, by assigning an essence to them, claims to enjoin them to be and do what by definition they are meant to be and do, classified and lowly classified men and women may reject the principle of classification which gives them the worst place. In fact, as history shows, it is almost always

under the leadership of those seeking a monopoly over the power to judge and to classify, who may themselves quite often be classified, at least from certain points of view, in the dominant classification, that the dominated are able to break out of the grip of the legitimate classification and transform their vision of the world by liberating themselves from those internalized limits that are the social categories of perception of the social world. (Bourdieu 1990b: 180)

First, as you know, for me there is no *a priori* essence; and so what a human being is has not yet been established. We are not complete human beings. We are beings who are struggling to establish human relations and arrive at a definition of what is human. At this moment we are in the thick of the battle, and no doubt it will go on for many years. But one must define the battle: we are seeking to live together like human beings, and to be human beings. So it's by means of searching for this definition, and this action of a truly human kind—beyond humanism, of course—that we will be able to consider our effort and our end. In other words, our goal is to arrive at a genuinely constituent body in which each person would be a human being and collectivities would be equally human. (Sartre and Lévy 1996: 67)

4. "This structuration of quotidian life is arranged by hegemony: not so much in a whole of 'alien' ideas about the dependency or inferiority of the popular sectors as in a change interiorizing social inequality, below the level of unconscious dispositions, inscribed in one's own body, in the consciousness of what is possible and what is attainable."
5. "That which—local or infrastructural—comes to systemic men from structures and that which—undefined in the times—indicates humanity as *humanity to be made* to each man in the system; not just in the construction of a system (even if it were the *socialist system*), but in the destruction of each system."
6. "The practico-inert (imperative) demands the maintenance of structures; a contradiction, but *not moral*: in fact, one can ceaselessly reorganize in keeping these very men in their place."

Chapter 5 Dirty Hands and Making the Human: Fanon, the
Algerian Revolution, and an Ethics of Freedom

1. France 1843: 1–2; cited in Ruedy 1992: 49.
2. France 1834: 333–334; cited in Ruedy 1992: 50.
3. "If the colonial expeditions obey a given and known schema—the necessity of imposing order on the barbarians; protection of the European countries' concessions and interests; generous supplies from Western civilization—one has not sufficiently shown the stereotypical means used by the metropolitans to cling to their colonies."
4. Here, note the racialization of the terms, a tactic that Fanon uses to illustrate both the universality of the colonial situation and the racialization that he knows, as one who is embedded in the colonial system as both subject of the system and warrior against it, to be part and parcel of the constitution of the *colonisé*'s consciousness.

5. "The object of racism is no longer the particular man, but a certain form of existence...."; "... the time-honored call of the 'cross against the crescent.'"

6. The obvious parallel is to Marx's "Alienation and Social Classes," in which he argues that the proletariat feels their alienation from themselves and others more profoundly than does the bourgeoisie, which experiences it as "a sign of their power" (Marx 1978: 133).

7. The Manichaeism of the colonial situation presented by Fanon and Sartre in their works may very well be hyperbolically stated by them in order to make this larger point: that the structure of colonial society was drawn broadly along racial lines in the first instance, with deviations along class lines permitted occasionally. Regardless of its literary value, though, this Manichaeism becomes reality as the revolution proceeds, ultimately taking hold over the Algerian situation *in toto*.

8. As a personal conversation with Ron Aronson (2004b) has highlighted, there may even be a fourth position within Algerian society, namely that occupied by Muslim Algerians who also felt themselves to be fully French. Mouloud Feraoun might be most indicative of this position, being highly educated within the French system, having loyalties to France *and* to Algeria as "parent countries," much in the same way that a citizen of Switzerland might see themselves as a member of their national group (German, French, or Italian) and Swiss and equally feel loyalties to each. The existence of this fourth position, though, would not seem to change the analysis here much; those who could throughout their adult life maintain a loyalty to both France and Algeria without feeling betrayed by either would not be likely to join in the revolution (though Feraoun certainly maintained connections with the FLN, in large part as a manifestation of his fealty to Algeria), while those who felt betrayed by France would be more likely to rebel against continued colonial rule.

9. As Horne notes, the early phase of the Revolution after the All Saint's Day uprising was dismal for the fortunes of the revolutionaries, at least in terms of the measures of efficacy they might have laid out for themselves. The innocents who were rounded up (and perhaps inspired to join the Revolution after their arrest) were an asset, but only "a potential one"; and soon after the uprising, the *pieds-noirs*, the focal audience for the uprising beyond the French colonial and metropolitan government, returned to a state of normalcy for a time. In large part, this ignorance of the FLN left it unable to further its revolutionary activity, leaving its support base small for the early part of the Revolution (Horne 1977: 96, 104).

10. "The colonial society is a system where it is important to comprehend the logic and the internal necessity of the fact that it constitutes the context in reference which makes sense of all the behaviors, and in particular the relations, between the two ethnic communities. To the transformations inevitably resulting from contact between two profoundly different civilizations, as much in the economic domain as in the social domain, colonization adds the confusion knowingly and methodically provoked to assure the authority of the dominant power and the economic interests of its nationals."

11. "One says willingly that man is endlessly questioning himself, and that he disowns himself when he pretends that he no longer exists."

12. Muslim Algerians were legally defined as French subjects, not French citizens, and in order to gain citizenship were required to renounce their rights to maintain their Islamic religion and cultural practices. As such, making the leap toward French citizenship legally as well as ontologically required alienating oneself from their culture, religion, and heritage, as well as their community; and the obstacles that were frequently placed in the way of Muslim Algerians who did want to obtain French citizenship—and, by 1936, only 2,500 had worked to obtain it—meant that the French would be unlikely to genuinely accept these *évolués* as "truly French" (Horne 1977: 35).

13. Whether this is the result of Fanon's ethnographic efforts or his propagandistic work is in the end almost immaterial. The *intent* behind the writings Fanon did for *El Moudjahid* was to create the perception of a burgeoning nation in revolt; and if *métropole* or *colon* officials read that as an accurate presentation of the situation, or if non-revolutionary Algerians saw the opportunity to read themselves into this "narrative of liberation," the effect is the same: a mutually reinforcing cycle of increasing involvement of Algerians in the Revolution, increased efforts by French officials at pacification, and increased dissatisfaction in *l'Hexagone*.

14. "This event, commonly known as 'alienation,' is naturally very important. One finds it in official texts under the name 'assimilation.'

But this alienation is never totally successful. It would be because the oppressor quantitatively and qualitatively limits the evolution, unforeseen, disparate phenomenon manifest themselves.

The inferiorized group had admitted, the force of reason being relentless, that its misfortunes followed directly from their racial and cultural characteristics."

15. As Tillion points out, primarily in reference to her own work but also referring to the work of the ethnographer in general, "Ethnographers should hurry up and have a look at them, for in a little while it will be too late" (Tillion 1958: 28–29). It is part of the task of the ethnographer to engage in a kind of reportage, one that, in situations such as the colonial, requires a certain kind of advocacy. One could argue—and ethnographers certainly would argue in their behalf—that the reportage of "foreign" situations is important both for the preservation of human situations and for increasing the awareness of the world at large that the way they do things is just as "foreign" as the practices depicted in the ethnography.

There is also some issue surrounding the position of Fanon as ethnographer. Because of Fanon's clear relationship and solid involvement with the FLN, it could be argued that the representation of the Algerian situation serves a propaganda purpose—namely, that Fanon intentionally constructed the representation of the situation in Algeria in order to satisfy the needs of the FLN to motivate the population to revolt against French colonialism. On this issue, one could say, "But of course! That was his job with the FLN, after all." In the end, though, the question should not be whether or not Fanon was the FLN's propagandist, but whether or not what Fanon wrote while working with the FLN (a) served the purposes for which it was intended, and (b) in some way represented the existential experience of Algerians prior to and during the Revolution. To my mind, the response to (b) is in the affirmative.

16. This discussion of the tensions between the overall revolutionary goals of the FLN and the particular tactics utilized to attain those goals parallels Michel de Certeau's discussion of "strategy" versus "tactics" in *The Practice of Everyday Life* (1984, University of California Press), in which strategy refers to the larger-scale motivations and goals of some program of social action, while tactics describes the particular ways in which those goals are attained through action. This tension also parallels the discussions earlier in this work (chapters 2 and 3) of the bond between means and ends as understood by Sartre and Merleau-Ponty. As we will see, the latter parallel will become more important for the course of this analysis.

17. A statement more on the organizational problems of the FLN than the willingness of the revolutionaries to hold to their promises, an attack on French civilians in 1955 by FLN soldiers in Philippeville resulted in the deaths of 71 Europeans and 52 Algerians, including a number of Algerian politicians (Le Sueur 2001: 30). It appears that the decision to pursue this attack was either made by the "army over the fence" in Cairo, or independently by the leader of *wilaya* 2, Youssef Zighout (Horne 1977: 118–119; Clark 1959: 152, 172). Following the Philippeville attacks, dramatic reprisals against Algerians (totaling between 1,273 and 12,000 Algerian deaths) and the resultant flocking of Algerians to the FLN demonstrated the likelihood that FLN attacks on French civilians would ultimately strengthen their hand.

18. To be more faithful to Hutchinson's text, she utilizes the general term "revolutionary terrorism" to talk about all forms of violence utilized against non-military persons during a revolutionary war, and identifies each of the types of violence I discuss herein as "terrorism" (Hutchinson 1978: 21). However, this unproblematized description of revolutionary violence as "terrorism" is doubly loaded, as she herself later recognizes. First, it involves a moral valuation; to describe a form of violent political action as "terrorist" necessarily negates any perception of its legitimacy as a tool for those who utilize it. Second, Hutchinson later (Crenshaw 1983: 2–3) argues for a "neutral descriptive definition," to be utilized in conjunction with a "normative valuation" to determine the actual legitimacy of the violence. In order to separate the description of the violent tactics utilized by the FLN from any kind of ethical valuation—the ultimate point of the chapter—I have elected to refer to the various types of political violence Hutchinson labels as "terrorism" simply as "violence" or "tactics."

19. The MNA was the reformulated version of Messali Hadj's MTLD, made to sound tougher after the establishment of the FLN (Horne 1977: 128). Because the politics of both groups was so similar—both deriving their original positions from Messali, fiercely nationalist, and opposed to any continued French rule over Algeria—the main issue became the commitment the FLN had to political violence, not entirely shared by the MNA. The MNA's slight moderation made them an appealing interlocutor for

de Gaulle; and it was this perceived threat to FLN dominance that resulted in the internecine conflict that resulted in as many as 10,000 Algerian deaths—even more than the number of French killed during the war (Crenshaw 1995: 483).

20. Following from recent discussions over the differences, particularly in Sartre's discussions of the justness of political violence, between the "justification" of political violence and its "endorsement" (Aronson 2002, 2004a; Santoni 2002, 2003), I want to make clear here that this analysis proceeds along *justificatory* lines. That is, I see the ways in which the revolutionary practices of the FLN could be justified, given their particular social, political, economic, and military position during the Revolution. That said, I am not *endorsing* their use of certain tactics that would generally fit under the heading of "terrorism" (cf. Hutchinson 1978; Crenshaw 1983), and certainly do not endorse the FLN's settling of scores after independence was gained. This in no way means that I could not see other forms of political violence as justified or endorsable, given the parameters discussed throughout this work.

21. Some have posed the issue of Camus's call for a civilian truce in terms of a "was he right or wrong" question, which would tend to lock theorists and scholars into a "Camus versus Sartre" debate. To my mind, the point is not whether or not Camus was correct to ask for a truce against both *pied-noir* and Algerian civilians—to his mind, he was correct on this point, despite the fact that, as Aronson (2004a) notes, this was Camus's philosophical "blind spot," that element of his public pronouncements that did not coincide with his philosophical *oeuvre*. The fact that Camus's call for a civilian truce coincides with the FLN's Soummam Conference (1956) shows that when violence came to roost on *pieds-noirs*, only then was it time for him to speak out for the protection of civilians on both sides. The point is that by the time Camus did make his pronouncement, the essential contradictions of the Algerian colonial system had already been laid bare; the reciprocal violence between Algerians and French soldiers and civilians had already begun to heat up; and there appeared to all sides to be no way back from it.

22. Merleau-Ponty's *Humanism and Terror* was originally published in 1947, at a time in which France was recovering from the German Occupation and World War II and the Soviet Union was expanding its control over much of Central and Eastern Europe. Thus, its historical context is one in which the question of which form of violence—bourgeois or Communist—was more "just." However, Merleau-Ponty moved away from support of Communist forms of violence by 1950, and with the publication of "Sartre and Ultrabolshevism" in 1953 had seemed to move completely away from any support of revolutionary violence. However, Merleau-Ponty remained committed to the humanization of the world, even if through violent means; further, his position moved closer to the first of these quotations than the second with the discovery of the *gulags* in the Soviet Union. Still, his words early on can still inform our perspective on the violence in the Algerian Revolution. See Le Sueur (2001: 210, 227–228).

23. "But the object of value is already homogenous to the moment of inertia in praxis: because, in the synthetic unity of praxis, I make myself inert to

combat the inertia of the world, the inertia of the object and their unity in the false interiority returning to me my own inertia and its practical unification condensed and made passive. In fact, I make myself an instrument (contra-inertia) and the object makes me into an instrument. Thus the first time of a value—an object silently implicating the idea of myself as a value as much as power, that is to say forged inertia."

24. "In fact, the contradiction of the revolutionary morality is that it is the only one to be determined in the function of the integral man; but also limits its goal *in itself* in the service of the exigencies of the struggle, *and* produces at the same time praxis-process of morals highly esteemed that are alienated in the process.

The problem is therefore in knowing how to produce the dialectical movement that comes in posing these alienated *morals* that contest their limits in service of the same goal they seek to attain."

25. "In a word, the ethical possibility or norm (that is to say, the action producing its own means) is the *sens* of historical praxis: that one, correcting without end its deviations, appears as penetrated; in effect of a sort . . . where one sustains and nourishes itself, whatever the objective, and by relation to which it seems to control itself without end, it corrects its deviations and ceaselessly reshapes its practical field, poses the overtaking by invention, and refuses its practical limits of invention in perpetual reorganization as if by this temporal development (perpetually reshaping itself) it would have to climb on board with historical time as an *a priori* to praxis, that is to say, the unconditional action, or if one prefers, the end created by free invention arises through its own ends."

Chapter 6   "For Everyone, Everything": Social Ethics,
Consent, and the Zapatistas

1. Some of the finer examples of case studies of the EZLN include Victor Campa Mendoza's *Las insurrecciones de los pueblos indios en México: la rebelión en Chiapas* (n.d.: Ediciones Cuéllar); George Collier's edited *Basta! Land and the Zapatista Rebellion* (1994: Food First Books); Héctor Díaz-Polanco's *La rebelión zapatista y la autonomía* (1998: Siglo Veintiuno Editores); Neil Harvey's *The Chiapas Rebellion: The Struggle for Land and Democracy* (1998: Duke University Press); Tom Hayden's anthology, *The Zapatista Reader* (2001: Thunder's Mouth Press); Elaine Katzenberger (ed.), *First World, Ha Ha Ha! The Zapatista Challenge* (1995: City Lights Books); June Nash's *Mayan Visions: The Quest for Autonomy in an Age of Globalization* (2001: Routledge); John Ross, *The War Against Oblivion: Zapatista Chronicles, 1994–2000* (2000: Common Courage Press); Jan Rus's edited volume *Mayan Lives, Mayan Utopias: The Indigenous Peoples of Chiapas and the Zapatista Rebellion* (2003: Rowman and Littlefield); Bill Weinberg, *Homage to Chiapas: The New Indigenous Struggles in Mexico* (2002: Verso); and John Womack's anthology, *Rebellion in Chiapas* (1999: New Press).

2. "In this sense, this revolution will not conclude with a new class, class fraction or group in power, but in a free and democratic 'space' of political struggle. . . . A new politics located in the base will not be a confrontation between political organizations, but a confrontation of their political proposals with these distinct social classes . . ."

3. "It is only a discursive body that relates more to a methodology of construction than to a proposed shape; that is to say, it is about an invitation made to all those spaces of otherness to manifest their existence and begin to weave a worldwide network of resistances that permit the strengthening of a discontinuous front against power."

4. "On the other side, the project of the transition to democracy; not a transition made with the power that simulates a change in which all would be the same, but a transition to democracy as a project of the reconstruction of the country; the defense of national sovereignty; justice and hope as yearnings; truth and *mandar obedeciendo* as a rule of leadership; the stability and security that gives democracy and liberty; dialogue, tolerance and inclusion as new forms of making politics."

5. "The particularity of the Zapatista discourse is that it puts in question *moral discipline* and *definitions* from another ethics and other definitions based in societies not 'previous' or past, but currently living in the Mexican territory. Starting from this existence, they do not propose a regress to some other past but rather opening a dispute on the content and definition of this present modernity in which they also exist."

6. ". . . a platform of complex interactions between modern civil rights and antique conceptions of the world, heart that can revitalize a West guided by a distinct modernity, one that puts to pasture the idea-force of progress at all costs, of univocality and homogeneity of 'development,' imposing rational limits (in human terms) on instrumental reason."

7. "There are practices anchored in community life and encompass their forms of organization, political form, the imparting of justice and other increases in human relations. In their attention to weaving these processes, they join the very best of Indian peoples and coincide with the quest for rural and urban citizenship organizations. They coincide as well with the old dream of self-governance, with anarchistic provisions, or with the approaches of Deleuze, Foucault, as well as Ivan Illich."

8. "For us, pain and anguish; for us, joyous rebellion; for us, the negated future; for us, insurrectionary dignity. For us, nothing."

9. "To the minds of many, Zapatismo is the best example of the new revolutionary thought; it must not either convert itself into a new 'official ideology' of revolutionaries, nor must it be able to institutionalize itself."

10. "This imaginative form of doing politics is not without its risks. It requires force and security to include many disparate positions in its bosom, all providing debates and discussions that will be accessible. . . . The generous and inclusive Zapatista proposal—to locate power as useful if it has the allotted outline and is articulated like a fabric—it has an enormous potential because it submits the process of conformation and continuity to the

organization: order is not imposed, it is encountered, it is discovered, it is woven: 'to join moments in a single heart, a heart of all, it will make us all sages, a little more to confront that which will come. Only between us all do we know all'—so said a Huichol shaman."

11. "To expand our world defending the right of other worlds to exist implies modifying substantial characteristics of our own culture. Not only to relativize it, to take a critical distance from it, but also, for example, to ask about the forms of human knowledge. Somehow, we should be concerned with constructing a heuristic mass that permits us to know without evading responsibility for knowing the actual state of things in the world, outlined as the problem of generating notions that deconstruct dominant cognitive paradigms to open spaces for diverse life experiences, that of the many worlds that inhabit the world, and that today, we hope, redefine humanity."

12. "In Zapatista discourse, human emancipation supposes the elimination of alterity but not of diversity. All worlds are possible because none imposes itself on the others, because each one occupies its own space, because respecting difference is like attaining equality."

13. Recent works on developing a radical form of democracy include: Peter Bachrach and Aryeh Botwinick, *Power and Empowerment: A Radical Theory of Participatory Democracy* (1992: Temple University Press); Stephen Eric Bronner, *Imagining the Possible: Radical Politics for Conservative Times* (2002: Routledge); Archon Fung and Erik Olin Wright's *Deepening Democracy: Institutional Innovations in Empowered Participatory Government* (2003: Verso); Ernesto Laclau and Chantal Mouffe's classic *Hegemony and Socialist Strategy: Toward a Radical Democratic Politics* (2001: Verso); C. Douglas Lummis's *Radical Democracy* (1997: Cornell University Press); Chantal Mouffe's edited *Dimensions of Radical Democracy: Pluralism, Citizenship, Community* (1996: Verso); Ewa Ziarek Plonowska, *An Ethics of Dissensus: Postmodernity, Feminism, and the Politics of Radical Democracy* (2001: Stanford University Press); David Trend's anthology *Radical Democracy: Identity, Citizenship and the State* (1996: Routledge); Roberto Mangabeira Unger's *False Necessity: Anti-Necessitarian Social Theory in the Service of Radical Democracy* (2002: Verso), and *Democracy Realized: The Progressive Alternative* (1998: Verso); and Howard Zinn's *Disobedience and Democracy: Nine Fallacies on Law and Order* (2002: South End Press).

Chapter 7   Toward a Resisting Social Ethics

1. This is not to suggest that I rely upon or even agree with a rational choice theory of resistance. Rather, I take this quote to say that only a few changes in our current sociohistorical field—the proverbial "one paycheck from poverty," for example—would make it "rational" within this new context for people to revolt.

2. One reading of the September 11, 2001, attacks on the World Trade Center and Pentagon would take exactly this tack; namely, those who had been used for the exercise of American foreign policy interests and were then left behind were now exacting their revenge on the symbols of that foreign

policy—capitalism and military might. While the more important elements of my argument—namely, the reclamation of agency and freedom through an ethically revolutionary project—are not at all embodied by Al Qaeda or other terrorist entities fighting against American imperialism, the direction of anti-American propaganda and attacks is clear—this is seen as a struggle for someone's freedom, even if not those who actually do the fighting.

3. To those who might argue that voting does constitute a form of consent, I would respond in this way: if voting were truly a form of consent, we would not simply elect people (and even the word "elect" posits an oligarchical relationship between our representatives and ourselves), but would have the ability to vote for the continued existence of a certain institution. There are ways, for example, to radically democratize U.S. federal policy-making; however, this possibility will never be presented to us, either directly (for our representatives would know the result in advance) or through our representatives, who would never vote themselves and the representative body out of existence.

4. This, of course, presumes that we act in good faith with regard to the importance that others have for us in the world. A venture capitalist, for example, who might claim that the amassing of large amounts of capital for investment in multinational corporations is intended to further the freedom of others to have a good standard of living, and so on would not be acting in good faith by my analysis. The presumption of venture capitalism is, of course, the "never-ending pie"—the idea that money can be created *ex nihilo* and that the amassing of wealth doesn't impact negatively on others. As Marx's analysis of the impact of capitalism on workers and environmental disasters such as the demise of the rain forest show us, though, the creation of capital *does* negatively impact on others, whether on particular individuals suffering under poor working conditions or on the climate of the entire planet.

5. Sartre's own footnote to this quote illuminates the distinction between potential and actual freedom: "But it is very important not to conclude that one can be free in chains. Freedom is a complete dialectical development, and we have seen how it can become alienated or bogged down or allow itself to be caught by the traps of the Other and how simple physical constraint is enough to mutilate it. But still even the most oppressed slave, simply in order to be obedient to his master, both can and must perform a synthesis of the practical field" (Sartre 1985 [1960]: 578n68). Here, Sartre's intent is to contradict his early formulations of the freedom of a slave; in *Being and Nothingness*, for example, a good deal of space is given over to a discussion of how a slave is able to formulate an escape from their condition (the quintessential goal of Sartre's early notion of freedom). This, though, is *potential* freedom until *actualized* through escape, a rebellion, or the murder of the master. In the *Critique*, Sartre is here arguing that the slave must *act* in order to obey their master, but that this *praxis* is not free because it comes through the compulsion of another to whom the individual has not freely pledged themselves. Note, then, that *it is the sociohistorical condition that determines the quality of freedom in this case.*

6. In some sense, though, this runs directly counter to the argument Merleau-Ponty makes in "Sartre and Ultrabolshevism," in which he claims "Those who

will be shot *would understand* tomorrow that they did not die in vain; the only problem is that they will no longer be there to understand it. Revolutionary violence insults them most grievously by not taking their revolt seriously: they do not know what they are doing" (Merleau-Ponty 1973b: 130). Here, Merleau-Ponty's critique is directed against Sartre's seemingly unqualified support of the *Parti Communiste Français* and their Stalinist methods; put another way, Merleau-Ponty criticizes not revolutionary violence *in toto*, but rather the arbitrary use of violence within the liberatory movement. The contradiction is resolved, though, when one considers Merleau-Ponty's perspective on history: sometimes the pursuit of social freedom of humanity requires the abandonment of some human beings; or, put another way, "The contingency of the future, which accounts for the violent acts of those in power, by the same token deprives these acts of all legitimacy, or equally legit-imates the violence of their opponents. The right of the opposition is exactly equal to the right of those in power" (Merleau-Ponty 1969: xxxvi). Overall, though, I see Merleau-Ponty's position as this: "When one has the misfortune or the luck to live in an *epoch*, or one of those moments where the traditional ground of a nation or society crumbles and where, for better or worse, man himself must reconstruct human relations, then the liberty of each man is a mortal threat to the others and violence reappears" (Merleau-Ponty 1969: xvii; cf. Sartre and Lévy 1996).

7. "Morality is a certain relation of person to person. But this relation is not at its foundation an inert relation of interiority. It is an active rapport of reciprocity that is passivized and eternalized (the eternity of the instant) by the mediation of worked matter. Morality changes inasmuch as the worked matter changes and as (behaviorally) our relations change with worked matter."

WORKS CITED

Alessandrini, Anthony. 1995. " 'We Must Find Something Else': Fanon and the Search for Non-Western Marxism." *Research and Society* 8: 54–69.
Alexander, Jeffrey C. 1995. *Fin-de-Siècle Social Theory*. London and New York: Verso.
Anderson, Thomas C. 1993. *Sartre's Two Ethics: From Authenticity to Integral Humanity*. Chicago and LaSalle, IL: Open Court Press.
Anthony, Douglas. 2004. Personal conversation. Lancaster, PA.
Aronson, Ronald. 2002. "Sartre and Terror" (transcript). Panel presentation at the North American Sartre Society meetings, Loyola University, New Orleans.
Aronson, Ronald. 2004a. *Camus and Sartre: The Story of a Friendship and the Quarrel That Ended It*. Chicago: University of Chicago Press.
Aronson, Ronald. 2004b. Personal conversation. Lancaster, PA.
Arquilla, John and David Ronfeldt (eds.). 2001. *Networks and Netwars: The Future of Terror, Crime and Militancy*. Santa Monica, CA: RAND Corporation. Accessed at http://www.rand.org/publications/MR/MR1382.
Aussaressess, Paul. 2002. *The Battle of the Casbah: Terrorism and Counter-Terrorism in Algeria, 1955–1957*. New York: Enigma Books.
Bauman, Zygmunt. 1992. *Postmodern Ethics*. London: Basil Blackwell Publishers.
Beckett, Paul A. 1973. "Algeria vs. Fanon: The Theory of Revolutionary Decolonization, and the Algerian Experience." *The Western Political Quarterly*, 26, 1: 5–27
Bell, Derrick. 1992. *Faces at the Bottom of the Well: The Permanence of Racism*. New York: Basic Books.
Bell, Linda A. 1989. *Sartre's Ethics of Authenticity*. Tuscaloosa, AL: The University of Alabama Press.
Bennett, Ronan. 1997. *The Catastrophist*. London: Headline Book Publishing.
Berlin, Isaiah. 1969. *Four Essays on Liberty*. Oxford: Oxford University Press.
Bhabha, Homi. 1994. *The Location of Culture*. New York and London: Routledge.
Bourdieu, Pierre. 1958. *Sociologie de l'Algérie*. Paris: Presses Universitaires de France.
Bourdieu, Pierre. 1977. *Outline of a Theory of Practice*. Cambridge: Cambridge University Press.
Bourdieu, Pierre. 1984. *Distinction*. Cambridge, MA: Harvard University Press.
Bourdieu, Pierre. 1987. *Choses dites*. Paris: Editions de Minuit.

Bourdieu, Pierre. 1990a. "'Fieldwork in Philosophy.'" Pp. 3–33 in *In Other Words: Essays Towards a Reflexive Sociology.* Stanford: Stanford University Press.

Bourdieu, Pierre. 1990b. "A Lecture on the Lecture." Pp. 177–198 in *In Other Words: Essays Towards a Reflexive Sociology.* Stanford: Stanford University Press.

Bourdieu, Pierre. 1990c. "Social Space and Symbolic Power." Pp. 123–139 in *In Other Words.* Stanford: Stanford University Press.

Bourdieu, Pierre. 1991. *Language and Symbolic Power.* Cambridge, MA: Harvard University Press.

Bourdieu, Pierre. 1998. *Acts of Resistance: Against the Tyranny of the Market.* Translated by Nice, Richard. New York: The New Press.

Bourdieu, Pierre. 2002. "Sartrémoi. Émoi. Et moi, et moi et moi. À propos de 'intellectuel total.'" Pp. 44–48 in Pierre Bourdieu, *Interventions 1961–2001: Science sociale et action politique* (Franck Poupeau and Thierry Discepolo, eds.). Marseille: Agone.

Bourdieu, Pierre and Jean-Claude Passeron. 1965. "Langage et rapport au langage dans la situation pédagogique." *Les temps modernes* 21: 441–463.

Bourdieu, Pierre and Loïc J. D. Wacquant. 1992a. *An Invitation to Reflexive Sociology.* Chicago: University of Chicago Press.

Bourdieu, Pierre and Loïc J. D. Wacquant. 1992b. "The Purpose of Reflexive Sociology (The Chicago Workshop)." Pp. 61–126 in P. Bourdieu and L. J. D. Wacquant (eds.), *An Invitation to Reflexive Sociology.* Chicago: University of Chicago Press.

Bowman, Elizabeth A. and Robert V. Stone. 1991. "'Making the Human' in Sartre's Unpublished Dialectical Ethics." Pp. 111–122 in Hugh J. Silverman (ed.), *Writing the Politics of Difference.* Albany: State University of New York Press.

Bowman, Elizabeth A. and Robert V. Stone. 1992. "'Socialist Morality' in Sartre's Unpublished *1964 Rome Lecture:* A Summary and Commentary." *Bulletin de la Société Américaine de Philosophie de Langue Française* IV, 2–3: 166–200.

Brysk, Alison. 1996 (Spring). "Turning Weakness into Strength: The Internationalization of Indian Rights." *Latin American Perspectives* 23, 2: 38–57.

Burbach, Roger. 1994 (May–June). "Roots of the Postmodern Rebellion in Chiapas." *New Left Review* 205: 113–124.

Camus, Albert. 1958. "Appel pour une trêve civile." In A. Camus, *Chroniques algériennes, 1939–1958.* Paris: Éditions Gallimard.

Camus, Albert. 1960. "Defense of Freedom." Pp. 55–108 in Albert Camus, *Resistance, Rebellion, and Death.* New York: Vintage International.

Camus, Albert. 1991. *The Rebel.* New York: Vintage International.

Canclini, Nestor Garcia. 1984. "Gramsci con Bourdieu: Hegemonía, Consumo y Nuevas Formas de Organización Popular." *Nueva Sociedad* 71: 69–78.

Caputo, John. 1993. *Against Ethics.* Bloomington: Indiana University Press.

Ceceña, Ana Esther. 1999. "La resistencia como espacio de construcción del nuevo mundo." *Revista Chiapas* 7. Accessed at http://www.ezln.org/revistachiapas/ch7cecena.html.

Ceceña, Ana Esther and Andrés Barreda. 1998. "Chiapas and the Global Restructuring of Capital." Pp. 39–63 in John Holloway and Eloína Peláez (eds.), *Zapatista! Reinventing Revolution in Mexico*. London and Sterling, VA: Pluto Press.

Chomsky, Noam and Edward Herman. 1987. *Manufacturing Consent: The Political Economy of the Mass Media*. New York: Pantheon Books.

Clark, Michael K. 1959. *Algeria In Turmoil: A History of the Rebellion*. New York: Frederick A. Praeger Publishers.

Cohen, William B. 1980. "Legacy of Empire: The Algerian Connection." *Journal of Contemporary History*, 15, 1: 97–123.

Collier, David and James E. Mahon. 1993. "Conceptual 'Stretching' Revisited: Adapting Categories in Comparative Analysis." *American Political Science Review* 87: 845–855.

Compton, John J. 1998. "Sartre, Merleau-Ponty, and Human Freedom." Pp. 175–186 in Jon Stewart (ed.), *The Debate Between Sartre and Merleau-Ponty*. Evanston, IL: Northwestern University Press.

Contat, Michel and Michel Rybalka. 1970. *Les Écrits de Sartre: Chronologie, bibliographie commentée*. Paris: Gallimard.

Crenshaw, Martha. 1983. "Introduction," in Martha Crenshaw (ed.), *Terrorism, Legitimacy, and Power: The Consequences of Political Violence*. Middletown, CT: Wesleyan University Press.

Crenshaw, Martha. 1995. "The Effectiveness of Terrorism in the Algerian War." Pp. 473–513 in Martha Crenshaw (ed.), *Terrorism in Context*. State College, PA: The Pennsylvania State University Press.

David, Comandante. 2003. "Words for Indigenous Brothers Who Are Not Zapatistas." Accessed at http://www.laneta.apc.org/sclc/ezln/030809 david-en.htm.

Davies, Howard. 1987. *Sartre and "Les temps modernes."* Cambridge, UK: Cambridge University Press.

de Beauvoir, Simone. 1994 (1948). *The Ethics of Ambiguity*. Translated by Bernard Frechtman. New York: Citadel Press.

Debray, Regis. 1978. *Che's Guerrilla War*. New York: Penguin Books.

Dubar-Ortiz, Roxanne. 2002 (December). "Don't Mourn, Organize: Joe Hill's Children" (review essay). *Monthly Review* 54: 7. Accessed at http://www. monthlyreview.org/1202dubarortiz.htm.

Dufrenne, Mikel. 1998. "Sartre and Merleau-Ponty." Pp. 279–293 in Jon Stewart (ed.), *The Debate Between Sartre and Merleau-Ponty*. Evanston, IL: Northwestern University Press.

Durkheim, Emile. 1973. *Durkheim On Morality and Society*. Robert Bellah (ed.). Chicago: University of Chicago Press.

Durkheim, Emile. 1997. *The Division of Labor in Society*. New York: Grove Press.

Eagleton, Terry. 1999. "Utopia and Its Opposites." Pp. 31–40 in Leo Panitch and Colin Leys (eds.), *Necessary and Unnecessary Utopias: Socialist Register 2000*. Suffolk: Merlin Press.

Edinburgh-Chiapas Solidarity Group. 2003. "Zapatistas mobilise to defend Morelia Caracol." Accessed at http://www.vinhtran.pwp.blueyonder.co.uk/ edinchiapas/morelia.html.

EZLN. 1994. *Segunda Declaración de la Selva Lacandona*. Accessed at http://www.ezln.org/documentos/1994/19940610.es.htm.

EZLN. 1996a. *Crónicas intergalácticas: Primer Encuentro Intercontinental por la Humanidad y contra el Neoliberalismo*. México, D. F.: Planeta Tierra.

EZLN. 1996b. *Cuarta Declaración de la Selva Lacandona*. Accessed at http://www.ezln.org/documentos/1996/19960101.es.htm.

EZLN. 1997. "Mensaje del EZLN a los pobladores de San Pedro de Michoacán." Accessed at http://www.ezln.org/documentos/1997/19970526.es.htm.

Fanon, Frantz. 1963. *The Wretched of the Earth*. New York: Grove Press.

Fanon, Frantz. 1964a. *Pour la révolution africaine: écrits politiques*. Paris: François Maspero.

Fanon, Frantz. 1964b. "Racisme et culture." In *Pour la révolution africaine: écrits politiques*. Paris: François Maspero.

Fanon, Frantz. 1965. *A Dying Colonialism*. Translated by Haakon Chevalier. New York: Grove Press.

Fanon, Frantz. 1967. *Black Skin, White Masks*. Translated by Charles Lam Markmann. New York: Grove Weidenfeld.

Fédération des Amicales Régimentaires et des Anciens Combattants (FARAC). 2001. "La tragédie des Harkis." Accessed at http://www.farac.org/php/article.php3?id_article=55.

Fox, Richard and Orin Starn (eds.). 1997. *Between Resistance and Rebellion: Cultural Politics and Social Protest*. New Brunswick: Rutgers University Press.

France, Commission nommée par le Roi. 1834. "Procès verbaux et rapports de la Commission nommée par le Roi, le 7 juillet 1833, pour aller recueillir en Afrique tous les faits propres à éclairer le Gouvernement sur l'état du pays et sur les mesures que réclame son avenir." Paris.

France, Ministère de la Guerre. 1843. "Collection des actes du gouvernement depuis l'occupation d'Alger jusqu'au 1er octobre 1834." Ministère de la Guerre du France, Paris.

Fraser, Nancy. 1997. *Justice Interruptus: Critical Reflections on the "Postsocialist" Condition*. New York and London: Routledge.

Geras, Norman. 1999. "Minimum Utopia: Ten Theses." Pp. 41–52 in Leo Panitch and Colin Leys (eds.), *Necessary and Unnecessary Utopias: Socialist Register 2000*. Suffolk U.K.: Merlin Press.

Giddens, Anthony. 1979. *Central Problems in Social Theory: Action, Structure, and Contradiction in Social Analysis*. Berkeley and Los Angeles: University of California Press.

Giddens, Anthony. 1990. *The Consequences of Modernity*. Stanford: Stanford University Press.

Gillespie, Joan. 1960. *Algeria: Rebellion and Revolution*. New York: Frederick A. Praeger Publishers.

Gilly, Adolfo. 1997. *Chiapas: la razón ardiente. Ensayo sobre la rebelión del mundo encantado*. México, D. F.: Ediciones Era.

Good, Kenneth. 1976. "Settler Colonialism: Economic Development and Class Formation." *The Journal of Modern African Studies* 14, 4: 597-620.

Gordon, Lewis. 1994. *Bad Faith and Anti-Black Racism*. Atlantic Highlands: Humanities Press.

Gordon, Lewis. 1995. *Fanon and the Crisis of European Man: An Essay on Philosophy and the Human Sciences*. New York and London: Routledge.

Gorz, André. 1973. *Socialism and Revolution.* Translated by Norman Denny. Garden City, NY: Anchor Press/Doubleday.

Gramsci, Antonio. 1971. *Selections from the Prison Notebooks.* New York: International Publishers.

Gramsci, Antonio. 1985. *Selections from the Cultural Writings.* Cambridge, MA: Harvard University Press.

Hall, Ronald L. 1998. "Freedom: Merleau-Ponty's Critique of Sartre." Pp. 187–196 in Jon Stewart (ed.), *The Debate Between Sartre and Merleau-Ponty.* Evanston, IL: Northwestern University Press.

Hayim, Gila J. 1980. *The Existential Sociology of Jean-Paul Sartre.* Amherst, MA: University of Massachusetts Press.

Heggoy, Alf Andrew. 1969. "The F.F.S., An Algerian Opposition to a One-Party System." *African Historical Studies,* 2, 1: 121–140.

Heggoy, Alf Andrew. 1972. *Insurgency and Counterinsurgency in Algeria.* Bloomington, IN: Indiana University Press.

Hellman, Judith Adler. 1999. "Real and Virtual Chiapas: Magical Realism and the Left." Pp. 161–186 in Leo Panitch and Colin Leys (eds.), *Necessary and Unnecessary Utopias: Socialist Register 2000.* Suffolk UK: Merlin Press.

Hoare, Quentin and Anthony N. Smith. 1971. "Introductory Notes." In *Selections from the Prison Notebooks.* New York: International Publishers.

Holloway, John. 1998. "Dignity's Revolt." Pp. 159–198 in John Holloway and Eloína Peláez (eds.), *Zapatista! Reinventing Revolution in Mexico.* London and Sterling, VA: Pluto Press.

Honneth, Axel. 1995. *The Struggle for Recognition: The Moral Grammar of Social Conflicts.* Cambridge, MA: The MIT Press.

Horne, Alistair. 1977. *A Savage War of Peace: Algeria, 1954–1962.* New York: The Viking Press.

Hutchinson, Martha Crenshaw. 1978. *Revolutionary Terrorism: The FLN in Algeria,* 1954–1962. Stanford: Hoover Institution Press.

Jameson, Frederic. 1991. *Postmodernism, or The Cultural Logic of Late Capitalism.* Durham, NC: Duke University Press.

Kleinman, Arthur, Veena Das, and Margaret Lock. 1997. *Social Suffering.* Berkeley and Los Angeles: University of California Press.

Le Sueur, James D. 2001. *Uncivil War: Intellectuals and Identity Politics During the Decolonization of Algeria.* Philadelphia: University of Pennsylvania Press.

Lewis, William H. 1969. "Algeria: The Cycle of Reciprocal Fear." *African Studies Bulletin,* 12, 3: 323–337.

Leyva Solano, Xochitl. 1998. "The New Zapatista Movement: Political Levels, Actors and Political Discourse in Contemporary Mexico." Pp. 35–56 in Valentina Napolitano and Xochitl Leyva Solano (eds.), *Encuentros Antropologicos: Politics, Identity and Mobility in Mexican Society.* London: Institute of Latin American Studies.

Locke, John. 1988. *Two Treatises on Government.* Cambridge: Cambridge University Press.

Lorenzano, Luis. 1998. "Zapatismo: Recomposition of Labor, Radical Democracy and Revolutionary Project." Pp. 126–158 in John Holloway and

Eloína Peláez (eds.), *Zapatista! Reinventing Revolution in Mexico*. London and Sterling, VA: Pluto Press.

Löwy, Michael. 1998 (November). "Globalization and Internationalism: How Up-to-Date is the *Communist Manifesto*?" *Monthly Review* 50: 6. Accessed at http://www.monthlyreview.org/1198lowy.htm.

MacLeod, Jay. 1987. *Ain't No Makin' It: Leveled Aspirations in a Low-Income Neighborhood*. Boulder, CO: Westview Press.

Maran, Rita. 1989. *Torture: The Role of Ideology in the French-Algerian War*. New York: Praeger.

Marcos, Subcomandante. 1995. *Shadows of Tender Fury: The Letters and Communiqués of Subcommandante Marcos and the Zapatista Army of National Liberation*. Translated by Frank Bardacke, Leslie López, and the Watsonville CA Human Rights Committee. New York: Monthly Review Press.

Marcos, Subcomandante. 1999. "The consulta, the victories and the questions of the moment." Accessed at http://flag.blackened.net/revolt/mexico/ezln/1999/marcos_post_consult_ap99.html.

Marcos, Subcomandante. 2000 (January). "Letter to Leonard Peltier." *Monthly Review* 51: 8. Accessed at http://www.monthlyreview.org/100sub.htm.

Marcos, Subcomandante. 2001 (May/June). "The Punch Card and the Hourglass." (Interview with Gabriel García Márquez and Roberto Pombo.) *New Left Review* 9: 69–79.

Marcos, Subcomandante. 2003a. "Chiapas: The Thirteenth Stele" (parts 1 through 7). Accessed at http://flag.blackened.net/revolt/mexico/ezln/2003/marcos/resistance13.html.

Marcos, Subcomandante. 2003b. "Message sent by the Subcommandante Marcos [to the Inauguration of the *Juntas de Buen Gobierno*]." Accessed at http://www.zmag.org/content/showarticle.cfm?SectionID=8&ItemID=4038.

Marx, Karl. 1978. "Alienation and Social Classes." Pp. 133–135 in Robert F. Tucker (ed.), *The Marx-Engels Reader*. New York: W. W. Norton.

McBride, William L. 1991. *Sartre's Political Theory*. Bloomington and Indianapolis: Indiana University Press.

McManus, Susan. 2002. "Creating the Wor(l)ds of Theory: Zapatismo as a Deconstructive and Utopian Political Imagination." Conference paper presented at Social Theory 2002, Dubrovnik, Croatia.

McNally, David. 2002. *Another World is Possible: Globalization and Anti-Capitalism*. Winnipeg: Arbeiter Ring Publishing.

Merleau-Ponty, Maurice. 1962. *The Phenomenology of Perception*. Translated by C. Smith. London: Routledge and Kegan.

Merleau-Ponty, Maurice. 1963. *The Structure of Behaviour*. Translated by A. L. Fisher. Boston: Beacon Press.

Merleau-Ponty, Maurice. 1964a. "Author's Preface." Pp. 3–8 in Maurice Merleau-Ponty, *Sense and Non-Sense*. Chicago: Northwestern University Press.

Merleau-Ponty, Maurice. 1964b. "Hegel's Existentialism." Pp. 63–70 in Maurice Merleau-Ponty, *Sense and Non-Sense*. Chicago: Northwestern University Press.

Merleau-Ponty, Maurice. 1964c. "The War Has Taken Place." Pp. 139–152 in Maurice Merleau-Ponty, *Sense and Non-Sense*. Chicago: Northwestern University Press.

Merleau-Ponty, Maurice. 1969. *Humanism and Terror*. Boston, MA: Beacon Press.

Merleau-Ponty, Maurice. 1973a. *Adventures of the Dialectic*. Evanston, IL: Northwestern University Press.

Merleau-Ponty, Maurice. 1973b. "Sartre and Ultrabolshevism." Pp. 95–202 in Maurice Merleau-Ponty, *Adventures of the Dialectic*. Evanston, IL: Northwestern University Press.

Millán, Márgara. 1998a. "En otras palabras, otros mundos: la modernidad occidental puesta en cuestión." *Revista Chiapas* 6. Accessed at http://www.ezln.org/revistachiapas/ch6millan.html.

Millán, Márgara. 1998b. "Zapatista Indigenous Women." Pp. 64–80 in John Holloway and Eloína Peláez (eds.), *Zapatista! Reinventing Revolution in Mexico*. London and Sterling, VA: Pluto Press.

Nolasco, Patricio. 1997. "Cambio Político, estado y poder: un bosquejo de la posición zapatista." *Revista Chiapas* 5. Accessed at http://www.ezln.org/revistachiapas/ch5nolasco.html.

Omi, Michael and Howard Winant. 1994. *Racial Formation in the United States: From the 1960s to the 1990s*. New York: Routledge.

Paulson, Justin. 2001. "Peasant Struggles and International Solidarity: The Case of Chiapas." Pp. 275–288 in Leo Panitch and Colin Leys (eds.), *Socialist Register 2001: Working Classes, Global Realities*. New York: Monthly Review Press.

Quandt, William B. 1969. *Revolution and Political Leadership: Algeria, 1954–1968*. Cambridge, MA: The MIT Press.

Roberts, Hugh. 2003. *The Battlefield Algeria, 1988–2002: Studies in a Broken Polity*. New York and London: Verso.

Rojo Arias, Sofia. 1997. "Las tres llaves que abren las tres cadenas: los valores políticos." *Revista Chiapas* 4. Accessed at http://www.ezln.org/revistachiapas/ch4rojo.html.

Ross, John. 2003. " '*Los Caracoles*': Dramatic Changes in Zapatista Structure Bolster Rebels' Regional Autonomy." *MexBarb* 1221. Accessed at http://www.globalexchange.org/countries/mexico/975.html.

Ruedy, John. 1992. *Modern Algeria: The Origins and Development of a Nation*. Bloomington, IN: Indiana University Press.

Santoni, Ronald E. 2002. "Sartre and Terror" (transcript). Panel presentation at the North American Sartre Society meetings, Loyola University, New Orleans.

Santoni, Ronald E. 2003. *Sartre on Violence: Curiously Ambivalent*. State College, PA: Pennsylvania State University Press.

Sardar, Ziauddin. 1998. *Postmodernism and the Other*. Oxford: Oxford University Press.

Sartre, Jean-Paul. 1948a. "Présentation des *Temps Modernes*." In *Situations II*. Paris: Gallimard.

Sartre, Jean-Paul. 1948b. *Qu'est-ce que la littérature?* Paris: Gallimard.

Sartre, Jean-Paul. 1963. "Preface." Pp. 1–23 in Frantz Fanon, *The Wretched of the Earth*. New York: Grove Press.

Sartre, Jean-Paul. 1964a. "Conférence à l'Institut Gramsci." Unpublished manuscript. Paris: Bibliothèque Nationale de France.

Sartre, Jean-Paul. 1964b. "Manuscript on Ethics Prepared by Gallimard." Unpublished manuscript. New Haven, CT: Beinecke Rare Book and Manuscript Library.

Sartre, Jean-Paul. 1965. "Reply to Albert Camus." Pp. 54–78 in Jean-Paul Sartre, *Situations*. Greenwich, CT: Fawcett Crest Books.

Sartre, Jean-Paul. 1966. "Materialism and Revolution." Pp. 85–109 in G. Novack (ed.), *Existentialism versus Marxism: Conflicting Views on Humanism*. New York: Delta Books.

Sartre, Jean-Paul. 1973 (1956). *Being and Nothingness*. Translated by Hazel Barnes. New York: Washington Square Press.

Sartre, Jean-Paul. 1976 (1948). *Anti-Semite and Jew: An Exploration of the Etiology of Hate*. Translated by George J. Becker. New York: Schocken Books.

Sartre, Jean-Paul. 1985 (1960). *Critique of Dialectical Reason, Volume One: Theory of Practical Ensembles*. London and New York: Verso.

Sartre, Jean-Paul. 1991 (1985). *Critique of Dialectical Reason, Volume Two (unfinished): The Intelligibility of History*, vol. 2. Edited by Arlette Elkaïm-Sartre. Translated by Quintin Hoare. London and New York: Verso.

Sartre, Jean-Paul. 1993a. "The Humanism of Existentialism." Pp. 31–62 in Wade Basking (ed.), *Essays in Existentialism*. New York: Citadel Press.

Sartre, Jean-Paul. 1993b. *Notebooks for an Ethics*. Chicago: University of Chicago Press.

Sartre, Jean-Paul and Benny Lévy. 1996. *Hope Now: The 1980 Interviews*. Chicago: University of Chicago Press.

Schaffer, Scott. 1997. "Reactivating Consent." Unpublished paper, Department of Sociology (Arts). York University, Toronto.

Schalk, David L. 1991. *War and the Ivory Tower: Algeria and Vietnam*. New York: Oxford University Press.

Scott, James C. 1987. *Weapons of the Weak: Everyday Forms of Peasant Resistance*. New Haven, CT: Yale University Press.

Scott, James C. 1990. *Domination and the Arts of Resistance: Hidden Transcripts*. New Haven, CT: Yale University Press.

Sekyi-Otu, Ato. 1996. *Fanon's Dialectic of Experience*. Cambridge, MA: Harvard University Press.

Sewell, William. 1992. "A Theory of Structure: Duality, Agency, and Transformation." *American Journal of Sociology* 98, 1: 1–29.

SIPAZ. 2003. "Resistance and Autonomy: The Creation of the Zapatista Juntas of Good Government." *SIPAZ Report* 8: 2. Accessed at http://www.sipaz.org/vol8no2/updatee.htm.

Spurling, Laurie. 1977. *Phenomenology and the Social World: The Philosophy of Merleau-Ponty and Its Relation to the Social Sciences*. London, Henley and Boston: Routledge and Kegan Paul.

Stewart, Jon. 1998. "Merleau-Ponty's Criticisms of Sartre's Theory of Freedom." Pp. 197–215 in Jon Stewart (ed.), *The Debate Between Sartre and Merleau-Ponty*. Evanston, IL: Northwestern University Press.

Stone, Robert V. and Elizabeth A. Bowman. 1986. "Dialectical Ethics: A First Look at Sartre's Unpublished 1964 Rome Lecture Notes." *Social Text* 13–14: 195–215.

Stone, Robert V. and Elizabeth A. Bowman. 1991. "Sartre's *Morality and History*: A First Look at the Notes for the Unpublished 1965 Cornell Lectures." Pp. 53–82 in Ronald Aronson, and Adrian van den Hoven (eds.), *Sartre Alive*. Detroit: Wayne State University Press.

Talbott, John. 1980. *The War Without a Name: France in Algeria, 1954–1962*. New York: Alfred A. Knopf.

Taylor, Patrick. 1989. *The Narrative of Liberation: Perspectives on Afro-Caribbean Literature, Popular Culture, and Politics*. Ithaca, NY: Cornell University Press.

Tillion, Germaine. 1958. *Algeria: The Realities*. Translated by Ronald Matthews. New York: Alfred A. Knopf.

Vera, Ramón. 1997. "El infinito devenir de lo nuevo." *Revista Chiapas* 4. Accessed at http://www.ezln.org/revistachiapas/ch4vera.html.

Wacquant, Loïc J. D. 1992. "Toward a Social Praxeology: The Structure and Logic of Bourdieu's Sociology." Pp. 1–60 in Pierre Bourdieu and Loïc J. D. Wacquant (eds.), *An Invitation to Reflexive Sociology*. Chicago: University of Chicago Press.

Whiteside, Kerry. 1988. *Merleau-Ponty and the Foundation of an Existential Politics*. Princeton: Princeton University Press.

Wolin, Richard. 1992. *The Terms of Cultural Criticism: The Frankfurt School, Existentialism, Poststructuralism*. New York: Columbia University Press.

Wood, Ellen Meiksins. 1995. *Democracy Against Capitalism: Reinventing Historical Materialism*. Cambridge: Cambridge University Press.

INDEX

C

caciques, 206

Camus, Albert, xii, 28, 94–5, 185, 188, 257, 276, 283
  and call for "civilian truce," 185
  debate with Sartre, 276

Canclini, Nestor Garcia, 110

capitalist development, 4, 245

Caputo, John, 6–7

caracoles
  and relations with non-governmental organizations, 232

caracoles (EZLN "encounter spaces"), 230–1, 233–4

Casbah, 129

Catholicism, 149, 176

Ceceña, Ana Esther, 206, 208, 215, 218, 220, 224, 229
  and Barreda, Andrés, 206, 208

Chechnya, rebellion in, 2

Chiapas (Mexico), 11, 205–6, 211–14, 221–2, 229, 236, 284
  and *caciques*, 206
  and material conditions, 232
  indigenous peoples, 125, 205–7, 216, 222, 236, 241
    disenfranchisement of, 206
    material conditions, 206
    material conditions in, 222

choice, 8, 11, 18–19, 22, 25, 29, 32–4, 40, 42, 44–6, 50, 54, 56, 60, 69, 74, 94–5, 100–1, 139–40, 143, 170–2, 177–82, 185, 199, 203, 210, 219, 237, 256, 259, 261, 267–8, 272, 286

civil society, 208–9, 211, 219–20, 227, 230–2
  and National Democratic Convention (CND), 216
  and solidarity between social movements, 209–10

as basis for revolutionary action, 209

as political force, 216

Clark, Michael, 282

class condition, 103

class consciousness, 35–6, 39–40, 65–6, 126, 155

Clinton, Bill, 205

COCOPA Laws, 231

cogito, 13, 16–17, 29, 32

Cohen, William, 169

Cold War, 28

"collective responsibility," 161, 164

collective unfreedom, 85, 267

Collier, David
  and James E. Mahon, 102

colonial domination, 138, 145

colonial system, 77, 133, 175, 188, 193

colonial violence, 131–2, 145–7, 157, 175, 180, 186

colonialism, 72, 77, 130, 132–60, 163, 171–3, 175, 177–8, 180–1, 183–4, 186, 190–1, 196, 247, 253, 278–81
  and bad faith, 181
  and civilizing impulse, 129, 134, 136–7, 139, 157, 281
    paradox of, 139, 178
  and complicity, 182
  and construction of alterity, 142
  and desire for recognition, 140, 179
  and distinction (*la distinction*), 137
  and "good intentions," 135
  and imposition of culture, 139–40, 143–4, 155, 180
  and maintenance of, 182
  and mutual recognition, 143
  and objectification of individuals, 185
  and "passing," 136
  and practico-inert, 139, 157

R

racialization, 134–5, 139–40, 151, 155
    as elimination of freedom, 135
racism, 77, 133–5, 213, 222, 180
    and subhumanity, 138
    as legitimation of colonialism, 134
radical democracy, 11, 241, 252, 265
reciprocity, 37–8, 54, 56, 62, 81, 96–7, 103, 262, 275, 277–8
    and alterity, 56
    and facticity, 38
recognition, struggle for, 48
reflection, 15–17, 34, 48
reflexivity
    and embodiment, 109
relations between individual and social, 107, 131
Rémy, Gilbert Renault (Col.), 146
repetition, 81–3, 85, 121–2, 248, 251, 267
    refusal of, 95
resistance, x, 5, 7–11, 13, 22–3, 25–6, 28, 31, 36, 39–41, 77–9, 87, 90, 95, 98–103, 115–17, 119, 124–7, 130–2, 137, 139, 141, 143, 145, 148, 155, 157–8, 160–2, 177, 182, 188–90, 197–8, 203–4, 209, 211, 221, 224, 227, 235, 240–2, 245–7, 252–3, 255, 257, 262–3, 268–9, 271, 273–4, 286
    and authenticity, 46
    and being-with-others, 254
    and collective meaning, 77
    and ethical orientation, 255
    and ethics (lower-case E), 9, 91, 95–6, 99, 255, 269
    and existential ethics, 77
    and hegemony, 124
    and immoralism, 255
    and mutual recognition, 77

and "pastiche attitude," 124
as process, 98, 252
construction of paths, 157, 183
construction of paths for, 148, 246
ethical orientation to, 245
necessity of, 253
resisting social ethics, 11, 98, 172–3, 190, 194, 202–3, 221, 230, 255, 257, 269
    and agency, 249–51
    and ambiguity, 255–6
    and "bottom-up" governance, 264–5
    and collective self-determination, 5, 8, 227–8, 258, 265
    and concrete freedom, 258
    and consent, 250–1, 265–6
    and decolonization of the habitus, 261
    and democracy, 251
    and "dirty hands," 255, 257, 272
    and Ethics (capital E), 256
    and fact of choice, 75, 261
    and flexibility of social order, 269
    and immoralism, 255–6
    and integral humanity, 21, 199–202, 257
    and material conditions, 262
    and "minimum utopia," 257, 264
    and obligation/requisition, 256
    and processuality, 253, 268
    and resistance to serialization, 258
    and sacrifice, 261, 269
    and situatedness in History, 257, 265
    and situatedness of social life, 65, 257, 258
    and social distance, 255
    and solidarity, 265–7
    and status quo, 254
    and violence, 261
    as political engagement, 269

Rojo Arias, Sofía, 219–20, 223, 229
Ronfeldt, David, 211
Ross, John, 233, 284
Ruedy, John, 136, 146–50, 154,
 157–62, 164, 175, 190, 279
Rybalka, Michel
 and Contat, Michel, 46, 81, 122,
 275

S
sacrifice, 75, 95, 130, 164, 182, 211,
 221, 224, 255, 259, 261, 275
Salinas de Gortari, Carlos, 205
San Andres Accords, 231
Santoni, Ronald, 194, 201–2, 283
Sardar, Ziauddin, 125
Sartre, Arlette El-Kaïm, 275
Sartre, Jean-Paul, ix, xii, 9, 13–39,
 41, 45–50, 53–70, 73, 77–91,
 93–9, 101, 104–7, 119, 121–2,
 126–7, 133–6, 142, 156, 168,
 176–7, 179–81, 183, 186,
 188–9, 193–4, 198–202, 217,
 225, 235–6, 239, 245–6,
 248–9, 250–2, 256–60, 262–3,
 269–70, 275–80, 282–3, 287–8
 and Algeria, 135
 and Bourdieu, Pierre, 104
 and "city of ends," 86, 87
 and example of prisoner, 18, 21
 and Fanon, Frantz, 135–6
 and "first ethics," 19–21, 86
 and fused group, 56–8, 60–2, 64
 and hope, 41, 72, 75, 205, 212,
 216, 285–6
 and integral humanity, 21,
 199–200, 202, 257
 and Lévy, Benny, 41, 69,
 89–90, 99, 236, 245, 256,
 279, 288
 and Liège (Belgium) infanticides, 94
 and membership in La Résistance,
 26–7, 147, 176

and pure future (l'avenir pur), 46,
 84, 274
and scarcity, 21, 30, 86, 152
and "second ethics," 20–1, 34
and seriality, 53–8, 60–3, 77–9,
 99, 150, 153, 174–5, 189,
 205–6, 209, 211, 263
and social ensembles, 53–64,
 77–80, 98–9, 150, 153,
 174–5, 189, 205–6, 209,
 211, 263
and "spirit of seriousness," 24, 36,
 106
and the gathering, 55–6
and unconditioned future, 81, 84,
 277
Anti-Semite and Jew, 54
Being and Nothingness, 9, 13–17,
 19–22, 32, 48, 85–6, 259,
 274, 287
Cornell Lectures, xii, 198, 275
Critique of Dialectical Reason, 22,
 36, 64, 97, 105, 107, 198,
 250, 258, 276
debate with Camus, 276
literature of commitment, 27
pledged group, 58, 60–1, 99,
 174–5, 199, 251, 258, 263
political engagement of, 269
Rome Lectures (*Conférence à
 l'Institut Gramsci*), xii, 21, 79,
 121, 183, 275
synthetic anthropology
 (*anthropologie synthétique*),
 27–8, 274, 277
The Wretched of the Earth, 156
scarcity, 21, 30, 86, 152
Schaffer, Scott, 239
Schalk, David
 process of *engagement*, 26–7, 29
Schalk, David L., 26
Scott, James C., 4, 124, 137, 160
Sekyi-Otu, Ato, xi, 145–6, 154, 156